MEL Scripting

a Character Rig in Maya

Chris Maraffi

New
Riders

MEL Scripting a Character Rig in Maya
Chris Maraffi

New Riders
1249 Eighth Street
Berkeley, CA 94710
510/524-2178
Fax: 510/524-2221

Find us on the Web at: www.peachpit.com
To report errors, please send a note to errata@peachpit.com
New Riders is an imprint of Peachpit, a division of Pearson Education

Copyright ©2009 by New Riders
Senior Editor: Karyn Johnson
Developmental Editor: Judy Walthers von Alten
Production Coordinator: Becky Winter
Proofreader: Elizabeth Welch
Composition: Danielle Foster
Indexer: Valerie Perry
Cover Design: Charlene Charles-Will
Cover Illustration: Chris Maraffi
Technical Editors: Michael Clavan and Ken Norman

ISBN-13: 978-0-321-38353-2

ISBN-10: 0-321-38353-2

9 8 7 6 5 4 3 2 1

Printed and bound in the United States of America

I dedicate this book to my beautiful wife Morgan for her tireless support and encouragement through the long process of writing. My love always and forever...

Acknowledgments

I want to thank all the dedicated professionals that worked on this book, including senior editor at Peachpit, Karyn Johnson, and developmental editor, Judy Walthers von Alten. All their feedback and suggestions were invaluable and contributed to making this book the best it could be. In addition, I want to thank all my colleagues at Full Sail University that helped me develop this material over the years, including the technical editors of this book—course directors Ken Norman and Mike Clavan—and lab specialists Carlos Breban, Monica Hyatt, Dan McCrummen, Kelly Wergin, and Shay Goldenberg. Also a special thanks to course director Ricardo Tobon for generously sharing his motion capture expertise.

Contents

Introduction

This introduction provides an overview of what this book offers to the intermediate Maya user, and gives you some information on how this book is unique in method and approach to Maya Embedded Language (MEL) scripting. Here you'll find a brief summary of each chapter, and details on how to download and use the book files.

Who Should Read This Book

This book is intended for intermediate Maya users who are interested in using MEL scripting to enhance the 3D production process in Maya, especially for character rigging. The reader should have a basic understanding of how to navigate in the Maya interface, as well as how to perform basic tasks, such as opening and saving files, and manipulating objects in the 3D views. If you're a new Maya user, it is recommended that you first complete the basic tutorials that come with the Maya software before starting the exercises in this book.

Why This Book?

The unique approach of this book is to teach scripting with a character rigging focus. While the MEL coding techniques shown here can be applied to any technical task in Maya, all the specific examples are targeted for rigging a biped character. There are other more general MEL books on the market, as well as rigging books that cover some MEL, but none matches the degree and focus presented here. Going through the exercises in this book will take you to an advanced level of coding, while also giving you a deeper understanding of character rigging than you can get by working solely in the Maya interface.

How This Book Is Organized

Throughout this book, you will first learn each major rigging task in the Maya interface, and then learn how to efficiently code the same task using MEL. In the interface this process will involve learning how to create skeletons and icons, parent nodes into a hierarchy, connect and constrain channels, and deform a skin model. In the coding techniques, you will learn to MEL script the same process, including how to declare variables and arrays, nest conditional statements and loops, create procedures with arguments and return statements, and use a variety of MEL commands with flags and arguments.

The book exercises are designed to take you step-by-step through the entire rigging and coding process, and each step builds on the previous examples. To get the most from the book, progress through the chapters in order. Each chapter features Maya scene files and MEL script files as examples.

Chapter 1: Starting to Rig a Character

This chapter gets you started on rigging a character by introducing you to the character rigging process, and teaching you how to create and edit skeletons. It also discusses some of the trends in the character rigging profession, as well as the main goals and responsibilities of a rigging artist.

Chapter 2: Learning to Script in MEL

The fundamental techniques of MEL scripting are introduced in this chapter. You learn how to find useful MEL commands in Maya, and how to specify options through flags and arguments. The chapter introduces other essential coding techniques, such as variables, loops, and procedures. These techniques are then applied to begin scripting the rigging process.

Chapter 3: Scripting a Basic IK Biped Rig

This chapter shows you how to build a basic biped rig in both the interface and through MEL scripts. Interface techniques include creating icons, parenting nodes, and constraining channels. Scripting techniques include creating procedures that create all the rig controls, and process the data so it is available to the advanced scripts.

Chapter 4: Adding Advanced Rig Controls

Here you'll learn advanced rigging techniques that involve creating and connecting channels on the icons to drive every control in the rig. You also learn how to create sophisticated controls on the limbs and torso, including a spline IK backbone. The chapter explains each technique in the interface, and then examines it in MEL.

Chapter 5: Finishing the IK Biped Rig

This chapter teaches you how to finish the rigging process by assigning the advanced rig to the skin model with a smooth bind. It shows you additional skin deformation techniques, such as binding a proxy skin to simplify the weighting tasks and using blend shapes to create facial morphing. Much of the binding process, and even some of the skin weighting, is also done through MEL scripts.

Chapter 6: Scripting an Advanced Character GUI

The final chapter shows you how to MEL script advanced character GUIs (graphical user interfaces) that are custom-designed for animation. You learn how to incorporate images, buttons, fields, sliders, and views into a multipanel window in Maya. This GUI streamlines and enhances the advanced rig controls, all through MEL.

How To Use This Book

As you go through the exercises in this book, the text will reference specific files. The companion files for this book consist of Maya scene files, MEL script files, and image files used in the advanced character GUI. Download all these files from the book web site at:

www.peachpit.com/melscripting

The files are organized into folders according to your system type. If you are using a Windows-based computer, download the Windows version. If you are using a Macintosh, download that version. A readMe.txt file on the download site contains any additional or updated downloading instructions.

Be aware that all the code was originally developed for the Windows version of Maya, so the book text and examples display the Windows version of the interface and scripts. The only difference between the Windows and Macintosh versions, however, is the file paths, GUI image types, and some keyboard shortcuts. The rigging and MEL scripting techniques, as well as all the MEL commands, are exactly the same on both versions.

The Windows version of the files use this default file path:

C:/CMaraffi_bookFiles/

Macintosh versions of the default file path look like this:

/Users/cmaraffi/Documents/CMaraffi_bookFilesMAC/

Be sure to change the default Macintosh path to incorporate your user name, rather than "cmaraffi." Also be sure to use the correct capitalization for your file path; this is critical on a Macintosh system.

Another difference is that the Windows version of the advanced character GUI uses BMP image files, while the Macintosh version uses XPM image files. These types of files are only used in the advanced character GUI in the last chapter. All the correct files should be in the version folder you download.

One other difference between Windows and Macintosh versions is in some of the keyboard shortcuts. When Windows specific keyboard modifiers are used in the text, such as Ctrl+[key], Macintosh users should use Command+[key].

To download, install, and run the book companion files:

1. Download and place the appropriate file folder for your version of Maya in the correct place on your hard drive.

2. Download and place the appropriate CMaraffi_setupRigGui.mel or CMaraffi_setupRigGui_MAC.mel script file in your Maya scripts folder in your user login. This will be the first script run in Maya that runs all the other scripts in the book folder. By placing this script in the main scripts folder, Maya will always be able to find it when you open the scene file.

For instance, here is an example of the scripts folder location in Windows:

C:\Documents and Settings\cmaraffi\My Documents\maya\scripts\

Here is an example of a Macintosh version of the scripts folder location:

/Users/Shared/Autodesk/maya/scripts/

3. Download and open the basicFkRig.mb script file, which should automatically launch Maya and run the setup GUI script. In the setup GUI, change the path in step 1 to be accurate for where you placed the book files folder on your system.

Clicking through the remaining steps in the setup GUI runs the scripts, and creates the advanced biped rig.

4. Before you begin working through the exercises, make sure that you click through the remaining steps in the setup GUI and create the advanced biped rig so that you can see what the script files do in Maya before you examine the code within the files.

Note: If you decide to use a variation of the default Windows path (or you're using the Macintosh path), change line 116 in the setup GUI script to permanently set the correct path. That way, you won't have to type the path in the GUI field each time you run the scripts.

Note from the Author

The content for this book developed out of the scripting and character rigging courses I taught at Full Sail University in Winter Park, Florida, from 2004 to 2008. Over this period, I continually revised my curriculum to incorporate more MEL scripting in direct response to industry trends as seen at conferences like SIGGRAPH, and through feedback from industry professionals. At Full Sail we had an advisory board composed of industry leaders, including rigging supervisors from Industrial Light & Magic, Sony Pictures Imageworks, and Blue Sky Studios, who related how much they were using MEL to automate their character rigging process. Although the particular rig and scripts presented in this book are generic examples developed for teaching these skills, the general rigging and coding techniques are consistent with what is being done at many industry studios that use Maya today.

Check my web site for more information on any book updates, live seminars, and webcasts on *MEL Scripting a Character Rig*. Please contact me about your experiences with the techniques presented in this book, and let me know if there are any issues with the book text or code. Also, feel free to use the Maya and MEL files I have provided, including the character and skeleton models, in your own rigging projects. I hope you enjoy exploring the artistry and power of coding.

Best regards,

Chris Maraffi
www.chrismaraffi.com

Starting to Rig a Character

THIS CHAPTER INTRODUCES you to the essential techniques for creating character animation controls in Maya, better known as creating a rig. You will learn how a rigging artist fits into the 3D production process, and what skills are required in today's animation industry to excel in this profession. Then you will learn the details of how to build a basic rig in the Maya interface by creating, editing, and binding skeletons. This knowledge will form the foundation for creating a more complex rig in later chapters in both the interface and ultimately through coding.

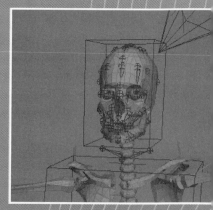

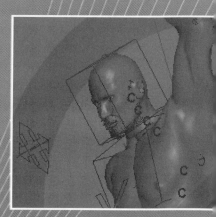

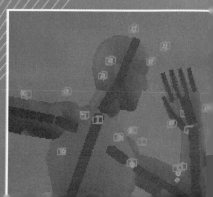

Rigging in Computer Animation

This section defines the job responsibilities of a rigging artist, and discusses how trends in the animation industry have changed what rigging artists need to know. You will also learn what skills are needed to excel at creating character controls, and what should be some of the main goals in building a rig.

The Job of a Rigging Artist

A character-rigging artist has the responsibility of creating the technical system that facilitates bringing a static character model to life. This involves talking to the animator or director to find out how the character should move, and then utilizing the tools available in Maya to achieve those goals. Generally this requires designing a set of logical controls to interactively move around the character's body, and to believably deform the model or skin accordingly.

Since Maya is a node-based 3D software, as seen in the Hypergraph or Hypershade, the technical side of making character controls requires creating and connecting a variety of nodes. The main types of nodes are skeletons and curves, and when you connect them together, they become a rig. Skeletons are specially designed to deform a character model like flexible skin, and curves are used to make 3D handles or icons for easily manipulating the skeletons. The most basic way of connecting these nodes is to simply parent them into a hierarchy, as seen by opening the basicFkRig.mb Maya file, and by looking in the Hypergraph (see **FIGURE 1.1**).

Other nodes typically used in such a hierarchy are group nodes, locators, and geometry. In complex rigs, additional connections between the nodes are made through attributes or channels to enhance the animation controls. Essentially, digital rigs are the equivalent of armatures or puppet strings on traditional 3D characters, but the rods, strings, and wires have been replaced by skeletons, icons, and channel connections.

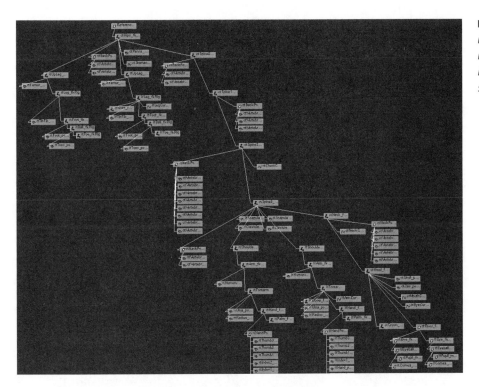

FIGURE 1.1 *In Maya node-based software, a rig in its most basic form is a hierarchy of nodes, as shown in the Hypergraph.*

In addition to the technical task of creating the rig hierarchy and connections at a node level, rigging artists also spend considerable time designing the rig interface in the 3D views. Digital rigs have traditionally had an iconic 3D interface, which means that although the rig is composed of many nodes, the icons are at the top level of the controls. Animators may not interact with most of the nodes in the rig, but they will directly manipulate the icons. Since many 3D animators originally came from puppetry and stop motion, where they manipulated physical objects, this often appeals to them. The rigging artist tries to create familiar real-world shapes from curves, such as boxes, spheres, arrows, text, and so on. Such shapes make it easy to select the controls in the 3D views (see **FIGURE 1.2**), and since curves are not rendered with surfaces in Maya, you don't have to worry about them showing up in the final animation.

FIGURE 1.2 *Rigs are animated through iconic controls, which are curves modeled into a variety of 3D shapes.*

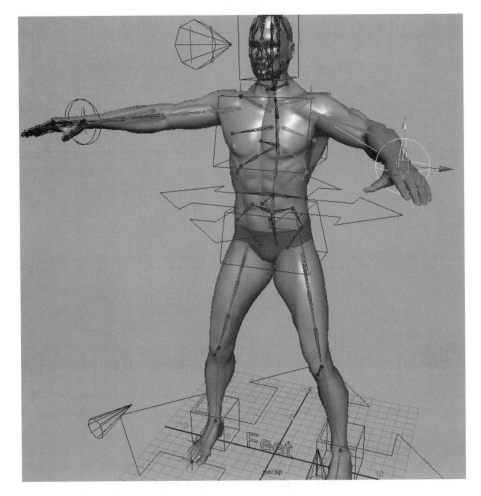

Iconic interfaces have been commonly used for character controls for many years and can become quite elaborate. I remember a rigging artist during a lecture in the late 1990s referring to such controls as "cockpits," because they had so many icons that they resembled the instrument panel in a jet airplane. Since then iconic interfaces have generally become more streamlined with the goal of being easier to animate.

Another type of interface is also becoming more common in the animation industry, and is designed by rigging artists. Since the implementation of Maya Embedded Language (MEL) in Maya, scripted graphical user interfaces (GUI) are possible. These can contain a wide variety of character controls that are made entirely from graphic icons or images (see **FIGURE 1.3**), such as the ones

Maya uses to create the software interface, or custom images that you create in a program like Photoshop.

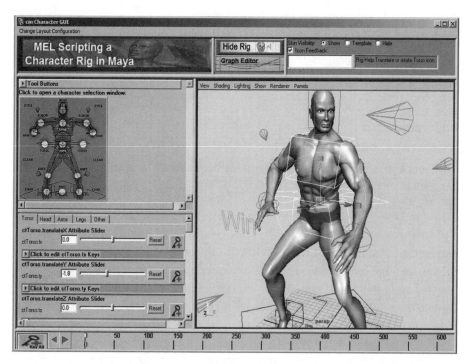

FIGURE 1.3 *A graphical user interface, or GUI, can be added to the iconic rig to enhance the character controls.*

This book will take you through the process of creating both kinds of interfaces as a part of scripting the advanced rig. You will begin by building the iconic controls in the Maya interface, and then automate the same rigging process entirely through MEL scripting. Throughout this process you will use a simple scripted GUI to more easily run your rigging scripts. Once the rig is complete, you will be shown how to create an advanced character animation GUI that can be used in conjunction with the iconic controls.

Character Rigging in a 3D Production

Rigging is one of the main components of any 3D character animation, and falls roughly in the middle of the production process before animation. Here is a general outline of the entire 3D production process:

PREPRODUCTION

1. Design: Create concept art, character designs, and storyboards.

2. Animatic: Scan and animate the 2D storyboard, or create a low-resolution 3D mockup of the storyboard.

PRODUCTION

3. Modeling: Model the character's skin and props.

4. Shading: Create skin and prop texture maps.

5. Rigging: Build the rig that will enable animating and deforming the character.

6. Animation: Use the rig to animate the character.

7. Lighting: Light the characters in the scenes for rendering.

8. Rendering: Render the character and scene into frames and layers.

POSTPRODUCTION

9. Effects: Add fluid or particle effects.

10. Compositing: Final compositing of rendered layers, and rotoscoping as needed.

Be aware, however, that this process is not entirely linear, but often overlaps in a fluid manner with related areas. On some productions, rigging may start in pre-production, and may continue well into post-production. For instance, rig design (5) can be done in tandem with the character design (1), can then be implemented and refined throughout the modeling process (3), may be continually updated or modified while the character is animated (6), and may be required to drive visual effects in post-production (9). Actually, it is good job security that the rigging artist's job is not done once the animation starts. Since rigs are continuously being refined, fixed, and customized for particular scene requirements throughout the animation, rigging artists are always needed.

Important Goals for a Rigging Artist

In the 3D production process, the rig becomes the main vehicle used by the animator to create the character animation. Character animators are mainly hired for their acting or performance talent, not their technical computer skills. As mentioned, many animators come from a traditional cell, stop motion, or puppetry background. Many do not know Maya beyond setting and editing animation keys on the timeline. So when building a rig, a character-rigging artist needs to be mindful that it may be used by someone who does not have the background to decipher the technical workings. Thus, the rigging artist must keep two goals in mind when creating a rig, regardless of whether it will have an iconic or graphical interface: the rig should be easy to use and hard to break.

Ease of use is mainly based on good interface design. For an iconic interface, this refers to how logical and intuitive the icons are shaped and positioned in relation to the character model. A rig with good iconic design makes it easy for an animator to understand what parts of the body each icon controls. Good design also balances between having too many or too few icons. Because a fully functional rig will have up to hundreds of controls to animate, you must prioritize which are going to require icons. I recommend creating icons for only the main body controls, and then adding custom attributes or channels to the icons for secondary controls (see **FIGURE 1.4**).

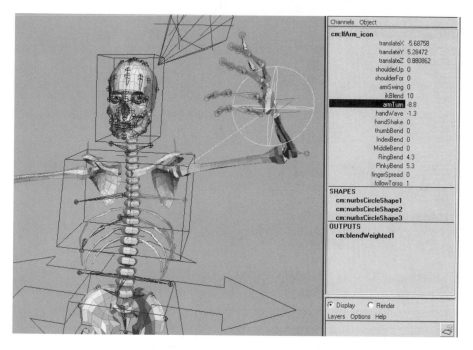

FIGURE 1.4 *Adding custom attributes or channels to your icons keeps character controls from becoming cluttered and hard to use.*

Breaking a rig refers to manipulating it in ways that were not intended, so that it stops working predictably during the animation. This can produce twisting of skeletons, which in turn causes unnatural deformations on the skin (see **FIGURE 1.5**).

FIGURE 1.5 *One of the goals in rigging is to make a rig hard to break, so that the skin doesn't deform badly, as in this example.*

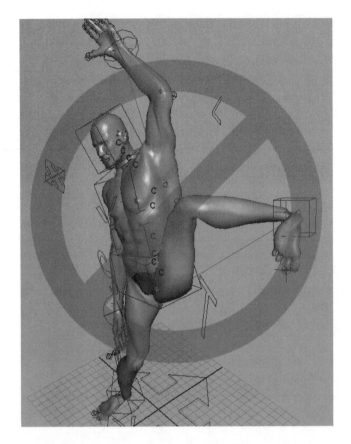

To make a rig hard to break, the rigging artist strives to provide intuitive animation controls that work well within the parameters of the storyboard and to limit access to controls that could push the rig beyond those parameters. This is done by locking and hiding nodes in the rig that should not be animated, and by limiting channels on nodes that should be animated.

How Digital Rigging Has Evolved

Various trends in the animation industry over the years have changed how rigging artists work and what they need to know. Some important trends include:

- Increasingly believable character movement through complex rigging solutions, including incorporating motion capture technology into the character controls.
- Scripting the rigging process using off-the-shelf software, including creating iconic and GUI character controls.

THE TREND TOWARD BELIEVABLE CHARACTER MOVEMENT

The trend toward believable characters has been developing in feature films since digital dinosaurs replaced Phil Tippett's Go-Motion dinosaurs in Steven Spielberg's 1993 hit *Jurassic Park*. Once it became clear that digital creatures could be animated with more realistic motion than any kind of traditional puppetry, animatronics, or stop motion techniques, a host of digital creatures followed. It wasn't long before more human monsters, such as seen in the films *The Mummy* and *Hollow Man*, were integrated with live actors in the late 1990s. Since then, films containing breakthrough realistic humanoid characters include the *Star Wars* prequels (Yoda), *Harry Potter and the Chamber of Secrets* (Dobby), and *Pirates of the Caribbean: Dead Man's Chest* (Davy Jones). In these films digital creatures rose to the status of virtual actors that were not only essential to the story, but in some cases overshadowed the performances of live actors. To create the controls for such believable characters, a rigging artist must first study anatomy and physiology on live humans and creatures, and then translate that knowledge into character controls that simulate bones, muscles, fat, and skin effects.

Part of this trend toward creating more believable characters is the use of some kind of motion capture technology to record realistic movement. Even in *Jurassic Park*, electronic armatures were used to input or capture the motion created by the traditional stop-motion animators, so that the data could be processed in the computer. Later in *The Mummy* and *Hollow Man* films, the animators used live-action footage as a motion guide for manually animating the characters' movements. This foreshadowed technology developed by Industrial Light & Magic for the *Pirates of the Caribbean* films to automatically drive the performance of the digital characters using film footage, called Imocap. At the same time, data-driven motion capture technologies have been steadily refined through films like *Polar Express*, *Monster House*, and *Beowulf*. These technologies allow the motion capture artist to record realistic movements directly into the computer using special suits with reflective markers or electronic transmitters attached. The motion data can then be processed in software like Autodesk Motion Builder (see **FIGURE 1.6**), and exported to Maya. The rigging artist must then connect that motion capture data to the Maya rig to drive the final character animation.

FIGURE 1.6 *Increasingly popular for creating realistic character movement, motion capture is done using simpler forward kinematics (FK) rigs in Motion Builder before importing the data to Maya.*

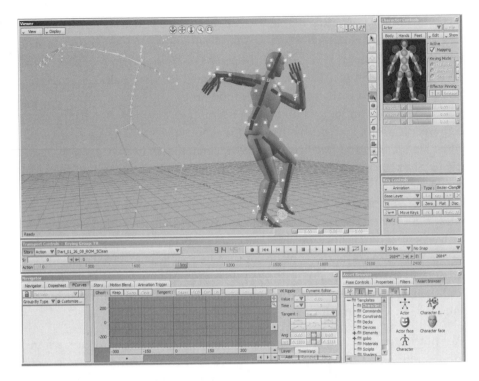

Along with creating or capturing realistic movement, it is often necessary for rigging artists to create additional controls that extend reality. Characters as seen in the film *Monster House* may have believable movement, but they also are clearly in the cartoon realm. Such cartoon characters may require subtle squash and stretch deformations that would not be part of the motion captured data. The rigging artist therefore must be able to accommodate broader cartoon controls into the rig, and still make it believable within the cartoon scene. Although you will be primarily creating realistic controls throughout this book, some broader squash and stretch controls will be added to the backbone of the rig.

THE TREND TOWARD SCRIPTING CHARACTER CONTROLS

The biggest trend that has influenced the writing of this book is the steady increase of scripting throughout the rigging process. Ever since Maya gave rigging artists access to MEL, it has been common for them to script small tools that make rigging tasks easier. However, scripting is increasingly being used to automate large portions of the character rigging process, even to the point of creating and assigning complete rigs to characters. For many years this was the job of dedicated coders, who wrote proprietary software tools for the rigging artists to use. But that began to change over the last ten years. Part of the change is undoubtedly due to productions incorporating more 3D characters, and thus requiring that the process be automated by people who know rigging. Part of the change also likely is due to off-the-shelf software like Maya becoming robust enough to not require separate proprietary tools, while also incorporating a simple coding language that lets users easily customize the software for particular tasks. Economic reasons also may have brought about this change for rigging artists: their coding eliminates the need to hire costly software developers, but in turn gives them more job security.

Another aspect of this trend in scripting character controls is the increasing use of GUIs for animating characters. Creating a GUI in Maya requires MEL scripting. As mentioned earlier in this chapter, animators are not necessarily technical, but will still be familiar with the basic Maya interface. A well-designed GUI will be easy to use for most people, because we interact daily with GUIs, whether surfing web sites, playing video games, or using computer software. As the world becomes more and more digital, GUIs are popping up everywhere, including in TVs, phones, cars, and even refrigerators. A logical extension of this is to have rigging artists design a GUI for character controls.

Designing a graphic character animation interface is not very different from designing a good website. Creating such an interface in Maya, however, does not so much involve HTML coding as MEL scripting (at least for now). Using MEL to script a GUI lets you use either the built-in Maya graphics to create controls, or import some of your own graphics to use for controls. In addition, MEL gives you the freedom to design a variety of character animation layouts that incorporate text labels, menus, panels, and custom views. Some common controls used in a GUI window are buttons, sliders, and checkboxes that run MEL commands to control any attributes on the iconic rig. A MEL-scripted GUI is not limited to character controls, however, but can be used to design any custom interface that is streamlined for a particular job.

Developing Skills

Now that you know some of the goals and trends influencing character rigging, let's look at what skills are required to achieve them as a rigging artist. Each job in the 3D animation process requires different kinds of talents, skills, and knowledge. For instance, storyboarding artists have drawing talent, modelers have sculpting talent, and animators have acting talent. Rigging artists, on the other hand, have a talent for technical design and are strong in logic. These are people who excel in research and development, and who enjoy solving technical problems. But they are more than just technicians, because their job often requires a combination of art and science, especially in the design of interfaces.

Ideally, a rigging artist in Maya has specific skills, knowledge, and talents. This artist:

- Has the ability to design iconic and graphical user interfaces for character controls.
- Can visualize and implement a logical hierarchy of nodes to generate a desired effect or movement.
- Has the ability to make attribute connections to have top-level controls drive other controls that are deep in the rig hierarchy.
- Is able to simulate real-world anatomy and physiology on a character using software tools and commands.
- Knows how to bind and weight the points on the skin model to the deformers in the rig.
- Can plan and write scripts using MEL to facilitate rigging a character.
- Has a creative mind for solving problems that occur when building rigs in the interface or through MEL code.

BEING A TECHNICAL ARTIST

If you examine art history, cutting-edge art has always been created using the latest technological advances, and many innovative artists have always been somewhat technical in nature. Cave artists used crude drawing tools, Renaissance artists created perspective and mixed their own paints, and contemporary artists use computers. Some universally recognized great artists, such as Leonardo Da Vinci, who made one of the first T-posed characters in the Vitruvian Man (see **FIGURE 1.7**), were also scientific visionaries and inventors. So it is perhaps not so surprising that some artists interested in animation are also technically minded, and gravitate toward jobs that involve rigging, dynamic effects, and technical directing. A close cousin to these kinds of artists is the web site designer, who has traditionally combined art with coding, such as HTML and Java.

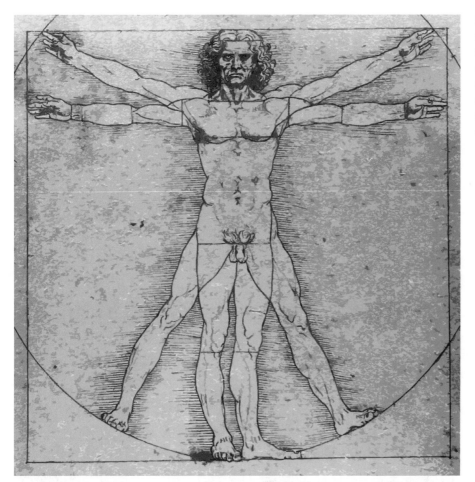

FIGURE 1.7 *Many artists are also technically minded, such as artist and inventor Leonardo Da Vinci, who created the Vitruvian Man—one of the first T-posed characters.*

Some people automatically assume that being technically inclined means being math-savvy. But the job of rigging characters has less to do with being a math wizard than simply being logical. Some high-level rigging operations do require math knowledge, especially if you stray into the area of software development to write a plug-in. But most standard rigging tasks can be done with the software commands and tools, and do not require any high-level math. Maya does the math for you, so you don't have to.

USING THE POWER OF LOGIC

Logic is what a rigging artist uses to come up with a plan to accomplish a complex task in both the software interface and in coding. It is also what is used to troubleshoot inevitable problems in the implementation of that plan.

Being logical mainly involves knowing and following the rules of the software or coding language, which were also created based on logic. When parenting nodes into a rig hierarchy, for instance, the rigging artist first finds out how the character should move, and then comes up with a logical plan for the hierarchical structure according to basic rules on how parented nodes work in Maya. The main rule is that all transforms of the parent nodes propagate to the child nodes.

With this in mind, if you want the backbone and hips to follow the torso controls, you make sure that the nodes controlling those areas of the body are child nodes of the torso node. But if you want the hips and backbone to be able to move separately from each other, you make sure that those nodes are on separate branches in the hierarchy (see **FIGURE 1.8**). You can follow a similar approach to keep the feet flat on the ground when the torso is moved, by making sure that the feet nodes are on a separate branch of the hierarchy than the torso node.

FIGURE 1.8 *Creating a rig hierarchy is based on logical choices, such as parenting the hips and backbone under the torso node, but keeping them on separate braches so they can move independently of each other.*

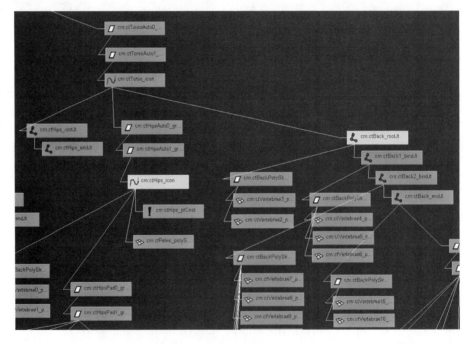

These logical choices are the basis for how most rigs are created in Maya. You can extend this logic to making specific connections between attributes on nodes that bypass parenting. Connecting attributes make rigs more complex and abstract, but all the connections are still based on logical rules. Attribute connections can be made in a variety of ways in Maya, including constraints, mathematical expressions, set driven keys, and direct connections in the Connection Editor. Such connection methods let you control particular transform attributes by simulating some parenting effects while filtering out others. For instance, instead of parenting one node to another, you can set a parent constraint that connects the translation and rotation channels, but not the scaling channels. The constrained node will then move and stay oriented to the target node, but won't scale with it. Since parenting is more straightforward than connecting channels, you should always default to it when building a rig. However, some controls will require more complex connections.

TROUBLESHOOTING RIG PROBLEMS

Coming up with a logical plan is the easy part of rigging. Implementing that plan without any problems to fix is the hard part. If you are trying to do something new and complex, there will invariably be some research and development that has to be done to streamline the plan. Sometimes the connections you make produce logic problems or cycles in the software that cause unpredictable results in the rig controls, or actual errors on the feedback field. The rigging artist should expect this as part of the process, and use the same logic and knowledge of the software to troubleshoot the problems until the rig is complete.

Since the main task in rigging is connecting nodes through parenting or other means, and nodes are connected through attributes or channels, most of the problems that crop up will be related to channel values. Channels are also what animators manipulate and set keys on when using the rig, so it is important for the rigging artist to understand how channel values are generated to make the animation controls work well. In Maya, transform channel values on any node are generated relative to the parent node channel values. When a node has no parent, the Maya world space is considered the parent, and channel values are generated relative to the position and orientation of the global axis. But as soon as you parent a node, the relative transform values on the child node change based on the position and orientation of the new parent node.

Essentially, when you connect a node to a hierarchy, the parent node becomes the global axis for the child node. Understanding this basic Maya rule will allow you to troubleshoot most problems that occur when creating rigs, and will enable you to manipulate channel values as needed to make the controls work well. Since the concept that attributes and channel values are generated relative to the parent is such an important aspect of creating rig controls, it's worth looking at an example in Maya.

To demonstrate how channel values are affected by parenting:

1. Create a primitive sphere by choosing Create > NURBS Primitives > Sphere.

2. Use the Move tool in Perspective view to move the sphere around, and watch the transform values change in the Channels panel.

Notice that the Translate values display the sphere's position in 3D space relative to the global 3D center.

3. In the Channels panel, type **0** in the Translate boxes to set the sphere back to where it was created.

4. With the sphere at the global center, create a group node parent for the sphere by pressing Ctrl+G (Command+G in Mac OS). Now if you move the group node, the sphere will move with it through the parenting connection.

5. Notice that translating the group node still generates channel values in relation to the global axis. But selecting the sphere shows that its channel values remain 0, even though the sphere is not at the global origin (see **FIGURE 1.9**).

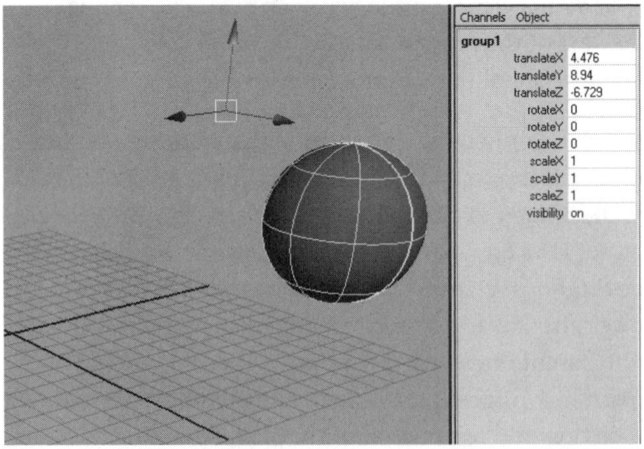

FIGURE 1.9

An important rigging concept is that channel values are generated in relation to the parent node in a hierarchy, such as this sphere's translation values in relation to a group node parent.

6. Move the sphere, and now notice that the Translate values are generated in relation to the parent's position, not in relation to the global center.

About Maya Skeletons

The main deformers in any character rig are skeletons, which in their most basic form are composed of a hierarchy of joints. The joints will ultimately be assigned to the character model through binding to drive the shape of the skin as the rig is animated. This section will introduce you to creating Maya skeletons by showing you how to draw, manipulate, and edit joints. You will also learn how to parent skeletons, which will culminate with an exercise in parenting joints into a simple hierarchy. Learning how to work with skeletons is the first step in building a rig in both the interface and through scripting.

Preparing to Create Skeletons

Since skeletons are so important to the function of a rig, you have to make a few preparations before creating them. First, make sure that you have good anatomical reference for placing the skeleton joints inside the character model. To make this easier when you do the exercise later in this chapter, you will open a scene containing a polygon reference skeleton, and use the polygon bones as a guide for placing the Maya joints. It is also helpful to acquire at least one good anatomy and physiology book to study how real joints are positioned and move in the human body. Of course, you also have unlimited access to one of the best references for a humanoid character: your own body. What's important to notice is how the joints in your body rotate, so that you can create similar effects with the Maya joints in the computer.

Another preparation is to set some user preferences to optimize the Maya interface for creating skeletons, and for some of the other rigging tasks in this chapter:

1. In the lower-right corner of the interface, click the Animation Preferences button.

2. In the Preferences dialog box that appears, in the Categories panel on the left, click Interface. Then in the Interface section, set the options as shown in **FIGURE 1.10**.

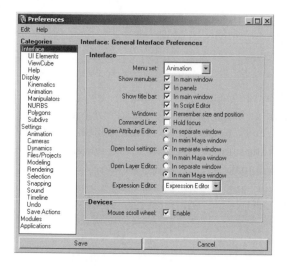

FIGURE 1.10

Set interface preferences to focus on animation and the Layer Editor in the main window, with tools and the Attribute Editor opening in a separate window.

3. In the Categories list on the left side of the dialog box, click UI Elements. Then set the preferences as in **FIGURE 1.11**.

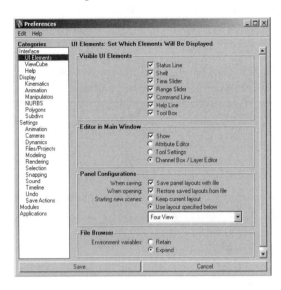

4. Click Save.

The options you've set will ensure that the Channel Box will always appear on the right side of the interface, which will allow you to examine attribute values and input connections on your joints. These options also set other editors and tools to open in separate floating windows, and will display the three main orthographic views for drawing skeletons.

5. To ensure that your primitives are created in the same manner as the book examples, in the Create menu, turn off the Interactive Creation option in both the NURBS Primitives and Polygon Primitives section.

Drawing Joints

You create skeletons by drawing joints in the 3D views using the Joint Tool. It is always best to draw the joints in the Orthographic view that allows you to place the joints most accurately within your character. At this point, you should draw all the joints for a given skeleton in the same orthographic view, rather than switch views while drawing. This will make sure that the skeletons you create have predictable components. For the same reason, do not draw joints in Perspective view until after you learn the basics of editing skeleton joints later in this chapter.

To draw a skeleton:

1. Choose Skeleton > Joint Tool ◘.

2. In the Joint Tool Settings dialog box, click the Reset Tool button in the lower section to use the default settings (see **FIGURE 1.12**).

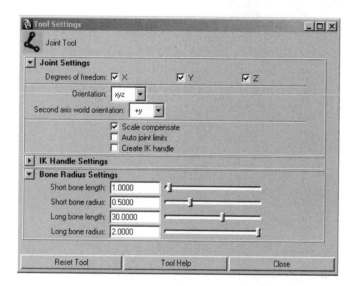

FIGURE 1.12 *Start drawing skeletons using the default Joint Tool settings, with IK turned off.*

3. Click the Close button in the lower section of the dialog to accept the settings.

4. Left-click to place a joint in the Front orthographic view. Hold down the left mouse button each time you draw a joint, and drag the cursor before releasing the left mouse button to set the joint exactly where you want it. If you position a joint badly, click the Z key to undo drawing the joint, and click again.

5. Click again in another spot in the Front view to see a bone drawn between the two spherical joints. Keep drawing joints until you draw a skeleton with at least four joints. If you make a mistake, click the Z key to undo the joint, and redraw it.

6. Press Enter to finalize the four-joint skeleton, which deactivates the Joint tool and selects the skeleton hierarchy (see **FIGURE 1.13**).

FIGURE 1.13 *Click and drag with the left mouse button to draw a skeleton in the Front orthographic view.*

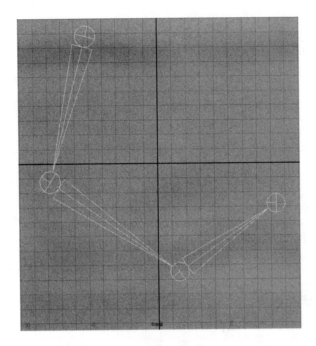

Take a moment to examine the structure of the skeleton in the 3D views. The joints are really just points in 3D space, but they appear as small wireframe spheres, connected by bones that appear as wireframe cones. The tapering bones indicate the direction in which the skeleton was drawn, and thus shows the hierarchy structure of the joints. As deformers that have no geometry, joints have position, direction, and length, but not width or thickness. In other words, a thick skeleton will not deform the model it is assigned to any more than a thin one. How much of the skin a skeleton deforms is instead based on the bind settings. For this reason, the display size of the joints and bones is based on user preference, and can be adjusted in the Display menu.

To change the display size of joints of bones:

1. Choose Display > Animation > Joint Size.

2. In the Joint Display Size panel, use the interactive slider to globally adjust the display size of the joints and bones according to the size of your character (see **FIGURE 1.14**).

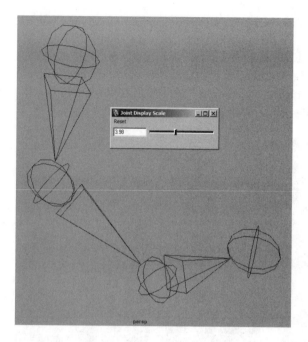

FIGURE 1.14 *Joints have only position and length, so the width can be interactively sized.*

Large models would require increasing the display size to more easily see the skeletons, while smaller models would require decreasing the size. To make the skeleton barely noticeable without actually hiding the joints, you can drag the slider to the lowest setting, which will display the skeleton as only a line.

A skeleton is really just a series of parented joints. To better see the hierarchy structure of the skeleton, open the Hypergraph.

To examine the skeleton nodes in the Hypergraph:

1. Open the Hypergraph by choosing Window > Hypergraph > Hierarchy to open a window that shows all the transform nodes in the scene, including the skeleton hierarchy.

2. In the Hypergraph, click the A key to frame all the nodes so you can see the entire skeleton in the window.

Skeleton nodes will always be labeled with some industry-standard naming conventions in this book. The first joint at the top of the hierarchy is known as the root joint of the skeleton, and should have the term "root" somewhere in the name. The last joint or bottom node in the hierarchy is known as the end joint, and should have "end" somewhere in the name. When you start parenting skeletons into a rig, adding these terms will indicate where a particular skeleton branch starts and ends in the hierarchy. Middle nodes should also have some kind of indication that they are joints by incorporating "joint" or "jt" in the name. This can be combined with other terms such as "bind" to create "bindJt" to indicate that it is a joint that will deform the skin. When you start scripting the rig, these terms will be combined with prefixes, suffixes, and increment values to ensure that all the nodes have unique names (see **FIGURE 1.15**).

FIGURE 1.15 *A common naming convention is to include the terms "root," "joint," and "end" in the names of skeleton joints.*

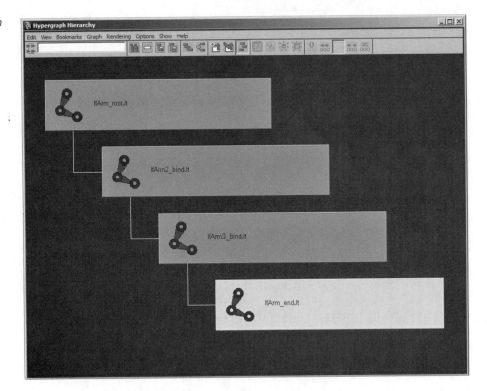

Understanding Joint Orientation

One of the unique properties of skeletons is the default center orientation of most joints. The default center orientation of other objects you create in Maya, such as primitives or group nodes, is always according to the global axis. Skeleton joints, however, are oriented according to the Joint Tool settings and how you draw the skeleton. If you use the default settings, and draw the skeleton in the Front view, Maya will orient a single axis to always point down the length of the bones. In other words, the orientation of the individual joints is designed to follow the direction of the skeleton.

To view the orientation of joints in the 3D views:

1. In the Hypergraph, drag a selection box around all the joints in a skeleton, and choose Display > Transform Display > Local Rotation Axes. This displays the rotation axes on the joints so that you can see the orientation of the centers in the 3D views (see **FIGURE 1.16**).

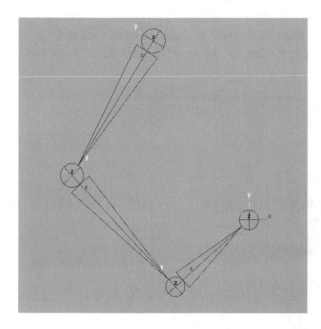

FIGURE 1.16 *In the default center orientation of skeleton joints, the X axis points down the bone toward the next joint in the skeleton; the end joint is oriented according to the global axis.*

2. Starting at the root joint, try rotating each joint of the skeleton hierarchy in the Z axis, and notice how the child joints in the hierarchy follow through the parenting connection.

3. To make rotating each joint easier, use the Up and Down arrow keys on the keyboard, called pickwalking, to move through the hierarchy.

Notice that all joints except the end joint are oriented so their X axis is pointing down the bone toward the next joint in the skeleton, with the Z and Y axes perpendicular to the X axis. This is the default joint orientation set by the Joint Tool when drawing a skeleton, and is important for the correct functioning of many body controls. The last joint in the skeleton, however, is oriented according to the global axis, because there is no next joint in the skeleton hierarchy to point at as a target. This doesn't affect the skeleton controls because the end joints are rarely animated in a rig. End joints are just used to determine the length and direction of the next-to-last joint in the skeleton.

As you rotate joints on the skeleton, check each joint's attribute values in the Channel Box. On a newly drawn skeleton, the root joint will always have translation values generated in relation to the global axis, just like all other objects in Maya. However, the rotation values will be 0, as they have been reset, known as freezing in Maya. This again reflects the special relative orientation of joints. The other joints in the skeleton have relative values for both translation and rotation, with 0 values in all the attributes except the X rotation channel. Since X points down the bone, the X translation value indicates the relative length of the bone, by showing the distance between joints in the skeleton (see **FIGURE 1.17**).

FIGURE 1.17 *Default rotation values of all joints on a skeleton are 0, while there is always an X translation value, which indicates the length of the bones.*

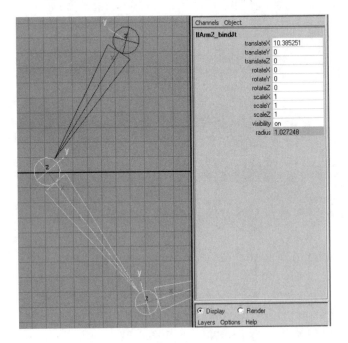

Fitting and Animating Skeletons

In general, individual joints are designed to be rotated, not translated, when animating a skeleton. It is standard to translate the root joint to fit the skeleton inside the character model, because it is the top node of the joint hierarchy. But be aware that translating other joints while manipulating a skeleton may change their default center orientation. Specifically, translating any joint below the root joint in the hierarchy may cause the previous joint's X axis to no longer face down the bone, which could be critical for some body controls to function properly, such as when the forearm rotates (see **FIGURE 1.18**). Manipulating skeletons through rotation, however, never adversely affects the center orientation of any joints.

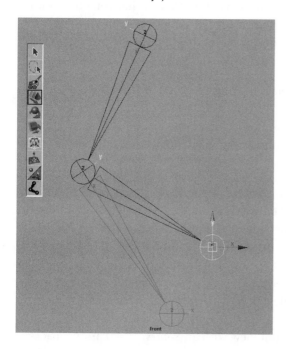

FIGURE 1.18 *Skeleton joints are meant to be rotated, because translating child joints won't update the center orientations correctly.*

Actually, there is an industry-standard name for rotating joints when animating: forward kinematics (FK). Rotating each joint from root to end is animating *forward* through the skeleton hierarchy, while setting keys is animating the movement or *kinematics*. FK is the most fundamental way of manipulating and animating a skeleton in Maya, and some basic rigs that only contain parented skeletons are considered FK rigs. Manipulating these types of rigs is very similar to manipulating the armature of a puppet, and many animators who have a puppeteer or stop motion background really like FK rigs. Also, most motion capture rigs are composed of FK skeletons, because the motion capture data is pretty straightforward and doesn't require extra connections in the nodes.

Setting Joint Tool Options

Although many of the Joint Tool options will remain at the default settings for skeletons created in this book, there are a few options that you need to know how to adjust (see Figure 1.12, shown earlier). Here is an overview of the main joint creation options, excluding details on the IK Handle Settings, which will be covered in Chapter 3, "Scripting a Basic IK Biped Rig":

Degrees of Freedom. Deselect the check box for any axis that you don't want to bend on the skeleton. This will lock the rotation attributes on all the joints. The default setting is to have all the degrees of freedom turned on, which will be used throughout this book.

Orientation. You will use the default setting of xyz for all the skeletons in this book, which is pretty standard in the industry. The first letter in this setting determines the main axis that points down the bone toward the next joint in the skeleton. If you set this option to None, it will orient the centers of all the joints according to the global axis.

Second Axis World Orientation. Use this option to keep the orientation of main joints consistent across the entire skeleton. Where the Orientation option sets the X axis to point down the bones, this option sets the direction of the other two axes on each joint. It is one of the few joint options that you may change for every skeleton you create, so it is important to understand how it works. For the XYZ orientation setting, Y is the second axis referred to in the name of this option. Using the default +Y setting for the second axis will always point the Y axis on each joint upward in global space. As a result, if you draw a skeleton upward in the Front view with an S-curve, such as on a backbone, using a +Y setting will cause some of the centers of the skeletons to flip 180 degrees in X (see **FIGURE 1.19**).

If you change the second axis setting to –X when drawing a similar skeleton, however, you will notice that the centers become consistently set with their Y axis pointed to the right side of the character, or global –X, and their Z axis points forward, or global +Z (see **FIGURE 1.20**).

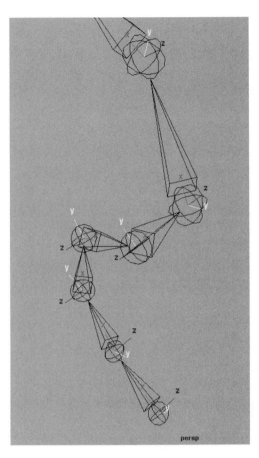

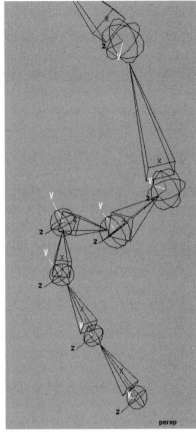

FIGURE 1.19 (left) *Using the default Second Axis World Orientation setting of +Y causes the joint centers to unpredictably flip 180 degrees in X, so that the Z axis is pointing forward on some joints and backward on others.*

FIGURE 1.20 (right) *Using a –X Second Axis World Orientation setting on a skeleton drawn upward forces the center orientations to be consistent, with the Z axis pointed forward for all the joints.*

Having consistent orientations on joints is preferable, because it simplifies scripting parts of the rigging process, such as making attribute connections.

Scale Compensate. This is another option that should remain in the default on setting. In its default setting, this option prevents scaling of joints to propagate through the rest of the skeleton hierarchy, which could cause deformation problems on the skin. By compensating for the scaling, the child joints move with the scaled joint without scaling themselves. Deselecting this option causes the scaling to propagate through the hierarchy from the pivot scaled joint, resulting in a stretching effect on the skin in the direction of the initial scaling.

Auto Joint Limits and Create IK Handle. By default this option is left off for all the skeletons in this book. If you draw a skeleton in an Orthographic view, it will be bent in only one axis and remain flat in all the others. In the Front view, for instance, the Z axis will be the main axis that shapes the skeleton. Turning this option on will automatically lock the two perpendicular axes to the main one facing you on all the joints except the root and end joints.

Create IK Handle. This option adds IK to the entire skeleton; it will be covered in detail in the section, "Using IK Skeletons in the Basic Rig," in Chapter 3.

Bone Radius Settings. Set these options to augment the display of your skeletons, in addition to using the menu sizing commands. This option lets you vary the display radius of individual bones based on the distance between joints as you draw them. Longer bones are sized larger, and vice versa, based on the upper and lower limits set.

Organizing Nodes in the Hypergraph

The Hypergraph is the best way to look at the parenting structure of nodes and to organize your hierarchy when building a rig in the interface. Since you will be using the Hypergraph extensively through the course of this book for rigging, it is important to set some basic options and to understand how to navigate in the window.

To use the Hypergraph to organize nodes:

1. If not already opened, again choose Window > Hypergraph > Hierarchy to open a standard Hypergraph window.

2. In the Hypergraph top menu bar, choose the following layout options:

■ Options > Layout > Freeform Layout to allow you to freely organize the nodes when creating a rig by just dragging them with the left mouse button (see **FIGURE 1.21**).

■ Options > Orientation > Horizontal to have Maya place newly created nodes to the right of existing nodes.

■ Options > Display. Deselect all options to ensure that you can see the parenting structure, which is the most important thing when initially building a rig. After the main parts of the rig are parented, you can display other connections as needed.

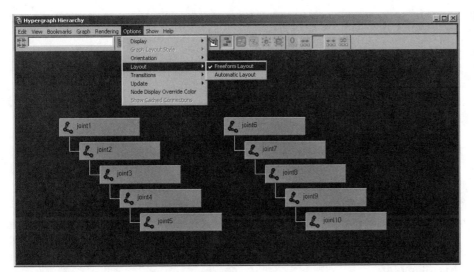

FIGURE 1.21 *Be sure to turn on Freeform Layout in the Hypergraph, which allows you to organize the nodes in a hierarchy by dragging them around.*

3. Use these techniques to navigate in the window:

   ■ Choose View > Frame All to show all the object nodes in the scene, or click the A key with your cursor in the window. You can also frame a selected node in the same menu by choosing Frame Selection, or click the F key.

   ■ To better view the nodes, navigate in the Hypergraph by holding down the Alt key.

   ■ To zoom in on a joint, drag with the left and middle mouse buttons held down; to navigate around the window, just drag with the middle mouse button held down.

4. To organize nodes in the Hypergraph:

   ■ Drag the nodes with the left mouse button to organize them while creating your rig, but keep the standard rule of placing parent nodes above the child nodes. This will make it easy to view the parenting at a glance.

   ■ Parent nodes by dragging one node on top of the other with the middle mouse button. Detach the parenting by using the middle mouse button to drag a parented node onto a black empty area in the Hypergraph.

   ■ As a good practice, organize nodes in the Hypergraph continuously as you create them. If you don't move the nodes, then they will automatically shift to the left when you start parenting. This can make nodes shift on top of other nodes, obscuring them from view. Moving the nodes even slightly will lock them down, and prevent this from happening. Maya remembers the positions of moved nodes, and saves that information with the scene file.

Editing Skeletons

While creating skeletons for a rig, you may need to adjust some of their components. Here is an introduction to some of the common skeleton editing tools and commands in Maya.

Making Basic Skeleton Edits

The Skeleton menu contains many basic editing tools and commands. Some of the commands—inserting, rerooting, removing, disconnecting, and connecting joints—will only be used if you make a mistake creating the skeletons in the interface. However, mirroring and orienting joints will be used throughout the book as a standard method of finalizing skeletons before parenting them into the rig in both the interface and through MEL scripting.

To edit a joint:

1. Choose Skeleton > Joint.

2. Select the joint you want to edit. The Skeleton menu appears (see **FIGURE 1.22**).

3. Choose an option from the Skeleton menu to edit the joint, as described in the following sections.

INSERTING JOINTS

Use the Insert Joint tool if you find the need to add an extra joint in a previously created skeleton. Simply choose Skeleton > Insert Joint Tool, and click any joint to insert a joint along the local X axis. Notice that the new joint slides along the length of the bone.

REROOTING A SKELETON

Use this command if a skeleton was drawn in the wrong direction. Select the end joint of the skeleton, and choose Skeleton > Reroot. Notice that the bones taper in the opposite direction, and the hierarchy has been rearranged in the Hypergraph. If you reroot a middle joint in a skeleton, it will split the skeleton into two branches from the selected joint.

REMOVING JOINTS

You can remove joints from a skeleton by selecting the joint and choosing Skeleton > Remove Joint. Always use this method of removing a joint rather than deleting it directly, which will break apart the hierarchy, deleting all child joints in the branch.

FIGURE 1.22

The Skeleton menu has several useful tools and commands for editing joints.

DISCONNECTING JOINTS

Sometimes you may need to separate a skeleton into multiple skeletons while preserving the positioning. To do this, Maya must create overlapping joints where the skeletons are separated. To disconnect joints, select a joint in the middle of a skeleton, and choose Skeleton > Disconnect Joint. In the Hypergraph, notice that the selected joint became the root joint of a new skeleton, and a new overlapping end joint was created for the original skeleton.

CONNECTING JOINTS

You can use this command if separate skeletons need to be parented, but parenting can just as easily be manually done in the Hypergraph. If you do use this command, make sure that you open the options dialog box to choose a connection method.

To connect joints:

1. Make sure that you have two separate skeletons in your scene.
2. Select the root joint of the skeleton you want to connect. Then Shift-click to select the end joint of the skeleton you want to add.
3. Choose Skeleton > Connect Joint.
4. In the options dialog box, choose from the following:
   - Connect Joint to move the joint you are adding to wherever the other joint is, and have it parented under the previous joint in the main skeleton.
   - Parent Joint to leave the new skeleton in place, and simply parent the root joint under the end joint of the main skeleton.
5. Click Connect to parent the skeletons and close the dialog box.

MIRRORING JOINTS

Many biped characters are symmetrical for the right and left sides of the body. Since this is the kind of character being rigged in this book, it saves time to create the skeleton on only one side, and mirror a duplicate to the other side. Mirroring differs from straight copying in that it automatically flips the orientation of the joints so that they generate the same channel values on both sides of the body when they are rotated. This is an industry-standard way of setting up biped character controls.

To mirror a skeleton:

1. In the Front orthographic view, draw a three-joint skeleton completely on the left side of the global Y axis.

2. With the root joint selected, choose Skeleton > Mirror Joint.

3. In the Mirror Joint Options dialog box, select:

   ■ Mirror Across YZ plane, which tells Maya that you want to go from the left to the right side across the Y axis.

   ■ Mirror Function Behavior to generate reverse values. (The Orientation option generates the same values for joints on each side of the body.)

4. Click Mirror to duplicate the skeleton and close the dialog box.

5. Select the joints on the mirrored skeleton, and notice that their channel values are the reverse of the original channel values.

To test the mirrored behavior, select the second joint on the left skeleton, and Shift-select the second joint on the right copy. Rotating both together produces the same movements on both skeletons (see **FIGURE 1.23**).

FIGURE 1.23 *Mirroring joints enables creating a duplicate skeleton on opposite sides of the body that have mirrored or flipped values. Industry-standard mirroring produces the same behavior on both sides of the body when the joints are rotated.*

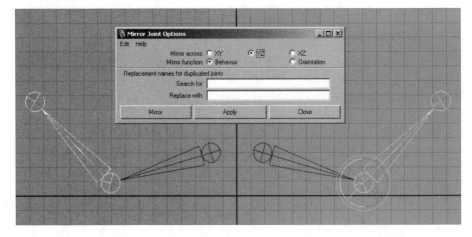

RESETTING JOINT ORIENTATION

You may have to reset the orientation of joints after fitting a skeleton into a character's body, or if you had to draw the skeleton in multiple views. Once you are comfortable working with skeletons, you may break some of the basic rules to create and place the skeleton joints as quickly as possible. In those cases, it is standard to orient the joints afterward to make sure the skeleton works correctly.

To reset a joint's orientation:

1. To try out this command, translate the second joint in one of your skeletons so the X axis of the root joint is no longer pointed down the bone. Make sure you display the centers of the joints to see the orientation. Then select the root joint.

2. Choose Skeleton > Orient Joint to open a dialog box that contains the same default settings as in the Joint tool. Use the default settings and click Apply to reset the orientations of all the joints in the skeleton (see **FIGURE 1.24**).

FIGURE 1.24 *Orient Joint settings are the same as for the Joint tool, and can be used to fix orientation problems after fitting skeletons into the skin model.*

FREEZING SKELETONS

When resetting the orientation of joints, you may get a warning that prevents the command from working. This occurs if you try to orient a skeleton that has values in the rotation channels. For instance, rotating joints to position them in the character, and then running the Orient Joint command, will produce a warning on the command line stating that there are nonzero rotations, and the centers on the joints will not change. To reorient joints on a manipulated skeleton, the rotation channels on all the joints of the skeleton must be first set back to their default 0 values. To reset the values without losing the manipulated shape of the skeleton, you run the Freeze Transformations command in the Modify menu.

To freeze a skeleton:

1. Select the root joint to freeze all the joints in the skeleton.

2. Choose Modify > Freeze Transformations ◘ in the Modify menu. Make sure that the Joint Orient option is deselected, which will set the values to 0, but preserve the current joint orientation. Turning this option on will set all the centers to the global orientation (see **FIGURE 1.25**).

FIGURE 1.25 *Turn off the Joint Orient check box when freezing FK skeletons to preserve their orientation while resetting their values.*

3. Click Freeze Transform to reset the transform values.

Only freeze FK skeletons after you first create them, when there are no connections to the joints. Do not freeze skeletons that were created with the Inverse

Kinematics (IK) option turned on in the Joint Tool Settings dialog box, as freezing could break the IK connection. This will be discussed further in Chapter 3, "Scripting a Basic IK Biped Rig."

Performing a Test Bind

Binding is assigning joints in a skeleton to the components of a model so that rotating any of the joints will move the points in the model to deform it. This is the best way to find out how well you made your rig, and is the main reason for creating the rig in the first place. The amount that a joint influences a point on the skin is called weighting, one of the main concepts in rigging that you need to understand.

Assigning a basic bind only takes a few seconds, so it is a good idea to do test binds early in the rigging process. If any joints are not placed correctly, you can then remove the bind and fix the placement before doing a final bind after the rig is finished. This section introduces you to how to create and edit a basic smooth bind, which will be expanded upon in Chapter 5, "Finishing the IK Biped Rig."

Introduction to Smooth Binding

In this section you will be introduced to the smooth binding method, and then additional details on other binding methods will be covered in chapter 5. The smooth binding method assigns a percentage of influence, called weighting, from multiple joints to the points on the skin model. The falloff in weighting between the joints causes the skin to deform in a smooth manner when the joints move and rotate.

Here, you will focus on learning how to assign and remove a basic smooth bind, so you can test bind the rig as you are building it throughout this book. Before binding a character, however, the easiest way to see how joints deform geometry is to bind a simple primitive.

To bind a simple primitive to a skeleton:

1. Create a polygon cylinder, and bind it to a three-joint skeleton.
2. To create the geometry, choose Create > NURBS Primitives > Cylinder ❐.
3. In the NURBS Cylinder Options dialog box, set the options as shown in **FIGURE 1.26**. This will create a tall cylinder with 12 subdivisions.

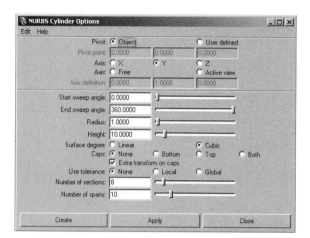

FIGURE 1.26 *Create a primitive cylinder with these settings to try smooth binding a skeleton.*

4. Then in the "Front view," draw a three-joint skeleton vertically within the cylinder, bending to the right at the second joint in the middle of the cylinder (see **FIGURE 1.27**).

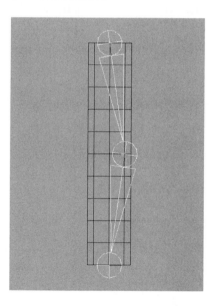

FIGURE 1.27 *Draw a three-joint skeleton from top to bottom of the cylinder, with a bend toward the right side at the middle.*

This is how you would draw a very simple limb skeleton, such as an arm or leg.

5. To bind the cylinder to the skeleton, select the cylinder, Shift-select the root joint of the skeleton, and choose Skin > Bind Skin > Smooth Bind ❐.

6. Set the options as shown in **FIGURE 1.28**. Binding options will be covered in detail in Chapter 5.

FIGURE 1.28 *Smooth bind the cylinder to skeleton joints using these basic settings as a test.*

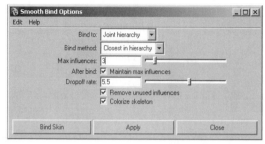

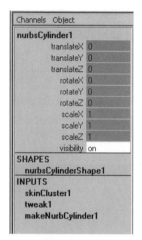

FIGURE 1.29 *Selecting the bound cylinder displays a skinCluster node in the Inputs and locked transform channels in the Channel Box's panel.*

FIGURE 1.30 *Smooth Bind looks smooth because the points in the bending area of the cylinder move with multiple joints.*

7. Click Bind Skin. You will see the cylinder turn purple, which indicates it has a connection to the component inputs to the skeleton joints.

To get more details on this connection:

1. Select the cylinder. In the Inputs section of the Channels Box, note the skinCluster1 node, which indicates that the model has a smooth bind connection (see **FIGURE 1.29**).

Also notice that the transform channels have turned dark gray, which means they have been locked. Maya automatically locks the transforms of a bound skin to prevent it from being moved. Once a skin is bound, it should only be moved through the bound components or points, when the joints transform.

2. Select the second joint of the bound skeleton.

3. Select the Rotate tool, and rotate the joint in the direction of the bend to see the cylinder deform.

4. Notice how the geometry smoothly compresses into the bending joint, as shown in **FIGURE 1.30**.

This compression is caused by the first and second joints sharing influence over the points close to the deforming area. A continuous falloff of weighting between the influences causes the points to move with both joints to create the smooth bend, with minimum intersections of geometry.

Once you test a bind by rotating some of the joints to see the deformation on the skin, you may decide joints must be moved, edited, or added to the skeleton. To make these improvements, you must first detach the bind, which removes all the connections to the skin.

To detach a smooth bind:

1. Set the joint you rotated to test the bind back to its default position by typing **0** in the Rotation channel in the Channel Box.

2. To remove the smooth bind, select the cylinder, and choose Skin > Detach Skin ❑.

3. In the Detach Skin options box, use the default settings of Delete History and Remove Joint Colors turned on.

In the Channel Box, notice that the transform channels are no longer locked, and that there is no longer a skinCluster node in the Inputs of the cylinder.

Introduction to Painting Skin Weights

No matter how well you make your rig and skin, you will always have to fix deformation issues by manually editing weights. The quickest and easiest way to edit the weighting on a smooth bind is to use the Paint Skin Weights tool.

To manually edit the weighting on the bound cylinder:

1. Middle-click to activate Perspective view, and make the view full size by pressing the spacebar on the keyboard. Optimize Perspective view for painting weights by selecting Smooth Shade All and X Ray Joints in the view's Shading menu (see **FIGURE 1.31**).

2. Before painting any weights, select the second joint in the skeleton and rotate it about 85 degrees. This should bend the skeleton to look similar to a bent arm. Bending the skeleton will make it easier to see the effects of your weight painting.

3. Select the bound cylinder, and choose Skin > Edit Smooth Skin > Paint Skin Weights Tool ❑. The advantage of the Paint Skin Weights tool is that it offers an intuitive way of adjusting the bind weighting without having to deal with exact numeric percentages of weighting values.

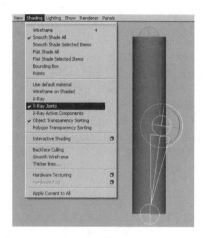

FIGURE 1.31 *When using the Paint Joint Weights tool, turn on Smooth Shading and X-Ray Joints in the Perspective view menu.*

4. Notice in Perspective view that the skin changes to a grayscale gradient to visually represent the weighting (see **FIGURE 1.32**).

This is called a weight map, and there is one generated for each joint in the influence list.

FIGURE 1.32 *Click a joint in the influence list to see the grayscale weight map for painting.*

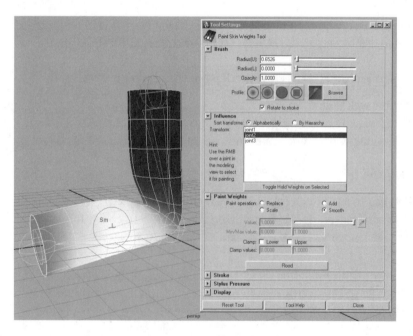

5. In the Influence section of the Paint Skin Weights Tool Settings dialog box, click the second and third joints in the list to change the default joint selected and see the weighting map change colors.

On the grayscale gradient, the color white represents a weighting value of 1, which influences the points 100%. The color black, on the other hand, represents a weighting value of 0, which has no influence on the points.

6. In the Paint Skin Weights Tool Settings dialog box, set these options:

■ In the Brush section, set the size of your brush by adjusting the Radius slider. You can also set the brush size interactively by holding down the B key and left mouse button as you move the mouse in Perspective view. The brush should be sized to fit the area you want to paint on your model. Keep in mind that although it will appear that you are painting on the surface, you are really just clicking on the surface points. So if your brush doesn't touch a point while painting, the weighting won't change.

■ From the list of Influences in the tool settings dialog box, choose the first joint assigned to the cylinder.

■ In the Paint Weights section, choose a value for the Paint Operation, and paint on the surface of the model as needed. For instance, with the first joint selected in the list, set the operation to Replace, and the value to 1.

7. Paint the area around the area where the skeleton bends at the second joint. Assigning weight to the first joint will prevent the points from moving with the second joint, making the surface of the cylinder stick out, and look more solid (see **FIGURE 1.33**).

You can then switch the Paint Operation to Smooth, which averages the weighting on the points and softens the effect.

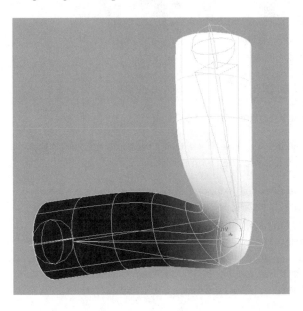

FIGURE 1.33 *Paint weights in the bend area to add weighting to the skeleton's root joint, to make an elbow or knee look more solid on a character.*

EXERCISE 1.1: CREATING A BASIC FK BIPED RIG

This exercise will take you through the steps for creating a simple FK rig in the Maya interface (see **FIGURE 1.34**), which will give you more experience in drawing, editing, and parenting joints. Creating a rig using only skeletons will facilitate building and MEL scripting a more complex rig throughout the rest of the book.

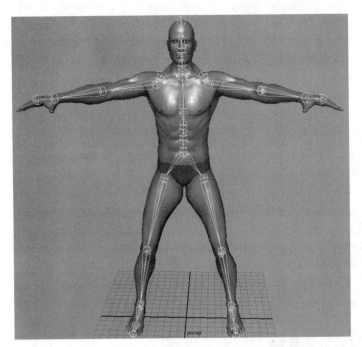

FIGURE 1.34 *This exercise creates a simple FK rig that fits inside the character's skin and will be used to create a more complex IK rig in later chapters.*

Step 1: Draw the Backbone Skeletons

You will begin this exercise by drawing skeletons in the 3D views for the biped character provided in the Maya scene files provided with the book.

1. Open the Maya file named Chapter1_skinBones.mb, which contains a character model with an anatomical reference skeleton composed of polygon bones.

The character model is named cm_skin, and has been placed on the skinModel layer so you can easily control its visibility. The polygon bones have already been fit inside the skin, and have been placed on the polyBones layer. You will use these polygon bones as reference for drawing your Maya skeletons accurately, and then will parent the polygon bones to the Maya joints to more easily see how they are moving and rotating.

2.   Start by drawing the backbone skeleton in the Side orthographic view so its shape follows the S-curve of the polygon backbone. This skeleton should be a five-joint skeleton drawn upward from the hips to the base of the neck.

3.   To more easily see the polygon bones to use them as a guide, template the skin by clicking the second empty box next to the skinModel layer name. A T should appear in the box, and the skin should become a transparent gray shade. Also make sure you have X-Ray Joints turned on in the Shading menu of any view you are working in.

4.   Open the Joint Tool Settings dialog box by choosing Skeleton > Joint Tool ◻, and change the Second Axis World Orientation setting to –X, leaving the rest of the options at their default settings.

5.   Then start drawing the skeleton at the base of the polygon vertebrae named ctVertebrae0_polySkel, continuing the skeleton upward through the backbone by clicking at the base of the following polygon vertebrae; ctVertebrae2_polySkel, ctVertebrae4_polySkel, ctVertebrae7_polySkel, and ctVertebrae15_polySkel (see **FIGURE 1.35**).

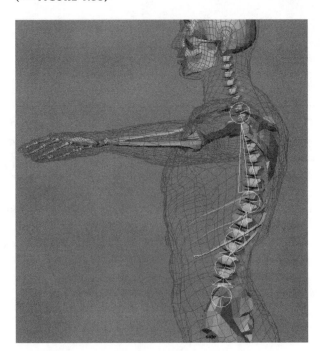

FIGURE 1.35 *Create a simple four-joint backbone skeleton that follows the contour of the polygon vertebrae.*

6.   Rename the joints with the following names from root joint to end joint: ctHips_fkRig, ctSpine0_fkRig, ctSpine1_fkRig, ctSpine2_fkRig, ctSpine3_fkRig.

7. Also in Side view, use the Joint Tool to draw a three-joint neck skeleton from the base of the vertebrae ctVertebrae17_polySkel to the base of the ctSkull_polySkel, and then to the top of the skull (see **FIGURE 1.36**).

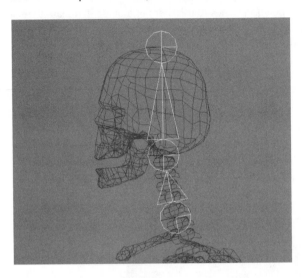

FIGURE 1.36 *Continue the neck skeleton up to the top of the head.*

8. Name the joints ctNeck_fkRig, ctHead_fkRig, and ctHeadEnd_fkRig.

9. Select the root joints of each skeleton and freeze transforms by choosing Modify > Freeze Transformations ❏, being sure to deselect the Joint Orient check box in the options.

10. Then check the centers on both skeletons by selecting all the individual joints in the Hypergraph, and choose Display > Transform Display > Local Rotation Axes.

The X axis should be pointing down the bones for all the joints except the end joint, and the Z axis should be pointed forward in Z. If any centers were changed while editing, you can reset them by using the Orient Joint command in the Skeleton menu using the same orientation settings as used in the Joint Tool options.

11. When done checking the centers, turn off their display by selecting the joints and running the Local Rotation Axes command again.

12. Save your work by choosing File > Save Scene As, and then type in the name **Exercise1Rig** and click Save.

Step 2: Draw the Arm and Leg Skeletons

When scripting the rig throughout this book, you will use a basic FK rig similar to the one you are creating as reference for creating the joints in the scripted rig. Because of the complex connections on the scripted rig, the FK rig arm and leg skeletons need to be bent in only one axis, known as being planar. This will be required to make connections like inverse kinematics work on the limbs correctly. To tell Maya what axis to use for bending the skeleton with IK, you must draw the skeleton in the appropriate orthographic view. This lets you create the appropriate angle for the limb, called the preferred angle, while still keeping the skeleton flat in the other axes. For the arms of a biped skeleton with the palms facing downward, you draw the skeleton in Top view, with a slight bend backward toward the elbows (see **FIGURE 1.37**).

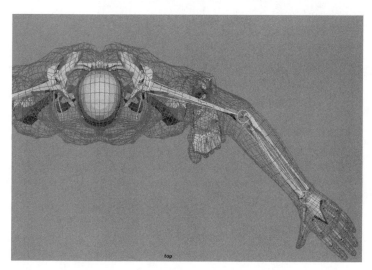

FIGURE 1.37 *Draw the arm skeleton in Top view to create a bend back toward the elbow, and to make the skeleton planar in the other axes.*

The leg skeletons, on the other hand, should be drawn in Side view, with a slight bend toward the front of the knees. To maintain the planar orientation, you transform the root joints to fit the skeletons correctly into the skin. Be careful not to rotate or translate the main joints at the elbows and knees when fitting them. Also, since the character is symmetrical, it is only necessary to draw the left skeletons, and use the Mirror Joint menu command to create the right skeletons.

To draw the arm and leg skeletons:

1. Begin by drawing the left arm skeleton in Top view to create a slight bend toward the back of the characters elbow.

2. In the Joint Tool Settings dialog box, change the Second Axis World Orientation setting to +Y.

You should draw this skeleton as four joints at the shoulder, elbow, wrist, and base of the middle finger. This creates a four-joint skeleton for the arm and hand that is created at the base of the character in Y. Since drawing a skeleton in an Orthographic view creates it flat in the other two axes, a skeleton drawn in Top view will always be positioned at 0 in the Y axis (see **FIGURE 1.38**).

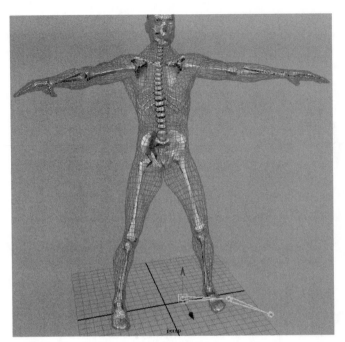

FIGURE 1.38 *Move the arm skeleton up into the shoulder area, and rotate the root joint in Z until it fits within the arm.*

3. To finalize the skeleton, translate the root joint upward in Y to the shoulder, and rotate it in Z to align the Maya joints with the polygon arm bones. Even though you shouldn't rotate the elbow joint to preserve the planar orientation, you can rotate the hand joint to create a better fit, because the hand will not be controlled in the same way as the arm.

4. Name the joints lfArm_fkRig, lfForearm_fkRig, lfHand_fkRig, and lfHandEnd_fkRig.

5. Finally, freeze the transforms on the skeleton, and double-check all the center orientations to make sure they are consistent. Y should be pointed upward, and Z should be pointed forward, and all the joints except the end joint.

6. In the Joint Tool Settings dialog box, change the Second Axis World Orientation setting to +X. Draw a five-joint left leg skeleton in the side view at the hips, knee, ankle, ball of the foot, and end of the toe. Draw a bend toward the front of the knee to create the correct preferred angle on that part of the leg. The foot part of the skeleton should bend downward at the ball of the foot, angling upward slightly at the toe. The skeleton is created at 0 in the X axis this time, and should be positioned inside the left leg of the character.

7. Transform the root joint in Front view to position it correctly in the leg. Try to position and rotate the root joint so the Maya bones are aligned with the polygon leg bones (see **FIGURE 1.39**). You can scale any of the joints in their local X to make them longer if needed, as long as you don't change the planar orientation.

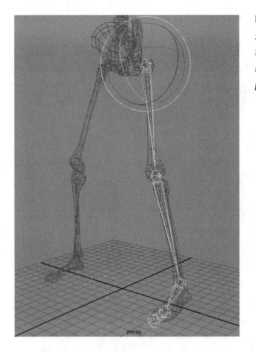

FIGURE 1.39 *Draw the leg skeleton in Side view and transform the root joint until it is aligned with the leg polygon bones.*

8. Name the joints lfUpLeg_fkRig, lfLeg_fkRig, lfFoot_fkRig, lfToeBase_fkRig, and lfToeEnd_fkRig.

9. Finalize the left leg by freezing the transforms on the skeleton, and double-check the center orientations. All the joints should have their Y axis pointed to the side, and their Z axis pointed forward.

10. Save your work by choosing File > Save Scene.

Step 3: Parent, Orient, and Mirror the Joints

Once all the main skeletons are created, you can parent them together to form the main part of the FK biped rig.

1. First open the Hypergraph to organize your four skeletons, and prepare to do all the parenting. Then make the neck skeleton child to the backbone skeleton by dragging the ctNeck_fkRig root joint on top of the ctSpine3_fkRig end joint with the middle mouse button in the Hypergraph.

Now the skeleton goes from the hips through the backbone to the top of the head.

2. To make sure the centers are oriented correctly across the entire skeleton, select the root joint at the hips and choose Skeleton > Orient Joint. Use the default XYZ orientation and set the Second Axis World Orientation to –X. This will ensure that the X axis points down the bones for all the joints except the end joint at the top of the head (see **FIGURE 1.40**).

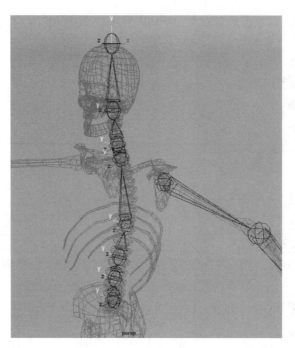

FIGURE 1.40 *Parent the neck skeleton under the end of the backbone skeleton, and orient the joints so the Z axes face forward.*

3. In the Hypergraph, drag the left leg root joint named lfUpLeg_fkRig on top of the node named ctHips_fkRig, or the root joint of the main skeleton created in Step 1. Once the left leg skeleton is parented into the torso, you can mirror it to the right side to create and automatically parent the other leg skeleton.

4. Select the lfUpLeg_fkRig joint, and choose Skeleton > Mirror Joint. In the Mirror Joint Options dialog box, mirror across the YZ plane, use the Behavior function, and type in the field labeled Search for: **lf**, and Replace with: **rt**. This renames the right skeleton joints with the correct prefix.

5. Notice that the right leg is automatically attached to the hips joint, and that the centers on all the main joints are flipped around to produce the mirror effect. At this point, your Hypergraph view of the hierarchy should look like **FIGURE 1.41**.

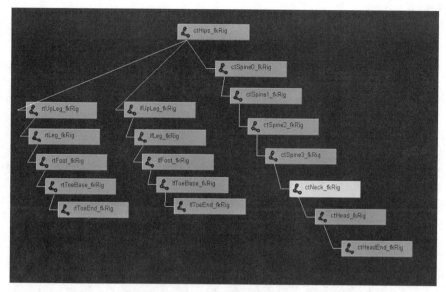

FIGURE 1.41 *How the hierarchy in the Hypergraph appears, after parenting and mirroring the leg skeletons under the backbone root.*

Lastly, you need to draw an extra joint to attach and finish the left arm skeleton before mirroring it over to the right side.

6.   Open the Joint Tool Settings dialog box, and make sure that you are using the XYZ orientation with a –X second axis world orientation.

7.   In Front view, click directly on the backbone joint named ctSpine3_fkRig, and then draw another joint where the left polygon clavicle bone ends at the shoulder, and finalize the skeleton (see **FIGURE 1.42**).

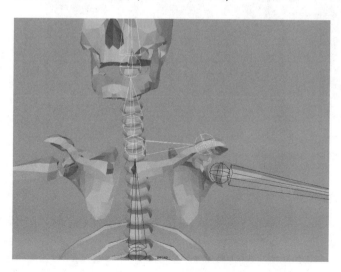

FIGURE 1.42
Click directly on the backbone joint to draw a clavicle skeleton branch out to the shoulder.

This joint should be positioned slightly above the root joint of the left arm skeleton, and should be named lfShoulder_fkRig. Clicking directly on a joint allows you to draw a new branch off an existing skeleton, fusing the roots of the branches into a single joint.

8. To complete the left arm skeleton, in the Hypergraph parent the left arm root joint under the new shoulder joint.

9. To make sure all the centers are oriented correctly, select the lfShoulder_fkRig joint and choose Skeleton > Orient Joint; use the XYZ orientation and the +Y second axis world orientation.

Checking the centers of the joints should show the X axis pointed down the bones, and the Z axis pointed forward on all the joints except the lfHandEnd_fkRig joint (see **FIGURE 1.43**).

10. To finalize the arms, select the shoulder joint again, and mirror it to the other side with the same settings you used when mirroring the legs.

11. Save your work by choosing File > Save Scene.

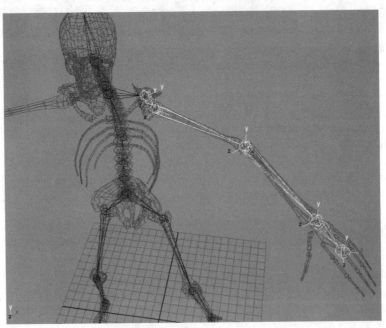

FIGURE 1.43 *Parent the root of the arm skeleton under the root of the shoulder skeleton, and orient the joints so that Z points forward.*

Step 4: Finish the FK Rig Hierarchy

At this stage all the skeletons are part of the FK rig. To finalize this rig you have to create a top group node for the whole hierarchy, parent the polygon bones under the appropriate Maya joints, and parent the eye geometry under the head joint. Parenting the polygon bones lets you use the polygon bones as visual reference for how the Maya joints are moving when animated.

Since Maya joints are only displayed as wireframe spheres and cones, it can be difficult to see if they are rotating incorrectly, especially if they twist around their local X axis. Making the polygon bones child to the Maya joints will show whether any problems occur on the joints when manipulating the rig controls before binding.

1.   Select the joint ctHips_fkRig, and choose Edit > Group, or press Ctrl+G (Command+G in Mac OS). The group node pivot should be created at the base of the character on the global center in world space.

2.   Organize the nodes in the Hypergraph so that the new top node is above the rest of the nodes, and rename it Reference.

3.   Parent the polygon bones under the appropriate Maya joints, so that rotating the joints moves the bones correctly.

For instance, the lfFemur_polySkel polygon bone should be child to the lfUpLeg_fkRig joint (see **FIGURE 1.44**).

Most of the parenting should be pretty intuitive, but you can use the basicFkRig.mb file as a guide.

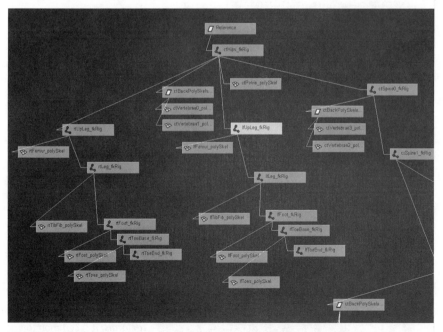

FIGURE 1.44 *Finish the hierarchy by parenting the polygon bones under the Maya skeletons, so that they move when the joints are rotated.*

4. Save your final FK rig by choosing File > Save Scene.

Step 5: Test Bind the Skin

Performing a test bind is when you temporarily assign a bind to assess deformations while you are still building the rig. Binding and moving the controls will show whether you need to make any fundamental changes to joint position, orientations, or hierarchy structure. Then you can detach the skin and edit the skeletons or node hierarchy as needed, and bind again.

1. To do a test bind, in the Hypergraph select the skin of the character, and Shift-select the top joint in your FK hierarchy, which is the ctHips_fkRig joint.

2. Choose Skin > Bind Skin > Smooth Bind. Set the bind options according to **FIGURE 1.45**, and click Bind Skin.

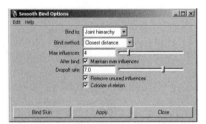

FIGURE 1.45 *Smooth bind the skin using these basic settings as a starting point for testing the deformations.*

3. Once bound, click the second box in the skinModel layer to turn off template mode, and display the shaded skin. Select and rotate the left arm joint in Z to lower the arm, and see how the skin deforms in the shoulder area. You will notice that the skin in the torso area under the arm collapses into the chest when the arm goes down (see **FIGURE 1.46**).

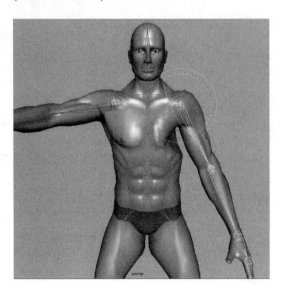

FIGURE 1.46 *Rotate the Maya joints to see how the skin deforms. It is common to find weighting issues on a basic bind, such as the chest caving in when an arm is lowered.*

The reason the skin collapses is that the points in this area have automatically been assigned too much weighting to the arm joint because of their close proximity. You could manually weight and smooth this area with the Paint Weights tool to improve the deformations in this area.

4. Undo the arm rotation by pressing the Z key. Then press the Down arrow key on the keyboard to pickwalk through the hierarchy to the left forearm joint, and rotate in Y to bend the arm at the elbow. Compare the deformation to how a real arm looks when it bends. Then undo the rotation again.

5. Keep selecting different joints in the FK rig to rotate the joints, and check how the skin deforms. Always use rotations on the different parts of the rig, and always undo the rotations after testing a joint.

As you check the deformations on the bound rig, you will notice that most of the major problems occur in the area that a limb or appendage attaches to the torso. This is because the joints from separate body areas are close to each other, so that the falloff of the weighting begins to bleed into each other. Actually, one of the reasons a T-pose is used when modeling the character is to minimize this problem. Having the arms lifted away from the torso keeps most of the arm joints away from the torso joints, and prevents incorrect weighting due to proximity.

6. When you have finished testing the skin deformation, remove the bind by selecting the model and choose Skin > Detach Skin ◻; be sure to delete History in the options dialog box.

After testing, you can adjust any joints that didn't look as if they were rotating around the correct pivots. If you make any edits to the skeletons that produce values in the transform channels, make sure that you freeze the joints afterward. Also display the center orientations, and reset the joint orientation if necessary.

WRAPPING UP

This chapter has introduced you to the character rigging process in the Maya interface. At this stage you have begun to learn about how to create skeletons, and how to parent them into a simple FK rig. You have also learned how to create a smooth bind, and seen some of the potential weighting problems that must be manually fixed on a bound skin. In the next chapter you will be introduced to MEL so you can start scripting the rigging process.

10 IMPORTANT POINTS TO REMEMBER FROM THIS CHAPTER

- Character rigs should be easy to use, and hard to break.

- Rigging artists should know how to create logical hierarchies.

- Rigging artists should know how to design iconic and graphical user interfaces for characters.

- Rigging artists must have strong knowledge of anatomy and physiology.

- In Maya the parent node becomes the world axis for the child node in a hierarchy, determining how channel values are generated.

- Skeletons are deformers that have position and length, but not width.

- The standard orientation of joints orients the X axis down the bone toward the next joint in the skeleton hierarchy, except the end joint, which is oriented according to the global axis.

- The most basic way to animate a skeleton is to rotate joints from the root joint to the end joint, called forward kinematics, or FK.

- The Second Axis World Orientation option determines the direction of the Y axis, which automatically determines the Z axis, and can make the joint orientation consistent across the entire skeleton.

- Smooth binding assigns multiple joints to a single point on a character model a percentage of influence called weighting, which determines how the skin deforms.

2

Learning to Script in MEL

THIS CHAPTER INTRODUCES you to MEL scripting in
Maya. You will learn how to find the MEL commands
and procedures that Maya uses to do everything that
occurs when working in the software interface. You will
also learn how to look up each command to see all the
options available, and how to streamline your code to
run more efficiently. This chapter also introduces essential
scripting techniques, such as using variables, arrays,
procedures, and loops. Learning such techniques will start
you toward the goal of scripting a character rig in Maya
through the rest of the book.

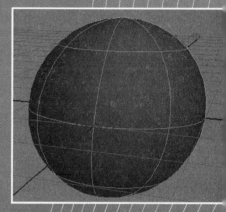

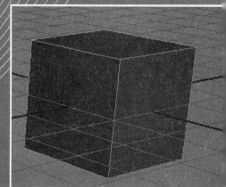

MEL Scripting Basics

This section gets you started learning MEL by examining how Maya runs MEL commands behind the scenes to execute everything you do in the interface. You will also learn the correct syntax and formatting for writing your own basic MEL commands, and how to look up the details of command options. You will learn how to combine MEL commands with intermediate coding techniques, such as variables and procedures, to create MEL scripts that can accomplish a variety of complex tasks in Maya. As a final step you will learn how to save your script into a MEL script file, so that the code can be further developed and edited in a dedicated script editor.

Starting to Code in Maya

Everything you do in the Maya interface is done through MEL code. The easiest way to see this is to look at the MEL command line, composed of a white-and-gray field below the timeline and next to the label MEL in the lower right of the Maya interface. The gray field on the right displays comments and error messages that occur as Maya runs MEL commands in the background while you are working. The white field on the left allows you to type in simple MEL commands to directly access Maya's core software. You can easily view some MEL commands by doing something in the Maya interface, such as creating a primitive NURBS sphere by choosing Create > NURBS Primitives > Sphere ◻. Look at the resulting options box to see what is available when creating a NURBS sphere in the interface, and then click the Create button to create a sphere with the default options. Also notice that code comes up in the gray feedback field in the command line (see **FIGURE 2.1**).

FIGURE 2.1 *Create a primitive sphere in the interface, and notice the MEL code displayed in the gray feedback field on the command line.*

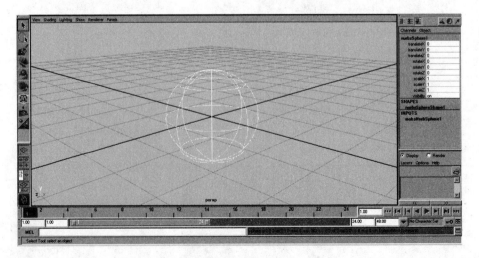

This is the best way to begin learning how to MEL script: by doing things manually in the interface, and then viewing through printed feedback the MEL commands that Maya executes.

USING THE SCRIPT EDITOR

Although you can access Maya's software core through the command line, it is extremely limiting because it only has the space to display or type a single line of code. Often Maya is printing more than one line of code, but you can't see the additional lines in the feedback field. Also, once you start using MEL regularly, you usually will want to type in more than one command at a time. So if you really want to take advantage of this access to Maya's software, then you must open the Script Editor.

To open the Script Editor, click the icon in the lower right of the interface next to the command line. Notice there are two main parts to the editor that correspond to the same color coding as on the command line, with a large gray panel above a large white panel (see **FIGURE 2.2**).

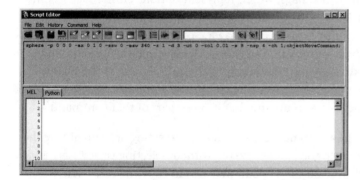

FIGURE 2.2 *Open the Script Editor to examine more details on MEL code being run by looking in the upper gray History field. Commands can also be typed into the white scripting field.*

The top gray panel is the Feedback or History field, and has the capability to print MEL code for most of what is done in the Maya interface. You should see several lines of code already printed in the field, with the bottom one displaying the last thing you did in Maya, which should be the line that created the primitive NURBS sphere. Below the History field is the white Input or Scripting field that has a MEL and a Python tab. When writing any code in the Script Editor for the exercises in this book, make sure that you are using the default MEL tab. This field is where you will begin writing and running your basic MEL scripts in this chapter.

ABOUT MEL SYNTAX

MEL scripting is a language, and like any language, it has specific rules that must be followed to communicate effectively. If you are learning to speak Spanish for instance, and break the basic grammatical rules, then native speakers may laugh at you because you are not making sense. If you break the rules, called syntax, in MEL, Maya will definitely laugh at you by giving you error messages and refusing to run your script. You can learn basic MEL syntax by examining the commands that Maya prints to the History field. Examining the previous command for creating a primitive sphere, you can see that the command name is sphere typed in all lowercase letters. Most scripting languages are case-sensitive, which is one of the main rules to follow in MEL: all commands start with lowercase letters. Following the command itself is a series of dashes, spaces, letters, and values:

```
sphere -p 0 0 0 -ax 0 1 0 -ssw 0 -esw 360 -r 1 -d 3 -ut 0 -tol 0.01 -s 8
-nsp 4 -ch 1;objectMoveCommand;
```

The dashed letters are called flags, which represent options on the sphere command, which you would normally set in an options dialog box when working in the interface. The numbers after each flag are called arguments, and are used to set the values of the creation options. The entire command ends at the first semicolon after the last argument. This means that objectMoveCommand after the semicolon is an entirely separate command. It may be running in conjunction with the sphere command, but it is not part of that command.

See for yourself how these commands are separate by selecting or highlighting the history code from sphere to the first semicolon, without selecting objectMoveCommand, and by pressing Ctrl+C (Command+C in Mac OS) to copy the code. Then click below in the white Scripting field, and paste the line of code by pressing Ctrl+V (Command+V in Mac OS). To run the code in the Script Editor, press Ctrl+Enter, which will create another sphere that is identical to the first one. (Pressing Enter by itself just moves to the next line in the field.) This demonstrates that objectMoveCommand is necessary only when creating a sphere in the interface, not when you create a sphere using MEL code. When you begin incorporating MEL commands that Maya runs in the Script Editor into your own scripts, use only the commands you really need, to avoid cluttering your scripts with nonessential commands.

Notice another syntax rule by looking at how objectMoveCommand is written. A command name can have multiple words in it, but never spaces, and although the first word will always be lowercase, the first letter of additional words will be uppercase. So to summarize MEL syntax:

- MEL commands always start with a lowercase name that may have multiple words indicated by capitalization of the first letter of each new word.
- The name is followed by flags that are preceded by a dash; these flags are used to specify command options through values called arguments. A space always separates flags and arguments.
- Each MEL command ends with a semicolon, called a terminator. Any code after the terminator is not part of the command, even if it is on the same line in the History field or in a script.

DECIPHERING ERROR MESSAGES

There are many kinds of error messages that may pop up when you start writing scripts. If you type something wrong, or use incorrect syntax, the feedback field will turn red, and Maya will print the error. The common name for an error is a bug in your script, and the common name for fixing errors is "debugging" your scripts.

Although sometimes Maya will print a generic syntax error message, usually it will try to tell you more specifically what and where the error is in your code. To view all the details, be sure to look in the Script Editor rather than the command line and have some options set in the Script Editor to get as many details as possible. In History, turn on History > Show Line Numbers, and in the Script Editor menu, select Command > Show Line Numbers. These options will specify the line number in which an error occurs in a multi-line script. Another option, History > Echo All Commands, is useful for tracking elusive commands that don't always show up in the History field. But this option can considerably slow down the software by forcing Maya to print everything it does in the background; so it is best to leave it off most of the time.

To see what an error actually looks like, find the `sphere` command you ran previously in the History field, and copy it again into the Scripting field. Change the first flag from a `-p` to a `-pl`, which simulates a simple typing error. Select or highlight the entire line of code, and then run the code again by pressing Ctrl+Enter. Selecting will ensure that the code stays in the Scripting field, to eliminate you having to copy and paste to run the code multiple times. Running the code produces the following error:

```
sphere -pl 0 0 0 -ax 0 1 0 -ssw 0 -esw 360 -r 1 -d 3 -ut 0 -tol 0.01 -s 8 -nsp 4 -ch 1;
// Error: line 1: Invalid flag: -pl //
```

If you change the flag back to -p and run it, the error message will disappear, and another sphere will be created. You can experiment with changing or deleting other parts of the code to see what kind of error messages it produces when you run it. As you progress in MEL, you will experience a variety of error messages. Read them carefully, and try to determine what Maya is telling you. The more code you write, the fewer error messages you will get; and when you do get one, you will easily be able to track it down and fix it.

Getting Basic Help on Commands

A couple of special MEL commands let you get details on other commands that you may come across in the Script Editor. Whenever a command comes up in the History field, the flags are written as the short-name versions. Most coders won't memorize every flag abbreviation, so you'll frequently have to look them up. If you are generally familiar with a command, but can't remember what a flag means, then you can run a help command. In the case of the sphere command, simply type help sphere; Maya will print a synopsis of the command to the History field that looks like this:

```
help sphere;
// Result:
Synopsis: sphere [flags] [String...]
Flags:
   -e -edit
   -q -query
  -ax -axis                Length Length Length
 -cch -caching             on|off
  -ch -constructionHistory on|off
   -d -degree              Int
 -esw -endSweep            Angle
  -hr -heightRatio         Float
   -n -name                String
 -nds -nodeState           Int
 -nsp -spans               Int
   -o -object              on|off
   -p -pivot               Length Length Length
  -po -polygon             Int
   -r -radius              Length
   -s -sections            Int
 -ssw -startSweep          Angle
```

```
 -tol -tolerance        Length
   -ut -useTolerance      on|off
//
```

The synopsis shows you the long names of the available flags, and what type of arguments are expected after each flag. Comparing this printout to the line of code that created the sphere, you can now see that the first -p flag represents the pivot position of the sphere. The arguments Length Length Length refer to three decimal values that represent positions in X Y Z space. Likewise, the second flag -ax followed by 0 1 0 sets the axis or pole of the sphere to point upward in positive Y. The flags -ssw and -esw show the start sweep and end sweep of the sphere. Since a NURBS sphere is made from isoparms, or curves, these start-and-end sweep flags indicate that a complete sphere is being created by revolving a curve 360 degrees. If you change the -esw flag to 180 and run the code again, it will create half a sphere. The -r flag represents the radius of the sphere, which determines the creation size of the sphere with the scale transforms at their default 1 value. Read through the rest of the long flag names and arguments to see if you recognize how they relate to creating a sphere.

The arguments listed after each flag refer to some of the data types in MEL; you should become familiar with the most common ones. In most cases, they will fall into three main categories: single whole or decimal numbers, groups of decimal numbers, and groups of numbers or letters. The individual numbers used in the flags are most often used to set individual attribute values on nodes that are created or connected. A whole number is referred to as an int or integer in MEL. A decimal number is most often referred to as a float, but may also be referred to in the help documentation as length or double. Groups of numbers, often referred to as a vector and matrix, are most often used to set groups of attributes, such as the XYZ values of transforms. A group of any keyboard characters, including numbers or letters, is called a string in MEL. Strings are most often used on flags for setting the names of nodes. When you specify a string in MEL, you should always enclose it in double quotation marks, even though Maya will sometimes let you use a string without the quotation marks.

In addition to names, strings are sometimes used to set attributes that are on or off, such as in the -ch, or construction history, flag. For these types of flags, you can specify "on"|"off", or "true"|"false", or even the integers 1|0. This illustrates that MEL sometimes features several ways to do the same operation. As you work through this chapter, you will see many more examples of how data types are specified and used in MEL.

An alternative to using the help command on unfamiliar commands found in the History field is to run a whatIs command. It's important to know when coding in Maya that not all the commands in the History field are single MEL commands. MEL commands are the main commands being run, but Maya has hundreds of scripts that contain groups of MEL commands, called procedures. These procedures have their own names, and won't be in the help documentation. If you run a help command and Maya reports that the command you are looking up is a procedure, then it is not a MEL command. For instance, the objectMoveCommand that came up after the sphere command is actually a procedure. Running a whatIs command on it will print these results:

```
whatIs objectMoveCommand;
// Result: Mel procedure found in: C:/Program Files/Autodesk/Maya2008/scripts/
startup/objectMoveCommand.mel //
```

Running the help or whatIs commands will tell you that the command is a procedure found in a MEL script file where the software is loaded. When you get to a more advanced level in coding, you can open and examine these script files in the Script Editor. You will learn more about procedures and even make some of your own later in this chapter.

LOOKING UP COMMANDS IN THE MEL COMMAND REFERENCE

One of the best resources for anyone writing MEL code is the MEL Command Reference, which details every MEL command in Maya. This resource is found in the Help menu, and opens a browser window listing commands both alphabetically and by category. To look up any command found in the History field, such as the sphere command, you would look it up alphabetically. Finding and clicking the word "sphere" in the S section opens another web page with extensive details on the sphere command (see **FIGURE 2.3**).

The top of the page contains a more detailed synopsis than that for the help command, giving a short explanation of what the command does and how to use it. Then the page displays important coding information, such as return statements and related commands. (Return statements are explained in "Catching Return Values" and used later in this chapter.) This page not only shows the long names

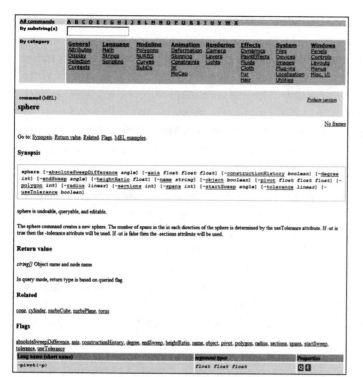

FIGURE 2.3 *Looking up help on the* sphere *command in the MEL Command Reference shows how the command should be run, coding details such as return statements, and more on flag arguments.*

of the flags, but lists additional details on both the flags and arguments. These details also are important for coding, and will be covered later in this chapter in the section on "Querying and Editing Attributes." The page also gives some examples of how the command is used, which you can copy and paste directly into the Scripting field in Maya, and run the code to see the result.

When coding, get used to looking up unfamiliar commands in the MEL Command Reference frequently, or running `help` commands if you only need a quick refresher. You may have noticed that each resource lists slightly different versions of argument types. Where the `help` command lists an argument type as `Length Length Length`, the MEL Command Reference may list it as `float float float`. Sometimes it is useful to look at both when trying to figure out how to use commands that you are seeing for the first time.

STREAMLINING YOUR MEL CODE

Looking up commands in the MEL Command Reference shows you all the flags available to a command and can help you streamline the code you found in the History field. One of the general goals of coding is to make your scripts as short and efficient as possible. This makes them less prone to errors, easier to read by other coders, and faster to process by Maya. To achieve this goal, use only the commands and flags needed to complete the intended task. It is even a good idea to get used to using the short names of flags, as this makes the lines of code shorter and leads to fewer typing errors.

Just as you didn't need to run the `objectMoveCommand` to create a sphere, you don't have to run all the flags Maya runs when creating objects in the interface. Looking up commands shows you which flags can be removed. For instance, when creating a sphere, the –tol or –tolerance flag is used only if the –ut or –useTolerance flag is turned on. The default argument value for the –ut flag is off. So, if you examine the sphere command that was run by Maya, because the –ut flag was off, the –tol flag is unnecessary. If this is the default setting, those two flags don't even need to be included in that line of code and can be removed. Maya will automatically set the default options for any flags that are not specified in the command. The documentation will state if a flag is required on the command. The resulting sphere command would look like this:

```
sphere -p 0 0 0 -ax 0 1 0 -ssw 0 -esw 360 -r 1 -d 3 -s 8 -nsp 4 -ch 1;
```

Examining the MEL documentation will also show you if any flags are available to complete tasks that couldn't be done in the interface. For instance, when you created a sphere in the interface, it didn't give you the option to name the sphere. Instead, Maya named it generically; you would have to manually change it by either right-clicking the sphere to choose rename, or by selecting it and by typing a new name in the Channel Box (see **FIGURE 2.4**).

FIGURE 2.4 *Maya creates primitives with a generic name; to customize the name, you must type a name in the Channel Box. MEL primitive commands have naming flags that let you input a custom name without renaming.*

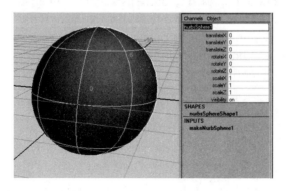

After typing in a name like mySphere to the Channel Box, Maya runs a rename command in the History field:

```
rename "nurbsSphere1" "mySphere";
// Result: mySphere //
```

Now that you know what a string is, you can see that the command is renaming the "nurbsSphere1" string to "mySphere". However, this step is not required when creating a sphere using MEL. If you look again through the list of flags in the MEL command reference for a sphere command, you will see there is a -n or –name flag that can be used to specify a string for naming the sphere. Try adding this flag to the sphere command you previously pasted into the Scripting field. Since the order of the flags doesn't matter in this case, you can type the new flag and argument anywhere you want in the line of code:

```
sphere -n "mySphere" -p 0 0 0 -ax 0 1 0 -ssw 0 -esw 360 -r 1 -d 3 -s 8 -nsp 8 -ch 1;
```

Running this code will create a sphere with mySphere as the name. Most object creation commands in Maya have name flags; you should always use these flags to efficiently name objects at creation time, rather than editing the name later.

Running the code additional times will create more spheres with similar names but incremented values. This is an important aspect of creating primitives, as well as most other objects in Maya, that can impact your scripts. Since names of nodes increment if the scene has another node with the same name, it is essential that you specify the correct names when editing nodes through MEL. Later in this chapter, in the "Catching Return Values" section, you will learn some coding techniques to prevent errors in your script from unexpected incrementing of names.

Following Scripting Conventions

When you start combining MEL commands into actual scripts, you must follow some basic scripting conventions to make your scripts more readable. These conventions involve formatting the code into related sections using tabs, adding comments, and writing print statements.

FORMATTING CODE

The main formatting you will put in your script is to tab in secondary lines of code that belong to a main command or section of code statements. When you start writing your scripts, you will find that many MEL commands require more flags than conveniently fit onscreen. To avoid having to scroll off screen to read the script, you will need to break many commands onto multiple lines. The best place to break commands is at the beginning of a flag, to make the second line start with a dash. To make it clear at a glance that the second line of code is a continuation of the first line, you tab in the second line.

Keep in mind there are no strict rules for formatting code. It is up to the coder how much space is inserted, from a full tab to just a few indented characters using the spacebar. However, it is important to not break command names or strings, as this will cause an error in your code. As your scripts become longer and more complex, you should increase the formatting to make them easier to read. For now, here is how you would format the previous sphere command if it spans multiple lines:

```
sphere -n "mySphere" -p 0 0 0 -ax 0 1 0 -ssw 0 -esw 360 -r 1 -d 3
    -s 8 -nsp 8 -ch 1;
```

ADDING COMMENTS

Another important formatting technique is to add comments throughout your scripts. Comments are not run as MEL code, but are inserted between sections of code to explain to anyone reading the script what the code is doing in lay terms. There are two kinds of comments: block and single line. A block comment is for comments that span multiple lines, such as a header that briefly explains the function and author of the script. Block comments start with /*, and end with a */ symbols, which tell Maya to not run anything between the symbols as commands:

```
/*
Scripting the Rig Header
by Chris Maraffi 2008
This script creates a biped rig…
*/
```

The more common type of comment is line comments. You will use these throughout your script to briefly explain a section of code, or point out the start or end of a process. These consist of placing // at the beginning of the line of text you want to comment out.

```
//Place line comments throughout the script to explain code…
```

WRITING PRINT STATEMENTS

Technically not used in formatting, print statements are used to send comments back to the History field after the script runs. This gives you another layer of information on what is happening in the script, and is essential for debugging your scripts. You know that when a particular print statement appears in the History field, Maya successfully made it through that particular section of the script. Printing will also be used extensively with intermediate coding techniques, such as variables and arrays introduced it later in this section.

To write a basic print statement, you type the `print` command, followed by a text string:

```
print ">>>>>>Look at me!<<<<<<<<";
```

Running this line of code will print >>>>>>Look at me!<<<<<<<< to the History field. You will learn more about printing throughout this chapter, especially in the next sections, "Using Variables" and "Using Arrays."

Learning Essential Coding Techniques

So far you have learned how to find and use individual MEL commands in the Script Editor. Writing a MEL script, however, involves more than writing a series of commands. There are some essential coding techniques and coding-related commands that are used throughout most, if not all, MEL scripts. Many of these coding essentials have to do with managing and moving information through the different parts of your script. Learning to incorporate these techniques into your MEL scripting will enable you to more efficiently code complex tasks in Maya, such as creating a biped rig.

USING VARIABLES

A *variable* is a placeholder or container for storing one piece of data of a particular type. The types of variables are similar to the types of arguments used for flags, such as strings, integers, floats, and so on. You first create or declare a variable in your script by telling Maya the type and the name, which is always proceeded by a $ sign. Try to keep your variable names short and descriptive of what they will contain. Declaring variables puts the name and type in Maya's memory while the script is running, such as declaring an integer variable that will contain a whole number.

```
int $num;
```

You specify the information you want to store into the variable on the other side of an equal (=) sign. Make sure that you use the same type of information as the variable, or you may get an error message. From that point on in the script you can use the variable name to reference the data that it contains or represents.

```
$num = 5;
```

It may help to visualize a variable as a single mailbox that has a label on it to only take one letter or package at a time. The nice thing about variables is that you declare them in one place in your script, and then can use them in lots of places. If you change the data where it is first declared, the change automatically propagates to all the other places the variable is used.

In the previous example, the variable name is declared first, and then the 5 is added to it. There will be times when scripting the rig that you won't know what the variable should contain until the script runs; so you will have to first declare an empty variable, and then add the appropriate contents later in the script. If you know what the variable should contain when it is created, then it is easier and more efficient to declare it and add the contents all in one line of code:

```
int $num = 7;
float $dec = 3.267;
string $name = "mySphere";
```

Once you have the data stored in the variable, you can insert the variable into the commands used in your script. For instance, you may put the name of the sphere in a $name variable, and then use the variable in the -n flag of the sphere command:

```
sphere -n $name -p 0 0 0 -ax 0 1 0 -ssw 0 -esw 360 -r 1 -d 3
        -s 8 -nsp 4 -ch 1;
```

Another MEL coding example would be to add the integer and float variables, and catch the sum in the appropriate variable type—in this case, a float variable named $sum. Also, when processing data through variables like this, it is common to print it so you can verify the contents.

```
float $sum = $num + $dec;
print $sum;
// Result: 10.267 //
```

When the print line runs, you should see 10.267 on the last line in the History field. If you change the numbers going into the variable and run all the lines of code again, the print results will change. Also notice that running the print code multiple times will result in the new print lines being appended to the previous lines, like this:

```
// Result: 10.267 //int $num = 7;
float $dec = 3.267;
float $sum = $num + $dec;
print $sum;
// Result: 10.267 //int $num = 7;
float $dec = 3.267;
float $sum = $num + $dec;
print $sum;
// Result: 10.267 //
```

The previous example shows how multiple print lines will appear when running a longer script. Since the goal of printing is to view the data easily inside the variable, appending print statements in this manner make the lines very difficult to read. To make the values stand out as the only information on a single line, you must add a new-line character, which is the string "\n", at the end of your print line of code. A new-line character is like pressing the Enter key on the keyboard, forcing the next printed data to go on a new line. In addition to placing a new-line character at the end of your print data, it can be useful to add some text before the variable to make it stand out. Here is an example:

```
print "The sum of adding my variables = $sum \n";
```

Running this line of code multiple times will place the print result on its own line, but the variable no longer displays its contents as 10.267. Instead, the command is just printing the variable name, which is not at all useful. This demonstrates an issue with variables: you cannot place them inside the double quotation marks of a string if you want Maya to process the variables to show their contents. Placing a variable inside a string simply converts it to text. So here is the technique to add variables to the strings without enclosing them in the double quotation marks:

```
print ("The sum of adding my variables = " + $sum + "\n");
```

Here the variable is outside of the double quotation marks, which allows Maya to process the variable to display its contents. Plus (+) signs are used to add the strings to each side, including the new-line character, and parentheses are used to group it all together. You must manually add to the strings any spaces you want to show up in the final result. You can also add other formatting to the string to make the result stand out, such as symbols or spaces:

```
print ("****The sum of adding my variables = >>" + $sum + "<<\n");
// Result: ****The sum of adding my variables = >>10.267<< //
```

USING ARRAYS

An array functions as a variable, except that it can contain multiple pieces of data of the same type. If a variable is like a single mail box, then an array is like a mail sorter in a mailroom that has many slots, and each slot will receive only a single letter from left to right as the letters come in. Creating or declaring an array is also similar to declaring a variable. The only difference is that brackets are inserted at the end of the name to tell Maya that it is an array and not a variable.

```
int $nums[];
```

You can insert the brackets in one of two ways: either place a number in the brackets representing how many pieces of data will be placed in the array; or leave the brackets empty, meaning that the array will automatically expand for however much data you put in it. The second method, called creating a dynamic array, is by far the most popular and flexible way of creating an array. Also, just as with variables, you can declare empty arrays and add the contents later with an equal sign, or you can declare and populate the array all at the same time. The main difference between entering data into a variable and into an array is that the array information is separated by commas and grouped inside curly brackets. Here are a couple of examples of declaring and populating arrays:

```
float $decs[5] = {7.23,1.0,20.7,0.567,12.0};
string $names[] = {"One","Two","Three"};
```

The first example creates a float array with exactly five positions, and then fills those positions with five decimal numbers. The second example creates a dynamic string array, and then adds three strings to it. What's important about arrays is that numbering of the slots or positions starts at 0, not 1. So in the mailroom analogy, if someone wants to get the letter in the fifth slot of the mail box, that person must ask for the letter in slot number 4. In the same manner, if you want to retrieve some information from the first slot in an array, you specify position 0 inside of the hard brackets on the name. For instance, to print the number 20.7 in the float array, you specify the second position in the array, while printing the second position in the string array will print the string "Three":

```
print ($decs[2] + "\n");
// Result: 20.7 //
print ($names[2] + "\n");
// Result: Three //
```

Arrays will be used extensively in the scripts that you'll write to create the biped rig, so you want to be clear on how they work. Try printing out other positions to see what they contain. Also, if you want to print all the positions in an array in order, then simply leave out the hard brackets in your print statement:

```
print $names;
/* Result:
      One
      Two
      Three */
```

CATCHING RETURN VALUES

There are two ways of using variables and arrays: by manually adding information, as shown in the last section; or by adding information through the return statement of a command. Now that you know how to create variables and arrays, you can learn how return statements are used in MEL scripts. (For an introduction to return statements, see "Looking Up Commands to the MEL Command Reference" earlier in this chapter.) Most commands have return statements, which send out information, in addition to whatever else the command does in Maya. Sometimes, some of this information is printed to the command line, such as the names of nodes that are created when you create a primitive. Regardless of whether the information is printed, if a command has a return statement, you can catch it in a variable or array for use in other parts of your script.

To catch the return statement of a command, you must first look it up in the MEL Command Reference to see whether you are required to use a variable or an array. Which to use depends on whether the return statement is one piece, or many pieces, of data. For instance, looking up the return statement of the sphere command states string[] Object name and node name. The documentation indicates that the return statement is multiple names, in this case two, of a type string array. To catch the names, you declare a dynamic string array in the same way as before, only this time put the sphere command on the other side of the equal sign, and enclose the command in single back quotation marks:

```
string $names[] = `sphere -n $name -p 0 0 0 -ax 0 1 0 -ssw 0
    -esw 360 -r 1 -d 3 -s 8 -nsp 4 -ch 1`;
```

Be aware that single back quotation marks, found on the tilde (~) key, are not the same as single quotation marks. Surrounding a MEL command with these symbols tells Maya to run the command and send out the return statement. If you then print the resulting array contents, you will see that it contains the name of the transform node in the 0 position, and the name of the creation node in the 1 position:

```
print $names;
/* Result:
        mySphere
        makeNurbSphere1 */
```

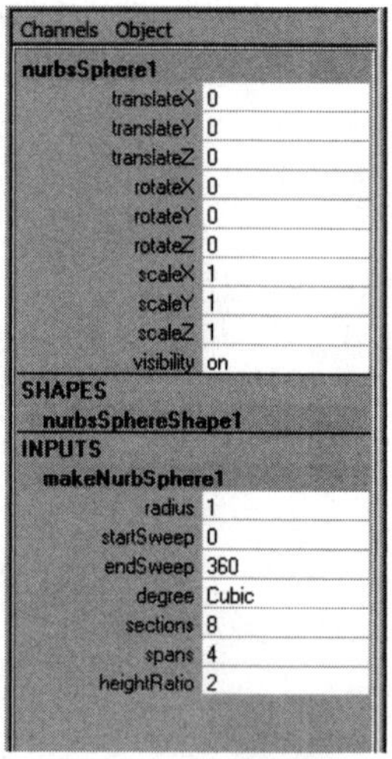

FIGURE 2.5 *Attributes on the creation node of a primitive correspond to flags on the primitive command, and can be queried and edited.*

The big advantage to catching the names of objects when they are created, as opposed to using hard-coded names in the script, is knowing that the correct names are going into the array. This is especially useful if the names get incremented because other objects with the same names already existed in the scene. If you then exclusively use the names caught in the array for anything that needs to be done to the object, such as transform or parent it, then you won't have to worry about script errors due to referencing the wrong name.

Catching the node names from the return statement of a primitive command also illustrates an important technical aspect of Maya. Creating objects often results in the creation of multiple nodes. In this case, creating a sphere produces a transform node containing transformation attributes, and a creation node containing creation attributes. You can see both nodes in the Channel Box, with the standard transform attributes at the top. You can also see the creation attributes by clicking the name of the creation node, makeNurbSphere1, so that the node expands to reveal the channels (see **FIGURE 2.5**).

Notice that the channels have the same names as many of the options in the interface options box and in the MEL flags. Some creation options produce attributes that can later be edited on the creation node. For instance, you can type 3 into the radius channel to make the sphere larger, or you can type **12** into the spans channel to add curves to the sphere. In the next section, you will learn how to edit creation channels through MEL.

QUERYING AND EDITING ATTRIBUTES THROUGH FLAGS

Some flags produce attributes on the creation node of objects; you can reference those channels using MEL. You do this in a script to get attribute values from a node you created, called querying, or to change attribute values on a node you created, called editing. To query or edit node attributes, you run the same command again that initially created the node, but only use a -q or -e flag in front of the flag that created the attribute. The MEL Command Reference has a Properties column that details what flags can be queried and edited.

Look up the sphere command again, and notice that the Properties column on the far right of each flag contains a letter *Q*, *E*, *C*, or *M*. The letters *Q* and *E* indicate whether a flag will create attributes that can be queried or edited (see **FIGURE 2.6**).

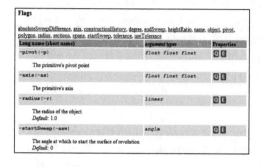

FIGURE 2.6 *Look at the Properties column in the MEL Command Reference to see what flags can be queried and edited.*

The letter *C* in the column indicates that the flag can be used only at creation time, and is not creating any attributes that can be queried or edited. Sometimes you will also find the rare letter *M* property, which means a flag can be run multiple times on a single command. Here is an example of querying the number of spans on the sphere created previously with code, and then printing the result:

```
int $spans = `sphere -q -nsp $names[1]`;
print ($spans + "\n");
// Result: 4 //
```

When you use MEL to query attributes, the order of the flags in the command matters: always place the -q before the flag that you want to query, remove all other flags, and then specify the node name at the end of the command. If the name is an array containing multiple node names, you must specify the correct array position. In this case, the creation node of the sphere is in the [1] position of $names array. Also, if you are querying an attribute, it is because you want to do something with the data in another part of your script, such as run the attribute in another command. The return statement for the sphere command changes to the result of whatever you are querying. So to catch and store the returned data, you again use single back quotation marks around the command. Here is another example of querying the radius attribute:

```
int $radius = `sphere -q -r $names[1]`;
print ($radius + "\n");
// Result: 1 //
```

When querying attributes in this way, make sure that you catch the data in the appropriate variable type, in this case an integer. Then add a new-line character \n to the integer variable to have the value print on its own line. Once the attribute value is stored in the variable, you can use it for other tasks like changing attributes on other nodes. To use the queried data to edit another attribute on the same creation node, you run the sphere command again with an -e flag followed by the flag corresponding to the creation attribute you want to change. Run the following code to edit the radius attribute to the same as the number of spans queried previously:

```
sphere -e -r $spans $names[1];
```

Running this code scales the radius of the sphere to four times the previous size. Check the radius attribute on the creation node to make sure that the value was edited to 4. You can experiment with querying and editing other creation attributes on the sphere, or any other primitives you create with MEL code. Notice, however, that none of the flags on the sphere command corresponds to transform attributes. You can only query and edit creation channels on the creation node using primitive commands, not on transformation channels on the transform node. Other attribute commands are used specifically for transforms.

RUNNING LIST AND SELECT COMMANDS

Listing and selecting nodes are common functions in Maya, so you should begin to familiarize yourself with the ls and select commands. Listing nodes can be quite involved, so to get started, this introduction covers only a few of the most common listing functions. Be sure to look up the ls command in the MEL Command Reference to see the options available. Before running the ls command, make sure that you have created several primitives in the scene, such as spheres and cubes, and so on.

To begin printing a list of nodes, simply run the list command without any flags in Maya, and notice all the names that print to the History field. These will include most nodes in Maya, making it difficult to even find the primitives you created. To view a more manageable list of nodes, run the command again with the transform and shape flags to produce these results:

```
ls -tr;
// Result: front myCube mySphere mySphere1 persp side top //
```

```
ls -s;
/* Result: frontShape myCubeShape mySphere1Shape mySphereShape perspShape
        sideShape topShape */
```

You could, of course, run both flags on the same list command, which would print both types of nodes, but often it's better to be as specific as possible. Notice the transform and shape nodes include camera view nodes, as well as any primitive you created. You could also catch the return of the list command in arrays, to use the node names in your script. You would do this by using single back quotation marks, as shown here with a print command:

```
string $trNodes[] = `ls -tr`;
print $trNodes;
/* Result:
        front
        myCube
        mySphere
        mySphere1
        persp
        side
        top */
```

Another important use of the ls command is to list selected objects using the -sl flag. This is particularly useful for interacting with a user through a MEL scripted tool or GUI. Sometimes it is easier and more intuitive to instruct users to select an object on which to run the code, than to have them type a name in a field, where a typing mistake could cause an error. For example, the setup GUI for the rigging scripts in this book instructs the user to select the skin, and then click a button to set the name of the rig. The button runs code that lists the selected, and extracts the name of the rig from the skin name. To try listing a selected object, again use the single back quotation marks to catch the return, which will always be caught in an array, even if there is only one node selected. Select a primitive in your scene (in this example a sphere is being selected), and run the following code to catch and print the name:

```
string $selNodes[] = `ls -sl`;
print $selNodes;
// Result: mySphere1 //
```

You can also incorporate selection into your MEL scripts by using the select command. It is usually unnecessary to select nodes for most MEL commands, as affected nodes can normally be specified by name. What is more useful is to deselect nodes. You may have noticed that some commands in Maya automatically select nodes; for example, the sphere command automatically selects the transform node after creating the sphere. Having a node selected can change how the next MEL command runs in the script, so it is best to clear the selection before starting another type of operation. Dragging a selection box in an empty area of any 3D view will clear the selection, and print the following command to the History field:

```
select -cl;
```

Running this command at the end of major sections of code will clear any nodes of selection. However, if you need to select a node using MEL, you would run the same command with an -r flag. This code will replace any current selection with the specified object. For instance, running this command on the original sphere using the array position for the transform node would look like this:

```
select -r $names[0];
```

You can also specify the creation node by using $names[1] in a similar select command which will select the creation node while deselecting the transform node. To select multiple nodes, use the toggle flag, which is equivalent to holding down the Shift key while selecting in the interface. The following code toggle-selects two spheres, and lists and prints the results:

```
select -r $names[0];
select -tgl $names3[0];
string $selNodes[] = `ls -sl`;
print $selNodes;
/* Result:
        mySphere
        mySphereThree */
```

GETTING, SETTING, AND LISTING ATTRIBUTES

Because attributes are so important for everything you do in Maya, there are some attribute-related commands that you must learn before going further in MEL. A pair commands work in a similar way to querying and editing creation attributes, but can be applied to any attribute on any node; these are getAttr and setAttr. You can use the getAttr command to query or get information, and you can use the setAttr command to edit or set any attribute to a value. Although the functions of these commands are similar to querying and editing, the syntax contains no flags:

```
getAttr ($names[0] + ".sx");
setAttr ($names[0] + ".ty") 5;
```

The first example gets the value of the X scaling on the sphere transform node, while the second example sets the Y translation on the same node to 5. Notice that attributes are specified as strings beginning with periods, and are added to the node name in the same manner as shown in the "Using Variables" section for printing.

Another example shows retrieving the value of the sections, storing it in a $sections variable, and then using the variable to set the number of spans. Notice that to reference the creation node, you must use the 1 position of the $names array, not the 0 position:

```
int $sections = `getAttr ($names[1] + ".s")`;
setAttr ($names[1] + ".nsp") $sections;
```

You can do the same type of operation with transform attributes. In the following case, the Y translation of the sphere is used to set the X scaling on the same node.

```
float $transY = `getAttr ($names[0] + ".ty")`;
setAttr ($names[0] + ".sx") $transY;
```

You should also be aware of one other attribute command, the listAttr command. This lets you list all the attributes on a node. Running the command without any flags produces a long list of attributes, most of which you won't need. Instead, run the command with the -k or -keyable flag, as in this example, which lists the attributes on the transform node of the sphere that can be animated through setting keys:

```
listAttr -k $names[0];
/* Result: visibility translateX translateY translateZ rotateX
        rotateY rotateZ scaleX scaleY scaleZ */
```

ADDING CUSTOM ATTRIBUTES

In addition to working with default attributes, eventually you will need to add your own custom attributes to nodes.

To create a custom attribute in the Maya interface:

1. Select the sphere and choose Modify > Add Attribute. In the resulting options box, type the long name myAttr for the attribute that uses the same syntax as MEL commands (see **FIGURE 2.7**).

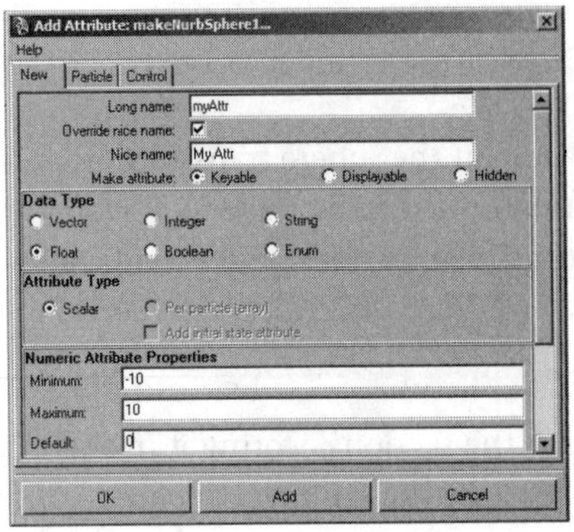

FIGURE 2.7 *You can add a custom attribute to nodes in the interface in the Modify menu.*

2. Turn on the Override Nice Name option to see an alternative name generated that contains capitalized letters and spaces. Then use the default options of Keyable, Float, and Scalar. Set the Minimum, Maximum, and Default values to -10, 10, and 0. Click OK to add the attribute and close the options box.

A new myAttr attribute appears on the transform node of the sphere in the Channel Box. Selecting the channel and scrubbing it with the middle mouse button shows the channel limits of -10 to 10. Currently this channel doesn't do anything in Maya, but eventually you will connect similar custom channels to other nodes to create the advanced rig controls.

Open the Script Editor to see the MEL command Maya ran to create the custom channel:

```
addAttr -ln "myAttr" -nn "My Attr" -at double -min -10 -max 10 -dv 0 |mySphere;
setAttr -e-keyable true |mySphere.myAttr;
```

You can see that Maya is creating the channel, and then editing it to take animation keys or be keyable. Looking up the addAttr command in the MEL Command Reference, however, shows you a -k or -keyable flag that is available on the initial command, as well as other useful flags not available in the interface options. For instance, here is how you would add the same custom attribute in MEL with the additional flags:

FIGURE 2.8 *Using a short-name flag on primitive commands makes the channel names consistent in the Channel Box when switching the Channel Names format.*

```
addAttr -ln "myAttr" -sn "ma" -nn "My Attribute" -at "float"
        -min -10 -max 10 -dv 0 -k 1 -r 1 -w 1 $names[0];
```

In addition to the long and nice names, a short-name flag has been added to keep the attribute display consistent in the Channel Box when changing the Channel > Channel Names format in the menu (see **FIGURE 2.8**).

The -at flag sets the channel to use float or decimal values, and is the same as the default Maya double setting that you may have noticed printed to the History field when creating a channel in the interface. The next three flags set the limits and default setting for the channel. If you do not set these flags, the channel will have no limits. Setting limits when you create a custom channel is more efficient than having to set the limits later by editing the channel. The last flags were added to make the channel keyable, readable, and writable. These flags facilitate animating the channel and later writing channel data to files.

TRANSFORMING WITH THE XFORM COMMAND

The xform command is more efficient and flexible than the standard transform commands because it allows you to consolidate multiple types of transforms with one command. To compare the xform and standard transform commands, try this.

Select the sphere you created previously, and translate it in Perspective view using the Move tool in the main toolbar. Then transform the sphere randomly with the Rotate and Scale tools. Open the Script Editor to examine the commands Maya is running to transform the sphere. Here is an example of how transform commands commonly come up when moving an object around in Perspective view:

```
move -r 1.741694 3.600385 -4.441983 ;
rotate -r -os 23.83278 0 0 ;
rotate -r -os 0 0 -37.478284 ;
scale -r 1.434608 1.434608 1.434608 ;
move -r -2.080461 0.825088 1.461645 ;
```

Looking up these commands in the MEL Command Reference, you can see they have some obvious limitations. None of the flags can be queried or edited, and no return statement is available. Maya uses these commands for relative transformations, as the -r flag indicates, which is why some are repeated as you move the object around. If you were going to transform another object to the exact same global position in your script, it wouldn't be very efficient to copy this code. A better command to use for transformations in your scripts is the xform command, which will never come up in the History field when moving objects in the interface.

Looking up the xform command, you can see that it has flags for translation, rotation, and scaling. Also notice that these flags can be queried to produce re-turn values that can be stored in arrays for use in other areas of your script. For example, you can query the current transformations of the sphere like this:

```
float $trans[] = `xform -q -t $names[0]`;
float $rots[] = `xform -q -ro $names[0]`;
float $scls[] = `xform -q -s $names[0]`;
```

Disregard the standard warning that comes up in the History field that states absolute scale cannot be queried; this warning won't affect the result at this point. The reason you have to use arrays to store the queried values is because the xform command is returning all three float values for X, Y, and Z. You can then create another sphere and transform it to exactly the same values by using the array values in a single xform command.

```
string $name2 = "mySphereTwo";
string $names2[] = `sphere -n $name2 -p 0 0 0 -ax 0 1 0 -ssw 0 -esw 360
     -r 1 -d 3 -s 8 -nsp 4 -ch 1`;
xform -ws -t $trans[0] $trans[1] $trans[2] -ro $rots[0] $rots[1] $rots[2] -s
$scls[0] $scls[1] $scls[2] $names2[0];
```

You can see how the [0], [1], and [2] array positions are being specified to insert the queried values for each transform into the final xform command. However, another type of variable was designed for use specifically with transforms, known as a vector variable. Here is a simple example of manually creating a vector variable, and then printing the entire contents:

```
vector $vects = <<3.1,7.6,1.008>>;
print ($vects + "\n");
print (($vects.y) + "\n");
/* Result: 3.1 7.6 1.008
7.6 */
```

To create another sphere, and transform it using vector variables to the same position as the previous one, you would write it like this:

```
vector $tranV = `xform -q -t $names[0]`;
vector $rotV = `xform -q -ro $names[0]`;
vector $scalV = `xform -q -s $names[0]`;
string $name3 = "mySphereThree";
string $names3[] = `sphere -n $name3 -p 0 0 0 -ax 0 1 0 -ssw 0 -esw 360
     -r 1 -d 3 -s 8 -nsp 4 -ch 1`;
xform -ws -t ($tranV.x) ($tranV.y) ($tranV.z) -ro ($rotV.x) ($rotV.y)
       ($rotV.z) -s ($scalV.x) ($scalV.y) ($scalV.z) $names3[0];
```

Notice how the individual values are specified with the .x, .y, and .z labels. Using either arrays or vectors works about the same for storing transform values.

Either one will work well, although vectors with their xyz labeling may make it easier to spot the individual transform values in a complicated script.

Using Procedures

One of the most powerful techniques you can use in a script is to group all the code for a particular function under a name, so it becomes a new custom command, called a procedure in MEL. Using procedures makes your code more modular, and helps to organize the data in your scripts into smaller pieces. Procedures will be the main contents of all the scripts used to create the biped rig throughout this book.

CREATING A PROCEDURE

Creating a procedure is like making your own MEL command that does a particular task. It's done by grouping the code in curly brackets, to create a code block. Then you specify a name for the grouped code. The basic syntax is:

```
proc name () {code block}
```

A good way to get started creating procedures is to use some of the code you created earlier to create and transform primitives. First, you group the code that you want to run in your procedure into a block by surrounding it with curly brackets. Then you type the word proc at the beginning, and in front of the code block, specify a unique name. Adding an empty pair of parentheses after the name tells Maya to run just the code in the code block when the procedure name is used in the script. When creating more advanced procedures later, you will add arguments into the parentheses to allow users to input options. It is not necessary to end a procedure with a semicolon, because the code block terminates itself.

For instance, here is a simple procedure that uses similar code to what you ran earlier, but changes a few things such as the names and primitive types to make it less generic. Running the code creates and transforms a NURBS sphere according to the values declared in variables at the beginning, and then creates and transforms a polygon cube in the same manner by first querying the transforms of the sphere.

```
proc cmMyProc ()
{
//These values will be used to translate the sphere:
  int $num = 7;
  float $dec = 3.267;
```

```
    float $sum = $num + $dec;
//Declare variables containing the primitive names:
    string $ball = "myBall";
    string $box = "myBox";
//Create and translate the sphere using xform:
    string $sphereNodes[] = `sphere -n $ball -p 0 0 0 -ax 0 1 0 -ssw 0
        -esw 360 -r 1 -d 3 -s 8 -nsp 4 -ch 1`;
    xform -t $num $dec $sum $sphereNodes[0];
//Create and translate the cube by querying the sphere translations:
    string $cubeNodes[] = `polyCube -n $box -w 2 -h 2 -d 2 -sx 1 -sy 1
        -sz 1 -ax 0 1 0 -cuv 4 -ch 1`;
    vector $tranV = `xform -q -t $sphereNodes[0]`;
    xform -ws -t ($tranV.x) ($tranV.y) ($tranV.z) $cubeNodes[0];
    select -cl;
}
//Run the procedure:
    cmMyProc;
```

It is important that your procedure names are unique, and not the name of a
MEL command or procedure. Because the name of any new procedure potentially can overwrite others already in memory, industry standard is to type
your own initials at the beginning of all your procedure names.

The main rule for using procedures in your MEL scripts is always to run them
first, placing their entire contents in Maya's memory, which doesn't actually
run the code inside the code block. Then you run the procedure name somewhere in your script, which tells Maya to run the contents of the code block.
This is called running a local procedure, because you are running the name
somewhere in the same script in which the procedure was created or declared.
Local procedures stay in Maya's memory only while the script is running.

Some procedures, however, must remain in memory because you want to use
them in multiple scripts, or because they are constantly being referenced by GUI
commands. These are called global procedures, and will be used later in the setup GUI script in this chapter's exercise. Procedures that pertain to GUI controls
must be global, because they have to stay in memory as the user clicks the controls, even after the GUI script runs. A global procedure is created in the same
way as a local procedure, except that you add the word global to the beginning:

```
global proc name () {code block}
```

USING ARGUMENTS AND RETURN STATEMENTS

The code inside any given procedure is made to be entirely self-contained. The curly brackets act like walls that keep information from getting in or out of the procedure. This quality is called scope, and it prevents naming conflicts, especially for variables and arrays. Scope allows you to put multiple procedures in a single script, and reuse generic variable and array names like $dec or $sum for different operations, without the variables overwriting or referencing each other. Because of scope, however, it is necessary to have some way of moving data into and out of your procedures. This is done by adding arguments and return statements, which work like flag arguments and return statements on MEL commands. Procedure arguments let you input optional data for processing inside the code block, while return statements let you send data out of the code block, such as the names of created nodes. You can then catch the returned data in variables or arrays to send it through other procedures using more arguments. This is the way data is moved through long MEL scripts that are performing complex tasks in Maya, such as building a character rig.

To add arguments to a procedure, you declare empty variables in the parentheses after the name. When the procedure name is then run in the script, Maya will expect the user to input the correct data for each argument. Place the data inside parentheses after the name, separated by commas, in the same order as the variables. It is just like manually declaring variables in a script, only you don't have to include the equals sign. You can then use the variables or arguments anywhere inside the code block. For instance, your procedure may contain the generic code for creating and translating primitives as done previously, but you may want the user of the procedure to be able to add the names and positions of the primitives. Here is what such a procedure would look like:

```
//Local procedure with arguments:
proc cmMyProc (int $num,float $dec,string $ball,string $box)
{
//Process arguments to determine the Z position of sphere:
  float $sum = $num + $dec;
//Create and translate the sphere using xform:
  string $sphereNodes[] = `sphere -n $ball -p 0 0 0 -ax 0 1 0 -ssw 0
      -esw 360 -r 1 -d 3 -s 8 -nsp 4 -ch 1`;
  xform -t $num $dec $sum $sphereNodes[0];
//Create and translate the cube by querying the sphere translations:
  string $cubeNodes[] = `polyCube -n $box -w 2 -h 2 -d 2 -sx 1 -sy 1
      -sz 1 -ax 0 1 0 -cuv 4 -ch 1`;
```

```
  vector $tranV = `xform -q -t $sphereNodes[0]`;
  xform -ws -t ($tranV.x) ($tranV.y) ($tranV.z) $cubeNodes[0];
  select -cl;
}
//Run the procedure:
  cmMyProc (7,3.267,"myBall","myBox");
```

Next, you may want to add a return statement to send information out of the procedure. As mentioned, a common type of data to send out is strings, such as the sphere and cube names, that you may want to input into another procedure for transforming, parenting, shading, and so on. To add a return statement to your procedure, you must declare it in two places: at the beginning and end of the procedure. If you include one statement, but not the other, an error message will appear stating that you don't have a return.

Start by declaring the type of return statement at the beginning of the procedure between the term `proc` and the name of the procedure. In this example, you are going to send out the names of the primitive node. Since there are multiple names, you declare a string array as the type of return statement. Then toward the end of the procedure, you place the names of the primitive nodes you caught in the string array named `$names`. Do this by referencing the positions in the arrays in which you caught the names. Then add the second part of the return statement by typing the word `return`, followed by the array containing all the names. This line must be the last line in the procedure, just before the final curly bracket, as in this example:

```
//Local procedure with arguments and a string array return:
proc string[] cmMyProc (int $num,float $dec,string $ball,string $box)
{
//Process arguments to determine the Z position of sphere:
  float $sum = $num + $dec;
//Create and translate the sphere using xform:
  string $sphereNodes[] = `sphere -n $ball -p 0 0 0 -ax 0 1 0 -ssw 0
      -esw 360 -r 1 -d 3 -s 8 -nsp 4 -ch 1`;
  xform -t $num $dec $sum $sphereNodes[0];
//Create and translate the cube by querying the sphere translations:
  string $cubeNodes[] = `polyCube -n $box -w 2 -h 2 -d 2 -sx 1 -sy 1
      -sz 1 -ax 0 1 0 -cuv 4 -ch 1`;
  vector $tranV = `xform -q -t $sphereNodes[0]`;
  xform -ws -t ($tranV.x) ($tranV.y) ($tranV.z) $cubeNodes[0];
```

```
  select -cl;
//Place the names of the nodes in an array to return:
  string $names[] = {$sphereNodes[0],$sphereNodes[1],
      $cubeNodes[0],$cubeNodes[1]};
  return $names;
}
//Run the procedure, and catch the return:
string $return[] = cmMyProc (7,3.267,"myBall","myBox");
print $return;
/* Result:
      myBall
      makeNurbSphere1
      myBox
      polyCube1 */
```

In this example, notice that single back quotation marks are not used when
catching the return statement of a procedure, as you do for a MEL command.
Printing the contents of the $return array shows all the transform and creation
node names for the sphere and cube. Arrays can be used in both return statements and arguments.

WRITING AN XFORM QUERY GLOBAL PROCEDURE

Now that you know how to create a basic procedure with arguments and return
statements, you can start writing more useful procedures that can complete a
particular Maya task. For instance, you may need to retrieve all the transform
values for an object you created in the interface, so you can move an object
in your script to the same position. This requires running multiple xform commands in query mode, and then composing a final xform command using the
queried values. A drawback of using the xform command to query transforms is
that you cannot query all of them at once. But you can write a procedure that
queries all the transforms of a target object, as specified in the arguments. This
time the procedure is made global, to keep it in memory for running multiple
times. Here is how you can write such a procedure:

```
//Global procedure to query xforms of target, and return xform string:
global proc string cmQryXforms (string $target,string $constrain)
{
//Query all three transforms:
  float $cmQueryTrans[] = `xform -q -t $target`;
  float $cmQueryRot[] = `xform -q -ro $target`;
```

```
      float $cmQueryScale[] = `xform -q -s -r $target`;
//Create strings that can be combined in a final xform command:
  string $string1 = (" -t " + $cmQueryTrans[0] + " " + $cmQueryTrans[1]
      + " " + $cmQueryTrans[2]);
  string $string2 = (" -ro " + $cmQueryRot[0] + " " + $cmQueryRot[1] + " "
      + $cmQueryRot[2]);
  string $string3 = (" -s " + $cmQueryScale[0] + " " + $cmQueryScale[1]
      + " " + $cmQueryScale[2] + " ");
//Combine the strings into the final xform command, and return:
  string $return = ("xform " + $string1 + $string2
      + $string3 + $constrain + ";");
  return $return;
}
```

This procedure has two string arguments, a $target and $constrain, and a string return statement. After the queried values are stored in several arrays, the procedure combines the contents into several strings. This is possible because both numbers and letters can be strings, to allow combining the float transform values with flags in a single string. When dealing with long strings—in this case all the transforms of the target object—it is easier to break up the strings to combine them later. Then you combine the three strings with an xform command and the $constrain argument to create the final string return—an xform command containing all the transform flags and values to move the object that you want to constrain. Catching and printing the return lets you copy the final command with all the correct values into your script.

To successfully test the procedure, make sure that your sphere from the previous procedure is moved, rotated, and scaled differently than the cube. Input the sphere name as the $target argument, and input the cube name as the $constrain argument:

```
//Run the procedure, catch the return, and print final xform command:
      string $xformGo = cmQryXforms ("myBall","myBox");
print ($xformGo + "\n");
/* Result:
xform  -t 7.388139313 10.36046578 4.558761351 -ro 0 -33.16811871 -23.61789112 -s
1.973460548 1.973460548 1.973460548 myBox; */
```

Copy and paste the printed xform command into the Scripting field. Running the command should move the cube right on top of the sphere, as well as rotate and scale it to match the sphere perfectly. Check the transform channels in the

Channel Box for both objects to make sure that they are the same. Such a procedure can be useful when writing many kinds of scripts designed to place objects in 3D space, such as positioning skeleton joints or icons in a rigging script. Since it is nearly impossible to know the values for such placement, you first manually position the objects in the interface, and then use the procedure to query the values for positioning the objects in the script.

CREATING AN XFORM QUERY TOOL

You could make the cmQryXforms procedure into a custom MEL tool to constrain objects in Maya without having to type in the names of the objects as arguments, and without having to copy and paste the return statement. A custom MEL tool is something a Maya user might use on a daily basis while working in the interface. This particular tool could be designed to transform one object to another based on selection. To modify the previous section's cmQryXforms procedure to have this functionality, you need to remove the arguments and return statement, and list the selected node instead. Here is how to write such a procedure:

```
//Local procedure to use as xform tool to transform objects to target:
proc cmXformTool ()
{
 //List selected transform nodes:
   string $selTrans[] = `ls -sl`;
   string $target = $selTrans[0];
   string $constrain = $selTrans[1];
 //Query all three transforms:
   float $cmQueryTrans[] = `xform -q -t $target`;
   float $cmQueryRot[] = `xform -q -ro $target`;
   float $cmQueryScale[] = `xform -q -s -r $target`;
 //Create strings that can be combined in a final xform command:
   string $string1 = (" -t " + $cmQueryTrans[0] + " " + $cmQueryTrans[1]
       + " " + $cmQueryTrans[2]);
   string $string2 = (" -ro " + $cmQueryRot[0] + " " + $cmQueryRot[1]
       + " " + $cmQueryRot[2]);
   string $string3 = (" -s " + $cmQueryScale[0] + " " + $cmQueryScale[1]
       + " " + $cmQueryScale[2] + " ");
 //Combine the strings into the final xform command, and return:
   string $xformGo = ("xform " + $string1 + $string2
       + $string3 + $constrain + ";");
   select -cl;
   eval ($xformGo);
```

```
}
//Run the procedure:
cmXformTool;
```

Because the final xform command was converted into a string, running it as
a command requires the use of a new command called eval. This command
forces the string to be evaluated as code at runtime. As your coding becomes
more advanced, sometimes the eval command will be required to run strings
correctly. Also, because the procedure is run automatically after it goes into
memory, it is not necessary to make it global at the beginning of the procedure.

To use this cmXformTool procedure as a tool, select or highlight the code in the
Script Editor, depress the middle mouse button, and drag the code to the Maya
shelf. This action creates a shelf button that will run the MEL procedure whenever you click the button. Then all you have to do is select the target object,
Shift-select the object you want to transform, and click the shelf button. The
second object will transform to the same position, orientation, and scale as the
first object you selected. Shelf buttons are one of the easiest ways to run MEL
commands and procedures. "Working with Shelf Buttons" in the next section
covers more details on creating shelf buttons, and other ways of storing and
saving your MEL code for easy access.

Saving MEL Code

Now that you have written some significant sections of code, it is time you
learned how to save them. Although the code you have been writing will remain
in the Script Editor even after Maya is closed, inevitably you will need to load
other scripts, and the procedures you wrote will be replaced. There are several
ways of securely saving your code so it can be edited and run both inside and
outside of Maya. Each method has advantages and disadvantages; generally you
will want to use the best method for the kind of code you are writing.

WORKING WITH SHELF BUTTONS

In the previous section, "Creating an Xform Query Tool," you saved the
cmXformTool procedure into a shelf button that made it easy to access and run the
procedure in Maya. Although there are other similar ways of saving MEL code,
such as creating hot keys and marking menus, shelf buttons are the simplest and
most common way of storing small sections of MEL code in the Maya GUI. This
section will give you more details on editing the contents of shelf buttons.

The code stored in a shelf button is saved locally in the Preferences folder of
your user login in Microsoft Windows:

```
C:\Documents and Settings\LoginName\My Documents\maya\2008\prefs\shelves
```

It is useful to know where Maya saves this data on your computer, for copying
to other machines if necessary, and take your shelf buttons with you. Just copy
the entire Preferences folder, and overwrite the one on the new machine. In
addition, you should know how to edit the display and contents of your shelf
buttons in the Shelf Editor.

To edit the shelf button created for the cmXformTool procedure in the last section,
follow these steps:

1. Click the Down arrow button to the left of the shelf, and choose Shelf Editor. The editor opens to the Shelf Contents tab, displaying a vertical list of
buttons for the current shelf. The list references the buttons on the shelf from
left to right; the last button saved on the far right of the shelf is at the bottom
of the list.

2. Use the Shelf Contents tab to add a label to the button you created in the
previous section, "Creating an Xform Query Tool." Click the name of the last
button in the list, and in the Icon Name field, type a short label no longer than
four or five characters, such as xTool. The text label will appear on the button to
make it easier to identify (see **FIGURE 2.9**).

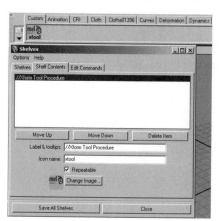

FIGURE 2.9 *Use the
Shelf Editor to add text
labels to shelf buttons and
edit MEL code contained
in a button.*

In the Label & Tooltips field, you can type a longer label, which will appear
when your pointer moves over the shelf button. If desired, use the Change
Image button that lets you load a custom bitmap image to use on the shelf.
Size any button images to 30 x 30 pixels to properly fit them on the shelf.

3. If you need to edit the MEL contents of the button, select the Edit Commands tab, which will give you access to the MEL procedure. Make any edits and click Save All Shelves to update the button and close the editor.

SAVING MEL SCRIPT FILES

A script file is just a text file with a .mel extension that contains your MEL code. Script files are most commonly used to save one or more procedures, because of how Maya manages the procedural data in memory. When you run a local procedure inside the Script Editor, Maya changes it to be a global procedure. Even any variables and arrays run outside of code blocks in a script are converted to global variables and arrays. Being global, they remain in memory until Maya is closed. By staying in memory, running large amounts of code could slow Maya's processing, and could cause clashes between variable names.

Saving your MEL code into a script file and running it from outside Maya, called sourcing, prevents Maya from subtly changing the code. This way you decide which procedures can be local and which must be global to work correctly and efficiently use Maya's memory. Sourcing a MEL script file uses a directive that tells Maya to search through all its scripts folders to open the named script file and run the code that it contains. An added benefit of saving your code into a MEL script file is that you can then edit the code in an external script editor, as described in "Using a Dedicated Script Editor," later in this chapter.

To save your code from the Script Editor into a MEL script file:

1. Using the cmMyProc procedure from the previous section "Creating an Xform Query Tool," simply highlight the code you want to save; or if you are working with a large block of MEL code that takes up the entire Scripting field, choose Edit > Select All to select all of the code.

2. Choose File > Save Script.

3. In the Save dialog box that appears, type cmMyProc.mel as the name of your script file (see **FIGURE 2.10**).

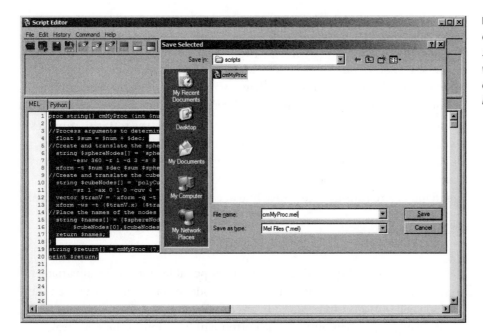

FIGURE 2.10 *Save more complicated scripts in the Script Editor as a text file with a .mel extension, and the text file becomes becomes a MEL script file.*

If you are saving only one procedure in a script file, it is standard to use the procedure name as the filename. However, if the script file has multiple procedures, you can use any descriptive name, or choose the name of the last procedure in the file.

4. Verify that the file is being saved into your Maya Scripts folder. Then click Save.

Once saved in the Maya Scripts folder, bring the contents of the MEL script files into Maya's memory by sourcing the filename in the Script Editor like this:

```
source cmMyProc.mel;
```

Sourcing a MEL script file doesn't necessarily run the MEL command or procedure; instead, it uses a directive to have Maya search through its script folders to open the named script file and run whatever code is in the file. If the file contains local procedures, then they will be run somewhere in the file. However, if the file contains global procedures, they may not be run in the file, but instead may be run in sections of code anywhere in Maya or in other scripts. In the case of the cmMyProc file, Maya puts the local procedure into memory, runs it to create and transform the primitives, and clears the procedure back out of memory when it is done.

When saving MEL script files, keep the following points in mind:

■ Make sure that you are using a unique name, by adding your initials, and save only one version in one Scripts folder. Maya looks through multiple script folders when it sources a script. If it finds different scripts with the same name in multiple folders, then it will get confused, and your scripts may not work correctly.

■ Maya caches the contents of all its scripts folders when the software launches. If you save a new script, as you just did, and then try to source it without re-launching Maya, Maya will display an error message stating that it can't find your script. To re-cache the folders without closing Maya, simply run a `rehash` command before running the source line of code; the command looks like this:

```
rehash;
source cmMyProc;
```

■ Always save your MEL code as script files if possible, and use local variables, arrays, and procedures if you don't need the code to stay in memory. Even the code in shelf buttons can be saved in a script file, and just the source directive is saved in the shelf button. The button will function in the same way, but memory will be managed better in Maya. An easy way to see how running code inside of Maya can cause problems is to declare a variable, and then try to re-declare it as a different type. Because the variables are placed in memory as global, you will always get an error message:

```
string $name;
int $name;
/* Error: Line 2.13: Invalid redeclaration of variable "$name" as a different
type. */
```

Generally, the Maya documentation recommends to always use local variables in your MEL scripts, unless you have a specific need to keep a variable permanently in memory. To purposely create a global variable or array, type `global` at the beginning, just as when you create a global procedure. Be aware that once you create a global variable or array, you can empty or clear its contents using a `clear` command, but you cannot delete the global variable or array without closing Maya.

USING A DEDICATED SCRIPT EDITOR

A big plus of saving your code into a MEL script file is that you can then work on it in an external script editor. Several external script editors are available for most platforms, including free ones you can download, like JEdit (www.jedit.org) or ConTEXT (www.contexteditor.org). Using these editors has several advantages over using the Script Editor in Maya. One advantage is that these editors have color-coding plug-ins for MEL. They assign different colors to the contents of your MEL script, such as making strings green, commands blue, and comments light gray in ConTEXT (see **FIGURE 2.11**).

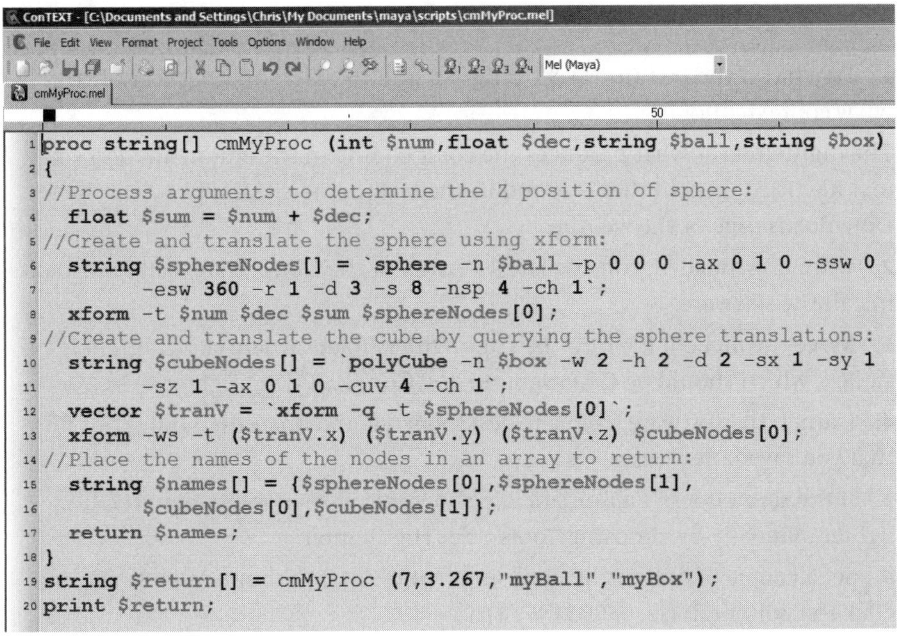

FIGURE 2.11 *Saving your code in a MEL script file lets you open it in an external script editor like ConTEXT.*

```
1 proc string[] cmMyProc (int $num,float $dec,string $ball,string $box)
2 {
3 //Process arguments to determine the Z position of sphere:
4   float $sum = $num + $dec;
5 //Create and translate the sphere using xform:
6   string $sphereNodes[] = `sphere -n $ball -p 0 0 0 -ax 0 1 0 -ssw 0
7        -esw 360 -r 1 -d 3 -s 8 -nsp 4 -ch 1`;
8   xform -t $num $dec $sum $sphereNodes[0];
9 //Create and translate the cube by querying the sphere translations:
10   string $cubeNodes[] = `polyCube -n $box -w 2 -h 2 -d 2 -sx 1 -sy 1
11        -sz 1 -ax 0 1 0 -cuv 4 -ch 1`;
12   vector $tranV = `xform -q -t $sphereNodes[0]`;
13   xform -ws -t ($tranV.x) ($tranV.y) ($tranV.z) $cubeNodes[0];
14 //Place the names of the nodes in an array to return:
15   string $names[] = {$sphereNodes[0],$sphereNodes[1],
16        $cubeNodes[0],$cubeNodes[1]};
17   return $names;
18 }
19 string $return[] = cmMyProc (7,3.267,"myBall","myBox");
20 print $return;
```

Using such color-coding makes it easier to view the components of your scripts and catch mistakes. For instance, if you forget to close the double quotation marks of a string in ConTEXT, the text won't turn green. Other advantages are search and replace functions that facilitate making global changes to your code, like changing a prefix or suffix; and the ability to work and save outside of Maya, so that your code remains local.

The most efficient way to work with an external script file in ConTEXT is to edit and save, and then switch to Maya to source the updated code using a shelf button. Make sure that the button contains the source directive to the file, and have the Script Editor open so that you can look at print statements and errors in the History field. Then just click the shelf button and examine the results. Switch back to ConTEXT to further edit the code, and to track down errors using line numbers.

Avoid copying and pasting code directly from ConTEXT into the Script Editor, as this technique may produce errors caused by formatting. Also, never work on a script in document programs like Microsoft Word, as the text formatting will cause many errors that are difficult to correct. Notepad is the only acceptable text program for coding, other than dedicated script editors.

Here's an example of how to load and set the preferences for ConTEXT in Microsoft Windows.

1. Download the free ConTEXT program and the MEL highlighter at http://www.contexteditor.org.

The highlighter is what produces the color coding in the editor, and is a small text file titled mel.chl that is found in the Highlighters [M...P] link on the Downloads page of the website.

2. Once downloaded, run the latest version of the ConTEXT executable file to install the software.

3. Move the mel.chl file into the Highlighters folder where the program is installed, which should be C:\Program Files\ConTEXT\Highlighters.

4. Launch the software from the desktop icon, and open the MEL script file that you saved previously.

5. If the script doesn't automatically show colors, then select the MEL highlighter manually by choosing Tools > Set Highlighter.

6. Set a couple of options by choosing Options > Environment Options, and click the Editor tab (see **FIGURE 2.12**).

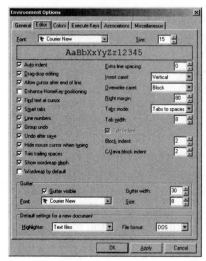

FIGURE 2.12 *Set options in ConTEXT to show line numbers; that way, you can easily track down errors you find in the Maya Script Editor.*

Since clearly seeing the code can impact the accuracy of your writing, increase the font size to 15. Also turn on the visibility of line numbers in the editor for tracking down and fixing errors that Maya returns in the Script Editor.

7. When you have finished, click Apply and then OK.

SAVING MEL CODE IN A MAYA SCENE FILE

At times, you will want to save MEL code in a Maya scene file, especially if you want to ensure that the code automatically runs when the scene is opened. To save MEL code in a Maya scene file, you use the Expression Editor (usually reserved for creating math expressions) with a special filter for creating MEL script nodes. When you save the scene, Maya automatically includes the script node with all the other nodes in the file.

To save your MEL code in a Maya scene file:

1. Choose Window > Animation Editors > Expression Editor.

2. Click Select Filter on the menu bar to change from the default By Object/At-tribute Name filter to the By Script Node Name filter (see **FIGURE 2.13**).

FIGURE 2.13 *Save MEL code in a Maya scene file using the Script Node filter inside the Expression Editor. Using script nodes can automatically run MEL code once a scene is opened.*

This filter is not intended for creating expressions, but rather for saving MEL code with the scene file. Be careful to use the correct filter; if you do not, your code will not work correctly. MEL and expressions are two distinct languages, and although there may be some similarities, you should not mix them up for now.

3. When you have selected the correct filter, use the middle mouse button to drag your procedure code from the Script Editor to the Expression Editor.

4. With the code in the Script field, type a script node name, and click Create. The new node appears in the Script Nodes list.

5. If you create multiple nodes in one scene file, select the name in the list of the node you want to test or edit. Whenever you make changes to the code, click the Edit button to update the script node.

6. Choose an Execute On option to determine how the code will be run:

- To manually run the code, choose Demand. Then click the Test Script button to run the code. Unlike running MEL code in the Script Editor, you never run the code in the Expression Editor by selecting the code and pressing Ctrl+Enter.

- To have your code run automatically when the scene file opens, choose GUI Open/Close. You could, for instance, save source lines to external MEL scripts, which cause them to run automatically when someone opens the scene file, as done in the basicFkRig.mb example file to automatically source and open the setup GUI for the advanced rig.

Refining Your Scripts

This section introduces you to more essential techniques for refining your scripts, including using conditional statements to control the flow of data and several types of loops to automate repetitive coding tasks. Other intermediate techniques will introduce how to code Maya name spacing, hierarchy creation, matrices for transform data, writing and reading data to custom text files, and a basic GUI.

Using Conditions and Loops

A condition is a statement that is evaluated as either true or false by Maya. Conditions use standard operators found also in expressions, with the most common being:

- A is greater than B: (A > B)
- A is less than B: (A < B)
- A is exactly equal to B: (A == B)
- A is not equal to B: (A != B)

Such conditions are used in if, else, and else-if statements to enable you to evaluate the condition, and then have Maya run different commands or procedures depending on the result. This allows you to control the flow of data through your script as the script executes and as the scene changes.

Loops, on the other hand, are one of the best techniques for making your scripts more efficient by automating repetitive code. Loops also incorporate conditions to control how the loop runs. There are several types of loops you need to learn to make your code more efficient, including while, for, and for-in loops.

IF, ELSE, AND ELSE IF STATEMENTS

The most common conditional statement in Maya is an if statement. This statement evaluates a condition in parentheses, and then runs a specified command or procedure if it evaluates as true. If the condition evaluates as false, on the other hand, then Maya ignores the command or procedure as it continues through the script. This makes your script more interactive and flexible, rather than just running through a predictable series of linear commands the same way every time. Here is a simple example of such a conditional statement using static numbers manually entered or hard-coded into a couple of variables:

```
float $A = 7.2;
float $B = 3.5;
if ($A > $B) print "A is greater than B!\n";
// Result: A is greater than B! //
```

You can add a second statement to allow running a second command or procedure if the condition evaluates as false. An else statement allows you even more control and flexibility over what your script does by making it possible to switch between two different results. Keep in mind that this statement is used only in conjunction with an if statement and cannot be used by itself. Here is a simple example of adding the else statement:

```
float $A = 1.3;
float $B = 5.7;
if ($A > $B) print "A is greater than B!\n";
else print "A is less than B!\n";
// Result: A is less than B! //
```

This is a powerful technique for making your script more interactive with changes that occur as the script runs in Maya. Instead of using static numbers in the conditional statement, you could reference values generated by Maya commands or attributes. For instance, you could have Maya generate random numbers using the `rand` command, and then evaluate which is greater. Here is a simple example that will generate different random numbers between 0 and 10, every time you run it, and store the results in two variables. Then it runs a conditional statement comparing the variable contents, and prints whether the random number in `$A` is less or greater than `$B`:

```
$A = `rand 0 10`;
$B = `rand 0 10`;
  print ("A is " + $A + "\n");
  print ("B is " + $B + "\n");
if ($A > $B) print "A is greater than B!\n";
else print "A is less than B!\n";
/* Result: A is 2.125328649
B is 5.330603067
A is less than B! */
```

Yet another way to make this condition more flexible is to add another option. In comparing the two values, an obvious third possibility not covered in the previous condition is that the values could be equal to each other. One way to incorporate this third possibility is to add a second condition using an `else if` statement. This statement is also used only with an initial `if` statement, and works similarly to running two `if` statements in a row, except there is more interaction between the conditions.

```
if (condition #1) {code block};
else if (condition #2) {code block};
else print {code block};
```

The `else if` statement is placed between the `if` and `else` statements, and the second condition will be evaluated only if the first condition evaluates as false. The `else` code block will run only if both conditions turn out to be false. Be aware that you can add as many `else if` statements as you like between the `if` and `else` statements. Here is an example of inserting such a statement in a condition to determine if the user chose different random values or equal static values for storing in variables. This is done by setting the initial `$change` argument to either 1 or 0 when running the procedure.

```
/*Set procedure argument to 1 or 0:
        Note!: 1 = Rand #s, 0 = Both 0 */
```

```
proc string cmCondition (int $change){
//Use condition to determine values:
    float $A;
    float $B;
    if ($change == 1) {
        $A = `rand 0 10`;
        $B = `rand 0 10`;
    }
    else {
        $A = 0.0;
        $B = 0.0;
    }
//Print values inside variables:
    print ("A is " + $A + "\n");
    print ("B is " + $B + "\n");
//Runs three conditionals to compare values:
    string $return;
    if ($A > $B) $return = "A is greater than B!";
      else if ($A == $B) $return = "A is equal to B!";
        else $return = "A is less than B!";
 return $return;
}
//Run procedure:
string $result = cmCondition (0);
print ($result + "\n");
/* Result:
A is 0
B is 0
A is equal to B! */
```

Notice that code blocks are used for the first conditional statements. Code blocks are necessary to group multiple lines of code to run together when the condition is evaluated as true or false. In the previous examples, you used conditional statements to compare abstract numbers; there will be many other applications when you get to scripting the rig. For instance, you may compare queried attributes of objects, and then run code based on evaluating how the values compare to each other.

WARNINGS AND ERRORS

Now that you have started using conditional statements, you can begin adding warning or error messages to further refine your code. The error and warning commands can be used in conjunction with conditional statements to give feedback, and in the case of a user error, prevent the script from breaking. Generally, you will check whether a user action or input was done in a particular way, such as selecting something before running a selection-based procedure; if the action or input was done wrong, then the warning or error message will run instead of the main code. The advantage of displaying a warning or error message is that these messages turn the feedback field purple or red, and thus may get the user's attention more than standard printing.

For instance, the cmXformTool procedure created previously in this chapter required selecting two objects to work correctly. You could check for this at the beginning of the procedure, and print an error message if it is done incorrectly. Here is how you add such an error message to that procedure:

```
proc cmXformTool ()
{
//List selected transform nodes:
  string $selTrans[] = `ls -sl`;
//Error check for selection:
  int $sizeSelect = `size ($selTrans)`;
  if ($sizeSelect != 2)
     error "Select a target object followed by an object to constrain!";
//Query all three transforms:
  float $cmQueryTrans[] = `xform -q -t $selTrans[0]`;
  float $cmQueryRot[] = `xform -q -ro $selTrans[0]`;
  float $cmQueryScale[] = `xform -q -s -r $selTrans[0]`;
//Create a strings that can be used in an xform command
  string $string1 = (" -t " + $cmQueryTrans[0] + " " + $cmQueryTrans[1]
      + " " + $cmQueryTrans[2]);
  string $string2 = (" -ro " + $cmQueryRot[0] + " " + $cmQueryRot[1] + " "
      + $cmQueryRot[2]);
  string $string3 = (" -s " + $cmQueryScale[0] + " " + $cmQueryScale[1]
      + " " + $cmQueryScale[2] + " ");
//Combine the strings into the xform command, and return:
  string $xformGo = ("xform " + $string1 + $string2
      + $string3 + $selTrans[1] + ";");
  select -cl;
```

```
  eval ($xformGo);
}
cmXformTool;
```

Notice that the `size` command is used to determine how many objects are selected, by calculating how many node names are in the `$selTrans` array. The value returned from the `size` command is stored in an integer variable that can then be run in a conditional statement. The `not equals` operator is used to find out if any number other than two is in the variable. If this evaluates as true, then the `error` command will run and stop the script, printing a message in red stating that two objects must be selected. The `warning` command is used in the exact same way, except that it does not stop the rest of the script from running. For an example of a `warning` command, see the next section on switch statements.

SWITCH STATEMENTS

You use `switch` statements to run a series of conditions to see if any evaluate as true, and then run commands or procedures. It is similar to running a series of `if` statements, without any `else` statements to run if the conditions are false. A `switch` statement is especially useful for checking through an array of names, and then doing something when the statement finds a particular one.

Here is an example that checks whether a user-defined integer value contained in the `$num` argument matches one of the cases in the `switch` statement, and then prints the number if it does:

```
//Change the integer value in the procedure argument:
proc string cmfindNum (int $num){//Open procedure...
 //Run warning if numbers are not 5,10,15, or 20:
   if (($num != 5) && ($num != 10) && ($num != 15) && ($num != 20))
       warning "Input a multiple of 5 under 25!";
 //Run switch statement to set string return:
   string $return;
   switch ($num) {//Open switch...
     case 5:
       $return = "Your number is 5!";
       break;
     case 10:
       $return = "Your number is 10!";
       break;
     case 15:
```

```
        $return = "Your number is 15!";
        break;
     case 20:
        $return = "Your number is 20!";
        break;
   }//Close switch.
  return $return;
}//Close procedure.
//Run procedure to catch return and print:
string $result = cmfindNum (1);
print ($result + "\n");
// Result: Warning: Input a multiple of 5 under 25! //
```

In this procedure, the switch statement checks whether the argument contains the integers 5, 10, 15, or 20. The incoming argument is placed in parentheses, followed by case statements that compare the numbers. If any of these cases evaluate as true, then the statement will print the value, and the break statement will stop the switch. If you enter a number that doesn't fit these cases, such as in the example argument of (1), then the if statement at the beginning prints a warning telling the user to input a multiple of 5 that is under 25. The warning is generated using a not-equals (!=) operator.

Let's look at another similar example that uses primitives instead of numbers. In this procedure, the argument is a short string that indicates one of four primitives. The conditional checks the strings and prints a warning if one of the target strings is not used. Then the switch statement creates the appropriate primitive and returns the node names. The return statement this time is a string array to facilitate printing both node names returned from the primitive command:

```
//Change the short primitive name in the procedure argument:
proc string[] cmCreatePrim (string $primitive){//Open procedure...
 //Run warning if numbers are not 5,10,15, or 20:
   if (($primitive != "sph") &&
      ($primitive != "cub") &&
      ($primitive != "con") &&
      ($primitive != "cyl"))
      warning "Use short primitive name (sph,cub,con,or cyl)!";
 //Switch statement to create prim and set string array return:
   string $return[];
   switch ($primitive) {//Open switch...
```

```
      case "sph":
        $return = `sphere`;
        break;
      case "cub":
        $return = `polyCube`;
        break;
      case "con":
        $return = `polyCone`;
        break;
      case "cyl":
        $return = `cylinder`;
        break;
    }//Close switch.
  return $return;
}//Close procedure.
//Run procedure to catch return array and print:
string $names[] = cmCreatePrim ("sph");
print ("Nodes created: " + $names[0] + "," + $names[1] + "\n");
// Result: Nodes created: nurbsSphere1,makeNurbSphere1 //
```

Also notice the additional formatting and comments that were incorporated to make it clear where code blocks in the procedure start and end. Since a line comment only comments out the text after the (//) on that particular line, the comment can be placed to the right of the curly brackets without affecting the code block. This formatting is especially useful when you start placing code blocks within other code blocks, called nesting. The important thing is to make sure that you don't leave a code block open, which would produce an error in your script.

WHILE LOOPS

Now you'll start looking at how loops can automate repetitive tasks. A while loop, for instance, continues to repeat a block of code until a stated condition evaluates as false. In the following example, the code block creates a sphere, and then translates it in Y based on the increasing $i integer variable. The variable starts at 0, and then increments by 2 each time the code block runs, stopping when the variable is no longer less than or equal to (<=) the number 10. This will create a total of six spheres stacked on top of each other (see **FIGURE 2.14**).

```
//While Loop example creating spheres:
int $i = 0;
while ($i <= 10)
```

```
{//Open loop:
  string $name = "mySphere";
  string $names[] = `sphere -n $name -p 0 0 0 -ax 0 1 0 -ssw 0 -esw 360
      -r 1 -d 3 -s 8 -nsp 4 -ch 1`;
  setAttr ($names[0] + ".ty") $i;
  select -cl;
  $i = $i + 2;
}//Close loop.
```

FIGURE 2.14 *Running the* while *loop example creates and transforms six spheres so they are stacked on top of each other.*

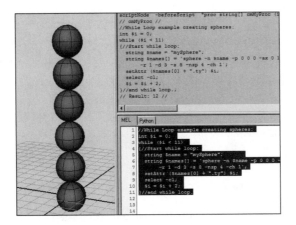

The important issue with a while loop is to not create a never-ending loop, because it could crash Maya. To prevent an infinite loop, you always write a condition that will prove false at some point. Although while loops can be useful, and will be used in the rigging scripts, they are used less than the for-in and for loops covered next.

FOR-IN AND FOR LOOPS

The most common loops used in MEL scripting are for-in and for loops. The for-in loop is specifically designed for running commands or procedures on every element in an array. This kind of loop is very useful for automating tasks on a series of names contained in a string array, such as deleting history and freezing transforms on a series of primitives you created. These are basic tasks that are often done to finalize rig nodes before parenting them into a hierarchy. You would do these operations in the interface, find the relevant commands in the Script Editor, and look up the required flags in the Maya documentation, and then include the commands in the loop. The following example shows running these commands in a loop to delete history and freeze transformations on any number of selected primitives:

```
//Shift-select primitives to delete history and freeze:
  string $selObjs[] = `ls -sl`;
string $obj;
for ($obj in $selObjs){//Open loop…
    delete -ch $obj;
    makeIdentity -apply true -t 1 -r 1 -s 1 -n 0 $obj;
}//Close loop.
```

After the selected primitive names are listed and stored in a $selObjs array, an empty $obj string variable is declared to hold each primitive name while the loop runs. The loop itself automatically moves the first name in the $selObjs to the $obj variable, and runs the commands on the named primitive. Maya continues in this fashion until all the names in the array have been run through the loop.

Useful for many repetitive coding operations, for-in loops are limited in only being able to page through the contents of a single array. Completing more complex repetitive operations that reference multiple arrays of various types requires using a more sophisticated loop. The for loop has a built-in increment value that allows paging through the contents of multiple arrays. To create this kind of loop, you set up a condition that states the starting value of the $i variable, the ending value, and how the variable should increment each time the loop runs.

```
//For loop general structure for looping 4 times:
int $start = 0;
int $stop = 4;
int $i;
for ($i = $start ; $i < $stop ; $i++)
    {code block}
```

The following application declares three arrays that contain four different types of data for creating and moving spheres. The data in the arrays is accessed in the loop by inserting the $i variable within the array name brackets. Each time the loop runs, the variable increments, and the next position in the arrays are referenced. The commands inside the loop will then create four spheres, translate them in four directions, and then finalize the nodes by deleting their history and freezing them (see **FIGURE 2.15**).

```
//Create arrays containing data to loop through:
  string $names[] = {"ltSphere","topSphere","rtSphere","botSphere"};
```

```
    string $attrs[] = {".tx",".ty",".tx",".ty"};
    float $values[] = {-2.0,2.5,3.0,-3.5};
//Run loop to create, transform, delete history, and freeze spheres:
    int $i;
for ($i = 0 ; $i < 4 ; $i++){//Open loop…
        string $name[] = `sphere -n $names[$i] -p 0 0 0 -ax 0 1 0 -ssw 0
        -esw 360 -r 1 -d 3 -s 8 -nsp 4 -ch 1`;
        setAttr ($name[0] + $attrs[$i]) $values[$i];
        delete -ch $name[0];
        makeIdentity -apply true -t 1 -r 1 -s 1 -n 0 $name[0];
                select -cl;
}//Close loop.
```

FIGURE 2.15 *Running the* for *loop example creates and transforms four spheres in four different directions.*

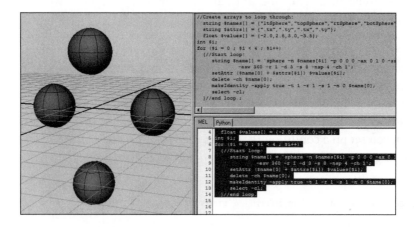

EXAMINING SOME MAYA PROCEDURES

Maya runs many procedures, in addition to the standard MEL commands. Procedures differ from MEL commands in that you can open the MEL script file containing the procedure and examine the contents of the procedural code block. You cannot, however, dissect a MEL command. The only reference to how commands work is the Maya documentation. To further your understanding of how to write your own scripts and procedures, you can examine the contents of a Maya script file. In "Getting Basic Help on Commands" earlier in this chapter, you saw how running the whatIs command on the objectMoveCommand showed it was a procedure found in one of Maya's script folders.

```
whatIs objectMoveCommand;
/* Result: Mel procedure found in:
C:/Program Files/Autodesk/Maya2008/scripts/startup/objectMoveCommand.mel */
```

Go to the appropriate folder and open this script in the Script Editor or ConTEXT to see what it contains. Opening the objectMoveCommand MEL script file shows some comments stating mostly warnings that you shouldn't modify the code, followed by the objectMoveCommand procedure:

```
global proc objectMoveCommand()
{
      if (!`optionVar -exists primitivePlacementRule`) {
            optionVar -sv primitivePlacementRule "AtOrigin" ;
      }

      string $placementRule = `optionVar -q primitivePlacementRule`;
      switch ($placementRule) {
            case "AtOrigin":
                  move 0 0 0;
                  break;
            case "ViewCenter":
                  float $pos[] = `autoPlace`;
                  move $pos[0] $pos[1] $pos[2];
                  break;
      }
}
```

You don't have to completely understand this procedure to recognize some coding techniques already covered in this chapter: a command being run with single back quotation marks inside a conditional statement; other commands being queried with a -q flag; the return caught in a string variable; and a switch statement with cases containing strings that, if evaluated as true, will run move commands. The main thing to understand is that procedures in Maya contain the same coding techniques you are learning to incorporate in your own procedures and scripts. This particular procedure is run when creating a sphere in the interface if interactive creation is turned off in the Create > NURBS Primitives menu. The procedure automatically places the created sphere at the world origin.

Now you'll look at another procedure that may be a little more useful for your rigging scripts. Open the script at this location:

```
C:\Program Files\Autodesk\Maya2008\scripts\unsupported\distance2Pts.mel
```

This file contains a procedure by the same name that can be used to find the distance between two points in 3D space. You can query the transform positions of two objects in conjunction with this procedure to find out the distance between the objects.

```
global proc float distance2Pts( float $p1[], float $p2[] )
{
    if( size($p1) != 3 )
        warning((uiRes("m_distance2Pts.kWarningNeedArray1")) );
    if( size($p2) != 3 )
        warning((uiRes("m_distance2Pts.kWarningNeedArray2")) );
    float $distance;
    float $v[3];
    $v[0] = $p1[0] - $p2[0];
    $v[1] = $p1[1] - $p2[1];
    $v[2] = $p1[2] - $p2[2];
    $distance = $v[0]*$v[0] + $v[1]*$v[1] + $v[2]*$v[2];
    $distance = sqrt( $distance );
    return $distance;
}
```

The two arguments in this procedure are float arrays expecting the three XYZ position values of two objects. In the code block of the procedure, the conditional statements check that the arguments contain three values, or else run a warning. Then the procedure runs some math computations and a square-root command to calculate the distance between the two float arguments; it then returns the distance as a float value. As you can see, except for a few new commands that you can always look up in the Maya documentation, these procedures contain the same techniques that you are now using. There are hundreds of these procedures that Maya uses all the time, and they are another important resource to use when you are writing your own scripts.

MEL Rigging Essentials

You need to know some intermediate MEL commands and techniques before starting to script the biped rig. These include the namespace command to prevent naming conflicts if there is more than one rig in a scene; the group and parent commands to facilitate creating the rig hierarchy; the matrix command to better organize position data of joints; several commands for writing and reading text files to move data between scripts; and some GUI commands to create a simple window for running your scripts.

PREVENTING NAMING CONFLICTS

The namespace command lets you specify a unique prefix for groups of nodes created in a scene. You use this command to make sure that the nodes in a rig hierarchy for a particular character do not conflict with the names in another rig hierarchy. This lets you use the same scripts to create multiple rigs without worrying about naming conflicts. Also, if you don't give the rig a namespace, then you have to specify the entire path for a node in a hierarchy, which can be quite long and involved in a large rig. Here is how the name looks for the right-hand node in the example FK rig if you list the entire branch hierarchy path:

```
ls -l "rtHand_fkRig";
/* Result: |Reference_fkTop|ctHips_fkRig|ctSpine0_fkRig|ctSpine1_fkRig|ctSpine2_
fkRig|ctSpine3_fkRig|rtShoulder_fkRig|rtArm_fkRig|rtForearm_fkRig|rtHand_fkRig */
```

The vertical pipe (|) symbols in the result indicate that the right-hand name is in a node hierarchy, one parented to the other. The top of the hierarchy is the Reference node, and the end of the hierarchy is the right-hand node. You can imagine how it would increase the length of your scripts if you had to use the entire naming path every time you referenced a node in your rig, and how it would increase the difficulty of reading your scripts. To avoid this complexity, you will place all the rig nodes in their own namespace.

Since the names of the nodes will have a prefix, main name, and suffix, it's best to use a short namespace prefix. When the names of nodes get too long, they are difficult to read in the Paint Skin Weights Tool and Component Editor. For this reason, it is advisable to use the character's initials as the namespace name. In this book, the namespace prefix will be extracted from the skin name, in this case the cm in cm_skin. Similarly, you could use your own initials, or any short unique name. Once you add the namespace prefix, Maya can then find the node in a hierarchy by the prefix followed by a colon, and then the main name, which looks like this:

```
cm:rtHand_fkRig
```

Be aware that even objects not parented are automatically part of a hidden namespace called the scene root. When you want to manually assign a custom namespace prefix to any nodes that are created in the scene, you run the namespace command with an -add flag, specifying the new prefix, and set the scene root as the parent. Then you run the namespace command again to set the current namespace as the custom prefix, in this case cm. Do not add a colon to the prefix; Maya will do that automatically as part of the command.

```
string $root = ":";
string $mySpace = "cm";
string $nameSpace = `namespace -p $root -add $mySpace`;
namespace -set $nameSpace;
```

After running this code, try creating some objects either in the interface, or by running code from the previous sections. Notice that every object has the prefix cm: before the rest of the name. Also notice that the prefix is on most nodes, such as the creation and shape nodes. This will be true of every object created while the current namespace is set to cm. To set the namespace back to the default root namespace so that no apparent prefix is added to node names, simply type the following:

```
namespace -set $root;
```

CODING HIERARCHIES

In addition to creating, transforming, and freezing nodes, you need to perform another Maya task to create a basic rig. Since a rig is primarily a hierarchy of nodes, you have to know the commands for parenting and grouping transform nodes. A basic FK rig may be composed primarily of parented skeletons, but more complex rigs will have many other nodes parented into the hierarchy, including group nodes.

Basic parenting is relatively simple, in that you follow the parent command with the names of the child nodes as required, and finish with the parent node specified. For instance, to parent a series of spheres like those created in the example while loop (in the same-named section) previously in this chapter, you would write the command like this:

```
string $parent = "mySphere";
string $child[] = {"mySphere1","mySphere2","mySphere3",
    "mySphere4","mySphere5"};
parent $child[0] $child[1] $child[2] $child[3] $child[4] $parent;
```

Running this code results in the sphere named mySphere becoming the direct parent of all the other spheres. Look in the Hypergraph after running the code to see how the spheres are parented. If you instead wanted to parent each sphere under the previously created sphere to create a branch hierarchy, you would have to run a series of parent commands. Since this process would be tedious and repetitive, and since you know how to write several types of loops now, it is better to use a for loop. The following example does this by placing the names of the spheres in an array in the order in which you want the parenting to occur. The first name will be the top parent node of the branch, while the last name will be the lowest child node in the branch (see **FIGURE 2.16**).

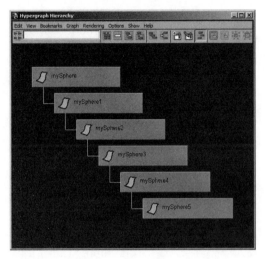

FIGURE 2.16
This procedure runs a loop on an array of sphere names to parent them in a branch hierarchy of nodes, as seen in the Hypergraph.

```
string $hierarchy[] = {"mySphere","mySphere1","mySphere2",
      "mySphere3","mySphere4","mySphere5"};
int $i;
for ($i = 1 ; $i < size($hierarchy) ; $i++)
  {//Start loop:
      int $p = ($i - 1);
      parent $hierarchy[$i] $hierarchy[$p];
  }//end loop.
```

A for loop is used instead of a for-in loop because the $i variable not only specifies the child node, but the ($i - 1) code is specifying the previous sphere name in the array as the parent node. Also notice that a size command, which counts the number of elements in an array, is used to set the upper limit of the loop to the exact number of names in the $hierarchy array.

Next is a similar but more complex example: it parents selected nodes into a branch hierarchy, and then prints the resulting hierarchy path. The size command is used in the procedure for error checking, parenting, and determining the last node in the array so that it can be listed.

```
//Local procedure to parent selected into branch and list:
proc string cmBranchParenter ()
```

```
{//Start proc:
//List selected nodes you want to parent:
  string $hierarchy[] = `ls -sl`;
  int $size = `size($hierarchy)`;
//Selection error check:
  if ($size < 1) error "Nothing selected!";
//Run loop to parent nodes in order of selection:
  int $i;
  for ($i = 1 ; $i < $size ; $i++)
    {//Start loop:
        int $p = ($i - 1);
        parent $hierarchy[$i] $hierarchy[$p];
        select -cl;
    }//end loop.
//Check resulting branch by listing last node:
  int $end = ($size - 1);
  string $branch[] = `ls -l $hierarchy[$end]`;
//Return hierarchy branch path:
  string $return = ("Branch path: " + $branch[0] + "\n");
  return $return;
}//end proc.
//Run proc:
string $branch = cmBranchParenter ();
print $branch;
```

The group command is also used to create hierarchies, but has extra features and creates a new transform node. In addition to being able to specify multiple children, the command has a -p, or parent, flag to specify a parent of the group node itself. These flags are useful for inserting the group node in the middle of a hierarchy. For instance, to parent the same spheres under a single group node and simultaneously parent the group node under mySphere, you could write:

```
string $hierarchy[] = {"mySphere1","mySphere2",
        "mySphere3","mySphere4","mySphere5"};
string $parent = "mySphere";
string $name = "myGroup";
string $group = `group -n $name -p $parent $hierarchy`;
print ($group + "\n");
//Result: myGroup //
```

Check the Hypergraph to see how the group node is inserted between the my-Sphere node and all the other nodes (see **FIGURE 2.17**).

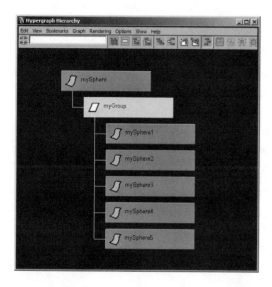

FIGURE 2.17 *Running the* group *command lets you insert a group node in a hierarchy.*

Notice that the code catches and prints the group name, as was done previously with primitives, but this time it uses a variable instead of an array. This illustrates that group nodes are really just a single transform node, with no creation node or attributes. Looking in the Channel Box you can see that the node doesn't have a shape or creation node in the Inputs. In later chapters, you will also insert group nodes into the rig hierarchy to create new pivot points for animating transforms.

MANIPULATING STRINGS

Often when MEL scripting a character rig, it's necessary to break names apart and replace parts of names. To manipulate strings in this way, Maya provides the tokenize and substitute commands.

The tokenize command lets you break a string into pieces at specified types of character or symbols. For instance, suppose a node has a suffix that starts with an underscore, like lfHand_fkRig, and you want to remove the suffix. You can do so like this:

```
string $name = "lfHand_fkRig";
//Declare an array to contain the strings:
  string $pieces[];
//Tokenize at the underscore:
```

```
tokenize $name "_" $pieces;
//Print array contents:
  print ($pieces[0] + "\n");
//Result: lfHand //
  print ($pieces[1] + "\n");
//Result: fkRig //
```

In this example the tokenize command breaks apart the string inside the $name variable at the underscore, and places the resulting two strings on either side of the underscore into the $pieces array, discarding the underscore. Printing out the first two positions of the array shows that the main name goes into the first position of the array, and the suffix goes in the second position.

Another use is to break up a hierarchy string, such as results when doing a long-name listing, as when previously working with the namespace command in the "Preventing Naming Conflicts" section. For instance, here is an example that breaks up an arm hierarchy path into four individual names at the vertical pipe (|) symbol:

```
string $path =
  "|rtShoulder_fkRig|rtArm_fkRig|rtForearm_fkRig|rtHand_fkRig";
string $nodes[];
tokenize $path "|" $nodes;
print $nodes;
/* Result:
  rtShoulder_fkRig
  rtArm_fkRig
  rtForearm_fkRig
  rtHand_fkRig */
```

Another frequent way you will manipulate strings is to replace one part of a string with another, such as changing a lf prefix to rt on a name. The substitute command lets you do this; you simply specify the part of the string you want to replace, followed by the entire string and the string you want to insert:

```
string $name = "lfHand";
string $newName = `substitute "lf" $name "rt"`;
print ($newName + "\n");
//Result: rtHand //
```

The substitute command will be used extensively in the rigging script to mirror left-side operations over to the right side.

USING MATRICES

A matrix is similar to a float array, but has a second dimension that allows it to contain multiple sets of floating numbers. This sounds complicated, but it will become easier to comprehend when you start using it to reference transform values of joints in a skeleton. Each joint position in 3D space will be described by three float values that represent X, Y, and Z, so describing several positions in a skeleton requires several sets of three numbers each. You could specify these values using multiple vectors or multiple arrays; using a matrix is another option you should know about.

In the following example, a matrix is used in the arguments of a procedure to translate four spheres to different positions in 3D space:

```
//Specify four spheres, and a matrix of four sets of three XYZ values:
 string $names[] = {"mySphere1","mySphere2","mySphere3","mySphere4"};
 matrix $trans[4][3] = << -3.5, 5.0, -1.2;
                          1.7, -1.2, 7.5;
                          -6.1, -1.3, 4.5;
                          2.2, 4.0, -2.6 >>;
//Local procedure using an array and a matrix as arguments:
proc string[] cmMatrixMove (string $names[],matrix $trans[][])
{//Open procedure...
 //Declare array to catch print strings in loop:
   string $printReturn[];
 //Use loop to create four spheres, and assign matrix values:
   int $i;
   for ($i = 0 ; $i < 4 ; $i++){//Open loop...
       string $name[] = `sphere -n $names[$i] -p 0 0 0 -ax 0 1 0 -ssw 0
           -esw 360 -r 1 -d 3 -s 8 -nsp 4 -ch 1`;
     //Use matrix positions to translate the spheres:
       setAttr ($name[0] + ".t") $trans[$i][0] $trans[$i][1]
           $trans[$i][2];
       delete -ch $name[0];
       makeIdentity -apply true -t 1 -r 1 -s 1 -n 0 $name[0];
       select -cl;
     //Query final values and assemble into string for printing:
       float $vals[] = `xform -ws -q -piv $name[0]`;
       string $print = ($i + ":" + $name[0] + ".t = " + $vals[0]
           + "," + $vals[1] + "," + $vals[2] + ";\n");
     //Use increment value in array brackets to add print strings:
```

```
      $printReturn[$i] = $print;
   }//Close loop.
 //Return string array for printing:
   return $printReturn;
}//Close procedure.
//Run procedure, catch return, and print:
string $result[] = cmMatrixMove ($names,$trans);
print $result;
/* Result:
      0:mySphere1.t = -3.5,5,-1.2;
      1:mySphere2.t = 1.7,-1.2,7.5;
      2:mySphere3.t = -6.1,-1.3,4.5;
      3:mySphere4.t = 2.2,4,-2.6; */
```

Running this procedure creates and moves the four spheres, and then queries and prints their final positions. The printed numbers should be the same as the values used in the matrix. In the first few lines of code, notice how the size of the $trans matrix is explicitly set after the name using numbers in brackets. The first set of brackets containing the number 4 specifies four sets of values, while the second set of brackets specifies three values in each of the four sets. The matrix is expected as the second argument of the procedure, and then is plugged into the setAttr command that moves the created sphere.

One of the main differences between arrays and matrices is that you cannot create a dynamic matrix, or leave the brackets blank when assigning the data into the matrix. This means you must know ahead of time how many positions a matrix will require—a drawback for using matrices for some rigging operations in Maya. Another drawback is that matrices can only contain float data, which is why you don't have to specify a type of matrix. This limitation means you cannot use matrices for storing string data. Instead, you will use the tokenize command in the rigging scripts to manipulate strings into a custom matrix-like configuration.

One of the main similarities between arrays and matrices, however, is that the positions in a matrix are numbered the same as in an array, or starting at 0. This means that you can use the same increment value in a loop for referencing positions in both arrays and matrices at the same time, as done in the previous example. Notice the $i variable is used to specify both names and values as the loop runs. Another useful technique used in this example is inserting the $i in the brackets of the $printReturn array to add a new string every time the loop runs. The array is first declared as empty before the loop, and then after querying and assembling the print string within the loop, the $i variable is used to assign the string to the array. Since the loop starts at 0 and the empty array starts at 0, the values are compatible for this technique. The array of strings is then sent out of the procedure through the return statement for printing.

On a side note, examine how the sphere values are queried within the loop. The main flag queried in the xform command is the -piv, or pivot, flag, not the -t, or translation, flag that was used in previous examples. The translation flag does not return accurate position values after you freeze transformations, as done on the spheres in the loop. Instead, query the pivot flag combined with a -ws, or world space, flag to return the accurate position of frozen objects.

WRITING AND READING FILES

When you start doing more complex tasks using MEL scripting, such as creating the biped rig in this book, the length of the code will increase dramatically. It is easier to deal with such large amounts of code by breaking it up into shorter segments. This is usually done by organizing the code into procedures within multiple script files that reference each other. This separation has the advantage of making the scripts shorter, and making them more modular by condensing the code within them to focus on particular tasks.

The issue then becomes how you can move data from one script file to the other so the scripts can work together. You may be creating and catching node names for skeletons in one script, and then you must be able to accurately move the names to another script that parents or binds them. Since you are storing the names in local variables and arrays inside of procedures, separate scripts cannot read them out of memory. You could try to move the names entirely through return statements and arguments of procedures. But using procedures to move large amounts of information, sometimes of different data types, is sometimes impractical. Another easier way to move information between multiple scripts is to write the data to a custom text file on the hard drive. Once written to file, the data can be read from within any other script.

The system commands that let you read and write custom text files in MEL are fopen, fprint, fgetline, and fclose. These commands interact with the operating system outside of Maya, so they do not follow the same syntax as other MEL commands. You can still look them up in the MEL Command Reference, however, like all other commands. Also, when running these commands, you will need to specify an existing system directory to contain the files, or create a new directory with the `sysFile` command. Here is an example of writing an array of sphere names to a `myFile.tmp` file in a folder you create on the C drive on a Windows system:

```
//Print array of sphere names to a file:
   string $names[] = {"mySphere1","mySphere2",
        "mySphere3","mySphere4","mySphere5"};
//Create temp directory on the C drive:
   string $fPath = "C:\\MEL_tempFiles";
   sysFile -md $fPath;
//Open the file for writing using file path:
   string $fName = ($fPath + "\\myFile.tmp");
   int $fNum = `fopen $fName "w"`;
//Write names to temp file using loop:
   for ($name in $names){//Open loop…
        fprint $fNum ($name + " ");
        print ($name + " printed to file: "
              + $fName + "\n");
   }//Close loop.
   fclose $fNum;
/* Result:
        mySphere1 printed to file: C:\MEL_tempFiles\myFile.tmp
        mySphere2 printed to file: C:\MEL_tempFiles\myFile.tmp
        mySphere3 printed to file: C:\MEL_tempFiles\myFile.tmp
        mySphere4 printed to file: C:\MEL_tempFiles\myFile.tmp
        mySphere5 printed to file: C:\MEL_tempFiles\myFile.tmp */
```

Notice that the file being written has a .tmp extension denoting it is a temporary file that will be deleted. You can customize the extension of the text file to anything that makes sense to you, such as .rig or .wts for files that contain rigging or weighting data. Regardless of the extension, the text file can be opened in any text editor like Notepad or ConTEXT. Be sure to open the myFile.tmp file to examine the contents.

In the resulting text file, the names of the spheres are on one line with a space between them. Actually, the default action of the `fprint` command is to add the names one after the other without any spaces. This would make it difficult, however, to separate the individual sphere names when Maya opens the file to extract the data in another script. To avoid this problem, an empty text string has been added to the name when the `fprint` command runs in the loop. After printing, the file is closed with the `fclose` command.

The following example shows the code used to open the file and read the names in another script. First you run the fopen command again, only in read mode instead of write mode. When retrieving the names with an fgetline command, Maya automatically combines them into a single string. To separate the individual sphere names into an array, use a tokenize command specifying an empty (" ") space. The command breaks up the string at the spaces you manually inserted when printing to file, and saves the individual sphere names into a $names2 array. Printing shows that the names have been placed correctly into the $names2 array in the original order:

```
//Open and retrieve the file contents:
  int $fNum = `fopen $fName "r"`;
  string $fContents = `fgetline $fNum`;
//Print to show the names have been combined into a string:
  print ($fContents + "\n");
// Result: mySphere1 mySphere2 mySphere3 mySphere4 mySphere5 //
//Break up the string to re-create string array of names:
  string $names2[];
  tokenize $fContents " " $names2;
  print $names2;
/* Result:
      mySphere1
      mySphere2
      mySphere3
      mySphere4
      mySphere5 */
```

Even though this example did not separate the code into multiple script files, you will use similar techniques throughout the rest of this book to move data through the biped rig scripts.

MEL SCRIPTING A BASIC GUI

Most people, even coders, don't like to remember all the details for running a large amount of procedures and scripts. It is much easier to set up a GUI that contains step-by-step text instructions, fields for inputting arguments, check boxes for making choices, and buttons for running procedures. A GUI lets the user interact with computers through a combination of images and normal text, rather than through a cryptic coding language. To make it easier for you to run the rigging scripts for this book, and to introduce you to coding a GUI, you will learn how to create a basic setup GUI in this chapter. This section will introduce you to the basic commands and controls; the exercise that follows shows you how to apply the commands in the main rigging scripts.

First you will learn how to create a floating window that contains a few simple controls with text included for instructions. Creating a window involves running a `window` command, then a layout command such as `columnLayout`, followed by various text and control commands such as `textField` and `button`, and ending in a `showWindow` command to display the GUI in the Maya interface:

```
//Creates a window to contain layout and controls:
  window;
//Adds a layout for controls:
  columnLayout;
//Creates text and controls:
  text;
  textField;
  checkBox;
  button;
//Displays window in Maya:
  showWindow;
```

FIGURE 2.18
This generic GUI code creates a floating window containing controls that look like the Maya interface, but don't do anything yet.

The layout command tells Maya how to arrange the controls in the window. In this case using `columnLayout` stacks the controls vertically flush left from top to bottom (see **FIGURE 2.18**).

The controls are the same ones Maya uses throughout its own interface. But with no flags specified, the controls are not very useful. Adding flags lets you run MEL commands when the controls are clicked or manipulated. Some controls even have flags that directly connect them to node attributes, such as transforms or visibility. Here is another example that has buttons and check boxes that control the selection and visibility of a sphere (see **FIGURE 2.19**).

FIGURE 2.19 *This GUI example connects the window controls to the selection and visibility of the sphere.*

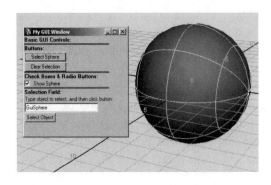

Just run the code, and follow the text instructions:

```
//Create an object to use with GUI controls:
  string $obj[] = `sphere -r 3 -n "GuiSphere"`;
  select -cl;
//Create and name a window to contain controls:
  if (`window -exists "MyWindow"`) deleteUI "MyWindow";
  window -t "My GUI Window" -wh 250 250 "MyWindow";
 //Column layout stacks controls vertically in window:
   columnLayout;
 //Text is used for instructions and headings:
   text -w 175 -al "left" -fn "boldLabelFont" -l "Basic GUI Controls:";
 //Separators are used to design groups of controls:
   separator -st "double" -w 200;
   text -w 150 -al "left" -fn "smallBoldLabelFont" -l "Click Buttons:";
 //Buttons run commands:
   button -l "Select Sphere" -w 100 -c ("select -r " + $obj[0]);
   button -l "Clear Selection" -w 100 -c "select -cl";
   separator -st "double" -w 200;
   text -w 200 -al "left" -fn "smallBoldLabelFont"
        -l "Check Boxes & Radio Buttons:";
 //Check boxes run different commands when on-off:
   checkBox -v 1 -l "Click to Hide Sphere"
        -onc ("setAttr " + $obj[0] + ".v 1")
        -ofc ("setAttr " + $obj[0] + ".v 0");
   separator -st "double" -w 200;
   text -w 150 -al "left" -fn "smallBoldLabelFont" -l "Selection Field:";
   text    -l "Type name of object to select, and then click button:";
 //Text fields allow you to input data, and then run it with a button:
   textField -text $obj[0] -w 175 "MyField";
   string $queryField = "string $MyText = `textField -q -text MyField`;";
   string $select = "select -r $MyText;";
   button  -w 75 -l "Select Object" -c {$queryField + $select};
//Display the window in  the Maya interface:
 showWindow "MyWindow";
```

There are some unique differences you should be aware of when scripting GUI controls, compared to coding regular objects in Maya. When you previously used MEL to create an object like a sphere or group node, you used -n flags to name the nodes, and caught the names in arrays to prevent problems if they incremented. GUI commands, on the other hand, never have naming flags and never increment custom names. Instead, you specify custom names for GUI elements by adding a string at the end of the command, after all the flags and before the semicolon. Since custom GUI names do not increment, it is not necessary to catch the names in variables. But you must explicitly name any GUI controls that you want to query or edit. Any GUI elements that you do not explicitly name will be named by Maya with a generic unique name. Maya will increment generic GUI names.

What happens if you attempt to name two GUI controls the same, since custom names do not increment? Simply, you will get an error message saying the name already exists, and your GUI window may not open. This GUI function can especially impact your script when you are required to name a window but later want to edit the name. Once a window name goes into memory, it doesn't go out of memory—even if you close the window—until you run a MEL command to delete it. Running the window code more than once can produce an error because the name is still stuck in memory. Notice the conditional statement at the beginning of the GUI code that has been added to prevent this error from occurring. The `if` statement checks whether the window name already exists in memory. If the condition evaluates as true, it runs a `deleteUI` command to remove the current window name from memory before running the window code again. An added benefit of adding this conditional statement is that it also automatically updates a new GUI without having to manually close the window while editing and testing.

Examining the contents of the previous window code, notice that the most common flag on GUI controls is the `-l`, or label, flag. Labels, by letting you add descriptive text or instructions, are what make controls easy to use. Width flags are also commonly used to improve the GUI design by sizing the controls consistently. Otherwise, controls like buttons will scale according to the amount of text in the label. The most important flag on the `button` command is the `-c`, or command, flag, which makes code run when the button is clicked. In this example window, the button flags are running `select` commands. The `-onc` and `-ofc` flags have similar functions on the `checkBox` command, by running different `setAttr` commands when the check box is turned on and off. The `-v`, or value, flag on the check box sets the default state of the control, which is checked.

The text field and following button in this example are more complex because they involve querying the field to use the typed text in a `select` command. This requires naming the field so that another `textField` command can query the `-tx` flag and store the result stored in a string variable. The variable is then added to a select command, and both commands are saved into string variables to facilitate combining them in a code block within the -c flag of the button command. Clicking the button then runs the commands, which select the object.

USING A GUI TO INPUT DATA TO A PROCEDURE

In this final basic GUI example, clicking a button runs a global procedure to query the state of the controls and input the resulting data into commands for creating and transforming a primitive (see **FIGURE 2.20**).

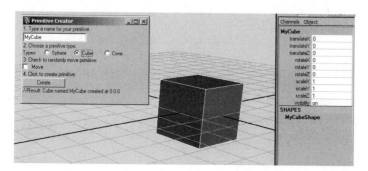

FIGURE 2.20 *This GUI window example lets the user input data into a global procedure that creates and transforms a primitive.*

This example illustrates how a GUI can allow the user to make choices that will change how a script runs. First run the code, and then follow the instructions in the resulting window to create a primitive:

```
//Global procedure to used with GUI to create primitive:
global proc cmPrimCreate (){//Open procedure...
  //Query GUI controls to determine type and transform:
    string $name = `textField -q -tx "myField"`;
    int $radio = `radioButtonGrp -q -sl "myRadios"`;
    int $check = `checkBox -q -v "myCheck"`;
  //Conditional to process radio data to create primitive:
    string $names[];
    string $type;
  //Third button on produces a cone:
    if ($radio == 3){//Open conditional...
      $type = "Cone";
      $names = `cone -n $name -p 0 0 0 -ax 0 1 0 -ssw 0 -esw 360
        -r 1 -hr 2 -d 3 -s 8 -nsp 1 -ch 1`;
    }//Close conditional.
    //Second button on produces a cube:
```

```
        else if ($radio == 2){//Open conditional...
          $type = "Cube";
          $names = `polyCube -n $name -w 2 -h 2 -d 2 -sx 1 -sy 1
            -sz 1 -ax 0 1 0 -cuv 4 -ch 1`;
        }//Close conditional.
        //First button on produces a sphere:
          else {//Open conditional...
            $type = "Sphere";
            $names = `sphere -n $name -p 0 0 0 -ax 0 1 0 -ssw 0
              -esw 360 -r 1 -d 3 -s 8 -nsp 4 -ch 1`;
          }//Close conditional.
    //Conditional to process check box data to position primitive:
      vector $vals;
    //Check box on randomly moves the primitive:
      if ($check == 1){//Open conditional...
        $vals = `rand <<-10.0,-10.0,-10.0>> <<10.0,10.0,10.0>>`;
        $vals = <<`floor (($vals.x) + .5)`,`floor (($vals.y) + .5)`,
          `floor (($vals.z) + .5)`>>;
        setAttr ($names[0] + ".t") ($vals.x) ($vals.y) ($vals.z);
      }//Close conditional.
      //Check box off positions the primitive at world center:
        else{//Open conditional...
            $vals = <<0.0,0.0,0.0>>;
            setAttr ($names[0] + ".t") ($vals.x) ($vals.y) ($vals.z);
        }//Close conditional.
    //Clear selection, delete history, and freeze transformations:
      select -cl;
      delete -ch $names[0];
      makeIdentity -apply true -t 1 -r 1 -s 1 -n 0 $names[0];
    //Print feedback about primitive to command line:
      string $print = ("//Result: " + $type + " named " + $names[0]
          + " created at " + $vals + "\n");
      print $print;
    //Edit text to add feedback to GUI window:
      text -e -l $print "myText";
    }//Close procedure.
    //End global procedure.
    //-----------------------------------------
    //Start GUI code to run global procedure:
```

```
//Set names for GUI controls that will be queried and edited:
  string $winName = "myWindow";
  string $fieldName = "myField";
  string $radioName = "myRadios";
  string $checkName = "myCheck";
  string $textName = "myText";
//Create GUI window with conditional:
  if (`window -ex $winName`) deleteUI $winName;
window -t "Primitive Creator" $winName;
 //Set layout to stack controls:
  columnLayout;
 //Create text field for entering primitive name:
    text -l "1. Type a name for your primitive:";
      textField -w 150 -tx "Name" $fieldName;
 //Create radio buttons for choosing primitive type:
    text -l "2. Choose a primitive type:";
      radioButtonGrp -sl 1 -nrb 3 -l "Types:" -cal 1 "left"
        -cw4 50 70 70 70 -la3 "Sphere" "Cube" "Cone" $radioName;
 //Create check box to choose primitive position:
    text -l "3. Check to randomly move primitive:";
      checkBox -l "Move" -v 0 $checkName;
 //Create button to run primitive creation procedure:
    text -l "4. Click to create primitive:";
      button -w 100 -l "Create" -c "cmPrimCreate";
    text -l " " $textName;
//Edit window size and position:
  window -e -wh 300 200 $winName;
showWindow $winName;
```

Clicking the button queries the controls, which then moves information from the field, radio buttons, and check box into the procedure. This functionality lets you input a name, choose a primitive type, and transform the primitive—all through the GUI. The beginning of the cmPrimCreate global procedure queries particular flags to find the state of the GUI controls and process that data to be meaningful to the primitive and transform commands. This includes queries of the -tx, or text, flag on the textField command, the -sl, or select, flag on the radioButtonGrp command, and the -v, or value, flag on the checkbox command.

Be aware that the results of querying the GUI controls may not be directly usable in other commands until processed to the required data types. Querying the text field does produce a string that can be used directly as the name of the primitive, while querying the radio buttons and check box does not produce any directly applicable results. Because the flags on these commands return integer values that reflect the state of the controls, the values cannot be directly inserted into primitive and transform commands. To evaluate and convert the integer values to have meaning for these applications, you must process them through a series of conditional statements.

After the procedure stores the queried data, if, else if, and else statements evaluate the radio button value. The 1, 2, or 3 value, indicating the user's choice of the first second or third radio button, is processed to create a sphere, cube, or cone. This process is done backward to make sure that the default choice of a sphere, indicated by the first button turned on, is always run in the else statement that does not evaluate a condition. The check box data is processed in the same way with two conditional statements to evaluate the state of the control. The default state is off or 0, indicating that the user does not want to randomly position the primitive in the scene. Turning on the check box to produce a 1 value in the queried data evaluates to run random, floor, and setAttr commands on the primitive. Because the random values generated can have up to 10 decimal values, the floor command is used to round off the number. This is primarily done for the print statement run at the end of the procedure, to fit the edited text feedback in the GUI window.

EXERCISE 2.1: BEGINNING THE BIPED RIG SCRIPTS

This exercise starts the process of learning how to MEL-script a biped rig. Make sure that you have the basicFkRig.mb example scene loaded, and open each script example in ConTEXT to examine each section of the code. You should always first run the code in Maya, and watch what is happening in the History field and the interface as the scripts run. Do this so you understand how the techniques and procedures used in the scripts relate to how the rig is being created in Maya. The goal is for you to understand MEL scripting well enough to customize the rigging scripts for your own needs or ultimately to compose your own MEL scripts from scratch.

The main contents of the two scripts covered in this exercise are global procedures that create the setup GUI used for running the rest of the scripts, and for processing important rig data into memory and text files. All of the procedures are global because either they are being run directly through the GUI controls or they are going to be used in multiple scripts throughout the rigging process.

Step 1: Format the Script Header

Start by opening the CMaraffi_setupRigGui script file in ConTEXT or another external script editor to examine the code. The first section of the script is formatted as a
header that quickly gives you a summary of the author and contents of the script. This
is useful information for anyone opening the script to understand the general purpose
of the script and what procedures it contains. Standard block comments using the /*
and */ symbols contain all the information. Additional formatting has been included
to make the header and following sections easily readable, without using too many
lines that would unnecessarily increase the length of the script. As the script runs, the
Script Editor displays print statements after the header, making it clear that the script
has started and that the procedures are going into memory.

```
/*=====================================================================
 Script Name:   CMaraffi_setupRigGui.mel
 by Chris Maraffi 2008.


 This script contains procedures that create a setup GUI for running all
 the scripts that create the biped rig for the book MEL Scripting a
 Character Rig in Maya, Peachpit 2008.


 Global procs: 1.checkCharName,2.setCharName,3.setNamespace,
         4.setupRigGui.
|=====================================================================*/
  print " \n";
  print "*******************************************************\n";
  print "Cmaraffi_setupRigGui script started!\n";
  print "-------------------------------------------------------\n";
  print "All procs are being put into memory...\n";
//*********************************************************************
```

Step 2: Determine the Rig Name and File Pathway

The first text instructions in the setup GUI ask the user to select the main skin node
before clicking the green button, which then runs the cm_checkCharName global procedure. This procedure lists the selected skin node to save the name in Maya's memory
for further processing. Ultimately, a variation of the skin name will become the main
rig name used for the top node of the hierarchy and for the namespace prefix added
to all the other nodes in the rig.

Next, a series of conditional statements check to make sure that only one node is
selected, and print a warning if necessary, or continue to process the skin name.
A tokenize command is used to remove the suffix at the underscore, so that only the

main skin name remains to use as the rig name. This name is presented to the user for approval, done by editing the GUI field. A new command is used to store the skin name in Maya's reserved system memory: putenv. Use this command only to store a few important strings that need to be accessed globally in many of your scripts. Because this command uses Maya's system memory, known as the software environment, it should not be used to store large amounts of data. Other scripts will later retrieve this data using a getenv command.

The procedure ends with a couple of button commands in edit mode to enable the next control in the setup GUI. The main flags being edited are the -en, or enable, flag to turn on, and the -bgc, or background color, flag to change the button color from red to green. The -vis, or visibility, flag is turned off and then back on to force the color of the button to update correctly. The edit commands direct the user through the setup GUI, while also preventing the user from clicking the buttons in the wrong order.

```
//1. Global proc used for finding the name of character:
global proc cm_checkCharName (){//Open procedure...
 //List selected to get the skin name:
   string $skinName[] = `ls -sl`;
 //Conditional checks to make sure only one node is selected:
   int $size = `size ($skinName)`;
   if ($size < 1) text -e -l "Warning: No skin selected!"
           "cm_guiWarning1";
   else if ($size > 1) text -e -l "Warning: Select only one skin!"
           "cm_guiWarning1";
   else {//Open conditional...
   //Tokenize to remove suffix from skin name:
     string $nameParts[];
     tokenize $skinName[0] "_" $nameParts;
     string $mainName = $nameParts[0];
     textField -e -tx $mainName -en 1 "cm_nameField";
   //Put skin name into environment for binding purposes:
     putenv "cm_skinName" $skinName[0];
     print ($skinName[0] + " put into env as cm_skinName\n");
   //Edit to enable and update the next button in Gui:
     button -e -vis 0 "cm_setCharacterButton";
     button -e -en 1 -vis 1 -bgc 0.0 1.0 0.0 "cm_setCharacterButton";
   }//Close conditional.
}//Close procedure.
   print "cm_checkCharName global proc is now in Maya's memory.\n";
   //************************************************************************
```

Step 3: Store the Rig Data in Maya's Memory

The second global procedure, `cm_setCharName`, prepares the scene for creating the biped rig by querying the final rig name and file path from the GUI fields, using the rig name to create the top group node of the hierarchy, and saving the names and file path into Maya's reserved memory. After the fields are queried, notice that the namespace is set to the scene root. This ensures that the group node created to be the top node in the rig hierarchy will not have a prefix. This is the only node in the rig that will not be assigned a namespace prefix.

In the next section, a `getenv` command is run to retrieve the default Maya script path. This data lets you source scripts without having to type the entire directory path every time, since Maya stores their location in environment memory. The procedure adds the custom file path from the GUI to Maya's default path, and saves it back into the environment using the `putenv` command. Because there are four strings to save into the environment, the names are first placed into an array, and then run with the `putenv` command in a loop.

One important preparation to creating the biped rig involves processing the FK rig in the example file so the nodes contain the new namespace prefix. You also need to list and sort all the FK rig nodes so they can be printed to a .rig file for referencing in the other scripts. The biped rig scripts will then use the names of the joints and polygon bones in the FK rig to create and position icons and skeletons. Much of this processing is done by global procedures contained in the CMaraffi_processNames script file, so the file must be sourced into memory.

The `eval` command is used to force the source line to process when the procedure is run through a GUI control, which is a runtime process. Then several global procedures are run to list and sort the FK rig hierarchy, add the namespace prefix to all the nodes, and print the new names to a file. These procedures will be covered later in this exercise, in Steps 6 through 10, so don't be concerned if you don't fully understand them yet. After the procedures run, the Hypergraph should show that the FK rig nodes have the rig namespace prefix on them. The `cm_setCharName` procedure ends with button commands that are run in edit mode to enable and disable the appropriate controls to continually guide the user through the setup GUI.

```
//2. Global proc used for processing the character name:
global proc cm_setCharName () {//Open procedure...
  //Query GUI fields to get user defined path and rig name:
    string $rigName = `textField -q -tx "cm_nameField"`;
    string $filePath = `textField -q -tx "cm_pathField"`;
  //Create the top node of the rig in the root namespace:
    namespace -set ":";
    string $topIkNode = `group -n ($rigName + "_topNode") -em`;
    print ("Basic rig top node has been created with the name: "
```

```
                        + $topIkNode + "\n");
      select -cl;
  //Add file path from GUI to Maya's environment paths:
    string $defaultMayaPath = `getenv "MAYA_SCRIPT_PATH"`;
    string $newMayaPath = ($defaultMayaPath + ";" + $filePath);
  //Use loop to put important rig names into environment:
    string $rigData[] = {$rigName, $topIkNode, $filePath,
        $newMayaPath};
    string $envNames[] = {"cm_rigName", "cm_topIkNode", "cm_filePath",
        "MAYA_SCRIPT_PATH"};
    int $i;
    for ($i = 0; $i < 4; $i++){//Open loop...
      putenv $envNames[$i] $rigData[$i];
      print ($rigData[$i] + " put into env as " + $envNames[$i] + "\n");
    }//Close loop.
  //Process FK hierarchy to have namespace and print:
    eval ("source CMaraffi_processNames");
    string $topFkNode = "Reference_fkTop";
    string $nSpace = cm_setNamespace(1);
    string $fkRigNames[] = cm_processNames($topFkNode,1,$nSpace);
    putenv "cm_topFkNode" $fkRigNames[0];
    print ($fkRigNames[0] + " put into env as cm_topFkNode\n");
    cm_printNames ($fkRigNames,1,"fkRig");
  //Enable next button and edit previous button in GUI:
    button -e -vis 0 "cm_basicIkRigButton";
    button -e -en 1 -vis 1 -bgc 0.0 1.0 0.0 "cm_basicIkRigButton";
    button -e -l "Done" -en 0 "cm_checkCharButton";
    button -e -l "Done" -en 0 "cm_setCharacterButton";
}//Close procedure.
  print "cm_setCharName global proc is now in Maya's memory.\n";
//************************************************************************
```

Step 4: Set the Rig Namespace

The cm_setNamespace global procedure is used throughout all the scripts to set the current namespace to either the scene root or the rig prefix. It does this using a single integer argument that is evaluated at the beginning of the procedure. If the argument is set to 1, then the namespace prefix is set to the rig name. Setting the argument to 0, on the other hand, sets the namespace to the scene root (:). In addition, nested conditional statements check whether the namespace prefix already exists. This check is necessary to avoid errors that may occur due to names incrementing. The conditional statement simply sets the namespace if it already exists, or creates and sets the namespace if it does not exist.

```
//3. Global procedure to set namespacing:
global proc string cm_setNamespace (int $setNspace){//Open procedure...
 //use conditional to set namespace to rig name or root:
   string $returnSpace;
   if ($setNspace == 1){//Open conditional...
   //Get names from the environment for the namespacing:
     string $rigName = `getenv "cm_RigName"`;
   //Set namespace to the main name from the top node and GUI:
     if (`namespace -exists $rigName`){//Open conditional...
       namespace -set $rigName;
       print ("Namespace has been set to: " + $rigName + ":\n");
     }//Close conditional.
     else {//Open conditional...
       $rigName = `namespace -p ":" -add $rigName`;
       namespace -set $rigName;
       print ("Namespace has been set to: " + $rigName + ":\n");
     }//Close conditional.
     $returnSpace = $rigName;
   }//Close conditional.
   else {//Open conditional...
   //Set the namespace to root:
     namespace -set ":";
     $returnSpace = "root";
     print ("Namespace has been set to root : \n");
   }//Close conditional.
  return $returnSpace;
}//Close procedure.
  print "cm_setNamespace global proc is now in Maya's memory.\n";
  //*********************************************************************
```

Step 5: Create the Rig Setup GUI

The fourth global procedure, cm_setupRigGui, is the main procedure in this script that creates the setup GUI window (see **FIGURE 2.21**).

The first part of this procedure is a series of GUI strings being declared in variables for naming the important GUI elements. Since GUI names do not incre-ment, it is best to declare unique names at the beginning of the procedure, to make sure that you don't accidentally repeat them. This also allows you to easily look up the names for use in query and edit commands in other scripts. After the names are declared, the remainder of the procedure contains the main window code, using a columnLayout command to vertically stack text, fields, and buttons that will be used to run all the procedures that create and bind the biped rig.

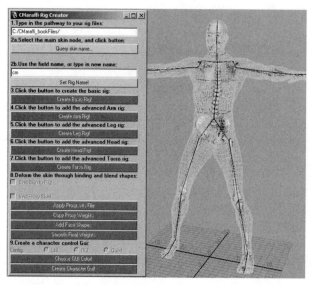

FIGURE 2.21 *The rig setup GUI is designed to make running your rigging scripts easier, by including instructions, input fields, and buttons to run all the procedures.*

The layout used in the setup GUI is the simplest available in Maya. More complex layouts, and additional details on how layouts work, will be covered in Chapter 6, "Scripting an Advanced Character GUI," when you learn how to create a more sophisticated character animation GUI. At this stage, just notice that the name of the layout is caught in a $layout variable, which is then used in the -p, or parent, flag on all remaining GUI commands. This flag assigns all the controls as children of the layout. The rest of the flags used on the GUI controls have been covered previously in the section "MEL Scripting a Basic GUI," or in this exercise.

The button commands at the end of the procedure in Step 2 were editing the background color, and enable flags of the buttons being created in this procedure, to control the user interaction with the GUI. These flags make most of the buttons red and disabled until other scripts are run to edit the buttons to turn green and be enabled for use. The -c, or command, flags on the buttons either run global procedures already in memory, or source scripts that contain additional procedures.

At the end of the procedure, notice a second window command in edit mode. The initial window command didn't contain any sizing flags, because Maya tends to ignore them when run at creation. Instead, running a -wh, or width-height, flag in edit mode forces the window to update at the intended size every time. Adding a -tlc or top-left-corner flag will always position the window a specific amount of screen pixels from the top-left corner of the Maya interface. These flags are useful for consistently displaying the setup GUI window whenever it is opened.

```
//4. Main global procedure to run setup GUI window:
global proc cm_setupRigGui (){//Open procedure...
 //Declare unique GUI strings for the path and names:
   string $defaultPath = "C:/CMaraffi_bookFiles/";
   string $nameWin = "cm_setupGuiWin";
   string $pathField = "cm_pathField";
   string $nameField = "cm_nameField";
   string $warning1 = "cm_guiWarning1";
   string $checkCharButt = "cm_checkCharButton";
   string $setCharButt = "cm_setCharacterButton";
   string $basRigButt = "cm_basicIkRigButton";
   string $armRigButt = "cm_advArmRigButton";
   string $legRigButt = "cm_advLegRigButton";
   string $headRigButt = "cm_advHeadRigButton";
   string $torsoRigButt = "cm_advTorsoRigButton";
   string $bindCheckBox = "cm_bindCheckBox";
   string $proxyCheckBox = "cm_proxyCheckBox";
   string $applyWtsButt = "cm_applyWeightsButton";
   string $copyWtsButt = "cm_proxyWeightsButton";
   string $blendsButt = "cm_blendWrapButton";
   string $smoothWtsButt = "cm_smoothWeightsButton";
   string $feedback = "cm_bindFeedback";
   string $configRadios = "cm_configRadios";
   string $colorButt = "cm_colorPickButton";
   string $charGuiButt = "cm_charGuiButton";
//----------------------------------------------------------------------
//Create the main setup GUI window:
   if(`window -ex $nameWin`) deleteUI $nameWin;
   window -t "CMaraffi Rig Creator" $nameWin;
   string $layout = `columnLayout -p $nameWin`;
//Create controls for running the rig scripts:
   text -w 400 -p $layout -fn "smallBoldLabelFont" -al "left"
        -l "1.Type in the pathway to your rig files:";
//Text field for to set directory path for all files:
   textField -w 300 -p $layout -tx $defaultPath $pathField;
   text -w 400 -p $layout -fn "smallBoldLabelFont" -al "left"
        -l "2a.Select the main skin node, and click button:";
   button -w 300 -p $layout -bgc 0.0 1.0 0.0 -l "Query skin name..."
        -c "cm_checkCharName" $checkCharButt;
//----------------------------------------------------------------------
//Set the name to be used for the top node and namespace:
   text -w 300 -p $layout -l " " $warning1;
   text -w 400 -p $layout -fn "smallBoldLabelFont" -al "left"
        -l "2b.Use the field name, or type in new name:";
```

```
//Text field for the rig name:
  textField  -w 300 -p $layout -tx "Name of Character" -en 0 $nameField;
  button -w 300 -p $layout -bgc 1.0 0.0 0.0 -en 0 -l "Set Rig Name!"
        -c "cm_setCharName" $setCharButt;
//----------------------------------------------------------------------
//GUI controls to run all the basic rig scripts:
  text -w 400 -p $layout -fn "smallBoldLabelFont" -al "left"
        -l "3.Click the button to create the basic rig:";
//Button to create the entire basic IK rig:
  button -w 300 -p $layout -bgc 1.0 0.0 0.0 -en 0 -l "Create Basic Rig!"
          -c "source Cmaraffi_basicIkRig" $basRigButt;
//----------------------------------------------------------------------
//GUI controls to run the advanced arm rig script:
  text -w 400 -p $layout -fn "smallBoldLabelFont" -al "left"
        -l "4.Click the button to add the advanced Arm rig:";
//Button to add the advanced arm rig:
  button -w 300 -p $layout -bgc 1.0 0.0 0.0 -l "Create Arm Rig!"
            -en 0 -c "source Cmaraffi_advArms" $armRigButt;
//----------------------------------------------------------------------
//GUI controls to run the advanced leg rig script:
  text -w 400 -p $layout -fn "smallBoldLabelFont" -al "left"
        -l "5.Click the button to add the advanced Leg rig:";
  button -w 300 -p $layout -bgc 1.0 0.0 0.0 -l "Create Leg Rig!"
            -en 0 -c "source Cmaraffi_advLegs" $legRigButt;
//----------------------------------------------------------------------
//GUI controls to run the advanced head rig script:
  text -w 400 -p $layout -fn "smallBoldLabelFont" -al "left"
        -l "6.Click the button to add the advanced Head rig:";
  button -w 300 -p $layout -bgc 1.0 0.0 0.0 -l "Create Head Rig!"
            -en 0 -c "source Cmaraffi_advHead" $headRigButt;
//----------------------------------------------------------------------
//GUI controls to run the advanced torso rig script:
  text -w 400 -p $layout -fn "smallBoldLabelFont" -al "left"
        -l "7.Click the button to add the advanced Torso rig:";
  button -w 300 -p $layout -bgc 1.0 0.0 0.0 -l "Create Torso Rig"
            -en 0 -c "source Cmaraffi_advTorso" $torsoRigButt;
//----------------------------------------------------------------------
//GUI controls to run the bind rig script:
  text -w 400 -p $layout -fn "smallBoldLabelFont" -al "left"
          -l "8.Deform the skin through binding and blend shapes:";
//Check boxes and buttons for binding the rig:
  checkBox -v 0 -l "Bind Skin to Rig!" -en 0 -onc "cm_bindSkin(0)"
            -ofc "cm_bindDetach(0)" $bindCheckBox;
  text -w 300 -p $layout -l " " $feedback;
```

```
    checkBox -v 0 -l "Bind Proxy Skin!" -en 0 -onc "cm_bindSkin(1)"
            -ofc "cm_bindDetach(1)" $proxyCheckBox;
    button -w 300 -p $layout -bgc 1.0 0.0 0.0 -l "Apply Proxy .wts File"
            -en 0 -c "cm_getProxyWts" $applyWtsButt;
    button -w 300 -p $layout -bgc 1.0 0.0 0.0 -l "Copy Proxy Weights"
            -en 0 -c "cm_copyWeights" $copyWtsButt;
    button -w 300 -p $layout -bgc 1.0 0.0 0.0 -l "Add Face Shapes"
            -en 0 -c "cm_blendWrap" $blendsButt;
    button -w 300 -p $layout -bgc 1.0 0.0 0.0 -l "Smooth Final Weights"
            -en 0 -c "cm_smoothWts" $smoothWtsButt;
  //------------------------------------------------------------------
//GUI controls to run the advanced character GUI scripts:
    text -w 400 -p $layout -fn "smallBoldLabelFont" -al "left"
         -l "9.Create a character control Gui:";
    radioButtonGrp -p $layout -sl 0 -nrb 3 -cal 1 "left" -cw4 80 70 70 70
    -en 0 -l "Config:" -la3 "Lf3" "Rt3" "Quad"
    -on1 "button -e -en 1 cm_charGuiButton"
    -on2 "button -e -en 1 cm_charGuiButton"
    -on3 "button -e -en 1 cm_charGuiButton" $configRadios;
  //Button to open color picker for GUI background color:
    button -w 300 -p $layout -bgc 1.0 0.0 0.0 -l "Choose GUI Color!"
            -en 0 -c "cm_runLocals(\"setColor\",{\"1\"})" $colorButt;
    button -w 300 -p $layout -bgc 1.0 0.0 0.0 -l "Create Character Gui!"
            -en 0 -c "source Cmaraffi_characterGui" $charGuiButt;
  //------------------------------------------------------------------
    window -e -wh 325 600 -tlc 130 50 $nameWin;
    showWindow $nameWin;
}//Close procedure.
  print "cm_setupRigGui global proc is now in Maya's memory.\n";
  //*******************************************************************
```

Step 6: Run the Procedure and Format the End of the Script

The last section of code adds print statements and comments to make it clear that the setup GUI procedure is being run. Running the procedure opens the setup GUI window to let the user begin clicking controls to create and bind the biped rig. After running the procedure, the script prints that it has finished, and then runs a new-line character (\n) to place a space in the History field where this script ends and the next one begins.

```
  print "------------------------------------------------------\n";
  print "Running all procs to create the rig setup Gui!\n";
  print "------------------------------------------------------\n";
//Run proc to create setup Gui for rig:
  cm_setupRigGui;
```

```
print "-------------------------------------------------------\n";
print "cm_setupRigGui script done!\n";
print "*******************************************************\n";
print " \n";
```

Step 7: List and Sort the Rig Node Names

In Step 3 of this exercise, you saw the cm_setCharName global procedure source the CMaraffi_processNames script, and then run procedures that the script contains, to process and write the FK rig node names to a custom text file. Now open this script to examine the contents for the rest of this exercise. The script contains four global procedures that will be used extensively throughout all the rigging scripts. The procedures are mainly designed to facilitate moving rig hierarchy data from file to file, so that names are available to any rigging procedures.

This script starts with similar formatting as the setup GUI script, with a header, line comments, and print statements. Then the cm_processNames global procedure has code for listing the names in a hierarchy and alphabetically sorting the resulting array. There is also an argument to optionally add a namespace prefix to the list of names. The previous script used this argument to add the rig namespace prefix to the FK rig names before printing.

The code in the procedure uses a listRelatives command with a –ad, or all-descendents, flag to list all the transform node children of a $topNode name specified in the arguments. Then a sort command is used to alphabetically sort the resulting array of names. The appendStringArray command is run to add the sorted names to an array containing the $topNode argument name in the first or [0] position. Then a loop nested inside a conditional statement evaluates the optional namespace argument and, if true, runs a rename command on all the nodes in the $arrayNames array. Renaming nodes in this way is how you add a namespace prefix to existing objects, as done on the FK rig nodes. Once the names are processed, the string array is returned out of the procedure for printing.

```
/*======================================================================
 Script Name:    CMaraffi_processNames.mel
  by Chris Maraffi 2008.
 ──────────────────────────────────────────────────────────────────────
 This script contains three global procs that enable the user to list
 and sort names, print names to .rig files, and read names from files.
 The fourth global procedure lets you search through an array of names
 using just the short main name, and returns the full name with prefixes
 and suffixes.
 ──────────────────────────────────────────────────────────────────────
 Global procs: 1.cm_processNames, 2.cm_printNames, 3.cm_getNames,
       4.cm_returnName.
======================================================================*/
```

```
print " \n";
print "*********************************************************\n";
print "CMaraffi_processNames script started!\n";
print "--------------------------------------------------------\n";
print "All procs are being put into memory...\n";
//***********************************************************************
//1. processNames lists and sorts a hierarchy with namespace option:
global proc string[] cm_processNames (string $topNode,int $addNspace,
        string $nSpace){//Open procedure...
  //List all nodes in the hierarchy:
    string $arrayNames[0] = {$topNode};
    string $listNames[] = `listRelatives -ad -typ "transform" $topNode`;
    string $sortedNames[] = sort($listNames);
    int $size = size ($sortedNames);
    appendStringArray($arrayNames, $sortedNames, $size);
    string $returnNames[];
  //Add namespacing to all the sorted nodes:
    if ($addNspace == 1){//Open conditional...
      string $newNames[];
      int $i;
      for ($i = 0; $i < size($arrayNames); $i++){//Open loop...
        namespace -set ":";
        $newNames[$i] = `rename (":" + $arrayNames[$i])
            ($nSpace + ":" + $arrayNames[$i])`;
      }//Close loop.
      $returnNames = $newNames;
    }//Close conditional.
    else {//Open conditional...
      $returnNames = $arrayNames;
    }//Close conditional.
return $returnNames;
}//Close procedure.
print "cm_processNames global proc is now in Maya's memory.\n";
//***********************************************************************
```

Step 8: Print the Rig Node Names to Files

Printing the FK rig names to a file used the cm_printNames procedure in this script. This procedure has three arguments: for the array of names you want to print; an option to print to both the command line and to a custom text file, and the name of the .rig file if you choose to print to file. Conditional statements evaluate the second $printFile argument to determine if the names should be printed to file, or just to the History field. Nested loops inside the conditional statement run the appropriate fprint and print commands for each name in the $nodeNames array. In addition, if printing to file, getenv commands are run to use the appropriate rig name and file path for the .rig file; in the process, fopen and fclose commands are run.

Notice that printing to the command line is done a little differently than the printing to file with the fprint command. The tokenize command is used to remove the namespace prefix from the names printed to the History field, and instead a number representing the array position that contains the name is printed. Replacing the namespace prefix with a number makes it easier to read the main name and array position of each node in the History field, but removing that information on the printed names would produce an error because the names are not accurate.

```
//2. printNames prints array names to .rig file and/or command line:
global proc cm_printNames (string $nodeNames[],int $printFile,string
$fileName)
{//Open procedure...
  //Print to both file and command line, or just to command line:
    if ( $printFile == 1){//Open conditional...
    //Get the name of the rig from the environment:
      string $rigName = `getenv "cm_rigName"`;
      string $filePath = `getenv "cm_filePath"`;
    //Set file name that will contain array names:
      string $rigFile = ($filePath + $rigName + "_" + $fileName + ".rig");
    //Open the .rig file for writing:
      int $fileId = `fopen $rigFile "w"`;
    //Use loop to print names to the command line and to file:
      print ($fileName + " array names printed to file:\n");
      int $i;
      for ($i = 0; $i < size($nodeNames); $i++){//Open loop...
      //Print to command line without namespacing:
        string $names[];
        tokenize $nodeNames[$i] ":" $names;
        int $size = `size ($names)`;
        if ($size == 1) print ("[" + $i + "]" + $names[0] + "\n");
        else print ("[" + $i + "]" + $names[1] + "\n");
      //Print to file with namespacing:
        fprint $fileId ($nodeNames[$i] + "\n");
      }//Close loop.
      fclose $fileId;
      print ($fileName + " finished printing to file!\n");
    }//Close conditional.
    else {//Open conditional...
    //Use loop to print names only to the command line:
      int $i;
```

```
        for ($i = 0; $i < size($nodeNames); $i++){//Open loop...
      //Print to command line without namespacing:
        string $names[];
        tokenize $nodeNames[$i] ":" $names;
        int $size = `size ($names)`;
        if ($size == 1) print ("[" + $i + "]" + $names[0] + "\n");
        else print ("[" + $i + "]" + $names[1] + "\n");
      }//Close loop.
    }//Close conditional.
}//Close procedure.
  print "cm_printNames global proc is now in Maya's memory.\n";
//*********************************************************************
```

Step 9: Retrieve the Rig Node Names from Files

The third global procedure, cm_getNames, is used throughout the rigging scripts to retrieve names printed into .rig files, and then place the names back into the same kind of array in which they were originally created. This procedure uses the same commands and techniques shown in the section "Writing and Reading Files" earlier in this chapter. After opening the file specified in the $fileOpen argument, the code runs an fgetline command to retrieve the first line in the .rig file. Notice that the tokenize command is used to remove the new-line character (\n) added in the previous procedure. Placing the names on separate lines in the file increases readability, but would cause naming errors if the new-line character is not removed from the strings when they are retrieved. The main part of the procedure retrieves the rest of the lines using a while loop, adding each name to a $nodeNames array, and then returning the array at the end of the procedure.

```
//3. getNames reads names from .rig files, and re-creates array:
global proc string[] cm_getNames(string $fileName){//Open procedure...
 //Get the name of the rig and file path from the environment:
  string $rigName = `getenv "cm_rigName"`;
  string $filePath = `getenv "cm_filePath"`;
  string $readFile = ($filePath + $rigName + "_" + $fileName + ".rig");
 //Read names from .rig file:
  int $fileId = `fopen $readFile "r"`;
  string $nodeNames[];
  string $nextLine = `fgetline $fileId`;
  string $buffer[];
  tokenize ($nextLine,"\n",$buffer);
  int $i = 0;
  $nodeNames[$i] = $buffer[0];
 //Use while loop to retrieve names:
  while ( size( $nextLine ) > 0 ) {//Open loop...
```

```
      $i++;
      $nextLine = `fgetline $fileId`;
     //Use tokenize to remove new line character:
      string $buffer[];
      tokenize ($nextLine,"\n",$buffer);
      $nodeNames[$i] = $buffer[0];
    }//Close loop.
    fclose $fileId;
    print ("Node list retrieved from " + $readFile + "\n");
    return $nodeNames;
}//Close procedure.
    print "cm_getNames global proc is now in Maya's memory.\n";
//*********************************************************************
```

Step 10: Match Particular Node Names in an Array

The last global procedure is used to match the main part of a name in a large array
of names, and return the accurate full name of the desired node. The cm_returnName
procedure is designed to make it easier to find particular hierarchy names retrieved
from the file by the cm_getNames procedure. The procedure saves coders from having
to search through a long list of names as long as they can remember the main name,
and what type of node it is they are searching for.

The first argument in this procedure specifies the array to search in, while the second
argument specifies the main part of the name, and the third argument specifies the
type of node based on the suffix. As you progress through the rigging scripts, you
will see that the suffixes added to the node names describe node types, such as
"_root" denoting the first joint in a skeleton and "_icon" denoting a 3D curve used as
a rig control. The main part of this procedure uses a loop to go through each name in
the array, running a tokenize command to break the name string at the "_", and run
match commands on the pieces contained in the $nameParts array. A match command
lets you compare one string with any part of another string and return the matching
part. Then a nested conditional statement in the loop returns the entire array name
when the match is found.

This procedure is used extensively in the basic and advanced rigging scripts. For now, look
at it, and come back to it later to examine it after you've seen it used. After the procedure
closes, the script is ended with the same print formatting as the previous script. The beginning and ending of all the rigging scripts consistently follow this kind of formatting.

```
//4. returnName matches short string in array, and returns the full name:
global proc string cm_returnName (string $names[],string $find,string $suffix)
{//Open procedure...
    string $returnName;
```

```
    //Use loop to match main name:
    for ($name in $names){//Open loop...
        string $nameParts[];
        tokenize ($name,"_",$nameParts);
        string $match = `match $find $nameParts[0]`;
        string $match2 = `match $suffix $nameParts[1]`;
    //Use condition to return the full name with prefix and suffix:
      if ($match == $find && $match2 == $suffix) {//Open conditional...
          $returnName = $name;
      }//Close conditional.
    }//Close loop.
return $returnName;
}//Close procedure.
print "cm_returnName global proc is now in Maya's memory.\n";
//*********************************************************************
print "--------------------------------------------------------\n";
print "CMaraffi_processNames script done!\n";
print "*****************************************************\n";
print " \n";
```

WRAPPING UP

You should now have a good foundation for understanding many of the commands and techniques that will be used to MEL-script the biped rig through the rest of this book. The chapter exercise applied much of the information introduced earlier in the chapter. Next, you will learn how to manually build, and MEL-script, all the main tasks required to create a basic biped rig—including creating skeletons and icons, and parenting all the nodes into a rig hierarchy.

10 IMPORTANT POINTS TO REMEMBER FROM THIS CHAPTER

- MEL command names are case-sensitive; always start lowercase and include no spaces. Names are followed by flags and arguments separated by spaces, and end in a semicolon.

- Use the MEL Command Reference to look up all MEL commands, such as the return statement, flag details, and whether a flag can be queried or edited.

- Variables and arrays are used to store either one or many pieces of information of a particular type. Array positions always start at 0.

- Names, attributes, and text are stored in variables as strings, and should always be enclosed in double quotation marks.

- Printing variables and arrays is important for debugging your scripts and tracking down errors.

- To avoid script errors due to incremented names, run object creation commands with single back quotation marks, and catch the names in arrays.

- Custom procedures function like MEL commands, complete with arguments and return statements. Save procedures in MEL script files.

- Loops and conditional statements are essential for writing efficient scripts, and let you direct the flow of data through a script.

- Writing and reading data to custom text files lets you move information from one script to another for further processing.

- A scripted GUI window enables you to more easily run your procedures without having to remember names and arguments.

Scripting a Basic IK Biped Rig

THIS CHAPTER TAKES you through the process of scripting a basic biped rig, as the basis for adding more advanced controls through the rest of this book. First, you'll learn how to create the rig in the Maya interface, and then learn how to apply the techniques through MEL code. You'll examine a total of six scripts, four containing procedures for creating skeletons and icons, and two containing procedures for processing, transforming, and parenting all the rig nodes.

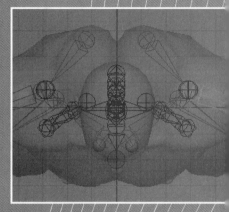

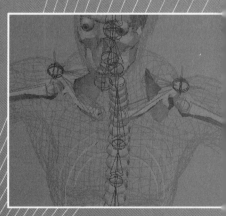

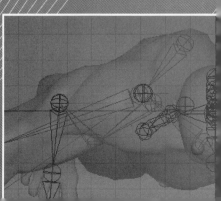

Creating the Basic Rig Components

In this section, you will learn how to create the essential components of IK biped rigs, namely IK skeletons and icons (see **FIGURE 3.1**).

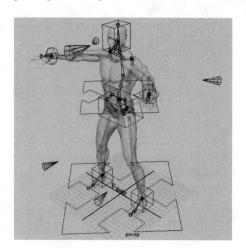

FIGURE 3.1 *Before creating the basic rig hierarchy, you must first create all the IK skeletons and control icons.*

You will start by learning how to add an IK solver to your skeletons in the interface, and where IK is most useful on biped rigs. Then you will examine MEL scripts containing procedures that draw skeletons from querying the positions of nodes in the FK rig and add IK wherever needed. After creating all the basic rig skeletons, you will learn how to draw 3D curves in the interface to create the main icons required for animating the rig. Lastly, you will examine MEL procedures that instantly create all the icons needed for the basic rig scripts.

Using IK Skeletons in the Biped Rig

You already know a lot about FK skeletons from Chapter 1, "Starting to Rig a Character," including how to draw, transform, and edit joints. But most biped rigs use IK as well as FK skeletons, so you must also understand how to add and manipulate IK solvers and handles. Adding IK to a biped rig is important for creating limb controls that are easy to animate. When creating a rig, you implement whatever kinematics will most easily simulate the appropriate movement for each part of your character's body. FK is often used in highly flexible areas of the body like the backbone, and IK is used in less flexible areas like the arms and legs.

ADDING AN IK SOLVER TO SKELETONS IN THE JOINT TOOL

When you add standard IK to skeletons, Maya uses an IK solver to constrain the joints, and creates an IK handle at the end of the skeleton. The constraint "solves" the rotation of each joint in the skeleton when the IK handle is moved. Thus, translating the IK handle, which is normally positioned at the end of the skeleton, inversely rotates all the joints higher up in the skeleton hierarchy.

To see how IK works, create a simple three-joint IK skeleton:

1. Choose Skeleton > Joint Tool ☐ to open the tool's options box, and select the Create IK Handle option. Make sure that the current solver is set to ikRPsolver (see **FIGURE 3.2**).

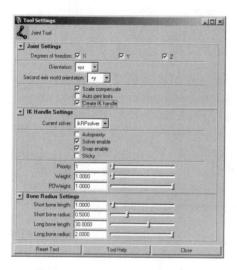

FIGURE 3.2 *For all the rigging scripts, most IK Handle options for the Joint tool will stay at their default settings, including the solver type, which should be set to ikRPsolver.*

Leave all the other IK settings at their default values, and click Close to activate the tool.

2. In Front view, draw a three-joint skeleton with a downward bend at the middle joint, and press Enter (see **FIGURE 3.3**).

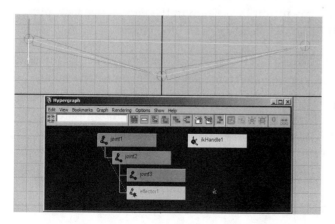

FIGURE 3.3 *Draw a typical IK skeleton in Front view with a downward bend to set the preferred angle. In the Hypergraph, view the hidden effector node and separate IK handle.*

3. Notice that a green line runs through all the joints. This line represents the IK solver, and the purple color on the joints indicates there is a connection to the IK solver and handle.

The handle is automatically selected after creating an IK skeleton. It is located at the end of the skeleton, and looks like a locator sticking out of the end joint.

4. Move the handle to see the solver rotate the joints, and bend the skeleton.

5. Open a Hypergraph view to examine the IK skeleton and separate IK handle. Notice that a dotted red line runs through the skeleton to a hidden effector node parented to one of the joints. The effector is part of the solver, and constrains the IK handle to stay with the skeleton, even though the handle is not actually parented (again, see Figure 3.3).

ENSURING A PREFERRED ANGLE ON IK SKELETONS

As you manipulate the IK handle, notice that the skeleton only bends in one direction. More specifically, if you select the middle joint of the skeleton after moving the handle, you can see in the Channel Box that the joint only rotates in one axis (normally the Z axis). Moving the handle until the skeleton straightens generates values in one direction on the channel, while bending the arm generates values in the other direction. This property of an IK skeleton is called the *preferred angle*, and is based on how the skeleton was originally drawn.

When drawing IK skeletons in the interface, you must always draw them with a slight bend to set the preferred angle. If you were to hold down the Shift key and draw an IK skeleton completely straight, the joints would not be able to rotate when the IK handle is moved. Also, because IK-constrained joints are only meant to bend in one axis, you always draw them in the orthographic 3D views. Drawing IK skeletons in these views makes them planar, or flat, in every view except that in which you are drawing. This tells Maya which axis to constrain with the IK solver. Drawing an IK skeleton in the perspective view may not result in a planar skeleton and could cause IK problems.

The main advantage IK has over FK is that it allows you to animate the rotation of multiple joints with one control object, namely the IK handle. The main disadvantage, however, is that the solver constrains the rotation of the joints to bend according to the preferred angle; that means that IK is appropriate only for body parts that have a limited range of motion, such as an arm that only bends in one direction at the elbow.

ABOUT STANDARD IK SOLVER TYPES

Maya has two standard IK solvers, and some more exotic solvers (one of which will be used to create an advanced spine rig in Chapter 4, "Adding Advanced Rig Controls"). Of the two standard solvers, known as the SC (single chain) and RP (rotate plane) solvers, the biped rig in this book will use only the RP solver. These two options differ mainly in how they manipulate the rotate plane, which is an important secondary control on an IK skeleton.

As mentioned in the previous section, the main skeletal motion produced by the standard IK solver is to rotate the joints according to the preferred angle when you translate the IK handle. A secondary motion also exists that twists the entire skeleton around a hidden axis, which corresponds to the flat perpendicular plane on which the skeleton was drawn. To visualize the rotate plane, imagine shading in the space between all the green lines that show up when you select the IK handle. The axis for the rotate plane is the straight green line that connects the root joint to the IK handle.

To see how the rotate plane works on the two types of IK solvers:

1. In Front view, create another identical three-joint skeleton with a downward bend, but change the current solver option in the Joint Tool to ikSCsolver. Notice that the only difference between the two IK skeletons is the orientation of the IK handles.

2. In X, rotate the handle for the skeleton with the SC solver, and notice how the entire skeleton twists around the rotate plane. Rotating the handle of the RP solver skeleton does nothing.

3. With the IK handle of the skeleton with the RP solver still selected, click the lowest icon in the Maya toolbox to activate the Show Manipulator tool and display a circular manipulator at the end of the skeleton. Grab the handle to move the manipulator, and notice that it drives poleVector channels on the IK handle as it rotates the skeleton around the rotate plane (see **FIGURE 3.4**).

FIGURE 3.4

The rotate plane creates an important secondary IK motion that involves rotating the entire skeleton around the green line that appears on selecting the IK handle. Skeletons with an RP solver have special channels to manipulate this motion.

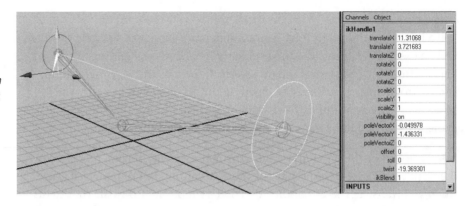

Now reset the solver and IK skeleton options, in preparation for creating the IK skeleton: Open the Joint tool again, and make sure that the current solver is set to ikRPsolver, which should remain at this setting for creating all the standard IK skeletons in basic rig. In addition, leave the other IK options at their default settings for all the exercises in this book (again, see Figure 3.2). If for some reason you need to adjust the IK handle or solver settings, you can do so by right-clicking the handle and choosing its name to open the handle in the Attribute Editor. Click the arrow next to the IK Handle Attributes and IK Solver Attributes to open the sections for editing (see **FIGURE 3.5**).

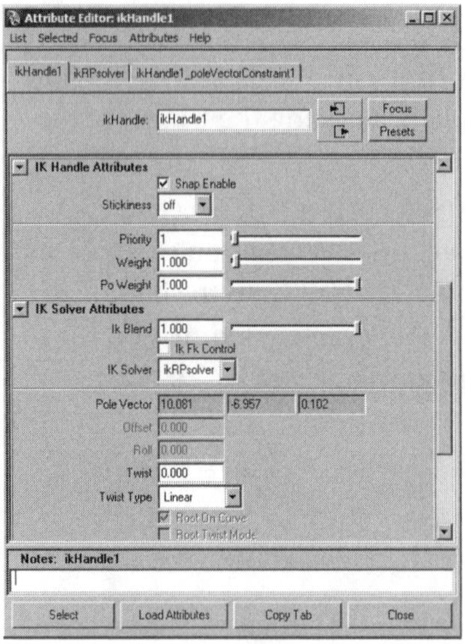

FIGURE 3.5 *Besides adjusting IK handle and solver settings manually, you can adjust them in the Attribute Editor.*

MANIPULATING THE ROTATE PLANE WITH A CONSTRAINT

In practical application, the RP solver is more flexible than the SC solver because the rotate plane controls are separated onto special channels that are not
part of the transforms. This independence lets you separate controls for the
two types of IK motion. On the limbs of the biped rig, for instance, you will
create arm and leg controls that move the IK handles, while creating elbow and
knee controls by constraining the poleVector channels to objects.

To use an object to control the rotate plane of the skeleton with the RP solver:

1. From the Create menu, create a locator to use as a separate control object for
the rotate plane. Position the locator by holding down the V key to drag and
snap it to the second joint of the RP skeleton. Then move the locator beyond
the joint on the side the skeleton bends.

For instance, if the skeleton were an arm, you would move it directly behind
the elbow joint. It is important to keep the control object in the same plane as
the IK skeleton, so that no numbers are generated in the rotate channels of the
joints when the constraint is applied.

2. Then set the constraint by holding down the Shift key as you select the
locator and the IK handle, and choose Constrain > Pole Vector. You should see
a green line appear that connects the locator to the IK solver through the constraint (see **FIGURE 3.6**).

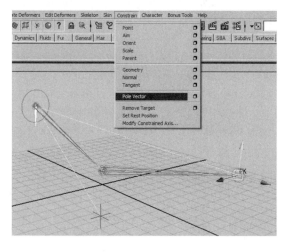

FIGURE 3.6 *The RP
solver allows using a
Pole Vector constraint to
connect the rotate plane
channels to a control
object. You can translate
this object to manipulate
the rotate plane.*

3. In Perspective view, translate the locator in Z to see the constraint manipulate the rotate plane, and twist the skeleton.

DRAWING THE BIPED RIG SKELETONS

The basic IK biped rig is a more complex version of the FK rig created in the Chapter 1, "Starting to Rig a Character." In fact, the scripts that create the basic IK rig skeletons later in this chapter reference the FK rig skeletons and the polygon bones as guides for creating and positioning the new joints. You can also use them as visual guides when drawing the IK skeletons in the 3D views.

There are a few things to keep in mind when creating skeletons for a biped rig in the Maya interface:

■ When first learning how to create skeletons for a rig, it is best to draw them in the orthographic views rather than the Perspective view, and transform them into place using the FK skeletons and polygon bones as a guide. If you hold down the V key while drawing to snap the joints to the FK rig nodes in the Perspective view, you have to check all the joint centers, and manually orient them afterward. This is quick to do in a script, but very time-consuming when creating skeletons in the interface. And if you forget to reorient some joints, it may cause problems on your final rig.

■ After positioning skeletons, avoid freezing transformations on joints connected to IK, as doing so traditionally has caused problems in Maya. If you are going to manipulate a skeleton extensively to fit it inside the character, then it is better to add the IK using the IK Handle tool after transforming and freezing the joints. Located in the Skeleton menu, the IK Handle tool has the same IK options as the Joint tool. Simply activate the tool, and click the root joint and end joint of the skeleton to add the IK.

■ It's important when drawing IK skeletons in the interface to use the correct orthographic view to produce a good preferred angle. For instance, legs need to bend forward at the knee when the IK handle is raised, so you draw them in Side orthographic view. With the palms facing downward on the model, the elbows should bend backward, so you draw the IK skeletons in Top view (see **FIGURE 3.7**).

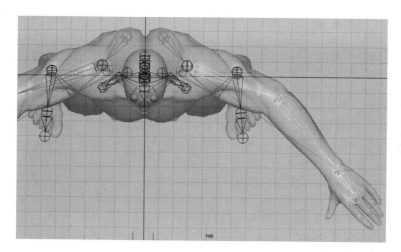

FIGURE 3.7 *Be sure to draw IK skeletons in the correct orthographic view to create a good preferred angle, such as drawing an arm skeleton in Top view for a character whose palms are facing downward.*

Normally you draw biped skeletons only for the left half of symmetrical characters; mirroring the skeleton using behavior mode ensures that the limbs also bend correctly on the right side.

■ When creating skeletons manually, you name all the main nodes with standard naming conventions, but you don't have to be as detailed with prefixes and suffixes as when scripting the entire process. Be sure to use "root" on the first joint, and "end" on the last joint, and add "lf", "rt", and "ct" prefixes for skeletons on the left, right, and center sections of the body.

With these points in mind, you're ready draw all the basic biped skeletons for the biped rig, using the following steps to guide you. If you get stuck, just look at how it was done in the basicIkRig.mb example file (see **FIGURE 3.8**).

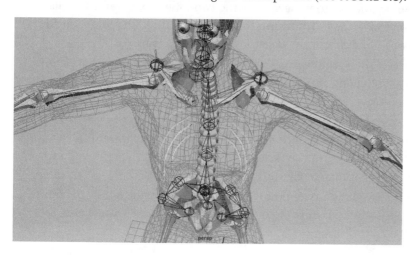

FIGURE 3.8 *When drawing the basic rig skeletons in the interface, refer to the basicIkRig.mb example file to see exactly how to position all joints inside the character.*

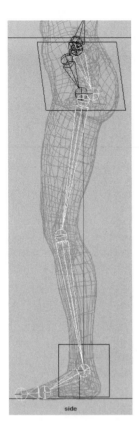

side

FIGURE 3.9 *In Side view, use the polygon bones to guide you as you draw the leg, foot, and hip skeletons.*

To draw a basic IK biped rig skeleton:

1. Open the basicFkRig.mb file, and examine the FK rig in the 3D views and in the Hypergraph. You will use the Maya joints, polygon bones, and character skin as guides, so make sure that you can see all of them. Template the skin in the Layers menu, and adjust the other layers as needed to clearly see your new skeletons while also seeing the guides. Whenever you need to see the joints more clearly, also turn on X-Ray Joints in the Shading menu of the orthographic views.

2. In the Joint tool, turn on IK. In Side orthographic view, using the polygon bones as a guide, draw the left leg skeleton as a three-joint skeleton from hip to ankle, with a slight bend toward the front of the knee.

3. Mirror the leg across the YZ plane using the behavior setting to create the right leg IK skeleton.

4. Then turn off IK to draw the rest of the skeletons for the feet, hips, and backbone:

■ In Side view, draw a three-joint left foot skeleton, transform it according to the polygon bone positions, and mirror it to the right side. Then draw the two-joint center hip skeleton, angling it back slightly toward the pelvis (see **FIGURE 3.9**).

■ In Front view, draw the left-side hip skeleton, contouring the pelvis bone, and then mirroring to create the right hip skeleton (again, see Figure 3.8). Then in Side view draw the four-joint backbone skeleton from the center of the hips to the base of the neck, using the polygon vertebrae as a guide.

5. Turn on IK, and in Front view, draw the two-joint clavicle and scapula skeletons on the left side. Transform the root joints and IK handle to fit the polygon bones, and mirror the skeletons (again, see Figure 3.8).

6. In Side view, draw the two-joint neck and head skeletons as FK skeletons (turn off IK), following the spine up through the center of the skull. Then draw the three-joint jaw skeleton to the end of the jaw (see **FIGURE 3.10**).

7. In Top view, turn on IK to draw the three-joint left arm skeleton from the shoulder to the wrist. Make sure that there is a slight bend toward the back of the elbow. Then transform the skeleton into place inside the arm, and mirror to the other side (again, see Figure 3.7).

8. In Front view, draw a two-joint FK skeleton to create the left hand; transform appropriately, and mirror to create the right-hand skeleton (again, see Figure 3.7).

PREPARING TO SCRIPT THE BASIC RIG SKELETONS

Creating skeletons in the interface displays in the Script Editor many of the commands you will use to code the creation of skeletons for your rig. The main command will be the `joint` command, with a series of decimal values to specify joint positions in 3D space. It is best to consolidate all the necessary code into a couple of procedures that also specify naming conventions, set the orientation of joints, and have arguments for adding IK and mirroring. For a symmetrical biped rig, this approach makes the scripting process more efficient by letting you write procedures that only require left-side data, and use arguments and conditional statements to mirror the skeletons to the right side. Later scripts will extend this same process to most rigging procedures. Eventually, all the scripts will be designed to create the left side of the character first, and then create the right side by using the established prefixes and arguments.

One of the main differences between creating skeletons in the interface and scripting the entire process is how much detail you put into the names of the nodes. When scripting, other than specifying the main names, you must also specify prefixes and suffixes that clearly categorize the nodes. For instance, in addition to using prefixes that label each joint as belonging to the left, right, or center section of the body, you also add suffixes to all the names in the rig to clarify the node type. For instance, group nodes have a `_group` suffix, while icons have an `_icon` suffix. Since skeleton joints have the additional option of being bound, they will follow an even more complex naming convention for suffixes. This is because not all skeleton joints need to be part of the bind, but instead are used as controls for other bound joints. The binding script makes this distinction by looking for particular suffices on the joints. The joint suffixes will be explained in detail in the following exercise.

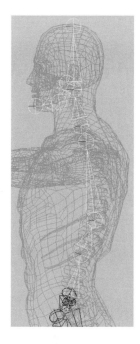

FIGURE 3.10 *Draw the backbone and neck skeletons in Side view so they contour the polygon vertebrae, and draw the head skeleton from the base to the top of the skull.*

EXERCISE 3.1: EXAMINING THE SKELETON CREATION SCRIPT

In this exercise, you examine the two main scripts that create the skeletons for the basic IK rig. The first script contains a couple of global procedures that create a single skeleton by placing the joints in 3D space according to target pivots or vertices, and then names and orients the joints. It also has options for adding IK and mirroring skeletons. The second script runs the main global procedure from the first script to create all the basic IK rig skeletons, as you just did in the interface in the "Drawing the Biped Rig Skeletons" section. These scripts also source and run procedures from the CMaraffi_processNames script covered in the Chapter 2 exercise ("Beginning the Biped Rig Scripts") as needed for retrieving names from files and arrays.

Step 1: Set the Joint Suffixes

Begin by examining the CMaraffi_skelCreate MEL script in an external script editor like ConTEXT. This script has similar formatting to the scripts from the previous chapter with a header comment and print commands, followed by procedures. (This header and formatting will be skipped in the following book example to conserve space.) The first local procedure named cm_drawJoints has seven arguments required for creating a single skeleton. The arguments let you specify joint position values, naming specifications, the number and orientation of joints, and options for IK and binding.

The main code begins with evaluating the $bind argument, which is an integer-based on-off switch for determining the suffix for each joint that is created. The code also declares the three main joint types of root, joint, and end, and then uses a conditional statement to assign a suffix for each type based on how the bind argument evaluates. If the argument is turned on or set to 1, then the script assigns the standard _rootJt, _bindJt, and _endJt as the suffix. However, if the argument is turned off or set to 0, then the script adds _ctrl to the joint suffixes: _ctrlRoot, _ctrlJoint, and _ctrlEnd. Later in the book, a binding script will be run to search for particular suffixes (_rootJt and _bindJt) in all the rig names, to bind the joints, and ignore all other names (see "Creating a Final Bind" in Chapter 5, "Finishing the IK Biped Rig").

```
//1. Local procedure for creating joints and IK of skeleton:
proc string[] cm_drawJoints (string $cmMatrix[],string $prefix,
  string $nameJoints,int $skelSize,string $orient2ndAxis,
  int $createIk,int $bind) {//Open procedure...
 //Use conditional to determine joint suffixes based on binding:
   string $rootSuffix;
   string $jointSuffix;
   string $endSuffix;
   if ($bind == 1){//Open conditional...
     $rootSuffix = "_rootJt";
     $jointSuffix = "_bindJt";
     $endSuffix = "_endJt";
   }//Close conditional.
   else {//Open conditional...
     $rootSuffix = "_ctrlRt";
     $jointSuffix = "_ctrlJt";
     $endSuffix = "_ctrlEd";
   }//Close conditional.
```

Step 2: Create an Individual Skeleton

The next section of the cm_drawJoints script uses a loop and nested conditional statements to draw and name each joint in the skeleton. To name the joints, the code first sets up some requirements for running the loop. Since the loop is creating joints using arrays, you must specify the array positions for the different name suffixes. By default, the $jointNames[0] array position always contains the joint that should have the root suffix added to the name.

To determine the end joint position in the arrays, the procedure subtracts one integer from the $skelSize argument, which determines the total number of joints to create in the skeleton. The conditional statement then adds the $endSuffix string to the end joint name when it is created. All other joints in the skeleton will be assigned the standard joint suffix by the conditional in the else statement. Notice that because there is potentially more than one middle joint in the skeleton, the statement also adds a $i incrementing value to the name:

```
($prefix + $nameJoints + $i + $jointSuffix)
```

Other data required by the loop include arguments to specify each joint's positions in 3D space. This specification requires three float values for each joint in the skeleton, which would ideally be specified by a matrix. For instance, a four-joint skeleton would use a matrix[4][3], or four sets of three float values. Notice, however, that the first argument called $cm_Matrix is actually a string array, not a true matrix. Using a string array gets around one of the inherent limitation of matrices in Maya: you cannot declare a dynamic matrix. This limitation makes it impossible to declare different sizes of real matrices in a loop to accommodate different sizes of skeletons. Instead, by using a string array like a matrix, you can create a much more flexible pseudo-matrix than a real matrix.

The reason that creating a pseudo-matrix is done with a string array, even though the position values are really floats, is that strings can combine a variety of characters and then can be broken up again using a tokenize command. This is exactly how the float positions of the joints are set when the rigging scripts run. The cm_skelCreate global procedure you will examine in step 4 of this exercise combines the three xyz float values with commas to form a single string, such as 1.5,0.5,3.2, along with other similar strings to create a string array that mimics a matrix. Each string in the array contains three float values. Then the script enters the array into the procedure as the $cmMatrix argument. Inside the cm_drawJoints procedure, the first tokenize command breaks down each string in the array into the individual float values, specifying commas as the breaking point. The code then converts the resulting three strings in the $tmpPos array back to float values by transferring them to float variables named $xPos, $yPos, and $zPos.

The float values from the custom string matrix are used in the -p, or position, flag of the joint command. After the procedure creates and positions all the joints, it selects the root joint, freezes the skeleton, and edits the joints to be oriented correctly. This is a necessary step when creating skeletons entirely in code, as you are not actually drawing the joints in any orthographic view (similar to the results of drawing skeletons in Perspective view).

Also notice that the code clears selection before and after creating the skeleton. The joint command automatically parents new joints to the currently selected joint, which is how the loop creates a skeleton hierarchy without any parenting commands or flags. Because of this feature, you would not want any other joints to be selected when creating a new skeleton.

```
//Use loop and conditionals to create joints based on suffix:
   select -cl;
   string $jointNames[];
   int $lastJoint = ($skelSize - 1);
   int $i;
   for($i = 0; $i < $skelSize; $i++){//Open loop...
   //Convert joint matrix from string to float array:
      string $tmpPos[];
      tokenize ($cmMatrix[$i],",",$tmpPos);
      float $xPos = $tmpPos[0];
      float $yPos = $tmpPos[1];
      float $zPos = $tmpPos[2];
      if ($i == 0){//Open conditional...
        //Adds root suffix:
          $jointNames[size ($jointNames)] = `joint -p $xPos $yPos $zPos
          -n ($prefix + $nameJoints + $rootSuffix)`;
      }//Close conditional.
      else if ($i == $lastJoint){//Open conditional...
        //Adds end suffix:
          $jointNames[size ($jointNames)] = `joint -p $xPos $yPos $zPos
          -n ($prefix + $nameJoints + $endSuffix)`;
      }//Close conditional.
      else {//Open conditional...
        //Adds joint suffix:
          $jointNames[size ($jointNames)] = `joint -p $xPos $yPos $zPos
          -n ($prefix + $nameJoints + $i + $jointSuffix)`;
      }//Close conditional.
   }//Close loop.
 //Select root to freeze and orient joints by propogation:
   select -r $jointNames[0];
   makeIdentity -apply true -r 1;
   joint -e -oj xyz -sao $orient2ndAxis -ch;
   select -cl;
```

Step 3: Add IK and Return Skeleton Node Names

The last section of code in the cm_drawJoints procedure uses a conditional statement to evaluate the IK argument, and adds the default RP solver to the entire skeleton if true. The statement also sets up the array of names to return at the end of the procedure. Notice that the procedure does not return all the node names in the skeleton, but instead returns only the root joint, end joint, and IK handle name if applicable. These are the most important names needed for parenting the rig hierarchy. However, to retrieve other required joint names, the rigging scripts will use other procedures shown in Exercise 3.3, "Step 1: Examine the CMaraffi_runLocals Script."

```
//Add IK solver and set up return names:
   string $rootJoint = $jointNames[0];
   string $endJoint = $jointNames[$lastJoint];
   string $ikSuffix = "_rpIk";
   string $IkHandle[];
   string $returnArray[];
   if ($createIk == 1) {//Open conditional...
     $IkHandle = `ikHandle -w 1 -pw 1 -fs 1 -shf 1
      -s 0 -sol "ikRPsolver" -n ($prefix + $nameJoints + $ikSuffix)
        -sj $rootJoint -ee $endJoint`;
     $returnArray = {$rootJoint,$endJoint,$IkHandle[0]};
   }//Close conditional.
 //Set up return names if no IK:
   else {//Open conditional...
     $returnArray = {$rootJoint,$endJoint};
   }//Close conditional.
   select -cl;
   return $returnArray;
}//Close procedure.
   print "cm_drawJoints local proc is now in Maya's memory.\n";
//*********************************************************************
```

Step 4: Create a Custom String Matrix to Position Joints

Now, you'll examine the main global procedure in the CMaraffi_skelCreate script that the other rigging scripts will run to create all the skeletons for the biped rig. This procedure has all the arguments needed to run the cm_drawJoints local procedure, as well as additional arguments for determining joint positions and for mirroring skeletons after they are created. The first code in this procedure runs a conditional statement on the $mirror argument to automatically determine the prefix to use for the skeleton. If the $mirror argument evaluates as turned on, then it sets the prefix to left; otherwise it gets set to center. This procedure assumes that all skeletons will be for a symmetrical biped rig, and that the left-side skeletons will always be mirrored to the right side. Otherwise, the procedure assumes it is creating a center skeleton that does not need to be mirrored.

The next section of code creates the custom matrix used to position the joints created by the `cm_drawJoints` procedure. The code uses conditional statements nested inside a loop to find the three float positional values for each joint. The conditional statements evaluate the `$vtxs` argument to determine whether the target is an object or point, and runs the appropriate MEL command to find the target's position in 3D world space. Notice that the `xform` command queries the pivot of the object, which works correctly even if the transforms have been frozen. The `pointPosition` command is designed to return the position of polygon or NURBS vertices or points. Both of these commands return three float values in an array. The code then converts and combines these commands into a single string, adding commas between the values, and saving it into the `$jtPos` variable. The loop increment value in the matrix, `$cmMatrix[0]`, adds the `$jtPos` string to the array, creating the custom string matrix. This array is then run in the `cm_drawJoints` procedure, broken up with a `tokenize` command, and used to position the newly created skeleton joints.

```
//2. Main global procedure to create, position, and mirror skeletons:
global proc string[] cm_skelCreate (int $numJts,string $objs[],
      string $vtxs[],string $skelName,int $mirror,string $orient,
      int $ik,int $bind){//Open Procedure...
 //Use conditional to set the prefix:
   string $pfx;
   if ($mirror == 1)$pfx = "lf";
   else $pfx = "ct";
 //Run loop to get custom string matrix joint positions for skeleton:
   string $cmMatrix[];
   int $i;
   for ($i = 0; $i < $numJts; $i++){//Open loop...
   //Get the 3D float position values for each joint:
     float $xyzPos[];
     if ($vtxs[$i] == "obj") {//Open conditional...
       $xyzPos = `xform -q -piv -ws $objs[$i]`;
     }//Close conditional.
     else {//Open conditional...
       $xyzPos = `pointPosition ($objs[$i] + $vtxs[$i])`;
     }//Close conditional.
   //Add position values into the custom string matrix:
     string $jtPos = ($xyzPos[0] + "," + $xyzPos[1] + "," + $xyzPos[2]);
     $cmMatrix[$i] = $jtPos;
   }//Close loop.
   //Run local procedure to create the skeleton using custom matrix:
     string $skelNames[] = cm_drawJoints($cmMatrix,$pfx,$skelName,
           $numJts, $orient,$ik,$bind);
```

Step 5: Mirror Skeleton Nodes from Left to Right

Once the skeleton is created with the cm_drawJoints procedure, the final section of
code uses the prefix to determine if the skeleton should be mirrored to the right side.
The code runs nested conditionals to evaluate whether the skeleton has IK added to
it, which changes the mirroring code and return statement. The reason the code is
different, and more complex, is because the mirrorJoint command does not have
a return statement. However, when you mirror a skeleton, different nodes will be
selected on the new skeleton depending on whether it has IK or not. This requires
pickwalking, equivalent to using the arrow keys to move through node connections,
to list and return the right-side names.

When all the necessary nodes are selected, listed, and saved into a $mirrorNames array,
the code appends the array to the left skeleton names array, and places it in the return
statement at the end of the global procedure.

```
//Run proc to mirror skeleton to create right joints:
    if ($pfx == "lf"){//Open conditional...
    //Use conditional mirror skels with or without IK:
      string $mirrorNames[];
      if ($ik == 1) {//Open if statement...
       //Mirror joints has no return, but does select new skeleton:
          mirrorJoint -myz -mb -sr "lf" "rt" $skelNames[0];
          string $mirrorIk[] = `ls -sl`;
          pickWalk -d left;
          select -hi;
          string $mirrorJoints[] = `ls -sl`;
          int $endJoint = size($mirrorJoints) - 2;
          $mirrorNames = {$mirrorJoints[0],$mirrorJoints[$endJoint],
                     $mirrorIk[0]};
          select -cl;
      }//Close if statement.
      else {//Open else statement...
          mirrorJoint -myz -mb -sr "lf" "rt" $skelNames[0];
          select -hi;
          string $mirrorJoints[] = `ls -sl`;
          int $endJoint = size($mirrorJoints) - 1;
          $mirrorNames = {$mirrorJoints[0],$mirrorJoints[$endJoint]};
          select -cl;
      }//Close else statement.
      int $numStrings = `size ($mirrorNames)`;
      appendStringArray($skelNames,$mirrorNames,$numStrings);
    }//Close conditional.
return $skelNames;
}//Close procedure.
```

Step 6: Create All the Basic Rig Skeletons

To see the `cm_skelCreate` procedure put into action, just open the CMaraffi_basicSkels script, and examine the main global procedure. The `cm_basicSkels` procedure has no arguments and is pretty straightforward. It starts by sourcing the scripts containing the procedures needed for creating skeletons, and uses the `cm_getNames` procedure to retrieve the basic FK rig names from file. Next, it sets up some necessary string variables, and sets the namespace to the rig name so that all the skeleton nodes will have a namespace prefix.

The majority of the code in the rest of the procedure simply creates each skeleton in the basic IK rig. The organization is the same in each section of code. First the `cm_returnName` procedure retrieves the target object names from the FK rig file. Then the code sets up the arrays to specify the target object or vertex that will be queried to establish the joint positions, and runs the name in the `cm_skelCreate` procedure with all the other arguments. Lastly, an array catches the returned names of the skeleton nodes and prints them to the command line.

```
//1. Main global procedure for creating the basic rig skeletons:
global proc string[] cm_basicSkels (){//Open procedure...
 //Source files containing local and global procs used for skeletons:
   eval ("source CMaraffi_skelCreate");
   eval ("source CMaraffi_processNames");
 //----------------------------------------------------------------
 //Run proc to access FK rig names from file:
   string $fkRigNames[] = cm_getNames("fkRig");
 //----------------------------------------------------------------
 //Set prefixes, joint names, and print strings:
   string $pfx0 = "ct";
   string $pfx1 = "lf";
   string $pfx2 = "rt";
   string $printSkelNames = "Skeleton created with node names: \n";
 //----------------------------------------------------------------
 //Set namespace and create the skeletons:
   cm_setNamespace (1);
 //Feet: Set all necessary names into variables:
   string $lfFkFootRoot = cm_returnName ($fkRigNames,"lfFoot","fk");
   string $lfFkFootBall = cm_returnName ($fkRigNames,"lfBall","fk");
   string $lfFkFootEnd = cm_returnName ($fkRigNames,"lfToe","fk");
   string $footName = "Foot";
 //Create arrays for procedure arguments:
   string $targetFk[] = {$lfFkFootRoot,$lfFkFootBall,$lfFkFootEnd};
   string $targetVtx[] = {"obj","obj","obj"};
 //Run procedure to create the skeleton:
```

```
    string $footSkels[] = cm_skelCreate (3,$targetFk,$targetVtx,
          $footName,1,"yup",0,1);
//Print names of main skeleton nodes:
  print $printSkelNames; print $footSkels; print " \n";
//-------------------------------------------------------------
//Legs: Set all necessary names into variables:
  string $lfFkLegRoot = cm_returnName ($fkRigNames,"lfUpLeg","fk");
  string $lfFkLegKnee = cm_returnName ($fkRigNames,"lfLeg","fk");
  string $legName = "Leg";
//Create arrays for procedure arguments:
  string $targetFk[] = {$lfFkLegRoot,$lfFkLegKnee,$lfFkFootRoot};
  string $targetVtx[] = {"obj","obj","obj"};
//Run procedure to create the skeleton:
  string $legSkels[] = cm_skelCreate (3,$targetFk,$targetVtx,
          $legName,1,"xup",1,1);
//Print names of main skeleton nodes:
  print $printSkelNames; print $legSkels; print " \n";
//-------------------------------------------------------------
```

Make sure that you open the actual script to examine the code that creates all the basic skeletons; to conserve space, the script won't be shown here. The code continues in a similar manner through the rest of the cm_basicSkels procedure, and then ends with the cm_setNamespace procedure setting the namespace back to the scene root. The final section of code manually places the skeleton node names into an array to use in the return statement of the procedure. These names will be used in the other scripts covered in this chapter that create the icons and the basic rig hierarchy. Before being returned, these names also are printed to the command line for error-checking.

```
//Set name space back to scene root:
  cm_setNamespace (0);
 //Create array of all the main skeleton nodes:
  string $basicSkelNames[] = {$footSkels[0],$footSkels[1],$footSkels[2],
    $footSkels[3],$legSkels[0],$legSkels[1],$legSkels[2],$legSkels[3],
    $legSkels[4],$legSkels[5],$ctHipSkels[0],$ctHipSkels[1],
    $sideHipSkels[0],$sideHipSkels[1],$sideHipSkels[2],$sideHipSkels[3],
    $ctBackSkels[0],$ctBackSkels[1],$ctNeckSkels[0],$ctNeckSkels[1],
    $ctHeadSkels[0],$ctHeadSkels[1],$ctJawSkels[0],$ctJawSkels[1],
    $clavicleSkels[0],$clavicleSkels[1],$clavicleSkels[2],
    $clavicleSkels[3],$clavicleSkels[4],$clavicleSkels[5],
    $scapulaSkels[0],$scapulaSkels[1],$scapulaSkels[2],
    $scapulaSkels[3],$scapulaSkels[4],$scapulaSkels[5],
    $armSkels[0],$armSkels[1],$armSkels[2],$armSkels[3],
    $armSkels[4],$armSkels[5],$handSkels[0],$handSkels[1],
    $handSkels[2],$handSkels[3]};
```

```
//Print skeletons to command line:
  cm_printNames ($basicSkelNames,0,"none");
//Return array of all the main skeleton nodes created:
  return $basicSkelNames;
}//Close procedure.
```

Creating Icons

Rig icons come in many shapes and sizes, but one thing they all have in common is that they are made from NURBS curves. Drawn in the shapes of 3D objects, icons are easy to select in the interface, but don't show up in a render of the geometry. Once you create the icons, you will parent them over many of the main nodes in the rig, making the icons function as the top-level controls. Although you could create icons for every part of the rig you want to animate, doing so would make the iconic interface too cluttered. It is better interface design to be selective about which icons to create, so that you focus on main body controls, and add custom channels on the main icons for animating secondary controls.

For instance, the basic biped rig scripts in this book create a main arm icon; the advanced scripts then add wrist, hand, and finger channels to the icon. These channels are then connected to the actual attributes of the arm to drive all the movements on the arm, hand, and fingers.

DRAWING ICON CURVES

Drawing the curves for most icons is like drawing any curve in the Maya interface, except that you need to use a guide to create a good 3D shape. For standard icon shapes like boxes and arrows, it is best to use a linear curve setting to produce straight edges.

To create a box icon using a linear NURBS curve:

1. In the Create > Polygon Primitives menu, create a polygon cube to use as a guide. Then choose Create > EP Curve Tool ▢. Set the curve settings to 1 Linear, leave the knot spacing to Uniform, and click Close.

2. In Perspective view, orbit around the cube until you can see all the corners where the points exist on the geometry.

3. Hold down the V key; this will snap the curve points to the cube points. Then start drawing the curve by clicking around the edges of the cube. You'll have to overlap the curve on top of itself to cover all the edges of the cube.

4. When you have finished, move the cube to the side and turn on Shaded mode in Perspective view to see the difference between your box icon curve and the cube geometry (see **FIGURE 3.11**).

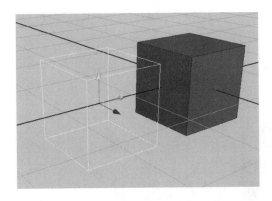

FIGURE 3.11 *To create many types of icons in the interface, simply snap a linear curve around the edges of a polygon primitive. Moving the icon afterward shows it has no geometry in the shaded view that can be rendered.*

If it looks as if it was done correctly, then you can delete the original polygon cube. You would then transform the box icon, both translating and scaling, so it fits around a body part like the hips. You can also move points in component mode to better shape the icon for the character. The important thing is to make sure that the icon is outside the character's skin and is easily selectable.

CREATING A COMPOSITE SPHERE ICON

You can create a variety of icon shapes drawing curves, but some shapes are difficult to create using this method. Smooth spherical shapes and text icons composed of several letters are more easily created using multiple curves combined into a single icon. You can create this type of compound curve icon by parenting the shape nodes of the separate curves under a single transform node; you do this by running a standard parent command with -r, or relative, and -s, or shape, flags. For instance, you can create such an icon in the shape of a sphere by combining two primitive NURBS circles.

To create a sphere icon from separate circles:

1. Choose Create > NURBS Primitives > Circle ◘, and set the options to create a cubic circle facing in the Z axis.

2. Duplicate the circle, rotating it 90 degrees in Y so that it is perpendicular to the first circle, and freeze it. Duplicate the second circle, rotating it 90 degrees in Z so that it faces upward, and also freeze it. You should have three circles facing down each axis, and it should look similar to a low-resolution sphere.

3. Next, create an empty group node to parent over the shape nodes of all three circles. Open the Hypergraph, and in its menu turn on Options > Display > Shape Nodes to see the shape nodes as well as the transform nodes (see **FIGURE 3.12**).

FIGURE 3.12 *Display the shape nodes in the Hypergraph; then create a composite curve icon by parenting the shapes of three separate circles under a single transform node.*

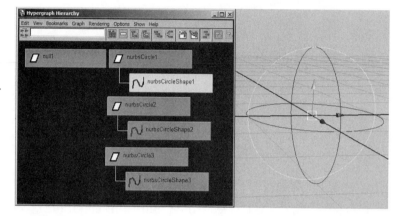

4. To parent all the shape nodes of the circles under the group node, run the following code:

```
parent -r -s nurbsCircleShape1 nurbsCircleShape2 nurbsCircleShape3 null1;
```

5. In the Hypergraph, view all the shape nodes now parented under the group node. Delete the original transform nodes of the circles.

6. In Perspective view, notice that selecting any of the circles automatically selects the group node. Essentially, they now function as a single object.

You can use this same method to create text icons, or any other compound curve icon. Since this process requires using MEL, it makes sense to script the creation of such icons, even if you are not scripting the entire rig. For instance, here is code that uses a loop to repeat what you just did in the interface:

```
//Create a transform node:
 string $iconNode = `group -em -n "sphere_icon"`;
//Use loop to create and parent circle shapes:
 string $curveNames[];
 int $x[] = {1,0,0};
 int $y[] = {0,1,0};
 int $z[] = {0,0,1};
for ($i = 0 ; $i < 3 ; $i++){//Open loop:
```

```
$curveNames = `circle -c 0 0 0 -nr $x[$i] $y[$i] $z[$i] -sw 360 -r 1
-d 3 -s 8 -ch 0`;
  string $shapeNode[] = `listRelatives -s $curveNames[0]`;
  parent -r -s $shapeNode[0] $iconNode;
  delete $curveNames[0];
  select -cl;
}//Close loop.
```

PREPARING TO SCRIPT ICONS

Looking in the Script Editor after manually drawing a curve icon in the interface shows all the commands needed for scripting the process. When drawing a curve by snapping to the points of a polygon primitive, the main code looks similar to this:

```
curve -d 1 -p -0.5 0.5 0.5 -p 0.5 0.5 0.5 -p 0.5 0.5 -0.5 -p -0.5 0.5 -0.5 -p
-0.5 0.5 0.5 -p -0.5 -0.5 0.5 -p -0.5 -0.5 -0.5 -p -0.5 0.5 -0.5 -p 0.5 0.5 -0.5
-p 0.5 -0.5 -0.5 -p -0.5 -0.5 -0.5 -p -0.5 -0.5 0.5 -p 0.5 -0.5 0.5 -p 0.5 0.5
0.5 -p 0.5 0.5 -0.5 -p 0.5 -0.5 -0.5 -p 0.5 -0.5 0.5 -k 0 -k 1 -k 2 -k 3 -k 4 -k
5 -k 6 -k 7 -k 8 -k 9 -k 10 -k 11 -k 12 -k 13 -k 14 -k 15 -k 16;
```

Copying this code into your script with similar code for other icons will allow you to easily create any icons you need for the biped rig.

EXERCISE 3.2: SCRIPTING THE ICONS FOR THE BIPED RIG

Open the CMaraffi_iconCreate and CMaraffi_basicIcons scripts to examine the procedures that they contain. The first script has procedures that create a single type of icon, and transform it as required. The second script runs the procedures in the first script to actually create all the icons for the basic IK rig.

Step 1: Create Icons

The series of local procedures at the beginning of the CMaraffi_iconCreate script all use the same formatting. Each procedure creates a different type of icon, such as a box, cone, and arrow, with a single string argument to input the name. The code is a cleaned-up version of the code found in the History field when creating the icon curves in the interface. The knot flags seen in the previous curve command have been removed because they are not really necessary for coding the icon. Since several of the icons use very similar code, they are not shown here to conserve space.

```
//1. Local procedure creates a box curve icon:
proc string cm_boxIcon (string $iconName){//Open procedure...
```

```
    string $returnName = `curve -n $iconName -d 1 -p 0.5 0.5 0.5
      -p -0.5 0.5 0.5 -p -0.5 0.5 -0.5 -p 0.5 0.5 -0.5 -p 0.5 0.5 0.5
      -p 0.5 -0.5 0.5 -p 0.5 -0.5 -0.5 -p 0.5 0.5 -0.5 -p -0.5 0.5 -0.5
      -p -0.5 -0.5 -0.5 -p 0.5 -0.5 -0.5 -p 0.5 -0.5 0.5 -p -0.5 -0.5 0.5
      -p -0.5 -0.5 -0.5 -p -0.5 0.5 -0.5 -p -0.5 0.5 0.5 -p -0.5 -0.5 0.5`;
    setAttr ($returnName + ".rotateOrder") 2;
    return $returnName;
}//Close procedure.
```

The sphere procedure creates a composite curve icon similar to the interface example shown in the previous section with three circles, except that it runs a createNode command instead of a group command to give the circle shape nodes a parent transform node. The code for the text icon is a little more complicated because it involves parenting the shape nodes of potentially many text components. The text icon code uses nested conditional statements inside a loop to search for all the shape nodes by matching parts of the name. Then it parents them all under the main transform node for the text, and deletes all the other nodes.

```
//4. Local procedure creates a sphere compound curve icon:
proc string cm_sphereIcon (string $iconName){//Open procedure...
    string $returnName = `createNode "transform" -n $iconName`;
    string $curveNames[];
    int $x[] = {1,0,0};
    int $y[] = {0,1,0};
    int $z[] = {0,0,1};
    for ($i = 0 ; $i < 3 ; $i++){//Open loop...
        $curveNames = `circle -c 0 0 0 -nr $x[$i] $y[$i] $z[$i]
                     -sw 360 -r 1 -d 3 -s 8 -ch 0`;
        string $shapeNode[] = `listRelatives -s $curveNames[0]`;
        parent -r -s $shapeNode[0] $returnName;
        delete $curveNames[0];
    }//Close loop.
    return $returnName;
}//Close procedure.
  print "cm_sphereIcon local proc is now in Maya's memory.\n";
  //*********************************************************************
//5. Local procedure creates a text compound curve icon:
proc string cm_textIcon (string $iconName,string $text){//Open proc...
    string $returnName = `createNode "transform" -n $iconName`;
    string $curveNames[] = `textCurves -f "Helvetica|h-8|w100|c0"
                -t $text -n "tempText"`;
    setAttr ($curveNames[0] + ".tx") -3;
    string $allNodes[] = sort (`listRelatives -ad $curveNames[0]`);
    int $i;
```

```
  for ($i = 0 ; $i < size($allNodes) ; $i++){//Open loop...
    string $match = `match "curve" $allNodes[$i]`;
    if ($match == "curve") {//Open conditional...
      string $match2 = `match "Shape" $allNodes[$i]`;
      if ($match2 != "Shape") {//Open conditional...
        parent -w $allNodes[$i];
        makeIdentity -apply true -t 1 -r 1 -s 1 -n 0 $allNodes[$i];
        parent -r $allNodes[$i] $curveNames[0];
      }//Close conditional.
      else {//Open conditional...
        parent -r -s $allNodes[$i] $returnName;
      }//Close conditional.
    }//Close conditional.
  }//Close loop.
  delete $curveNames[0];
  return $returnName;
}//Close procedure.
```

Notice that the return string for each procedure is the name of the icon. Also, by default, each icon is being created at the center or origin point of the 3D world space. The next procedure in the script will transform each icon into place using the returned name.

Step 2: Size, Position, and Mirror the Icon

The last local procedure in this script is the cm_processIcon procedure, which lets you size, position, and mirror the icon you are creating. The scaling is done by either direct input through arguments, or by finding the distance between points on guide curves or polygon bones on the FK rig. Notice that the FK rig contains circles around the left wrist and ankle, and around the chest. The circles were scaled manually to sit close to the surface of the skin, so that they can be used as sizing guides for these areas of the model. If you were to use the FK rig with another character, you would need to refit the circles.

To determine icon size, the procedure can also use vertices on polygon bones, such as the pelvis bone for the hips. The script runs the pointPosition command on the vertexes to determine their position in 3D space, and then it runs the Maya procedure distance2Pts to get the distance between the positions. The procedure combines the $addScale argument with the distance when sizing the icon to make it slightly larger than the model, and thus easier to select.

```
//6. Local procedure sizes, transforms, and mirrors an icon:
proc string[] cm_processIcon (string $iconName,string $scaling[],
    float $addScale[],string $target,int $mirror){//Open procedure...
  //Use conditional and loop to determine size of icons:
    float $scale[];
```

```
    int $i;
    int $size = `size ($scaling)`;
    if ($size == 3){//Open conditional...
      for ($i = 0 ; $i < 3 ; $i++){//Open loop...
      //Use distance of points for base size, then add argument:
        string $scaleData[];
        tokenize ($scaling[$i], ",", $scaleData);
        float $ptPos1[] = `pointPosition ($scaleData[0] + $scaleData[1])`;
        float $ptPos2[] = `pointPosition ($scaleData[0] + $scaleData[2])`;
      //Source and run distance procedure:
        source distance2Pts.mel;
        float $distance = distance2Pts($ptPos1,$ptPos2);
        $scale[$i] = ($distance + $addScale[$i]);
      }//Close loop.
    }//Close conditional.
    else {//Open conditional...
        string $scaleData[];
        tokenize ($scaling[0], ",", $scaleData);
        float $scaleX = $scaleData[0];
        float $scaleY = $scaleData[1];
        float $scaleZ = $scaleData[2];
        $scale[0] = ($scaleX + $addScale[0]);
        $scale[1] = ($scaleY + $addScale[1]);
        $scale[2] = ($scaleZ + $addScale[2]);
    }//Close conditional.
  //Convert string data to float data and add to increase size:
    xform -ws -s $scale[0] $scale[1] $scale[2] $iconName;
  //Clear selection:
    select -cl;
```

Once the icon is sized, the procedure moves it to the object specified in the $target argument by running a pointConstraint command. This command is a useful way of moving one object's center on top of another object's center, without the need to query any values. This method is very reliable, and works regardless of whether a node's channels have been frozen. After the script positions the icon, it deletes the constraint node. Lastly, the code runs a conditional to evaluate the $mirror argument, and if true, it duplicates the icon and moves it using the appropriate names for the right side of the body. Be aware that this mirror argument is not the same type of operation as mirroring joints, which flips the centers so that the rotation channels generate the same values for similar behavior. Instead, the mirror function of the cm_ processIcon procedure just duplicates the icon over to the other side. The code then adds the name of the new icon to the return array, and all the names are sent out of the procedure through the return statement.

```
    //Use point constraint to move icon to target object:
     string $tempCns[] = `pointConstraint -o 0 0 0 -w 1 -n "tempMvCns"
            $target $iconName`;
     delete -cn $tempCns[0];
     makeIdentity -apply true -t 1 -r 1 -s 1 -n 0 $iconName;
    //Create right icon based on mirror argument:
     string $returnNames[];
     if ($mirror == 1){//Open conditional...
       string $rtName = `substitute "lf" $iconName "rt"`;
       string $rtIconName[] = `duplicate -n $rtName $iconName`;
       string $rtTarget = `substitute "lf" $target "rt"`;
       string $tempCns[] = `pointConstraint -o 0 0 0 -w 1 -n "tempMvCns"
            $rtTarget $rtIconName[0]`;
       delete -cn $tempCns[0];
       makeIdentity -apply true -t 1 -r 1 -s 1 -n 0 $rtIconName[0];
       $returnNames = {$iconName,$rtIconName[0]};
     }//Close conditional.
     else {//Open conditional...
       $returnNames = {$iconName};
     }//Close conditional.
    return $returnNames;
}//Close procedure.
```

Step 3: Create All the Basic IK Rig Icons

The main global procedure in the CMaraffi_iconCreate script contains all the arguments required for running the local icon procedures. In addition, the cm_iconCreate procedure has an $iconType string argument that is evaluated in the main switch statement to choose a particular icon to create. Types can be specified as box, cone, arrow, sphere, or text. As in the cm_processIcon procedure, the $mirror argument determines whether the prefix is set as left or center, which is then input into the local procedure arguments. Each case in the switch statement runs the appropriate icon procedure, catches the resulting icon name in a variable, and then inputs the name into the cm_processIcon procedure. (To conserve space, not all the cases are shown here.) This procedure sizes, positions, and mirrors the icon, sending out all the final icon names from the return, which in turn is caught in an array and sent out of the main global procedure for parenting in other procedures.

```
//7. Main global procedure to create an icon:
global proc string[] cm_iconCreate (string $iconType,string $name,
       string $text,string $scaling[],float $addScale[],
       string $target,int $mirror){//Open procedure...
  //Use conditional to set the prefix and icon name:
```

```
      string $pfx;
      if ($mirror == 1)$pfx = "lf";
      else $pfx = "ct";
      string $iconName = ($pfx + $name + "_icon");
//Set return variables and arrays:
      string $returnName;
      string $returnNames[];
//Use switch statement to choose icon from argument type:
      switch ($iconType){//Open switch statement...
        //Create a box icon from a curve:
          case "box": {//Open case:
            $returnName = cm_boxIcon ($iconName);
            $returnNames = cm_processIcon ($returnName,$scaling,
                      $addScale,$target,$mirror);
          }//Close case.
          break;
        //Create a compound text icon:
          case "text": {//Open case:
            $returnName = cm_textIcon ($iconName,$text);
            $returnNames = cm_processIcon ($returnName,$scaling,
                      $addScale,$target,$mirror);
          }//Close case.
          break;
      }//Close switch statement.
//Clear selection:
      select -cl;
      return $returnNames;
}//Close procedure.
```

Step 4: Position the Pole Vector Icons

The second icon script, CMaraffi_basicIcons, has one local and one global procedure for creating all the basic IK rig icons. The local cm_vectorPos procedure finds the correct position for the icons that will become the Pole Vector controls on the knees and elbows. Remember that IK skeletons are created on a flat plane called the rotate plane, and that the RP solver allows you to control the twisting of the skeleton around that plane. For the Pole Vector icon to work well and to ensure that the skeleton does not move out of position when the constraint is applied, the icon must be positioned correctly. For instance, the knee icons should be placed beyond the front of the bended knee joint, while remaining in line with the rotate plane of the leg skeleton.

Looking at the cm_vectorPos procedure, you can see that it starts by using commands to find the right-side name for the controls. Since this procedure is intended to be used on the arms and legs, it assumes that left Pole Vector controls will always be mirrored. Next it runs a loop to create and position the Pole Vector icon. Although you can eyeball the placement of the icon when building the rig in the interface, when scripting the rig you should use a more automatic method for finding the correct position. The procedure contains a loop that creates two target locators for positioning both the left and right Pole Vector icons. The procedure does this by placing each target locator on a half-circle that is constrained to be aligned with the rotate plane of the appropriate skeleton. The main code starts by creating and constraining another locator to the axis of the rotate plane by running a pointConstraint command to the joints at the start and end of the IK skeleton. Point constraining to two target objects averages the position of the constrained object halfway between the targets. The constraint in the procedure places the locator directly on the middle of the green IK solver line going from the root to the end joint.

In the code, the half-circle is also point-constrained, only to the middle joint of the skeleton. Then an aimConstraint command is run to align the locator with the rotate plane. An aim constraint forces a single axis to point at a target object. The axis that is aim-constrained on the circle is the X axis, and the target is the locator constrained to the rotate plane. The result is that the arc of the circle is aligned correctly to the rotate plane. Lastly, the procedure creates another locator and places it halfway along the arc of the circle using a pathAnimation command with an uValue attribute setting of 0.5.

After the locator is placed on the circle, the connection between the locator and the path is deleted with the CBdeleteConnection Maya procedure. Whenever you use a Maya procedure in your scripts, make sure that you first source the file containing the procedure. After breaking the connection, the procedure deletes the circle and the original locator, and then returns the names of the locators for both sides of the body.

```
//1. Local procedure for positioning pole vector icons:
proc string[] cm_vectorPos (string $skelRoot,string $skelMid,
    string $skelEnd){//Open procedure...
  string $rtSkelRoot = `substitute "lf" $skelRoot "rt"`;
  string $rtSkelMid = `substitute "lf" $skelMid "rt"`;
  string $rtSkelEnd = `substitute "lf" $skelEnd "rt"`;
 //Create arrays of names containing skel names for lf and rt:
  string $skelRoots[] = {$skelRoot,$rtSkelRoot};
  string $skelMids[] = {$skelMid,$rtSkelMid};
  string $skelEnds[] = {$skelEnd,$rtSkelEnd};
 //Run loop to create locators on the rotate plane:
  string $returnNames[];
  int $i;
  for ($i = 0 ; $i < 2 ; $i++){//Open loop...
   //Temporarily turn off cycle check to prevent warning:
     cycleCheck -e off;
```

```
        //Create locator and constrain between root and end joints:
          string $tmpLoc1[] = `spaceLocator -p 0 0 0`;
          pointConstraint -o 0 0 0 -w 1 $skelRoots[$i] $skelEnds[$i]
                $tmpLoc1[0];
        //Create a large half circle and constrain to rotate plane:
          string $tmpCirc[] = `circle -c 0 0 0 -nr 0 1 0 -sw 180
                -r 12 -d 3 -s 8`;
          string $tmpCns[] = `pointConstraint -o 0 0 0 -w 1
                $skelMids[$i] $tmpCirc[0]`;
          aimConstraint -u 0 1 0 -aim 1 0 0 $tmpLoc1[0] $tmpCirc[0];
        //Create target locator and place halfway on path of circle:
          string $pfx;
          if ($i == 0) $pfx = "lf"; else $pfx = "rt";
          string $name = ($pfx + "VectTrgt_tmp");
          string $targetLoc[] = `spaceLocator -n $name -p 0 0 0`;
          $returnNames[$i] = $targetLoc[0];
          string $path = `pathAnimation -fm true -stu 0 -etu 0
                 -c $tmpCirc[0] $returnNames[$i]`;
          setAttr ($path + ".uValue") .5;
          select -cl;
      //Run procedure to delete connections, extra nodes, and circle:
          eval ("source generateChannelMenu");
          CBdeleteConnection ($returnNames[$i] + ".tx");
          CBdeleteConnection ($returnNames[$i] + ".ty");
          CBdeleteConnection ($returnNames[$i] + ".tz");
          delete $tmpLoc1[0] $tmpCirc[0];
          cycleCheck -e on;
      }//Close loop.
    //Return the names of the target locators for pole vectors:
      return $returnNames;
  }//Close procedure.
```

Step 5: Create All the Basic IK Rig Icons

The main global procedure, cm_basicIcons, creates all the icons for the basic rig. The procedure has one string array argument that expects the basic skeleton names, so the cm_basicSkels procedure must be run before this procedure runs. Both of these procedures will be run one after the other inside the CMaraffi_basicIkRig script covered later in this chapter in Exercise 3.3, "Creating the Basic IK Rig."

As usual, this global procedure starts by sourcing all necessary previous scripts, retrieves additional names from the FK rig file, declares strings for prefixes and print statements, and sets the rig namespace. Then the procedure creates each icon, starting with an arrow for the character or "Char" icon, which will be used to move the entire character in 3D space. In the code, the target node for positioning the character icon is the Reference or top node of the FK rig hierarchy, which places the icon at the base of the character's feet. The sizing for this icon is manually set to the default 1,1,1 scale values, with nothing added, as shown by the $iconScale and $addScale arrays. Once the sizing is set, the cm_iconCreate procedure is run, and the name of the icon is caught in an array to return at the end of the cm_basicIcons procedure.

All the other icons in the script are created in a similar manner, and so most will be skipped in this exercise. Make sure that you open the actual script to look at how they are created.

```
//2. Main global procedure for creating the basic rig icons:
global proc string[] cm_basicIcons (string $skelNames[])
{//Open procedure...
 //Source files containing local and global procs used for icons:
   eval ("source CMaraffi_iconCreate");
   eval ("source CMaraffi_processNames");
 //---------------------------------------------------------------
 //Run proc to access FK rig names from file:
   string $fkRigNames[] = cm_getNames("fkRig");
 //---------------------------------------------------------------
 //Set prefixes, joint names, and print strings:
   string $pfx0 = "ct"; string $pfx1 = "lf"; string $pfx2 = "rt";
   string $noTxt = "none";
   string $printIconNames = "Icons created with node names: \n";
 //---------------------------------------------------------------
 //Set rig namespace and create the icons:
   cm_setNamespace (1);
 //Character: Set all necessary names into variables:
   string $refNode = cm_returnName ($fkRigNames,"Reference","fk");
   string $charName = "Char";
 //Set size data for the icon:
   string $iconScale[] = {"1.0,1.0,1.0"};
   float $addScale[] = {0.0,0.0,0.0};
 //Run global proc to create icon:
   string $charIcon[] = cm_iconCreate
         ("arrow",$charName,$noTxt,$iconScale,$addScale,$refNode,0);
 //Print name of the icon:
   print $printIconNames; print $charIcon; print " \n";
```

Creating the knee icons involve running the cm_vectorPos procedure for finding the correct Pole Vector position. Running the Pole Vector procedure requires finding the middle joint name on the leg skeleton, so select and pickWalk commands are run, and then the selected joint is listed. Before the cm_iconCreate procedure runs, notice that the cone icons are being scaled slightly smaller than the default; after the procedure runs, some transforms are done to the components to better orient the cone icons to point at the knees. The actual Pole Vector constraint won't be added until the basic rig script is run.

```
//Knees: Set all necessary names into variables:
   string $lfLegRoot = cm_returnName ($skelNames,"lfLeg","root");
   select -r $lfLegRoot;
   pickWalk -d "down";
   string $child[] = `ls -sl`;
   select -cl;
   string $lfKneeJt = $child[0];
   string $lfLegEnd = cm_returnName ($skelNames,"lfLeg","end");
   string $kneesName = "Knee";
//Set size data for the icon:
   string $iconScale[] = {"0.8,1.75,0.8"};;
   float $addScale[] = {0.0,0.0,0.0};
//Run local proc to get target for pole vectors:
   string $kneeTgts[] = cm_vectorPos ($lfLegRoot,$lfKneeJt,$lfLegEnd);
//Run global proc to create icon:
   string $kneeIcons[] = cm_iconCreate
        ("cone",$kneesName,$noTxt,$iconScale,$addScale,$kneeTgts[0],1);
//Delete target locator:
   delete $kneeTgts[0] $kneeTgts[1];
//Rotate the components so the cones point toward character:
   rotate -r -os -90.0 0 0 ($kneeIcons[0] + ".cv[0:21]");
   rotate -r -os -90.0 0 0 ($kneeIcons[1] + ".cv[0:21]");
//Freeze transforms:
   makeIdentity -apply true -t 1 -r 1 -s 1 -n 0 $kneeIcons[0];
   makeIdentity -apply true -t 1 -r 1 -s 1 -n 0 $kneeIcons[1];
//Print name of the icon:
   print $printIconNames; print $kneeIcons; print " \n";
```

This procedure ends in a similar manner to the cm_basicSkels procedure: by setting the namespace back to root, placing the names of all the icons in an array, and printing and returning the names. Again, this code will not be shown here to conserve space.

Building the Basic Biped Rig

This section shows how to group and parent all the skeletons and icons into a rig hierarchy. The rigging process expands the use of group nodes to facilitate the parenting process, create animation pivots, and clean up the rig interface.

In addition to parenting, the rig will also utilize constraints to make node connections. Lastly, this section examines in detail the main basic rig script that runs all the other scripts in this chapter.

Constructing the rig hierarchy in the interface will give you a good view of the relationship between nodes, because you'll do the parenting directly in the Hypergraph. Scripting the rig, however, requires more planning and organization, because there's a lot of data to manage. Learning how to do both will further your understanding of the entire rigging process.

Creating the Rig Hierarchy in the Hypergraph

Creating the basic IK rig hierarchy differs from how you created the FK rig hierarchy, mainly due to the many constraints on the nodes. These consist of standard node constraints like point, orient, and aim constraints, as well as skeleton-specific constraints like IK solver and Pole Vector constraints. These constraints add a layer of complexity to the rig because they connect nodes that are not directly parented, allowing for control nodes to be added as parents instead. Sometimes these control nodes are icons that are directly animated, and sometimes they are group nodes that are indirectly animated.

The hierarchy covered in this chapter is still pretty basic, however, with only a minimum amount of constraints and control nodes being inserted. In later chapters you will refine the rig by adding more skeletons, constraints, and control nodes. As the complexity of the rig increases, the controls become more robust, flexible, and more efficient to animate. Think of it as the difference between driving an antique manual transmission automobile and a modern automatic sports car. Both will take you where you want to go, but the one with more robust technology under the hood will get you there faster, with less effort, and in cool style.

PREPARING TO CREATE THE BIPED RIG

The easiest way to parent in the Hypergraph is to simply drag the nodes on top of other nodes using the middle mouse button. Make sure that Freeform Layout in the Options > Layout menu bar is turned on so that you can manipulate the nodes as you go along. It is generally a good practice to keep the default organization of parent nodes above child nodes when building a rig in the Hypergraph. This convention makes it easy to see the parenting relationship between the nodes. If you don't want to take the time to build the hierarchy manually, then simply open up the basicIkRig.mb scene file to examine the finished hierarchy in the Hypergraph.

You'll begin the parenting process with all the skeletons and icons already in place, either after creating them manually or by running the scripts covered in this chapter. The new skeletons and icons will be sitting loose in the Hypergraph, unconnected to any other nodes, and positioned to the right of the FK rig hierarchy. Before creating the main rig hierarchy, parent all the FK rig geometry, such as the polygon bones and eyeballs, under the appropriate new skeleton joints. You want the polygon bones to move with the joints in your new IK rig, to more easily see how the controls are working before the rig is bound to the skin.

To parent the existing FK rig geometry to the IK rig skeletons:

1. In the Hypergraph, starting with the left leg skeleton, drag the lfFemur_polySkel and lfTibFib_polySkel close to the left leg nodes. Then middle-mouse-drag the femur bone onto the root joint of the leg, and drag the tibia-fibula bone onto the middle or knee joint.

2. Rotate the left leg joints to see the polygon bones move. In the same way, continue parenting the rest of the polygon bones to the appropriate skeleton joints, testing them by rotating the joints afterward.

3. Parent any grouped polygon bones, such as the vertebrae and hand bones, under the main joints that move that part of the body (see **FIGURE 3.13**).

FIGURE 3.13 *Parent the groups of polygon bones, such as the backbone vertebrae, under the closest Maya joint in the basic IK rig.*

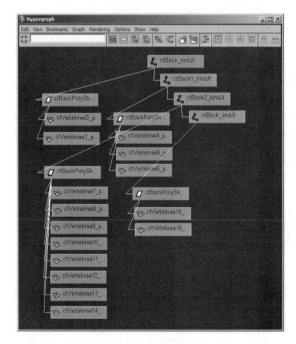

Simply drag the group node parent onto the joints instead of the individual bones. Parent the center group for the eyeball geometry, ctEyes_fkGroup, under the same head joint you parent the skull polygon under.

As you add more advanced controls in later chapters, you will re-parent these polygon bones under additional joints. Also, since the polygon bones will never be animated, it is not necessary to ever freeze the transformations of the bones. Freezing is important, however, when parenting the icons in the next few sections.

CREATING THE LOWER BODY HIERARCHY

You will now begin parenting the IK rig skeletons under icons and group nodes. You'll notice as you go along that two or more group nodes are inserted between many nodes in the hierarchy. This is done for three reasons: to create pivots that will facilitate controls added later through channel connections; to create a couple of pad nodes to manipulate the channel values of important nodes in the rig; and to prevent bones from being displayed between two parented skeletons that are not positioned close to each other. It is a function in Maya that parented joints always display a connecting bone. But inserting two nodes between the parented nodes overrides this function and prevents the interface from being cluttered with crossing bones.

After parenting control objects, especially icons and group nodes that will be animated, check the Channel Box and freeze their transforms if you notice any values in the channels (see **FIGURE 3.14**).

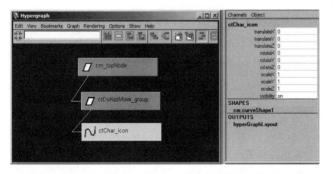

FIGURE 3.14 *When parenting nodes, such as icons in the rig, be sure to freeze the child nodes after parenting if channel values change. This freezing is unnecessary for the Char icon, because it sits right on top of the DoNotMove node.*

Numbers may reevaluate in the channels because the parent node becomes the new world axis for the child node, causing the channel values to change if the child is not directly on top of the parent. Since this always occurs when you parent nodes in Maya, it is a standard practice to parent first, and then always freeze the child afterward. The only time this practice is not advisable is when the child is an IK skeleton node. You also want to avoid freezing the top node of an entire hierarchy, as it will propagate down all the nodes, and could break any IK nodes in the branch.

To parent the lower body skeletons and icons:

1. Start by grouping the Char, or character, icon, and name the parent group node ctDoNotMove. This node should remain at the center of the 3D world space, and should never be animated. You will use this node to parent any nodes that are constrained and that should never be transformed manually.

2. Parent the feet icon under the character icon and the individual leg icons under the feet icon. Each leg icon is parented over the appropriate foot skeleton, leg IK handle, and knee icon.

3. Parent the torso icon under the character icon to create a second branch that will contain all the controls for the rest of the biped rig.

4. Insert a couple of group nodes between the character and torso icons, called ctTorsoAuto0 and ctTorsoAuto1. Position these group nodes right on top of the torso icon and freeze them before re-parenting the torso icon. All the channels on these nodes should be at their default frozen values.

5. Then parent the torso icon over the hip icon, and over the root of the four-joint backbone skeleton, to create two branches for the torso controls.

6. Again, insert two group nodes between the torso and hip icons, naming them ctHipsAuto0 and ctHipsAuto1. Position the group nodes on top of the hip pivot, and freeze them.

7. As a last step, group all the hip skeletons and the two leg skeleton roots, name the group node ctHipsPad, and parent the entire group under the hip icon.

This completes parenting the lower body hierarchy in the Hypergraph (see **FIGURE 3.15**).

8. Select some of the icons and move them around to see how they transform the skeletons. Moving the feet icon moves both feet and legs together, while lifting the individual leg boxes moves each foot and leg separately. Transforming the torso icon moves the hips, upper legs, and backbone together to make the character crouch. Notice that moving the torso bends the knees without the feet moving, because the feet are on a separate branch of the hierarchy. Rotating the hip icon with the knees bent causes the hips and upper legs to swing.

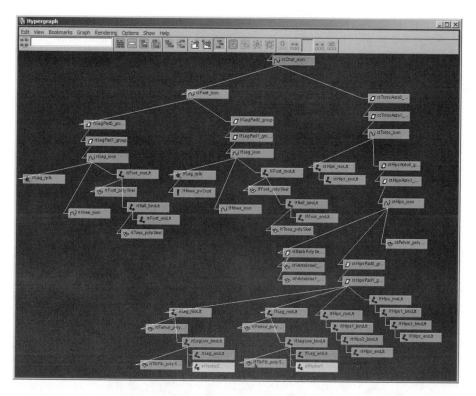

FIGURE 3.15 *Start building the basic IK rig by parenting the lower body nodes, which consist of the controls for the feet, legs, and hips.*

ADDING THE UPPER BODY HIERARCHY

You'll finish the basic rig by adding the upper body controls. The backbone skeleton should move all the skeletons in the shoulders, neck, head, and arms.

To begin parenting all the upper body skeletons and icons:

1. Create two group nodes between the skeletons to prevent bones from being displayed, and name them ctBackPad0 and ctBackPad1. Place the two group nodes on top of and parented under the backbone end joint.

Many skeletons will be parented under the backbone end joint. Adding the group nodes here keeps the rig structure from becoming cluttered with bones crossing over one another in the upper torso.

2. Parent the root joints for the clavicle, scapula, and neck skeletons under the second backbone pad group, or BackPad1.

3. Create another set of double group nodes for the shoulders, named ctShoulders0 and ctShoulders1, and parent the shoulders group under BackPad1 as well.

4. To finish the neck branch of the hierarchy, parent the head icon under the neck end joint, and the head and jaw skeleton roots under the head icon. This creates an FK rig setup through the backbone, neck, and head hierarchy (see **FIGURE 3.16**).

FIGURE 3.16 *Continue parenting nodes up the torso to create the controls for the backbone, neck, and head.*

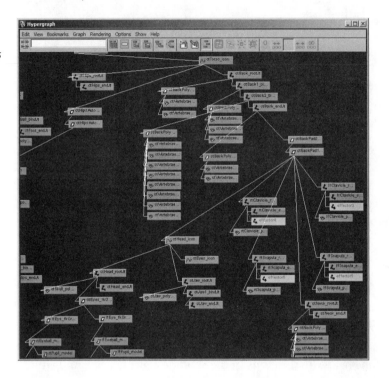

COMPLETING PARENTING OF THE BASIC RIG HIERARCHY

Now you'll continue parenting the nodes in the shoulders and arms to complete the upper body hierarchy of the basic rig. The IK arm branches of the hierarchy start at the shoulders with the clavicle and scapula skeletons. The clavicle IK handles will be the main individual shoulder controls, with group nodes inserted to create additional functionality.

To parent the nodes in the shoulders, arms, and hands:

1. First create two group nodes to place between the shoulder groups and clavicle IK, naming the new groups lfClavAuto0 and lfClavAuto1. These nodes will be used to automatically rotate the clavicles when the arm is raised, so place them on top of the clavicle root joints. Make lfClavAuto0 the child of ctShoulders1, and the left clavicle IK handle the child of lfClavAuto1.

2. Each left clavicle IK is parented over the appropriate scapula IK and the root joint of the arm skeleton. Repeat steps 1 and 2 on the right side to create the right shoulder hierarchy.

3. Create a couple of group nodes for the arm, named lfArmPad0 and lfArmPad1, and place them at the arm root. Make the lfArmPad0 node child to ctBackPad1, and parent both the left arm icon and the left elbow icon under lfArmPad1. This will make it easier to set limits on the arm icons, by making the parent node located at the shoulder. When the arm icon moves, for instance, the translation values will generate in relation to the position of the arm root.

4. To finish the arm branches of the hierarchy, parent the left IK handle under the left arm icon, and the left hand skeleton under the end of the left arm skeleton. This FK lower arm setup ensures that the hand stays oriented to the forearm as the arm icon is moved.

5. To facilitate rotating the hand, insert a couple of group nodes between the end of the arm and the root of the hand. Name the nodes lfWristTurn0 and lfWristTurn1. You will use these nodes as pivots for rotating the hand at the wrist.

6. Repeat steps 3 through 5 on the right side of the rig to create the right arm hierarchy. **FIGURE 3.17** shows the completed hierarchy of the basic IK rig.

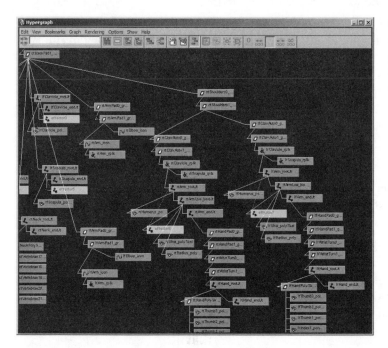

FIGURE 3.17 *Finish the basic IK rig hierarchy by parenting the nodes for the shoulders, arms, and hands.*

In step 5, separating rotations onto parented nodes creates a rotation order, which will reduce a common 3D rotation problem called Gimbel locking. This problem can occur whenever you animate the rotation of a node in multiple axes, especially if the rotation approaches 90 degrees. Creating a rotation order through parenting, or by setting it in the Attribute Editor, assigns a priority level to the different rotations. You should assign the parent node the broader rotation, and the child node the smaller rotation. In the case of the hand, the up and down wrist rotation should be done on lfWristTurn0, while the side-to-side wrist rotation should be done on lfWristTurn1.

ADDING CONSTRAINTS TO THE EYES AND LIMBS

To incorporate another layer of controls and complexity, you'll add constraints to the eyes, head, and hips. Constraints are one-way connections between like attributes on separate objects that force the constrained objects to follow the movements of the target objects. Constrained objects are indicated by blue channels. Always Shift-select the target object, and then the constrained object, before choosing the Constraint command in the Constraint menu.

To connect nodes through constraints in the hierarchy:

1. Use aim constraints to create some eye controls on the eye geometry. The eye icon is a cone with two locators as children. Position the locators and add constraints as follows:

■ Position the locators in front of each eye. Each locator is the target for aim-constraining the Z axis of the parent group node of the individual eye geometry. To set the aim constraint in the interface, Shift-select the locator and the group node, and choose Constrain > Aim ❏. In the dialog box, change the Aim Vector from X (set field to 0 value) to Z (set field to 1 value), and click Add. This constraint will force the eyeball to always point at the locator.

■ If desired, place a reverse aim constraint on the cone to force it to always point at the ctEyes group node. You reverse the aim constraint in the options, by using a –1 value in Z as the Aim Vector. This constraint makes it easy to see where the eyes are always pointing, even if you cannot see the eyeballs themselves.

2. In the head and hip areas, use point constraints to shift the head and hip icons when skeletons rotate. You apply the point constraint to the head icon so that you can use the FK neck rotation to shift the head from side-to-side and forward to backward, without any rotation on the head. Simply Shift-select the neck end joint and head icon, and choose Constrain > Point. Once the constraint is made, all translation of the head should only come from rotating the neck, not translating the head icon directly.

3. Lastly, add Pole Vector constraints to the elbows and knees of the character. To set the Pole Vector constraint on the left knee, for instance, simply Shift-select the left knee icon and the left leg IK handle, and choose Constrain > Pole Vector. In addition, you can again add reverse aim constraints to make the cone icons point at the limbs. Set the aim target as the second limb joints on the arm and leg skeletons (see **FIGURE 3.18**).

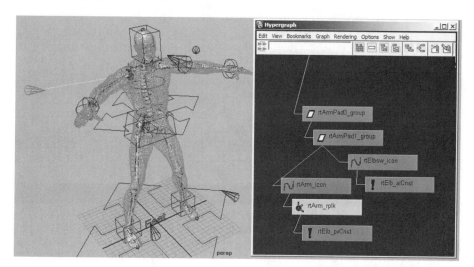

FIGURE 3.18 *Add a layer of complexity to the rig by connecting channels, such as using a Pole Vector constraint to control the twisting of the arms with the elbow icons.*

Preparing to Script the Basic Rig Hierarchy

When scripting something as complex as a character rig, which requires the interaction of multiple procedures in multiple scripts, it is a good idea to create a flow chart of how the scripts relate to each other and when they run in the rigging process. This type of chart is often roughed out in the early planning stages of the scripting process, and then refined as the scripts are created. As an example, **FIGURE 3.19** shows how all the basic IK rig scripts relate to each other, how information flows through the scripts, and where they are being run in the scripting process. Understanding this organization of the basic scripts is critical for progressing to the advanced scripts in future chapters.

On the basic rig, there are many fundamental rigging tasks, such as parenting and freezing, which are performed repetitively when building the rig in the interface. To script such tasks, it helps to organize a few operations into small local procedures. These procedures are very task-specific, and can be combined very efficiently throughout the rigging scripts. This is done in the CMaraffi_runLocals script, which contains many such local procedures for basic rigging tasks. To ensure that these local procedures can be accessed in all the rigging scripts, they are run through a `switch` statement in a global procedure at the end of the same script file. You will examine this file, as well as the main CMaraffi_basicIkRig file where the procedures are run, in the following exercise.

FIGURE 3.19 *To help organize the scripting process, create flow charts that show how scripts relate to each other and how data flows through the scripts. This chart shows the relationships between all the basic IK rig scripts.*

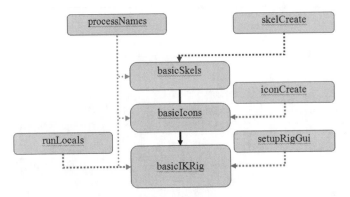

EXERCISE 3.3: SCRIPTING A BASIC IK RIG

This exercise examines the two main scripts that create the basic IK biped rig: CMaraffi_runLocals and CMaraffi_basicIkRig. Open each script, and make sure that you understand all the main concepts, and how the scripts are now working together to create the basic rig.

Step 1: Examine the CMaraffi_runLocals Script

The CMaraffi_runLocals script contains a series of local procedures that are run through the main global procedure at the end of the script. The `cm_runLocals` procedure incorporates a `switch` statement to choose and run the desired local procedure. A similar technique was used in previous scripts, but this time more data is being processed through the arguments and return statements. In many cases, data must be converted to different types to move it through both the local and global procedures successfully.

Start by examining the local procedures in this script. Each local procedure does a few particular tasks in the same order as they would be done in the interface. These include creating groups, moving and orienting nodes using constraints, parenting, renaming, querying a child joint's name in a skeleton, and querying the 3D position of an object or point. Many of these procedures also have arguments that freeze transformations and arguments for mirroring the operation to the other side of the rig. Because the main operations in these procedures are fairly basic and repeat many of the same argument types, only the first two will be examined in detail here.

The first local procedure, cm_doubleGrp, creates two parented group nodes, with arguments for parenting the groups into the hierarchy and mirroring the operation. The procedure itself runs two group commands, using the same names but adding 0 to the first name and 1 to the second. Both commands also incorporate a -p, or parent, flag, using the $parent argument on the first group, and then catching and running its name in the second group's parent flag. The result is two parented group nodes sitting on top of each other and parented into the rig hierarchy. If the mirror argument is turned on, then the process is repeated with right-side names for the parent and groups. Once created, the groups can be moved using the next local procedure in the script.

```
//1. Local proc creates two group nodes to use as pads or pivots:
proc string[] cm_doubleGrp (string $pfx,string $name,
              string $parent,int $mirror){//Open procedure...
  //Create two parented group nodes on top of each other:
    string $sfx = "_group";
    string $groupTop = `group -n ($pfx + $name + "0" + $sfx)
          -em -p $parent`;
    string $groupBot = `group -n ($pfx + $name + "1" + $sfx)
          -em -p $groupTop`;
    print ("Double groups created with names: " +
          $groupTop + "," + $groupBot + "\n");
    select -cl;
    string $returnGroups[] = {$groupTop,$groupBot};
  //Mirror option:
    string $rtGrpTop;
    string $rtGrpBot;
    if ($mirror == 1){//Open conditional...
      string $rtTopName = `substitute $pfx $groupTop "rt"`;
      string $rtBotName = `substitute $pfx $groupBot "rt"`;
      $rtParent = `substitute $pfx $parent "rt"`;
      $rtGrpTop = `group -n $rtTopName -em -p $rtParent`;
      $rtGrpBot = `group -n $rtBotName -em -p $rtGrpTop`;
      print ("Double groups created with names: " +
            $rtGrpTop + "," + $rtGrpBot + "\n");
      select -cl;
    }//Close conditional.
    string $rtGroups[] = {$rtGrpTop,$rtGrpBot};
    appendStringArray($returnGroups, $rtGroups, 2);
    return $returnGroups;
}//Close procedure.
```

The `cm_nodeMover` procedure uses a point constraint to transform a node on top of another node, and then deletes the constraint—a more reliable way of moving objects than querying transforms. The default procedure operation is to run a `pointConstraint` command, with an `$orient` argument being evaluated to specify running an `orientConstraint` command, which sets the `$constrained` object's rotation channels to follow the `$target` object. The orient constraint can be useful for orienting group node pads parented over controls that must have their channels generate numbers in a specific way when they're animated. Setting keys on attributes registers the orientations of the parent nodes, affecting the child values, which can cause unpredictable rotations on some controls. You will see the `cm_nodeMover` procedure used extensively for this purpose in the advanced rigging scripts.

Notice that this procedure also has a `$freeze` argument that, when turned on, runs a `makeIdentity` command to freeze the transformations of the constrained node after moving. This is used when moving group nodes that are already parented into the hierarchy. The `$mirror` argument is typical of how operations have been duplicated to the right side in other scripts, using the `substitute` command to determine the right names, and running the operation again on the other nodes. Mirroring is done the same way on all the other local procedures in this script.

```
//2. Local proc uses constraints to move and orient nodes:
proc cm_nodeMover (string $target,string $constrained,
    int $orient,int $freeze,int $mirror){//Open procedure...
//Move nodes with constraints, and then delete constraints:
  string $tempCns[] = `pointConstraint -o 0 0 0 -w 1 -n "tempMvCns"
        $target $constrained`;
  delete -cn $tempCns[0];
  if ($orient == 1) {//Open conditional...
    string $tempCns[] = `orientConstraint -o 0 0 0 -w 1
        -n "tempMvCns" $target $constrained`;
    delete -cn $tempCns[0];
  }//Close conditional.
  if ($freeze == 1) makeIdentity -a 1 -t 1 -r 1 -s 1 $constrained;
//Mirror option:
  string $rtTarget;
  string $rtConstrained;
  if ($mirror == 1){//Open conditional...
    string $pfx = "lf";
    $rtTarget = `substitute $pfx $target "rt"`;
    $rtConstrained = `substitute $pfx $constrained "rt"`;
    string $tempCns[] = `pointConstraint -o 0 0 0 -w 1 -n "tempMvCns"
        $rtTarget $rtConstrained`;
    delete -cn $tempCns[0];
    if ($orient == 1) {//Open conditional...
```

```
        string $tempCns[] = `orientConstraint -o 0 0 0 -w 1
                -n "tempMvCns" $rtTarget $rtConstrained`;
        delete -cn $tempCns[0];
    }//Close conditional.
    if ($freeze == 1) makeIdentity -a 1 -t 1 -r 1 -s 1 $rtConstrained;
}//Close conditional.
```

Step 2: Run the Local Procedures through a Global Procedure

The last procedure in the CMaraffi_runLocals script is the main global procedure that runs all the previous local procedures. Essentially, the local procedures are run through this procedure, so they must conform to its parameters, especially in regard to argument and return statement types. The cm_runLocals global procedure has two string arguments. The first $proc argument is used to specify the local procedure that should be run in the switch statement of the global procedure. The second string array argument allows the user to enter all the required local procedure arguments as strings that can later be converted if needed. The main body of the cm_runLocals procedure is a switch statement that compares the incoming $proc argument with the case statements, and runs the appropriate local procedure with arguments if they match. Notice that the return statement for the global procedure is also a string array, which likewise requires that any local procedures with return statements must be of the same string array type.

The advantage to using the global procedure to run the local procedures is that it makes them available to all the rigging scripts, but without making them global, which would require keeping all the local procedures in memory. On the other hand, the limitation of running the local procedures in this way is that the arguments and return statements must either be strings, or converted to and from strings within the local procedure. This is possible because strings can be composed of numbers and letters.

```
//7. Main global proc for running local procedures using switch:
global proc string[] cm_runLocals (string $proc,string $args[])
{//Open procedure...
    print ("Running local proc cm_" + $proc + " by cm_runLocals.\n");
    string $returnLocal[];
    switch ($proc) {//Open switch statement...
    case "doubleGrp"://1.
        $returnLocal = cm_doubleGrp($args[0],$args[1],$args[2],$args[3]);
      break;
    case "nodeMover"://2.
        cm_nodeMover($args[0],$args[1],$args[2],$args[3],$args[4]);
      break;
    case "parenter"://3.
```

```
            cm_parenter($args[0],$args[1],$args[2],$args[3]);
        break;
    case "reNamer"://4.
            $returnLocal = cm_reNamer($args[0],$args[1],$args[2]);
        break;
    case "getChild"://5.
            $returnLocal = cm_getChild($args[0]);
        break;
    case "getPos"://6.
            $returnLocal = cm_getPos($args[0],$args[1]);
        break;
    case "setColor"://7.
            $returnLocal = cm_setColor($args[0]);
        break;
    }//Close switch statement.
 //Return array of names specified in argument:
    return $returnLocal;
}//Close procedure.
```

Step 3: Run All the Scripts to Create the Basic IK Rig

The CMaraffi_basicIkRig script runs all the previous procedures to create the basic
IK rig. The script starts out with a cm_aimVector local procedure that will be used to
more easily create the aim and Pole Vector constraints on the eyes and IK limbs. The
arguments allow you to specify whether you want to create just an aim constraint, or
a Pole Vector constraint with an aim constraint. The extra combined constraints are
used to make the elbow and knee icons control the limbs, while also making the icons
point at the limbs. Since this procedure is pretty standard, it will not be shown here to
conserve space. However, make sure that you look at it in the actual script so that you
understand how the procedure works.

The main cm_basicIkRig global procedure in the script has no arguments, as all data
needed to create the basic IK rig will be retrieved from the environment or generated
within the procedure. This technique also makes it easier to run the procedure through
the setup GUI by simply sourcing the script when you click the GUI button. The procedure
starts by sourcing all the scripts necessary to get names, create skeletons and icons, and
run the local rigging procedures. Then the next section of code runs the cm_getNames
procedure to retrieve names from the FK rig script, and runs the cm_basicSkels and
cm_basicIcons global procedures to create and catch the names of all the skeletons and
icons needed to build the IK rig. By running these procedures inside the cm_basicIkRig
procedure, all the names are easily available for use in the parenting process.

```
//2. Main global procedure for creating the basic rig:
global proc string[] cm_basicIkRig (){//Open procedure...
```

```
//Source files with procedures needed to create the basic IK rig:
   eval ("source CMaraffi_basicSkels");
   eval ("source CMaraffi_basicIcons");
   eval ("source CMaraffi_runLocals");
   eval ("source CMaraffi_processNames");
//----------------------------------------------------------------
//Run procs to get FK names, and create basic rig components:
   string $fkRigNames[] = cm_getNames("fkRig");
   print "Create the the skeletons for the basic IK rig:\n";
   string $skelNames[] = cm_basicSkels();
   print "-------------------------------------------------------\n";
   print "Create the the icons for the basic IK rig:\n";
   string $iconNames[] = cm_basicIcons($skelNames);
   print "-------------------------------------------------------\n";
```

Step 4: Parent the FK Rig Polygons and Groups under the IK Skeletons

The main parenting part of the cm_basicIkRig procedure is divided into two sections: parenting polygon bones under skeleton joints, and then building the main rig hierarchy while inserting group nodes. The first section starts out by using the cm_returnName procedure to retrieve and store the names of the foot skeletons and polygon bones into string variables. Notice that the cm_runLocals global procedure is used throughout this section to run the cm_getChild local procedure for finding the name of obscure joints like the ball of the foot. Once the names of the nodes are set into memory, the cm_runLocals procedure is run again to parent the polygon bones under the foot joints. This is done on both sides of the body by turning on the mirror argument in the cm_parenter local procedure. If you cannot remember how the local rigging procedures work, open the CMaraffi_runLocals script and look over them again.

The rest of this section parents the polygon bones to the skeleton joints in the exact same way, so the entire code isn't included in this exercise example. The only variation is to run loops to reduce repetitive parenting of the same bone types, such as when parenting many backbone vertebrae.

```
//1. Set namespace and parent skeleton and FK components(polys):
//Note! Freezing not advisable on polygon bones.
   cm_setNamespace (1);
//Feet Skels and Polys: Set all necessary names into variables:
   string $lfFootRoot = cm_returnName ($skelNames,"lfFoot","root");
   string $lfFootPoly = cm_returnName ($fkRigNames,"lfFoot","poly");
   string $lfFootBall[] = cm_runLocals("getChild",{$lfFootRoot});
   string $lfToesPoly = cm_returnName ($fkRigNames,"lfToes","poly");
//Parent and rename nodes using local procs:
```

```
    cm_runLocals("parenter",{$lfFootRoot,$lfFootPoly,"1","0"});
    cm_runLocals("parenter",{$lfFootBall[0],$lfToesPoly,"1","0"});
    string $footBalls[] = cm_runLocals
            ("reNamer",{$lfFootBall[0],"lfBall_bindJt","1"});
  //Print check:
    print "Feet skels and polys are parented.\n";
```

Step 5: Create the Main Rig Hierarchy

The second section of code in the `cm_basicIkRig` procedure parents and groups all the main rig components to build the rig hierarchy. The parenting is done in the exact same way as shown previously in the interface, starting in the lower body and going through the upper body. Each section retrieves the necessary names, creates groups if required, parents the nodes, and then constrains the nodes if required. Much of the process is achieved by running local procedures like `cm_doubeGrp` and `cm_nodeMover` through the `cm_runLocals` global procedure. While looking through the code, notice that although most of the parenting and constraints are done through these custom procedures, occasionally others are done with straight MEL commands. When writing code, you choose which method is the most efficient for each application. In these cases, the custom procedures are not suitable, and MEL commands should be used.

Since the code for each part of the body is very similar, only a small portion will be shown here.

```
//2. Create groups and parent all nodes into the basic rig hierarchy:
 //Character-DoNotMove: Create empty group used for parenting constrained:
    string $charIcon = cm_returnName ($iconNames,"Char","icon");
    string $doNotMoveGrp = `group -n ($pfx0 + "DoNotMove" + $sfxGrp)
                -em -p $topNode`;
 //Parent the Character icon under DoNotMove group and freeze:
    cm_runLocals("parenter",{$doNotMoveGrp,$charIcon,"0","1"});
    //-----------------------------------------------------------------
 //Legs-Feet Rig: Set names:
    string $feetIcon = cm_returnName ($iconNames,"Feet","icon");
    string $lfLegIcon = cm_returnName ($iconNames,"lfLeg","icon");
    string $lfLegIK = cm_returnName ($skelNames,"lfLeg","rpIk");
    string $lfKneeIcon = cm_returnName ($iconNames,"lfKnee","icon");
    string $legGrpName = "LegPad";
    string $kneeGrpName = "KneePad";
 //Create groups for legs, and transform:
    string $legPads[] = cm_runLocals
            ("doubleGrp",{$pfx1,$legGrpName,$feetIcon,"1"});
    cm_runLocals ("nodeMover",{$lfLegRoot,$legPads[0],"0","1","1"});
 //Create groups for knees, and transform:
```

```
    string $lfKneePads[] = cm_runLocals
        ("doubleGrp",{$pfx1,$kneeGrpName,$lfLegIcon,"1"});
  cm_runLocals ("nodeMover",{$lfKneeIcon,$lfKneePads[0],"0","1","1"});
 //Parent and freeze the icons and IK for the feet, legs, and knees:
  cm_runLocals("parenter",{$charIcon,$feetIcon,"0","1"});
  cm_runLocals("parenter",{$legPads[1],$lfLegIcon,"1","1"});
  cm_runLocals("parenter",{$lfLegIcon,$lfFootRoot,"1","1"});
  cm_runLocals("parenter",{$lfLegIcon,$lfLegIK,"1","1"});
  cm_runLocals("parenter",{$lfKneePads[1],$lfKneeIcon,"1","1"});
 //Constrain knees using aim and pole vector constraints:
  float $aimVect[] = {0,0,-1};
  cm_aimVector ("Knee",$lfKneeIcon,$lowLegs[0],$aimVect,1,$lfLegIK,1);
```

Step 6: Run Basic IK Rig Procedure and Print Rig Names to File

The cm_basicIkRig procedure ends by listing and sorting the entire hierarchy from the top node. This process was also done previously with the FK rig hierarchy to use the names in all the basic rigging scripts. After the cm_basicIkRig procedure closes, the procedure is run at the end of the script to create the rig and catch the names in a $basicRigNames array. Then the cm_printNames global procedure is run to print all the names to the command line and to a file named basicRig. It is good debugging technique to print the names after the procedure is run, rather than inside the procedure, to make sure that all the names return correctly. See the actual script for additional formatting at the end to edit the next buttons in the setup GUI to be enabled, and to print that the script is done.

```
//List and sort all node names in the rig hierarchy:
   string $rigHierarchy[] = cm_processNames ($topNode,0,"none");
 //Return the top node name of the rig:
   return $rigHierarchy;
}//Close procedure.
//*********************************************************
print "cm_basicIkRig global proc is now in Maya's memory.\n";
//*********************************************************
//Run procedure to create the basic biped rig:
print "Running basic IK rig procedure:\n";
string $basicRigNames[] = cm_basicIkRig();
print "Basic Rig created!\n";
print "-----------------------------------------------------\n";
print "cm_basicIkRig proc returns the following rig names: \n";
//Run procedure to print return array to file and command line:
cm_printNames($basicRigNames,1,"basicRig");
```

WRAPPING UP

This completes construction of the basic IK rig through the interface and through scripting. By now, you should have a good understanding of the fundamental techniques that are used to create a rig in the interface, including creating skeletons and icons, as well as connecting nodes through grouping, parenting, and constraining. You have also learned how to script the entire process.

In the next chapter, you will use all the same rigging and scripting techniques again to create advanced rigging controls, plus you will learn additional techniques for making more complex IK systems and channel connections.

10 IMPORTANT POINTS TO REMEMBER FROM THIS CHAPTER

- IK uses a constraint called a solver to inversely rotate the skeleton joints in one axis when a separate IK handle is moved.

- Skeletons with standard IK must be planar, and must have a preferred angle set to be able to bend.

- IK produces a secondary motion accessed by manipulating the rotate plane.

- Do not freeze any skeleton components that are connected to IK.

- Icons are made from curves to make it easy to select rig components, while not showing up in a render of the character.

- Single icons can be made from multiple curves by parenting the shape nodes under a single transform node.

- Inserting two parented group nodes into the rig hierarchy is useful for creating pivot points for automatic controls, manipulating channel values, or keeping the interface from becoming cluttered with the display of unnecessary skeleton bones.

- Since the parent affects the child node channel values in a hierarchy, it is better to freeze the child after parenting, not before.

- Constraints add complexity to a rig because they connect nodes through channels, but otherwise allow the nodes to be separate in the hierarchy.

- To save memory, run small task-oriented local procedures through a global procedure; however, the arguments and return statement will have limitations.

4

Adding Advanced Rig Controls

THIS CHAPTER SHOWS you how to take the basic IK biped rig that you just created in the last chapter to an advanced level by adding skeletons and upgrading all the controls for the major body areas. This involves writing modular scripts that incorporate all the rigging and coding techniques previously covered in this book, while enhancing the process with new techniques for connecting and refining attribute connections. By the end of this chapter, you will have a fully functional character rig with many advanced controls, ready to bind and animate.

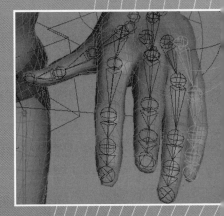

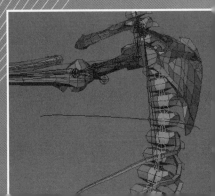

Enhancing the IK Limb Controls

This section focuses on upgrading the basic IK rig arm and leg controls to have a variety of new skeletons and attribute connections. You'll add both FK and IK skeletons to improve skin deformations, and add custom channels to allow a greater range of icon controls, especially in the hands and feet. The process will be first shown in the interface, and then reviewed in the advanced scripts.

Creating an Advanced Arm Rig

Rigging the advanced arm involves creating skeletons in the upper arm, fore-arm, and fingers. Many of the FK joints in these skeletons will be connected to custom channels that you'll create on the arm icons. New methods for creating and connecting channels will be introduced, such as math expressions and setting driven keys. These techniques will allow you to create a variety of custom controls on the rig, like channels on the arm icon that drive finger rotations (see **FIGURE 4.1**). Once you've created all the new controls, you'll see how to clean up the channels so they are ready to animate.

FIGURE 4.1 *Rigging the advanced arm involves creating skeletons in the forearm, hand, and fingers, and then driving the joints using custom channels added to the arm icon.*

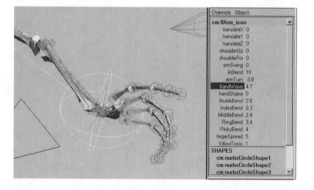

IMPROVING BIND DEFORMATIONS

When running the book scripts to create the basic rig, if you click the check box in step 8 of the setup GUI, you can test-bind the rig to see how it deforms the skin. Inevitably you will notice some deformation problems in areas where limbs or appendages attach to main body sections like the torso. For instance, moving an arm icon may produce too much movement in the neighboring chest area, causing it to cave in when the arm is lowered (see **FIGURE 4.2**). Or rotating the hip icon may cause the stomach skin to move too much. These are common problems for any simple character rig, because you are assigning only a minimum amount of deformers to the skin. Maya assigns points on the skin to the closest deformer or joint, and many of these areas do not even contain skeletons. Having few joints in these areas forces Maya to guess how much it should assign influence to these deformers, and frequently it assigns the wrong amount.

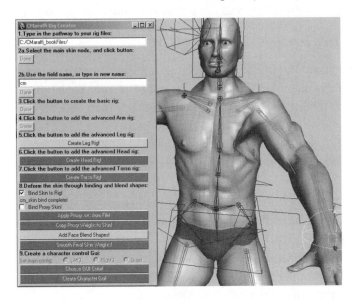

FIGURE 4.2 *Test-binding the basic rig reveals some inherent deformation problems where limbs connect to the torso, such as the chest caving in when an arm is lowered.*

You could fix many of these deformation problems by painting weights on the skin, but such work is time-consuming and tedious. Instead, it is often easier and faster simply to add secondary FK skeletons to these problem areas to force Maya to assign better weighting. Parenting these secondary skeletons under the closest joints in the main skeletons will force them to move correctly with the rig controls. Then when you bind the skin, the points will move indirectly with the main joints you originally intended them to move with, and you will have some extra joints to drive for additional controls. With this in mind, a major part of all the advanced scripts will involve adding such secondary skeletons.

ADDING UPPER ARM FK SKELETONS

One problem area on the upper arm is how the shoulder deforms when the rotate plane controls the arm. In the default pose, moving the elbow icon up and down uses the Pole Vector constraints to twist the arm. This movement produces too much movement at the shoulder because it globally rotates the entire skeleton the same amount, whereas in a real arm, the shoulder area has less apparent twisting because the shoulder muscle structure hides the bone rotation.

Since the goal of rigging is to achieve realistic effects as easily as possible without resorting to complex simulations, you want to just use joints and channels to create the desired rotation falloff at the shoulder. Do this by adding another upper arm joint that is segmented to rotate the shoulder area joints less than the elbow area joints. Here's how to create such a control in the interface using a math expression to divide the rotation, and drive the joints different amounts.

To add a multi-joint upper arm skeleton to the basic rig:

1. In Perspective view, create a two-joint FK skeleton on top of the left upper arm bone, going from shoulder to elbow. After activating the Joint Tool, hold down the V key to snap a joint on the left arm root joint, and then on the lower arm joint.

2. Then activate the Insert Joint tool in the Skeleton menu, and hold down the Shift key as you drag a new joint out of the left root joint. Holding down the Shift key ensures that the skeleton stays straight along the bone.

3. Repeat step 2 using the Insert tool until you have segmented the skeleton into three equal segments. Name the new skeleton joints something like **lfNewUpArmRoot, lfNewUpArm1**, and so on.

Now you'll use a parent constraint to make the new segmented FK arm skeleton stay attached to the IK upper arm skeleton. Parent constraints combine the effects of point and orient constraints into one command.

4. Shift-select the left arm root followed by lfNewUpArmRoot, and choose Constrain > Parent ❏. Set the options as shown in **FIGURE 4.3**, being sure to deselect Rotate All, and only select the Rotate Y and Z axes.

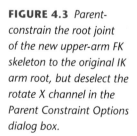

FIGURE 4.3 *Parent-constrain the root joint of the new upper-arm FK skeleton to the original IK arm root, but deselect the rotate X channel in the Parent Constraint Options dialog box.*

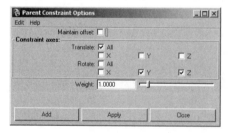

This constrains all the translations and rotations except the X axis, which will be driven at different rates to twist the skeleton. The new segmented FK skeleton should remain connected to the original IK skeleton when the arm icon is moved, but it won't twist yet when you move the elbow icon.

DRIVING THE UPPER ARM TWISTING

To twist the new upper arm joints at different rates, you can use math to divide the IK arm X rotation by different amounts, and have the resulting values rotate the FK joint segments. Attribute connections that involve math can be done by writing a math expression in the Expression Editor. Although expressions and MEL have some similarities, they are different languages, with different commands, syntax, and formatting.

To rotate the FK upper arm joints in X using a math expression:

1. Choose Window > Animation Editors > Expression Editor to open the Expression Editor. In the Select Filter menu, switch to By Expression Name, and then type the following math expression (being sure to use the correct names for your skeleton joints):

```
lfNewUpArm.rotateX = 0 + (lfArmRoot.rotateX / 3);

lfNewUpArm1.rotateX = 0 + (lfArmRoot.rotateX / 2);

lfNewUpArm2.rotateX = 0 + (lfArmRoot.rotateX);
```

This expression has several lines that increasingly divide the effect of the arm twisting as joints get closer to the shoulder. Notice at the end of the lines that the root joint rotation is divided by three (/ 3), the second joint rotation is divided by two (/ 2), and the third joint rotation is not divided at all. These values are then used to drive the rotationX channel of each new upper arm joint. The 0 + operation adds the divided value to the FK joints default 0 value.

2. Type **UpArmTwist** into the Expression Name field, and click Create to assign the expression to the new joints. Notice that the driven joints X channel turns purple, indicating there is an expression connection (see **FIGURE 4.4**).

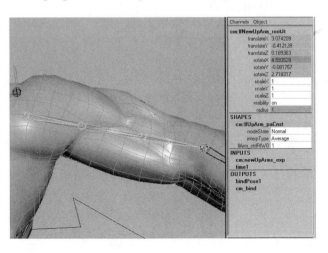

FIGURE 4.4 *Using an expression to divide the X rotation of the new upper-arm joints creates a falloff on the shoulder when the arm twists, turning the constrained channel purple.*

Be aware that this connection has the effect of constraining the driven channel, because the expression is always turned on, as indicated in the Expression Editor by the Evaluation setting of Always.

3. Click Close to close the Expression Editor, and move the elbow icon to test the expression. The effect of the expression on the bound skin produces an automatic falloff that smoothes out the twist deformation at the shoulder.

Math expressions are easy to understand and write, but you may need to use another method to create the same division effect. Since connecting nodes directly with a connectAttr command is the most basic kind of connection in Maya, it processes a little faster than math expressions. This may not be an issue with all animation projects, but some large productions may require the use of direct node connections to speed up scene interaction. To do the same operation manually with node connections requires that you connect the X rotation channels of the nodes through a Multiply-Divide utility node.

Although you can create and connect these types of nodes manually in the Hypergraph or Hypershade, it is easier and more reliable to use MEL. Here is how you would use MEL code to make the same type of connection to divide the new upper arm joint rotations:

```
//Set joint names into variables:
  string $limbRoot = "lfArmRoot";
  string $joint0 = "lfNewUpArm";
  string $joint1 = "lfNewUpArm1";
  string $joint2 = "lfNewUpArm2";
//Create a Multiply-Divide utility node:
  string $divide = `createNode multiplyDivide
         -n "armDivide_util"`;
//Set the operation to divide:
  setAttr ($divide + ".operation") 2;
//Connect and divide all the input attributes:
  connectAttr -f ($limbRoot + ".rx") ($divide + ".i1x");
  connectAttr -f ($limbRoot + ".rx") ($divide + ".i1y");
//Set the division values on the utility node:
  setAttr ($divide + ".i2x") 3;
  setAttr ($divide + ".i2y") 2;
//Connect th output attributes to the joints:
  connectAttr -f ($divide + ".ox") ($joint0 + ".rx");
  connectAttr -f ($divide + ".oy") ($joint1 + ".rx");
  connectAttr -f ($limbRoot + ".rx") ($joint2 + ".rx");
```

In this MEL code, the IK arm joint or $limbRoot is being connected to two XY input channels on the utility node (both input X rotation values even though one channel is labeled Y). Then setAttr commands set the division values on the utility node. Lastly, connectAttr commands connect the output channels containing the divided values to the new FK joints. After running this code, selecting the left arm root joint and choosing Window > Hypergraph: Connections will show you how the nodes are connected (see **FIGURE 4.5**).

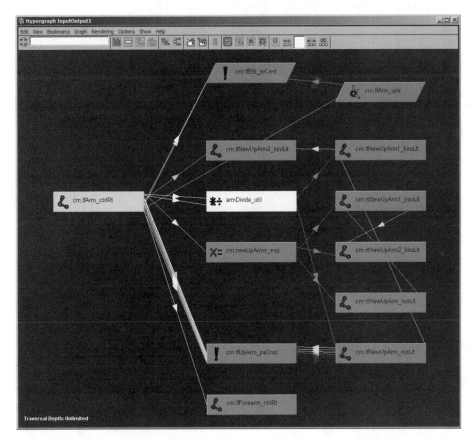

FIGURE 4.5 *Creating utility nodes in the Hypergraph allows editing direct node connections, such as multiplying or dividing a channel connection.*

CREATING FOREARM TWIST CONTROLS

The forearm is extremely complex in a real body. Muscles wrap around bones, contracting and relaxing to create the twisting motion of the lower arm and hand. Rather than try to simulate this complexity, you can simply create a new FK arm skeleton that contains a joint centered in the forearm that will drive the lower arm twisting. This joint will not only drive the hand skeleton, but will also drive two IK skeletons created for the radius and ulna.

To create a left forearm rig to control the lower arm twisting:

1. In Top view, draw a three-joint FK skeleton straight down the middle of the lower arm from elbow to wrist, placing the second joint midway down the forearm. Name the joints **lfForearmRoot**, **lfArmTurn**, and **lfForearmEnd**.

2. Transform the new forearm skeleton into place so it fits well inside the skin, and is positioned between the radius and ulna polygon bones. Use the main IK arm skeleton as a guide for positioning (see **FIGURE 4.6**).

FIGURE 4.6 *Create a new FK lower-arm skeleton with an extra armTurn joint in the middle of the forearm. This joint will be the main control for twisting forearm and hand skeletons.*

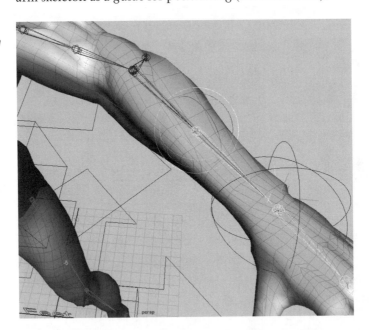

3. Make the root joint child to the lower arm joint of the main arm skeleton, creating some group nodes to be used as pads between the parented joints. Name the group nodes **lfForearmPad0** and **lfForearmPad1**. To make sure the FK skeleton produces the correct values when the joints rotate, orient the group nodes the same as the root joint before parenting.

4. Re-parent the wrist group nodes, lfWristTurn0 and lfWristTurn1, that were parented under the end joint of the IK arm skeleton in the basic rig, to the end joint of the new FK forearm skeleton. Rotating the new lfArmTurn joint in X will now rotate the hand.

5. To make the forearm set up a little more realistic, add ulna and radius skeletons. Use the polygon bones as guides for drawing two-joint IK skeletons from the elbow area to the wrist area on either side of the main forearm skeleton. Name the joints **lfUlnaRoot**, **lfUlnaEnd**, **lfUlnaIk**, and so on.

6. Parent both root joints of the ulna and radius skeletons under the root joint of the new forearm skeleton, with group nodes inserted as pads. Then make the IK handle for the radius skeleton child to the lfArmTurn joint. This will cause the radius to twist with the hand when the central forearm joint rotates in X.

The ulna, however, won't be parented in the same way as the radius, which would make the elbow appear to break when the forearm rotates.

7. To dampen the rotation effect, but still make the ulna move with the forearm, use a constraint rather than parenting. Create a locator positioned right on top of the ulna IK handle. Then point-constrain the ulna IK handle to the locator.

8. Parent the ulna IK under the forearm root joint, and parent the locator under the lfArmTurn joint. The point constraint simulates some of the parenting effect, while filtering out the rotation, preventing the elbow from breaking. This is easy to see once you re-parent the radius and ulna polygon bones under the new Maya joints, and rotate the lfArmTurn joint to test the control.

Your final hierarchy should look like the Hypergraph structure in **FIGURE 4.7**.

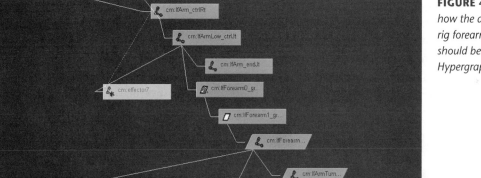

FIGURE 4.7 *Here is how the advanced arm rig forearm controls should be parented in the Hypergraph.*

9. After completing the left arm, repeat the entire process to complete the right arm. Although some of the individual skeletons can be mirrored to the other side, the whole hierarchy won't mirror correctly.

This setup technique has the advantage of easily creating an FK swinging control on the lower arm. To make a limb swing means that the upper limb joint stays still while the lower limb joint rotates. This is often an unconscious movement on the arms, and sometimes the legs, when walking. A slight swing can also occur on the arms after throwing something, or on a character's leg when sitting off the ground with the legs dangling. Because all the joints in an IK skeleton are constrained to rotate whenever the IK handle is moved, it is very difficult to create such a swinging effect with IK skeletons.

Since the FK forearm skeleton is child to the main arm skeleton, it will move with the IK; but you can also rotate the forearm root joint in Z to make the arm swing slightly (see **FIGURE 4.8**). Rotating the new lower arm skeleton will produce a minor swinging motion, but avoid animating the lower arm skeleton away from the IK arm and icon for long periods, which makes the controls less intuitive. Be aware that adding new child skeletons like this means you will not bind the parent IK arm joints. In fact, it is a good practice to rename the original arm joints to indicate that they should not be bound. For instance, in the advanced scripts covered later in this chapter, the IK arm joints are renamed with _ctrlRoot and _ctrlJoint suffixes, which causes the bind script to ignore them.

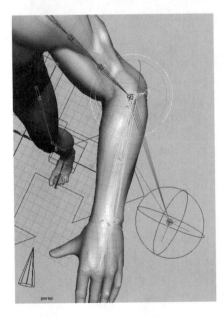

FIGURE 4.8 *The new lower-arm setup facilitates a simple FK swinging control on the arm through the parenting; only bind the FK joints, not the original IK joints.*

This type of arm setup does not use the method of constraining multiple skeletons to create IK-FK switching controls, which would really complicate the arm rig, and often have flipping problems. Unfortunately, you cannot make the IK parent skeletons and icon follow the FK child, because that sequence produces a computer cycle or never-ending loop. Computer cycles cause error messages, and make the rig unstable. Instead, use the new FK arm controls to animate minor swinging movements; later you can create IK-FK switching controls using the built-in ikBlend channel on the arm IK handle, and the IK/FK Keys in the Animate menu.

ADDING FK FINGER SKELETONS

All the controls in the wrist and hand, including the finger skeletons, should be FK controls that will later be driven by custom channels created on the arm icon. You can create the finger controls as five-joint skeletons starting from the metacarpals in the hand, or as four-joint skeletons starting from the knuckles, depending on the amount of control you want to have over deforming the palm of the hand. Adding metacarpal joints allows you to cup the hand, and can produce minor tendon deformations on the back of the hand.

To add FK finger skeletons:

1. Draw the finger skeletons in Top or Front view using the polygon bones as a guide. If your character is in a relaxed default pose, like the example character, you will have to transform the joints extensively to fit them correctly. It is often easier to draw and fit one finger skeleton, and then duplicate it to create the others. Since they are FK skeletons, you can freeze the transformations afterward.

2. After positioning the joints correctly, mirror them to the other side using behavior, and then parent them individually under the appropriate hand end joint.

3. Insert two group nodes as pads between the hand end joint and each finger root joint. Name them **lfIndexPad0**, **lfIndexPad1**, **lfMiddlePad0**, and so on. Be sure to position and orient these group nodes according to each finger root joint, which is required to generate the correct channel values for driving the finger joints in the next section (see **FIGURE 4.9**).

FIGURE 4.9 *Be sure to orient the group node parents of the finger skeletons the same as the finger joints, so that the channels on the finger controls will generate correct values in a single axis.*

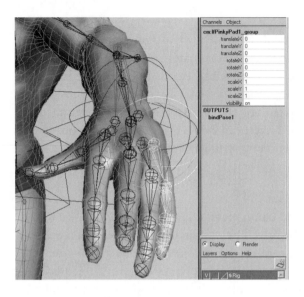

DRIVING ARM JOINTS WITH SDKS

Many of the joints in the lower arms, hands, and fingers have no icons to easily animate their rotations. Since creating individual icons for all the joints would clutter up the rig, you can instead add custom channels on the existing arm icons to control the joint rotations. The easiest and most intuitive way of doing this in Maya is to use set driven keys (SDKs). This feature is a useful way of connecting channels that don't require any math computations. As the name implies, SDKs generate special keys that are independent of the animation timeline. Setting the keys defines the values of the driven channel in relation to the values of the driver channel.

To create a SDK connection in the interface, you must define a driver channel and driven channel and then set the keys that connect them in the SDK dialog box. One advantage of this method over node constraints or math expressions is that it produces animation curves that can vary the timing in the connection. Also, SDKs allow multiple drivers to control the same driven channel, without inserting any additional nodes into the connection; this simplifies the controls. For these reasons, SDKs are used for the majority of controls on most rigs.

The typical SDK has three keys to set for the minimum, default, and maximum values of the driver and driven channels. You normally set your custom driver channel limits to generic values, while the driven channel values are specific to the range of motion of the body control. You can add more or fewer than this standard amount of keys for your SDK connections, depending on your needs.

To create a custom driver channel on the arm icon and use SDKs to drive the twisting of the forearm:

1. Select the left arm icon and choose Modify > Add Attribute. In the resulting dialog box, type **armTurn** for the custom attribute name and select the Override Nice Name option to create a label that is displayed with spaces and capitalization in the Channel Box Nice Name field. Use the default Float data type and Scalar attribute type, and set the Minimum, Maximum, and Default numeric attribute properties to –10, 10, and 0 (see **FIGURE 4.10**).

FIGURE 4.10 *Creating custom attributes or channels on the icons allows you to create additional controls to manually drive any control that doesn't have a control icon of its own.*

The numbers you choose for the channel limits are somewhat arbitrary, since you will key the SDKs at whatever values are set. You could create the same controls using limits of –0.5 to 1, or –50 to 100. Just try to be consistent with the values you use. The suggested values of 10 are neither too big nor too small, while still providing a good range of values to set keys.

2. Click OK to add the attribute to the arm icon, and test the limits by scrubbing the channel in the Channel Box.

3. Choose Animate > Set Driven Key > Set. The resulting dialog box has a Driver section on the top, with a Driven section on the bottom. Load Driver and Load Driven buttons across the bottom let you load the objects to connect.

4. Select the arm icon and click the Load Driver button to load the transform node and attributes. In the list of attributes on the right, select the armTurn custom attribute that is at the end of the list (see **FIGURE 4.11**).

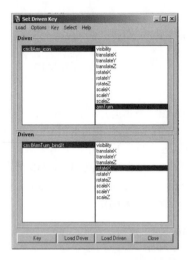

FIGURE 4.11 *Load the driver and driven nodes into the Set Driven Key dialog box, and select the channels you want to connect with driven keys.*

5. In the 3D or Hypergraph view, select the lfArmTurn joint, and click the Load Driven button, selecting rotateX in the attribute list.

6. With both driver and driven channels at their default values, click the Key button to set a driven key. You should see the X rotation channel in the Channel Box turn orange to indicate that a key is set.

7. Select the arm icon in 3D view or double-click the icon name in the SDK dialog box. In the armTurn channel, type a value of 10, and then double-click the lfArmTurn joint name in the SDK dialog box to select the joint; manipulate the rotation value to about 40 degrees. Click the Key button again.

8. Select the icon again and set the driver channel to –10, select and rotate the joint in the other direction to about –70 degrees, and set the final driven key.

9. When you have finished, set the icon driver channel back to 0, which should set the arm back to the default rest position. Then select the driver channel in the Channel Box and scrub it using the middle mouse button in the 3D views to see the arm twisting (see **FIGURE 4.12**).

Be sure to look at your own joints to see how the controls should work, and how far to set limits on custom channels. For instance, on the lower arm twist control, you keyed the rotation of the lfArmTurn joint at –70 and 40 degrees because that is the range of motion without moving the elbow. To twist the arm further, you translate the elbow icon, which rotates the entire arm around the rotate plane.

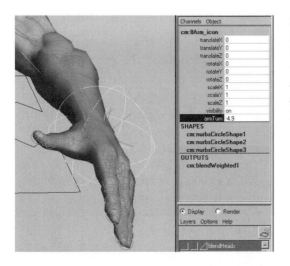

FIGURE 4.12 *Always test the SDK controls to ensure that they are working correctly, such as scrubbing the armTurn channel in the Channel Box to twist the arm.*

Once you get used to switching between driver and driven channels when creating SDK controls, the process is easy and fast. In addition to the armTurn channel, the advanced arm controls should include driver channels for the lower arm FK swing, as well as for the wrist rotations, and all the finger joint movements.

Also, if you are going to connect the same type channels to a single driver, you can load multiple driven nodes into the driven field of the SDK dialog box. This can speed up the process of using a single-finger channel to drive multiple-finger joints to rotate in Z. Just Shift-select the finger joints to load them together into the driven section of the SDK dialog box (see **FIGURE 4.13**).

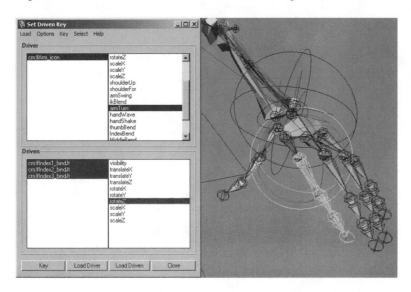

FIGURE 4.13 *Use the Shift key to load and simultaneously key multiple driven nodes in the Set Driven Key dialog box, such as setting keys on the rotate Z channels of several finger joints.*

CLEANING UP THE ARM ICON CHANNELS

One of the final rigging tasks when creating advanced controls is to clean up the icons that will be used by the animator. Cleaning up the icons streamlines the controls, and makes them harder to break by preventing the animator from easily manipulating unintended transformations. The task involves setting default manipulators for each icon, and setting limits on the main transform channels. It also involves hiding and locking channels that should not be animated, such as most scaling and constrained channels.

After you've cleaned up the channels, it is a good practice to set a key at frame 0 on the timeline for all the icons at their default positions. Doing this makes it easy to return the rig to the default T-pose whenever needed, such as for binding, by simply clicking the timeline at 0.

To clean up the channels on the left arm icon:

1. Select the left arm icon. In the main toolbox, turn on the Show Manipulator tool by clicking the tool button at the bottom of the main transform toolbox. Notice that no manipulator is displayed with the arm icon selected.

2. Choose Modify > Transformation Tools > Default Object Manipulator > Move, and notice that the Move tool appears whenever the arm icon is selected.

Try assigning some of the other choices in the Default Object Manipulator menu, including the transform manipulator, which assigns a tool that has all three transform functions (see **FIGURE 4.14**). However, since an arm icon is only meant to translate the arm IK handle, reassign the Move tool as the permanent default manipulator.

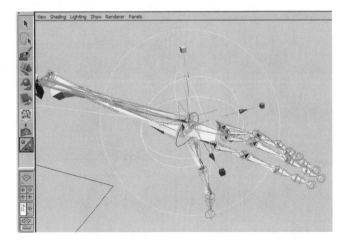

FIGURE 4.14 *A good way to streamline iconic controls is to set default manipulators and activate the Show Manipulator tool. The transform manipulator allows moving, rotating, and scaling the icon.*

3. Set the default manipulators on all the icons depending on how each icon should be transformed. For instance, the torso icon requires both translation and rotation, so set the transform manipulator. The head icon, on the other hand, only requires to be rotated, not translated, so set the rotate manipulator. Do not be concerned about scaling at this point, as you will be locking and hiding the scaling channels on most icons.

4. To set limits on transform channels that will be animated, right-click the icon to open the Attribute Editor, and click the Limit Information tab under Transform Attributes. Setting limits on all the icons is necessary to make the character GUI sliders generate correctly later. If you don't want to limit a particular control, then just set the limits on that icon to well beyond the normal values.

For instance, for an arm icon that will only be translated, setting a limit of 50 grid units on the translation channels will be more than enough to allow for a free range of motion on most normal sized characters. Or setting a rotation limit of 720 on the Char icon will allow the animator to completely turn the character twice, which is more than most scenes require.

5. Click the arrow button next to Limit Information to display the limit options, and select the check boxes for the attributes you want to limit (see **FIGURE 4.15**). Either type limit values manually, or manipulate the icons in the 3D interface, and click the arrows to set the limits.

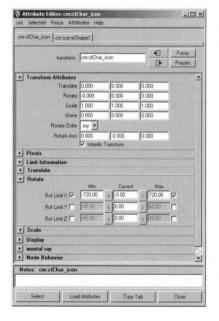

FIGURE 4.15 *Set transform limits in the Attribute Editor on icon channels that will be animated.*

6. To remove channels from view that you do not want to be animated, lock and hide them. Choose Window > General Editors > Channel Control. Notice the resulting dialog box has tabs for Keyable and Locked channels, with the visible and hidden keyable channels displayed.

To hide transform channels, select them in the left Keyable list, and click Move to move them to the middle Nonkeyable Hidden list (see **FIGURE 4.16**).

FIGURE 4.16 *A big part of cleaning up icons is to hide and lock icon channels that the animator should never manipulate, such as the scaling channels on the arm icon.*

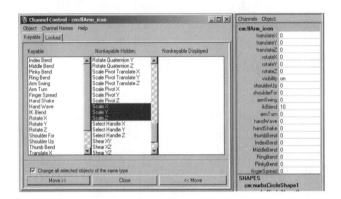

Hiding a channel doesn't necessarily keep it from being available to the animator. For instance, with the left arm icon selected, hold down the Ctrl key and select all the rotation, scaling, and visibility channels, and then click the Move button. Notice that the channels are no longer visible in the Channel Box. However, if you activate the Rotate tool, the rotation manipulator will still be available, even though all rotation channels have been hidden. To keep hidden channels from accidentally being manipulated, you should also lock them.

7. Click the Locked tab in the dialog box, and select the same channels you just hid, and then move them to the left Locked field. Now notice when activating the Rotate or Scale tools that the manipulators are grayed out and not available.

8. When you have finished hiding and locking all channels, click Close to exit the Channel Control editor.

Upgrading the Legs and Feet

You'll follow the same basic process just used for the advanced arm to create all the advanced rig controls for the leg and feet: node creation, hierarchy setup, connections, and channel cleaning. For the advanced leg controls, you should again add skeletons to the upper legs and knees to improve deformations when the limbs twist and bend. Simply apply the same setup and connection techniques as used on the upper arms. A new setup technique, however, will be shown for creating a rolling foot control, which will be useful whenever the character is animated to walk.

ADDING ADVANCED IK FEET CONTROLS

To upgrade the controls for the feet, you need to add locators and IK handles to the basic foot rig. Creating controls for rolling the foot through the heel, ball, and toe (otherwise known as a foot-roll rig), requires adding two new IK handles to each foot skeleton and inserting several group node pivots into the hierarchy.

To add an IK based foot-roll rig to the left FK foot skeleton:

1. Begin by disconnecting the basic foot hierarchy. In the Hypergraph drag the left foot root and IK handle nodes with the middle mouse button onto an empty area. This detaches them from the left leg icon. It is a good idea to also detach the polygon foot bones from the parent foot joints, so they don't shift when you add IK to the skeleton.

2. To add two IK solvers to the foot skeleton, choose Skeleton > IK Handle tool ⬚, and make sure that the standard RP solver is selected in the options. The IK Handle tool is used to add IK to an existing FK skeleton. To add the first IK solver, in Right view, click the left-foot root followed by the ball joint. Name the resulting IK handle located at the ball of the foot **lfBallIk**.

3. Add a second IK handle to the same skeleton by activating the tool again, and click the left-foot ball joint followed by the end joint. Name the resulting IK handle at the end of the foot **lfToeIk**. Notice that the two IK solvers have not overlapped, so there won't be any conflicts between the constraints.

You'll parent the two IK handles under three new locators that will be used as the main pivots for the foot-roll rig.

4. Choose Create > Locator to manually create each locator, and place them at the heel, ball, and toe of the foot. Use **FIGURE 4.17** as a guide for placing the heel locator where the heel of the foot touches the ground, which is where the foot should pivot from when rolling backward, and for placing the other two locators on the ball and end joints. Name the locators **lfHeelRoll**, **lfBallRoll**, and **lfToeRoll**.

FIGURE 4.17 *Place three main locators at the heel, ball of the foot, and toe to create the pivots for a rolling foot control.*

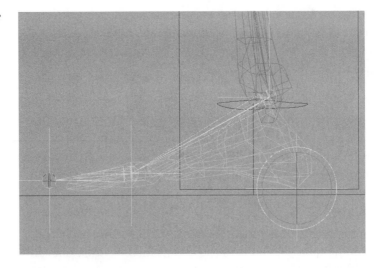

5. Parent the locators between the left leg icon and the foot skeleton in the following order: lfHeelRoll, lfToeRoll, and lfBallRoll. Parent the two new IK handles under the lfBallRoll locator, and parent the original leg IK handle under the lfToeRoll locator (see **FIGURE 4.18**). Make sure that you re-parent the polygon bones under the appropriate foot joints, and then rotate the locators to test out the controls.

FIGURE 4.18 *Here is the hierarchy setup for the standard foot-roll control. The more advanced version on the example rig inserts more locators to create additional pivots for the foot.*

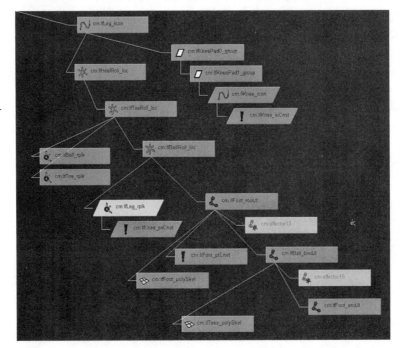

6. Repeat steps 1 through 5 of the process on the other foot. Mirroring a whole hierarchy can be problematic.

This foot-roll rig is a variation of the "reverse foot-roll" setup that has been common in the animation industry for many years. However, even though the foot-roll rig has all the controls needed to animate a rolling foot, it can be further enhanced by adding more locators or group nodes as pivots. For instance, you may have noticed that even though you have a pivot located at the ball of the foot, because of the way it is parented you cannot wiggle the toe joints. Instead, the toes stay still while the foot rotates upward, which is the direct result of the "reverse" parenting of the nodes.

Creating additional controls just involves thinking about how the three locators are moving, and then inserting new locators or group nodes to extend that movement. For instance, in addition to the standard pivots at the ankle and ball of the foot, try adding a pivot to rotate the foot at the outer edge. Some experimentation would show that such a node would need to be parented above the lfHeelRoll locator in the hierarchy, as would a node that will be used to rotate the foot at the ankle. On the other hand, a node that is intended to wiggle the toes should be inserted in the hierarchy below the lfToeRoll locator and above the left leg IK handle and left foot root joint.

DRIVING AND CLEANING THE IK FOOT CONTROLS

As with the advanced arm controls, the advanced leg controls must also be driven using math expressions, node connections, or SDKs. The foot-roll controls can be entirely driven by custom channels on the leg icon using SDKs. You'll create a custom channel named footroll to drive the three locators created in the last section. After driving the foot to roll, clean the leg icon by locking and hiding the scaling channels, and set the transform manipulator as default.

To drive the left foot-roll rig with SDKs:

1. Create a custom channel on the leg icon by choosing Channels > Attributes > Add Attribute in the Channel Box. Set the limits for your footRoll channel to minimum –5 and maximum 10, with a default setting of 0.

2. In the Set Driven Key dialog box, load the leg icon's custom footRoll channel as the driver, and load the lfHeelRoll locator's rotateX channel as the driven. Set two SDKs on the heel locator to roll backward about 35 degrees when the footRoll channel is manipulated from 0 to –5.

3. Load the lfBallRoll locator, and drive its rotateX channel to rotate upward about 30 degrees when the footRoll channel is manipulated from 0 to 5.

4. Move the footRoll channel to 10, and rotate the ball of the foot locator back down about 10 degrees to uncompress the foot. To complete the roll up onto the toes at 10 on the footRoll channel, load the lfToeRoll locator and set a driven key on the rotateX channel at about 30 degrees.

5. To test the control, set the driver channel back to 0, and scrub the channel. You should see the foot roll back onto the heel at –5, up onto the ball of the foot at 5, and up onto the toe at 10 with a slight decompression at the ball (see **FIGURE 4.19**). Of course, if you added other pivots for the foot and toes to your foot controls, make sure that you create driver channels on the foot icon and drive those pivots as well.

FIGURE 4.19 *Create custom channels to drive the foot-roll pivots, as well as other pivots on the advanced foot rig.*

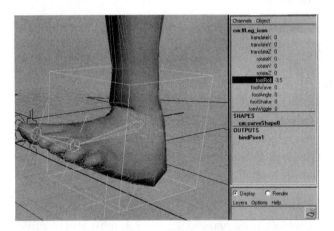

MEL SCRIPTING THE ADVANCED CONTROLS

Writing MEL code for the advanced controls involves all the commands and techniques used in the basic scripts, plus new commands for connecting channels and editing attributes. You can find most of these commands by doing the rigging tasks in the interface, and then examining the history in the Script Editor. Remember to always look up new commands in the MEL Command Reference to streamline the code by using available flags. For instance, after connecting channels with SDKs in the interface, the code in the History field will contain many select, setAttr, and rotate commands as you manipulate the driver and driven channels. The code will look something like this:

```
select -r cm:lfArm_icon ;
select -r cm:lfArmTurn_bindJt ;
setDrivenKeyframe -currentDriver lfArm_icon.armTurn lfArmTurn_bindJt.rotateX;
// 1 //
select -r lfArm_icon ;
```

```
setAttr "lfArm_icon.armTurn" 10;
select -r lfArmTurn_bindJt ;
rotate -r -os 36.379451 0 0 ;
select -r lfArm_icon ;
setDrivenKeyframe -currentDriver lfArm_icon.armTurn lfArmTurn_bindJt.rotateX;
// 1 //
setAttr "lfArm_icon.armTurn" -10;
select -r lfArmTurn_bindJt ;
rotate -r -os -115.024388 0 0 ;
setDrivenKeyframe -currentDriver lfArm_icon.armTurn lfArmTurn_bindJt.rotateX;
// 1 //
select -r lfArm_icon ;
setAttr "lfArm_icon.armTurn" 0;
setAttr "lfArm_icon.armTurn" -10;
```

You can consolidate all of this code into three SDK commands simply by adding the flags to set the driver and driven values, which is -dv, or driver value, and -v, or value (which specifies the driven value). Loops and procedures further streamline the code in the advanced scripts. Here is a simplified example:

```
//Set SDKs to create forearm twist controls:
setDrivenKeyframe -cd "lfArm_icon.armTurn" -dv 0
         -v 0 "lfArmTurn_bindJt.rotateX";
setDrivenKeyframe -cd "lfArm_icon.armTurn" -dv 10
         -v 35 "lfArmTurn_bindJt.rotateX";
setDrivenKeyframe -cd "lfArm_icon.armTurn" -dv -10
         -v -115 "lfArmTurn_bindJt.rotateX";
```

The advanced controls also require connecting channels using math expressions. Maya sees a math expression as a string, so you specify the expression using the string flag on the expression command. Since most expressions have multiple lines, it is advisable to store them in separate string variables that can be combined. Be careful to avoid breaking long strings onto multiple lines, as this will cause an "unterminated string" error. Also be aware that names won't be hard-coded in the advanced scripts, so names stored in variables and arrays will further break up the expression string. Here is one example of using MEL to declare an expression:

```
//Expression for twisting the upper arm joints:
string $exp1 = "lfNewUpArm_rootJt.rx = 0 + (lfArm_ctrlRt.rx / 3);\n";
string $exp2 = "lfNewUpArm1_bindJt.rx = 0 + (lfArm_ctrlRt.rx / 2); \n ";
```

```
string $exp3 = "lfNewUpArm2_bindJt.rx = 0 + (lfArm_ctrlRt.rx); \n ";
expression -name "newUpArms_exp" -string ($exp1 + $exp2 + $exp3);
```

Creating direct node connections in the advanced scripts is basically the same as described in "Driving the Upper Arm Twisting," earlier in this chapter. You run `createNode` commands to create utility nodes, and then use the `connectAttr` commands to connect these nodes to other transform channels. In addition, you'll use `setAttr` commands extensively to set how the utility nodes affect the connections. You'll use similar `setAttr` commands to lock and hide attributes, and set default manipulators. As a final step, you'll use a `transformLimits` command in the process of cleaning up icons to set limits on the icon transform channels. All of this will, of course, be organized into procedures with arguments for all the node names and values.

EXERCISE 4.1: EXAMINING THE ADVANCED LIMB SCRIPTS

This exercise takes you through the main parts of the scripts that generate the advanced limb controls. Procedures and commands are examined that facilitate connecting and cleaning channels, as well as creating new skeletons to improve deformation. The CMaraffi_advArms and CMaraffi_advLegs scripts follow the same formatting as the basic rig scripts, so some common code will not be reviewed; instead, you should refer to them in the actual scripts.

Step 1: Create an SDK Global Procedure

First, open the CMaraffi_advGlobals script, which contains global procedures for connecting channels with SDKs and cleaning icons by hiding, locking, and limiting channels. In addition to sourcing all the basic scripts for creating skeletons and icons, the advanced limb scripts will use procedures in this script extensively.

The `cm_setDrivens` global procedure has string arguments for the driver and driven names, and float arrays for the driver and driven key values. These arguments let you set the minimum, default, and maximum values to SDK. There is an integer argument to let the user decide whether creating a driver channel is needed, followed by arguments to set the channel name and limits. Lastly, a `$mirror` integer argument allows the user to create the SDKs on the right side as well.

The first conditional inside the SDK procedure evaluates the `$addDriverAttr` argument to determine if the `addAttr` command should be run to create a custom attribute on the driver icon. If true, the driver is an icon, and the conditional creates the channel using the procedure arguments.

The next section of code runs the setDrivenKeyframe command in a loop with all the argument values to key the SDK connection. Once the keys are initially set, a conditional statement evaluates the $mirrorSDK argument to determine if the keys should be mirrored from left to right. The code does not mirror the SDKs in the traditional sense, but just repeats the same SDK process on the other side of the body using the substitute command. Because the joints in the rig were all originally mirrored to generate the same values on both sides of the body when rotated, there is no need to mirror or flip the positive and negative SDK values.

The final conditional statement verifies that the prefix of the driver object starts with lf. This check is necessary with procedures that create SDKs on two sides of a center icon, such as on the head icon to drive controls on both sides of the face. In this case, the procedure doesn't try to create another custom driver channel of the same name on the same icon, which would produce an error. Instead, it uses the initially created channel to also drive the right-side controls. As the procedure ends, note that no return statement is needed.

```
global proc cm_setDrivens (string $driverObj,string $driverAttr,
        string $drivenObj,string $drivenAttr,float $driverValues[],
        float $drivenValues[],int $addDriverAttr,string $shortName,
        int $min,int $max,int $default,int $mirrorSDK)
{//Open procedure...
 //Add driver attribute if specified in arguments:
   if ($addDriverAttr == 1){//Open conditional...
      addAttr -ln $driverAttr -sn $shortName -at "float"
      -min $min -max $max -dv $default -r 1 -w 1
      -s 1 -k 1 $driverObj;
   }//Close conditional.
 //Use loop to set all driven keys:
   string $driver = ($driverObj + "." + $driverAttr);
   string $driven = ($drivenObj + "." + $drivenAttr);
   int $i;
   for ($i = 0; $i < size($driverValues); $i++){//Open loop...
      setDrivenKeyframe -cd $driver -dv $driverValues[$i]
          -v $drivenValues[$i] $driven;
      print ("SDK's have connected: " + $driver + " "
          + $driven + "\n");
   }//Close loop.
 //Repeat process on the right side if mirror argument is on:
   string $rtDriverObj;
   string $rtDrivenObj;
   if ($mirrorSDK == 1){//Open conditional...
     string $checkPfx = `match "lf" $driverObj`;
     if ($checkPfx == "lf"){//Open conditional...
```

```
        $rtDriverObj = `substitute "lf" $driverObj "rt"`;
        $rtDrivenObj = `substitute "lf" $drivenObj "rt"`;
        if ($addDriverAttr == 1){//Open conditional...
                addAttr -ln $driverAttr -sn $shortName -at "double"
                    -min $min -max $max -dv $default -r 1 -w 1
                    -s 1 -k 1 $rtDriverObj;
        }//Close conditional.
        string $rtDriver = ($rtDriverObj + "." + $driverAttr);
        string $rtDriven = ($rtDrivenObj + "." + $drivenAttr);
        int $i;
        for ($i = 0; $i < size($driverValues); $i++){//Open loop...
            setDrivenKeyframe -cd $rtDriver -dv $driverValues[$i]
                -v $drivenValues[$i] $rtDriven;
            print ("SDK's have connected: " + $rtDriver
                + " " + $rtDriven + "\n");
        }//Close loop.
    }//Close conditional.
    else{//Open conditional...
        $rtDrivenObj = `substitute "lf" $drivenObj "rt"`;
        string $rtDriven = ($rtDrivenObj + "." + $drivenAttr);
        int $i;
        for ($i = 0; $i < size($driverValues); $i++){//Open loop...
            setDrivenKeyframe -cd $driver -dv $driverValues[$i]
                -v $drivenValues[$i] $rtDriven;
            print ("SDK's have connected: " + $driver
                + " " + $rtDriven + "\n");
        }//Close loop.
    }//Close conditional.
  }//Close conditional.
  select -cl;
}//Close procedure.
```

Step 2: Clean Up and Finalize Rig Icons

The next few global procedures in the CMaraffi_advGlobals script clean up and finalize the rig icons. The first procedure, cm_cleaner, cleans up the channels by locking and hiding them, as well as by setting a default manipulator. Notice that the arguments expect an array of attributes to lock or hide, which will be processed together through a loop. Locking and hiding are actually node attributes that can easily be specified using a setAttr command. The procedure sets the –l, or lock, flag to 1, and –k, or keyable, flag to 0, which locks the channel while also hiding it.

To finish the cleaning process, a `setAttr` command is used to set the default manipulator by assigning the `showManipDefault` channel an integer value from 1 to 4. The value corresponds to the four manipulators available: move, rotate, scale, and transform. Lastly, a `$mirror` argument is evaluated to repeat the process on a corresponding right-side icon. No return statement is required for this procedure.

```
global proc cm_cleaner (string $object,string $attrs[],int $lock,
              int $hide,int $defManip,int $mirror){//Open procedure...
 //Loop used to lock and hide attrs:
   string $attr;
   for ($attr in $attrs){//Open loop...
        if ($lock == 1)setAttr -l 1 ($object + "." + $attr);
        if ($hide == 1)setAttr -k 0 ($object + "." + $attr);
     //Set the default manip to 1(tr),2(ro),3(sc), or 4(all 3):
        setAttr ($object + ".showManipDefault") $defManip;
   }//Close loop.
 //Mirror option to lock right side icon:
   if ($mirror == 1){//Open if statement...
     string $pfx = "lf";
     $rtObj = `substitute $pfx $object "rt"`;
   //Loop used to lock and hide rt attrs:
     string $attr;
     for ($attr in $attrs){//Open loop...
        if ($lock == 1)setAttr -l 1 ($rtObj + "." + $attr);
        if ($hide == 1)setAttr -k 0 ($rtObj + "." + $attr);
      //Set the default manip to 1(tr),2(ro),3(sc), or 4(all 3):
        setAttr ($rtObj + ".showManipDefault") $defManip;
     }//Close loop.
   }//Close if statement.
}//Close procedure.
```

The next `cm_limits` procedure uses the `transformLimits` command to set translation and rotation limits. A conditional statement at the beginning of the procedure checks the number of values in the array argument, and sets limits only if the array has more than 1 value. This allows the user to put a 0 in the argument to not set any limits on either the translation or rotation. Another conditional statement checks whether a corresponding icon exists on the right side of the rig, and creates the same limits on the channels if it does. This procedure also doesn't require a return statement.

```
global proc cm_limits (string $obj,float $tVals[],float $rVals[])
{//Open procedure...
   int $size = size ($tVals);
   if ($size > 1){//Open conditional:
     transformLimits -tx (-$tVals[0]) $tVals[0] -ty (-$tVals[1]) $tVals[1]
         -tz (-$tVals[2]) $tVals[2] -etx 1 1 -ety 1 1 -etz 1 1 $obj;
```

```
    //Limit right side objects if they exist:
      string $pfx = "lf";
      string $rtObj = `substitute $pfx $obj "rt"`;
      if (`objExists $rtObj`){//Open conditional...
          transformLimits -tx (-$tVals[0]) $tVals[0] -ty (-$tVals[1]) $tVals[1]
          -tz (-$tVals[2]) $tVals[2] -etx 1 1 -ety 1 1 -etz 1 1 $rtObj;
      }//Close conditional.
  }//Close conditional.
  int $size = size ($rVals);
  if ($size > 1){//Open conditional:
    transformLimits -rx (-$rVals[0]) $rVals[0] -ry (-$rVals[1]) $rVals[1]
        -rz (-$rVals[2]) $rVals[2] -erx 1 1 -ery 1 1 -erz 1 1 $obj;
    //Limit right side objects if they exist:
      string $pfx = "lf";
      string $rtObj = `substitute $pfx $obj "rt"`;
      if (`objExists $rtObj`){//Open conditional...
          transformLimits -rx (-$rVals[0]) $rVals[0] -ry (-$rVals[1]) $rVals[1]
          -rz (-$rVals[2]) $rVals[2] -erx 1 1 -ery 1 1 -erz 1 1 $rtObj;
      }//Close conditional.
  }//Close conditional.
}//Close procedure.
```

The last two global procedures in this script, cm_keyArray and cm_setColor, are pretty straightforward, so they won't be shown here. The cm_keyArray procedure uses a loop to run a setKeframe command on an array of objects at a particular frame. This lets the user easily set keys on several icons at once, or create a Key All button in a character-animation GUI. The last procedure, cm_setColor, is used in step 9 of the setup GUI to set a background color in the top panel of the character GUI. The procedure runs a colorEditor command to allow the user to pick an RGB color, and then use that color in -bgc, or background color, flags.

Step 3: Create the Advanced Arm Controls

In the CMaraffi_advArms script, the advanced arm controls are created by one local procedure that is run at the end of the script. Since the cm_advArms procedure is run only once in the rigging process, making it local conserves memory, but also requires that you source the script name in the setup GUI. The procedure itself has no arguments, and the return statement is a string array of arm hierarchy names.

The code inside the procedure begins by sourcing all necessary scripts, and runs procedures to put all required names into memory. After setting the names, the code creates group nodes to serve as the top nodes of the new arm hierarchy. Then the first main rigging section runs all the code to rig the upper arms so that the shoulder will deform better when the elbow icon twists the arm. The procedure renames the original IK upper-arm skeleton joints so that they won't bind, while the cm_skelCreate procedure creates a new four-joint FK upper-arm skeleton. Notice the joints of the new skeleton are positioned using the points on a curve specially created for that purpose. A curve command is run from the shoulder to elbow, and then a rebuildCurve command is run to subdivide the curve into four sections. Once the skeleton is created, the curve is deleted.

The rest of the code parents and constrains the skeleton into place, and a math expression is created to divide the rotateX channels of the joints to create a falloff from elbow to shoulder. To increase the efficiency of the code, a loop is used to create all six lines of the expression. After running the expression command, look in the Expression Editor to see the final result.

```
proc string[] cm_advArms (){//Open procedure...
 //Source files with procs needed to create the adv arm rig:
   eval ("source CMaraffi_processNames");
   eval ("source CMaraffi_skelCreate");
   eval ("source CMaraffi_runLocals");
   eval ("source CMaraffi_advGlobals");
 //-----------------------------------------------------------------
 //Run proc to get basic IK and FK rig names:
   string $basicNames[] = cm_getNames("basicRig");
   string $fkNames[] = cm_getNames("fkRig");
 //-----------------------------------------------------------------
 //Set prefixes and suffixes:
   string $pfx0 = "ct"; string $pfx1 = "lf"; string $pfx2 = "rt";
   string $sfxGrp = "_group";
 //-----------------------------------------------------------------
 //1. Set namespace, create new upper arm nodes, and rename:
   cm_setNamespace (1);
 //Shoulders: Set all necessary names into variables:
   string $backPad1 = cm_returnName ($basicNames,"BackPad1","group");
   string $shoulders0 = cm_returnName ($basicNames,"Shoulders0","group");
   string $lfArmPad0 = cm_returnName ($basicNames,"lfArmPad0","group");
   string $armsGrpName = "AdvArms";
 //Create new groups for the advanced arm, and transform:
   string $advArmGps[] = cm_runLocals
        ("doubleGrp",{$pfx0,$armsGrpName,$backPad1,"0"});
   cm_runLocals ("nodeMover",{$backPad1,$advArmGps[0],"1","1","0"});
 //Re-parent shoulders and arm pads under the adv Arm groups:
   cm_runLocals("parenter",{$advArmGps[1],$shoulders0,"0","0"});
   cm_runLocals("parenter",{$advArmGps[1],$lfArmPad0,"1","0"});
   select -cl;
 //-----------------------------------------------------------------
```

```
//Upper Arms: Set all necessary names into variables:
   string $lfArmRoot = cm_returnName ($basicNames,"lfArm","root");
   string $lfArmLow = cm_returnName ($basicNames,"lfArmLow","bind");
   string $lfArmPad1 = cm_returnName ($basicNames,"lfArmPad1","group");
   string $newUpArmName = "NewUpArm";
//Rename the suffix of the IK arm roots to NOT bind:
   string $armRoots[] = cm_runLocals
         ("reNamer",{$lfArmRoot,"lfArm_ctrlRt","1"});
//Create new upper arm skeletons to improve shoulder deformations:
   float $rootPos[] = `xform -q -piv -ws $armRoots[0]`;
   float $elbPos[] = `xform -q -piv -ws $lfArmLow`;
   string $tmpCurve = `curve -d 1 -p $rootPos[0] $rootPos[1] $rootPos[2]
         -p $elbPos[0] $elbPos[1] $elbPos[2] -k 0 -k 1`;
   rebuildCurve -s 3 -d 1 -rpo 1 -end 1 -kr 0 -kt 0 $tmpCurve;
   string $targetObj[] = {$tmpCurve,$tmpCurve,$tmpCurve,$tmpCurve};
   string $targetPt[] = {".cv[0]",".cv[1]",".cv[2]",".cv[3]"};
//Run procedure to create the skeleton:
   string $newUpArms[] = cm_skelCreate (4,$targetObj,$targetPt,
         $newUpArmName,1,"yup",0,1);
   delete $tmpCurve;
//Constrain the new arm skeletons to the original arm skeletons:
  parentConstraint -n "lfUpArm_paCnst" -sr "x" $armRoots[0]
         $newUpArms[0];
  parentConstraint -n "rtUpArm_paCnst" -sr "x" $armRoots[1]
         $newUpArms[2];
//Use an expression to constrain twist of limbs:
   string $lfUpArm2[] = cm_runLocals ("getChild",{$newUpArms[0]});
   string $lfUpArm3[] = cm_runLocals ("getChild",{$lfUpArm2[0]});
   string $rtUpArm2[] = cm_runLocals ("getChild",{$newUpArms[2]});
   string $rtUpArm3[] = cm_runLocals ("getChild",{$rtUpArm2[0]});
   string $newUpArmJts[] = {$newUpArms[0],$lfUpArm2[0],$lfUpArm3[0],
         $newUpArms[2],$rtUpArm2[0],$rtUpArm3[0]};
   string $sourceArmRoots[] = {$armRoots[0],$armRoots[0],$armRoots[0],
         $armRoots[1],$armRoots[1],$armRoots[1]};
   string $divs[] = {".rx / 3);\n",".rx / 2);\n",".rx);\n",
         ".rx / 3);\n",".rx / 2);\n",".rx);\n"};
   string $armExpLine[];
   int $i;
   for ($i = 0; $i < 6; $i++){//Open loop...
      $armExpLine[$i] = ($newUpArmJts[$i] + ".rx = 0 + ("
         + $sourceArmRoots[$i] + $divs[$i]);
   }//Close loop.
   expression -n "newUpArms_exp" -s ($armExpLine[0] + $armExpLine[1]
```

```
        + $armExpLine[2] + $armExpLine[3] + $armExpLine[4] + $armExpLine[5]);
//Parent the upper arm skeleton roots under the arm pad groups:
    cm_runLocals("parenter",{$lfArmPad1,$newUpArms[0],"1","0"});
    select -cl;
```

Step 4: Rig the Lower Arms

The second main section of code in the cm_advArms procedure rigs the lower arms,
including the elbow and radius-ulna section of the forearms. The code begins by creating a new three-joint FK forearm skeleton using a point constraint to position the
second joint mid-forearm, and then renaming the joint as armTurn. This joint will be
driven to twist the lower arm.

```
//2. Lower Arms: Set all necessary names into variables:
    string $lfArmEnd = cm_returnName ($basicNames,"lfArm","end");
    string $lfHandPad0 = cm_returnName
            ($basicNames,"lfHandPad0","group");
    string $forearmName = "Forearm";
//Rename the suffix of the IK forearm joints to NOT bind:
    string $armLows[] = cm_runLocals
            ("reNamer",{$lfArmLow,"lfArmLow_ctrlJt","1"});
//Create new lower arm with armTurn joint to rotate forearm:
    string $tmpLoc[] = `spaceLocator`;
    string $tmpCnst[] = `pointConstraint $armLows[0] $lfArmEnd $tmpLoc[0]`;
    string $targetObj[] = {$armLows[0],$tmpLoc[0],$lfArmEnd};
    string $targetPt[] = {"obj","obj","obj"};
//Run procedure to create the skeleton:
    string $forearms[] = cm_skelCreate (3,$targetObj,$targetPt,
            $forearmName,1,"yup",0,1);
    delete $tmpLoc[0];
//Rename the second joints in the new skeletons:
    string $lfArmTurn[] = cm_runLocals ("getChild",{$forearms[0]});
    string $armTurns[] = cm_runLocals
            ("reNamer",{$lfArmTurn[0],"lfArmTurn_bindJt","1"});
//Create pad nodes and transform:
    string $newLowArmGps[] = cm_runLocals
            ("doubleGrp",{$pfx1,$forearmName,$armLows[0],"1"});
    cm_runLocals ("nodeMover",{$armLows[0],$newLowArmGps[0],"1","0","1"});
//Parent the new lower arm skeletons, and re-parent the hand skeletons:
    cm_runLocals("parenter",{$newLowArmGps[1],$forearms[0],"1","0"});
    cm_runLocals("parenter",{$forearms[1],$lfHandPad0,"1","0"});
    select -cl;
```

The next section of code in the `cm_advArms` procedure creates a skeleton at the elbow that forces more skin-weighting to the upper-arm deformers when bound. Since this code is just creating and parenting a skeleton, it will be skipped in this review.

The last section of code for the lower arm adds radius and ulna IK skeletons to produce more realistic forearm controls. This is done in the same way as shown in "Creating Forearm Twist Controls" earlier in this chapter. The code creates two IK skeletons and parents the radius IK handle directly under the main armTurn joint. The code also runs a `spaceLocator` command, moves the resulting locator on top of the ulna IK handle using a `cm_runLocals` procedure, and point-constrains the ulna IK to the locator. Parent and group commands are then run to finish the hierarchy. Notice that many of the custom procedures have their mirror flags turned on, and the locator is created and constrained within a loop, to create the right-side forearm rig at the same time as the left.

```
//Forearms: Set all necessary names into variables:
    string $lfUlnaPoly = cm_returnName ($basicNames,"lfUlna","poly");
    string $lfRadiusPoly = cm_returnName ($basicNames,"lfRadius","poly");
    string $ulnaName = "Ulna";
    string $radiusName = "Radius";
    string $UlnaRadName = "UlnaRad";
 //Create Radius-Ulna joints in the forearm:
    string $targetObj[] = {$lfUlnaPoly,$lfUlnaPoly};
    string $targetPt[] = {".vtx[7]",".vtx[52]"};
 //Run procedures to create the skeletons:
    string $ulnaSkels[] = cm_skelCreate (2,$targetObj,$targetPt,
            $ulnaName,1,"yup",1,0);
    string $targetObj[] = {$lfRadiusPoly,$lfRadiusPoly};
    string $targetPt[] = {".vtx[27]",".vtx[0]"};
    string $radiusSkels[] = cm_skelCreate (2,$targetObj,$targetPt,
            $radiusName,1,"yup",1,0);
 //Use loop to create locators and pt constrain the Ulna Ik:
    string $ikNames[] = {"lfUlna","rtUlna"};
    string $ulnaIks[] = {$ulnaSkels[2],$ulnaSkels[5]};
    string $ulnaLocs[];
    for ($i = 0; $i < 2; $i++){//Open loop...
    string $locTmp[] = `spaceLocator -n ($ikNames[$i] + "_loc")`;
    $ulnaLocs[$i] = $locTmp[0];
 //Move locators to Ulna Ik position:
    cm_runLocals ("nodeMover",{$ulnaIks[$i],$ulnaLocs[$i],"0","0","0"});
 //Point constrain the Ulna Ik to the locator:
    pointConstraint -n ($ikNames[$i] + "_ptCnst") $ulnaLocs[$i] $ulnaIks[$i];
    }//Close loop.
 //Create pad nodes and transform:
```

```
   string $ulnaRadGps[] = cm_runLocals
         ("doubleGrp",{$pfx1,$UlnaRadName,$forearms[0],"1"});
   cm_runLocals ("nodeMover",{$forearms[0],$ulnaRadGps[0],"1","0","1"});
//Parent all the joints, IK handles, and locators:
   parent $ulnaSkels[0] $radiusSkels[0] $ulnaSkels[2] $ulnaRadGps[1];
   parent $ulnaLocs[0] $radiusSkels[2] $armTurns[0];
   parent $ulnaSkels[3] $radiusSkels[3] $ulnaSkels[5] $ulnaRadGps[3];
   parent $ulnaLocs[1] $radiusSkels[5] $armTurns[1];
//Re-parent the polygon bones under the new Maya joints:
   cm_runLocals("parenter",{$ulnaSkels[0],$lfUlnaPoly,"1","0"});
   cm_runLocals("parenter",{$radiusSkels[0],$lfRadiusPoly,"1","0"});
   select -cl;
```

Step 5: Create the Finger Skeletons

The next section of code in the cm_advArms procedure creates the finger skeletons, including double-group node pads for every finger. These group nodes are oriented according to the root joint of each finger, which ensures that the finger channels generate the correct channel values when rotated to bend. While the code for creating the thumb skeleton is fairly straightforward, the nested loops creating the rest of the finger skeletons are more complex because they are creating another custom string matrix. This technique is the same one used in the cm_skelCreate procedure, and is used to get the names of the finger polygon bones and then combine those names into a single string for each finger. The following loop that creates the finger skeletons breaks up the matrix of bone names with a tokenize command, uses the polygon points to draw the joints, and parents the polygon bones under the same joints. The last part of the code saves the names of all the finger joints in a single $allFingers array.

```
//3. Hands and Fingers: Set all necessary names into variables:
   string $lfHandEnd = cm_returnName ($basicNames,"lfHand","end");
   string $lfThumbPoly1 = cm_returnName ($basicNames,"lfThumb1","poly");
   string $lfThumbPoly2 = cm_returnName ($basicNames,"lfThumb2","poly");
   string $lfThumbPoly3 = cm_returnName ($basicNames,"lfThumb3","poly");
   string $fingersPadName = "FingersPad";
   string $thumbName = "Thumb";
//Create groups for all the fingers:
   string $fingersGps[] = cm_runLocals
         ("doubleGrp",{$pfx1,$fingersPadName,$lfHandEnd,"1"});
   cm_runLocals ("nodeMover",{$lfHandEnd,$fingersGps[0],"1","0","1"});
//Run procedures to create the skeleton and pad groups:
   string $targetObj[] = {$lfThumbPoly1,$lfThumbPoly1,
         $lfThumbPoly2,$lfThumbPoly3};
   string $targetPt[] = {".vtx[7]",".vtx[0]",".vtx[0]",".vtx[0]"};
   string $thumbSkels[] = cm_skelCreate (4,$targetObj,$targetPt,
```

```
          $thumbName,1,"yup",0,1);
  string $thumbGps[] = cm_runLocals
          ("doubleGrp",{$pfx1,($thumbName + "Pad"),$fingersGps[1],"1"});
  cm_runLocals ("nodeMover",{$thumbSkels[0],$thumbGps[0],"1","0","1"});
//Parent all the thumb nodes:
  cm_runLocals("parenter",{$thumbGps[1],$thumbSkels[0],"1","0"});
  string $lfThumb2[] = cm_runLocals ("getChild",{$thumbSkels[0]});
  string $lfThumb3[] = cm_runLocals ("getChild",{$lfThumb2[0]});
  cm_runLocals("parenter",{$thumbSkels[0],$lfThumbPoly1,"1","0"});
  cm_runLocals("parenter",{$lfThumb2[0],$lfThumbPoly2,"1","0"});
  cm_runLocals("parenter",{$lfThumb3[0],$lfThumbPoly3,"1","0"});
  select -cl;
//Use nested loops to create arrays of arrays for the fingers:
  string $fingerPolys[];
  string $fingersPolys[];
  string $fngrNames[] = {"Index","Middle","Ring","Pinky"};
  for ($i = 0; $i < 4; $i++){//Open loop...
    int $i2;
      for ($i2 = 0; $i2 < 4; $i2++){//Open loop...
        $fingerPolys[$i2] = cm_returnName
            ($basicNames,("lf" + $fngrNames[$i] + $i2),"poly");
      }//Close loop.
      $fingersPolys[$i] = ($fingerPolys[0] + "," + $fingerPolys[1]
        + "," + $fingerPolys[2] + "," + $fingerPolys[3]);
      print ($fngrNames[$i] + " finger poly names saved in string: "
          + $fingersPolys[$i] + "\n");
  }//Close loop.
//Use loop to create all the finger skeletons, and parent polys:
  string $fingerSkels[];
  string $allFingers[];
  string $allFingerGps[];
  for ($i = 0; $i < 4; $i++){//Open loop...
  //Tokenize to get individual finger poly names:
    string $fPoly[];
    tokenize $fingersPolys[$i] "," $fPoly;
    string $targetObj[] = {$fPoly[0],$fPoly[0],$fPoly[1],$fPoly[2],
        $fPoly[3]};
  //Create finger skeleton:
    string $targetPt[] = {".vtx[17]",".vtx[0]",".vtx[0]",
        ".vtx[0]",".vtx[0]"};
    $fingerSkels = cm_skelCreate (5,$targetObj,$targetPt,
        $fngrNames[$i],1,"yup",0,1);
  //Create finger pad groups:
    string $fingerGps[] = cm_runLocals
```

```
        ("doubleGrp",{$pfx1,($fngrNames[$i] + "Pad"),$fingersGps[1],"1"});
  cm_runLocals ("nodeMover",{$fingerSkels[0],$fingerGps[0],"1","0","1"});
  $allFingerGps[size ($allFingerGps)] = $fingerGps[0];
  $allFingerGps[size ($allFingerGps)] = $fingerGps[1];
//Parent finger skeleton and polygon bones:
  cm_runLocals("parenter",{$fingerGps[1],$fingerSkels[0],"1","0"});
  string $lfFinger1[] = cm_runLocals ("getChild",{$fingerSkels[0]});
  string $lfFinger2[] = cm_runLocals ("getChild",{$lfFinger1[0]});
  string $lfFinger3[] = cm_runLocals ("getChild",{$lfFinger2[0]});
  cm_runLocals("parenter",{$fingerSkels[0],$fPoly[0],"1","0"});
  cm_runLocals("parenter",{$lfFinger1[0],$fPoly[1],"1","0"});
  cm_runLocals("parenter",{$lfFinger2[0],$fPoly[2],"1","0"});
  cm_runLocals("parenter",{$lfFinger3[0],$fPoly[3],"1","0"});
//Add skeleton names to array of all joint names:
  $allFingers[size ($allFingers)] = $fingerSkels[0];
  $allFingers[size ($allFingers)] = $lfFinger1[0];
  $allFingers[size ($allFingers)] = $lfFinger2[0];
  $allFingers[size ($allFingers)] = $lfFinger3[0];
  $allFingers[size ($allFingers)] = $fingerSkels[1];
  select -cl;
}//Close loop.
```

Step 6: Drive the Arm, Hand, and Finger Controls

In the SDK section of the code, the cm_setDrivens global procedure is run to drive
the majority of the arm, hand, and finger controls. After placing the names for the
driver and driven nodes into variables, a keyTangent command is run to set the global
method for setting keys to "plateau" tangent type. Running this command ensures
that the animation curves created by the SDKs have smooth transitions between keys,
and slow down slightly as the controls are manipulated close to their limits, called an
ease-in and ease-out.

The first two SDKs automatically drive the shoulders to rise when the arm and elbow
icons rise, so they don't require creating any custom channels; both these SDKs have
0 and "none" in the arguments for creating a custom channel. The third procedure
instead has a 1 in the seventh argument, followed by a short name, minimum, maximum, and default values for the shoulderUp custom channel. All three SDKs have a 1
value in their last argument, which means they are being set on the left side of the rig,
and then mirrored to the right side.

Many of the remaining SDKs are similar, creating custom channels and being mirrored
to the other arm. View the actual script to examine the details on these procedures,
and manipulate the custom channels on the arm icons after running the code to see
how they all work.

```
//4. SDK's: Set all necessary names into variables:
    string $lfArmIcon = cm_returnName ($basicNames,"lfArm","icon");
    string $lfElbowIcon = cm_returnName ($basicNames,"lfElbow","icon");
    string $lfClavAuto1 = cm_returnName ($basicNames,"lfClavAuto1",
            "group");
    string $lfArmIk = cm_returnName ($basicNames,"lfArm","rpIk");
    string $lfWristTurn0 = cm_returnName
            ($basicNames,"lfWristTurn0","group");
    string $lfWristTurn1 = cm_returnName
            ($basicNames,"lfWristTurn1","group");
//Set the global key tangents to set ease-in and ease-out:
    keyTangent -global -itt "plateau" -ott "plateau";
//Icons drive the shoulders to raise automatically:
    float $driverVals[] = {-10.0,0.0,15.0};
    float $drivenVals[] = {-5.0,0.0,35.0};
    cm_setDrivens ($lfArmIcon,"ty",$lfClavAuto1,"rz",
            $driverVals,$drivenVals,0,"none",0,0,0,1);
    float $driverVals[] = {-8.0,0.0,8.0};
    float $drivenVals[] = {-10.0,0.0,15.0};
    cm_setDrivens ($lfElbowIcon,"ty",$lfClavAuto1,"rz",
            $driverVals,$drivenVals,0,"none",0,0,0,1);
    print "Auto SDK's set for the shoulders!\n";
//Create channels to manually drive the individual shoulders:
    float $driverVals[] = {-5.0,0.0,10.0};
    float $drivenVals[] = {-15.0,0.0,30.0};
    cm_setDrivens ($lfArmIcon,"shoulderUp",$lfClavAuto1,"rz",
            $driverVals,$drivenVals,1,"sup",-5,10,0,1);
    float $driverVals[] = {-10.0,0.0,10.0};
    float $drivenVals[] = {-25.0,0.0,25.0};
    cm_setDrivens ($lfArmIcon,"shoulderFor",$lfClavAuto1,"ry",
            $driverVals,$drivenVals,1,"sfr",-10,10,0,1);
```

Step 7: Set Warnings and Clean Up Icons

The next section of code uses a math expression to create a color warning on the polygon bones when a limb has reached its extended limit. The polygon bones turn red when the lower arm joint rotates to the point of straightening or locking. The warning is generated by a conditional expression that evaluates the lower arm joint rotation, and if the values go beyond a target amount, then an incandescent color channel is turned on. The color itself is on a material previously assigned to the polygon arm bones in the basicFkRig scene file. Choose Window > Rendering Editors > Hypershade, to view the materials assigned to the polygon bones. Here is what the expression will look like in the Expression Editor after the procedure is run:

```
if (cm:lfForearm_ctrlRt.rotateZ < -4.3) lfArmBone_mat.incandescenceR = 1;
else lfArmBone_mat.incandescenceR = 0;
```

The next several sections of code clean up the icons by using the custom procedures that lock, hide, and limit channels. The limit values used in the procedures can be adjusted according to animator preference, the scene requirements, and the character size. The value for the rotation limits on the arm and elbow icons is being set to 0 because the rotation channels are also being locked and hidden, which means there is no reason to set limits.

After the icons are cleaned up, the code turns on the Show Manipulator tool, sets a default key on the icon channels at frame 0, and resets the namespace to the default root namespace. Turning on the Show Manipulator tool automatically displays the default move manipulator set by the cm_cleaner procedure. Also, setting a key at 0 makes it easy to reset the character to the default pose after testing the controls: Simply click the timeline at 0, and the controls will snap back into place.

```
//5. Expression: Set color warnings for when the limbs lock:
   float $armLimits[] = {-4.3,-4.3};
   string $armJts[] = {$armLows[0],$armLows[1]};
   string $armColors[] = {"lfArmBone_mat","rtArmBone_mat"};
   string $armExps[] = {"lfArmWarn_exp","rtArmWarn_exp"};
   int $i;
   for ($i = 0; $i < size($armJts); $i++){//Open loop...
      string $warnExpLine1 = ("if (" + $armJts[$i] + ".rz < "
         + $armLimits[$i] + ") " + $armColors[$i] + ".ir = 1;\n");
      string $warnExpLine2 = ("else " + $armColors[$i] + ".ir = 0;\n");
      expression -n $armExps[$i] -s ($warnExpLine1 + $warnExpLine2);
   }//Close loop.
 //-------------------------------------------------------------
 //6. Clean: Limit, hide, and lock channels on the icons:
 //Use procedure to hide, lock and set default manip:
   string $cleanAttrs[] = {"rx","ry","rz","sx","sy","sz","v"};
   cm_cleaner ($lfArmIcon,$cleanAttrs,1,1,1,1);
 //Use procedure to set limits on the icons:
   float $tranVals[] = {20.0,15.0,10.0};
   float $rotVals[] = {0.0};
   cm_limits ($lfArmIcon,$tranVals,$rotVals);
 //Use procedure to hide, lock and set default manip:
   string $cleanAttrs[] = {"rx","ry","rz","sx","sy","sz","v"};
   cm_cleaner ($lfElbowIcon,$cleanAttrs,1,1,1,1);
 //Use procedure to set limits on the icons:
   float $tranVals[] = {20.0,20.0,20.0};
   float $rotVals[] = {0.0};
   cm_limits ($lfElbowIcon,$tranVals,$rotVals);
```

```
//--------------------------------------------------------------
//Set tool to the Show Manipulator tool to use default manips:
  setToolTo "ShowManips";
//Set a keyframe on all the icons at 0 in their default positions:
  string $keyIcons[] = {$lfArmIcon,$lfElbowIcon};
  cm_keyArray ($keyIcons,0);
//Clear selection and set namespace to root:
  select -cl;
  cm_setNamespace(0);
```

Step 8: Run the Procedure to Create the Advanced Arm Controls

The last few sections of code in the CMaraffi_advArms script complete the cm_advArms local procedure to process names and create the controls. At the end of the procedure, all the names in the new arm hierarchy are listed, sorted, and returned in a $armHierarchy array. Then the cm_advArms procedure is run and the names are caught in an $advArmNames array, and the cm_printNames procedure prints the names to the command line and to file for future reference. Lastly, the script edits buttons in the setup GUI to direct the user to run the next advanced rigging script. The remaining advanced scripts for the legs, head, and torso all will use this same organization.

```
//List and sort all node names in the rig hierarchy:
   string $armHierarchy[] = cm_processNames ($advArmGps[0],0,"none");
 //Return the top node name of the rig:
   return $armHierarchy;
}//Close procedure.
print "cm_advArms proc is now in Maya's memory.\n";
//************************************************************
//Run local procedure to create the advanced arm rig:
print "Running advanced arm rig procedure.\n";
string $advArmNames[] = cm_advArms();
print "Advanced arm rig is created!\n";
print "----------------------------------------------------\n";
print "cm_advArms proc returns the hierarchy names: \n";
//Run procedure to print names to the command line and to file:
cm_printNames($advArmNames,1,"advArms");
```

Step 9: Create the Advanced Foot Controls

The CMaraffi_advLegs script has many similarities to the advanced arm script, so this chapter won't review that code in detail. Go through the actual script on your own, reading the comments for each section, and examine the code after running it to compare the commands and procedures in the script to what is happening in Maya.

Creating Advanced Head and Torso Controls

This section covers the rest of the advanced controls, including skeleton controls for the head, face, and torso. Important new techniques will be shown in the interface, such as using spline IK for the backbone controls. At the end of the section advanced scripts for the main controls are explained in detail.

Upgrading the Head and Face Rig

In the basic rig only two skeletons were used for simple head controls: the main head skeleton and the jaw skeleton that was child to it. If you did a test bind of the basic rig and rotated the jaw joint, you would have noticed that the whole face collapsed in an unnatural way. If your head rig is too simple with too few joints, Maya is forced to guess at how to assign the weighting of the points. It will assign percentages of influence to the closest joint in 3D space. Because the jaw joint is close to many of the face points, Maya will automatically assign the joint too much influence, causing the face to collapse when the jaw is moved (see **FIGURE 4.20**).

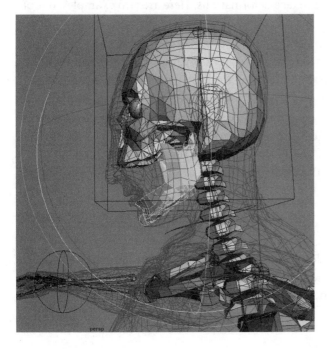

FIGURE 4.20 *Binding just the head and jaw joints on the basic rig makes the whole face collapse when the jaw is rotated, and requires extensive manual weighting to improve the deformation.*

ADDING SKELETONS TO THE FACE

To improve the face deformations without a lot of tedious manual weighting of points, it is best to add skeletons to all the main areas of the face, and then parent them under either the head or jaw joints. This will more clearly tell Maya how to weight the points on the face, and will reduce the amount of manual weighting required after binding. The best way to approach adding these skeletons is to define the main bone structures of the face, and examine how the muscles flex. Look at a good anatomy and physiology book to see how the muscles are structured on the face.

To add some face skeletons to the nose and jaw:

1. Start by drawing skeletons that contour the main features of the face, holding down the V key as you draw to snap directly to points on the polygon skull and jaw bones. The purpose for adding these skeletons is to define what parts of the face should move with the head, and what should move with the jaw. Although you could snap directly to the skin model if it is available, to build or script a generic rig that will fit most biped characters, use the polygon bones for joint placement.

2. Add skeletons to improve face deformations. Here are two examples, out of many possibilities:

    ■ To keep the nose points from being assigned to the jaw joint, draw a new skeleton in the nose area from between the eyes to above the mouth, and parent it under the head joint. Name the joints **ctNoseRoot**, and so on.

    ■ To ensure that points in the jaw area move with the jaw, and not the head, draw a skeleton around the contour of the left jaw edge from below the left ear to the center of the jaw (see **FIGURE 4.21**). Name the joints **lfJawRoot**, and so on. Mirror the skeleton to the right side, and parent both skeletons under the center jaw joint.

CREATING MUSCLE-FLEXING WITH SKELETONS

Other than adding static skeletons to improve weighting to the head and jaw, you can add skeletons to create muscle movements on the face as well. For instance, muscles on the forehead flex upward and downward to raise and lower the eyebrows. You can simulate this basic motion by adding three two-joint skeletons on the left, middle, and right sides of the forehead.

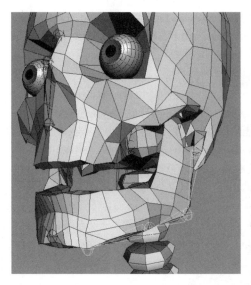 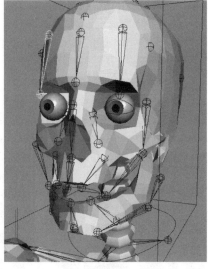

FIGURE 4.21 *Snap joints to points on the polygon bones to contour the bony parts of the face and define the weighting, and then parent the new skeletons under the main jaw and skull joints.*

FIGURE 4.22 *Create simple face controls by drawing skeletons in the direction that the muscles flex, such as on the forehead to create eyebrow controls.*

To add some face skeletons to the forehead that will flex the eyebrow muscles:

1. Draw the left eyebrow skeleton over the left eye, from a point on top of the forehead area of the skull bone to a point somewhere around the middle of the left brow area. Name the joints **lfBrowRoot**, and so on. Mirror this skeleton to the right side, and then draw another skeleton down the middle of the forehead between the eyebrows (see **FIGURE 4.22**). Name the center joints **ctBrowsRoot**, and so on.

2. Group all three skeletons together, and parent the group node under the head joint (double-group to keep bones from being displayed between the parented skeletons).

Just these three skeletons will let you shape the forehead to create simple brow movements by scaling them in their X axis. These movements can facilitate the creation of facial expressions such as sad, happy, and surprise. Most current facial rigs are a combination of joint transforms, which this chapter covers, and blend shapes, which will be covered in the next chapter.

ROTATING JOINTS AROUND FACIAL FEATURES

One reason joints are often used for face controls is that they rotate on arcs, while other methods like blend shapes morph in straight lines from shape to shape. On a basic blend shape without any in-between shapes, this movement could lead to unnatural deformations or intersections of surfaces in the middle of the morph. Joint controls can sometimes bypass this problem on the curved surfaces of the face. For instance, a good place on the face to incorporate the rotation of joints is in opening and closing the eyes.

To add some skeletons to open and close the eyes:

1. Draw a two-joint skeleton from the center of the eyeball to the middle of the top eyelid. Name the joints **lfEyeLidRoot**, and so on. Since the eyeball is round, the skeleton will rotate on the correct arc to close the eye without intersecting the eye surface (see **FIGURE 4.23**). Be aware that points on the lower and side corners of the eye will be assigned to the top eyelid joints if you don't also add other skeletons to these areas.

FIGURE 4.23 *Using the natural arcs produced by rotating joints can create good eyelid controls for opening and closing the eyes.*

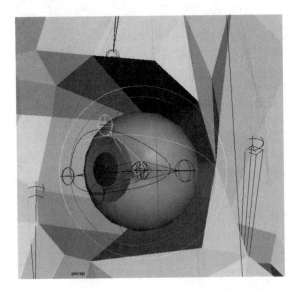

2. Experiment with adding other face skeletons, such as a skeleton drawn from the sides of the cheek down to the corner of the mouth, which allows you to scale and rotate the joints to create a smile or grimace expression. Be aware that some manual weighting of the points will still be required when binding, especially to smooth out the deformations on the skin.

Once you've created and parented the skeletons to the rig hierarchy, add custom channels to the head icon to drive the joints using SDKs. In some cases, as on the eyebrow joints, drive the scaling in X to raise and lower the brows; in other cases, like the eyelid joints, drive the rotations to open and close the eyes. Experiment with driving both directions on the driven channel, as this can produce unexpected, but sometimes useful, facial expressions.

Building an Advanced Torso Rig

Upgrading the torso involves adding new skeletons and controls to the backbone, chest, and waist. The backbone skeleton will incorporate a new type of IK solver called spline IK, which has properties of both FK and IK skeletons. After creating the advanced backbone, you will create additional FK skeletons in the chest and stomach, driven with SDKs and expressions. This section also implements some advanced connections to create automatic torso controls for breathing and moving the upper body with the feet.

PREPARING TO ADD SPLINE IK TO THE BACKBONE

Upgrading the backbone will be the most involved setup you do on the biped rig because there are so many nodes and connections involved. The process involves drawing skeletons, adding spline IK, binding spine IK curves to icons, connecting and setting advanced attributes, and parenting all the nodes into the basic rig hierarchy so everything works together.

The main part of the new backbone controls involves using the Spline IK solver, which creates and assigns a curve to a skeleton, so that the shape of the skeleton tries to mimic the shape of the curve. To continuously follow the shape of the curve, the solver calculates how the joints should rotate as the points on the curve are moved. Deforming the curve allows you to bend the skeleton in multiple directions, much like an FK skeleton, only with the ease of IK by moving points instead of an IK handle. Actually, moving points manually is not that easy, but you will be shown how to make icons easily control the curve points instead. Lastly, spline IK does create an IK handle, but it is used only to set spline IK attributes, not to animate transforms.

To better fit the curvature of the polygon vertebrae, you must draw a new spine skeleton that has more joints than currently exist in the basic backbone rig. Such a skeleton will also better follow the points on a spline IK curve, and produce smoother deformations on the skin. Keep in mind, however, that you won't delete the original backbone skeleton, but use it as an FK control for the new spline IK backbone. These types of backbone controls were widely popularized by Jason Schliefer over the years at several Maya master classes held during SIGGRAPH conferences. Since then they have become an industry standard for creating a flexible backbone; as a result, any character rigging artist should know some variation of this type control.

DRAWING THE NEW BACKBONE SKELETONS

You'll begin by creating two new FK backbone skeletons in the spine area from center hip to shoulder, and then a separate neck skeleton from center shoulder to head. Two main spine skeletons are necessary to move the neck independently from the back when you add the spline IK in the following section. In addition, several two-joint skeletons will be created in the hip, chest, and head areas to facilitate controlling the spline IK curves.

To create the new backbone skeletons:

1. In the Joint Tool options dialog box, make sure that standard IK is turned off. Using the polygon vertebrae as a guide, draw both of the new backbone skeletons in Side view, clicking between every other vertebra. This creates a Maya joint for every two polygon bones.

You should draw the back spine skeleton from the center pelvis to the base of the neck (vertebrae 0 to12). You should draw the neck spine skeleton from the base of the neck to the base of the skull (vertebrae 16 to 21). Make sure that the joints are positioned between the vertebrae (see **FIGURE 4.24**).

FIGURE 4.24 *Draw the new backbone skeletons in Side view to center the joints between every two vertebra of the spine.*

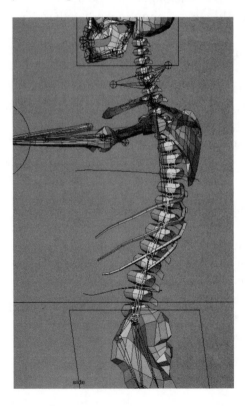

2. Name the new back spine joints **ctLowSpineRoot**, **ctLowSpine1**, and so on, and name the neck spine joints **ctUpSpineRoot**, **ctUpSpine1**, and so on.

3. Create a two-joint FK skeleton in the neck area from where the back spine skeleton ends at vertebra 12, up to where the neck spine skeleton starts at vertebra 16. Name the joints **ctMidSpineRoot** and **ctMidSpineEnd**. This skeleton will be used to bind the spline IK curves of the other two skeletons, which will partially control the shape of the curves.

4. Create similar skeletons in the head and hip areas. Actually, these skeletons should be duplicates of the main center head and hip skeletons. Name the skeletons **ctTopSpineRoot**, **ctBotSpineRoot**, and so on. These skeletons will also be used to bind the spline IK curves.

5. So that you can better see the effect of spline IK on the skeletons, re-parent all the polygon vertebrae under the appropriate joints. Because of how the skeletons were drawn, make sure you parent every two joints under the lower and upper skeleton joints. Parent vertebrae 12 to 15 under ctMidSpineRoot, and then make the pelvis and skull polygon bones children of the bottom and top skeletons.

6. To prevent redundancy and weighting conflicts when binding, rename the original center hip, head, and backbone skeletons so they will not be bound. For instance, in the rigging scripts the joints are given a new suffix indicating they are now control joints (_ctrlRt and _ctrlJt).

Keep in mind that whenever you work on a character, you must choose how much resolution a particular control really needs. On the two main spine skeletons, for instance, too few Maya joints won't be flexible enough, while too many joints will be more difficult to bind and weight. Drawing a Maya joint for every polygon vertebrae produces too many joints. Creating a skeleton with a Maya joint for every two vertebrae produces a much more manageable skeleton, while still being flexible enough for a backbone. Though not an issue when creating a rig through code, working with fewer nodes speeds up the whole manual rigging process.

ADDING SPLINE IK TO THE SKELETONS

To add spline IK to the two main backbone skeletons:

1. Choose Skeleton > IK Spline Handle Tool ❒ to activate the tool, and then click Reset Tool in the dialog box to use the default settings. Once the tool is activated, click Close to close the dialog box.

2. In Perspective view, click the root joint followed by the end joint of the lower spine skeleton. You should see a new IK handle appear, and if you also look in the Hypergraph you will see a new curve has automatically been created (see **FIGURE 4.25**). Name the IK handle and curve **ctLowSpineIk** and **ctLowSpineCurve**.

FIGURE 4.25 *Adding spline IK to the spine skeleton creates an IK handle and curve that is used to rotate the joints.*

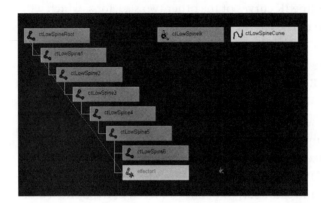

3. Select the spline IK curve in the Hypergraph, and press the F8 key to switch to component mode in Perspective view. The default IK spline handle settings, with a Number of Spans set to 1, creates a curve with four points. This is normally enough points for a human backbone, but if necessary you can increase the number of points, and thus the complexity of the curve, by increasing the span setting. Try moving some of the points to see how that flexes the skeleton by the solver rotating the joints.

4. Repeat steps 1 to 3 on the upper spine skeleton in the neck area of the character, naming the spline IK nodes **ctUpSpineIk** and **ctUpSpineCurve**.

Do not be alarmed if you see a pink warning appear in the feedback field when you add the spline IK to the skeletons. This occurs because the spline IK handle is automatically selected, and you are never supposed to transform it like a standard IK handle. Maya is just indicating that spline IK should be controlled only by transforming the curve components. You'll learn how to do that in the next section

CREATING THE SPINE ICON CONTROLS

Since manually moving points on a curve is tedious, it is best to indirectly control the shape of the curve through icons. In the past, this was often done by creating clusters on the points and parenting the clusters under different icons. Instead, the technique shown here smooth-binds the spline IK curves to the two-joint skeletons created at the bottom, middle, and top of the spine.

1. Bind the lower spline IK curve by Shift-selecting the root joints of the bottom and middle skeletons followed by the curve, and choose Skin > Bind Skin > Smooth Bind ❒. In the dialog box, set bind to Joint Hierarchy using the Closest Distance method, set the Max Influences to 5, the Dropoff Rate to 4, and turn on all the other check boxes (see **FIGURE 4.26**). Then click Bind Skin to apply the settings.

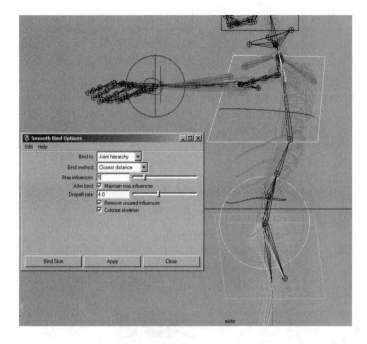

FIGURE 4.26 *Binding the spline IK curve to joints parented under the icons allows easy manipulation of the points on the curve.*

2. Repeat the same binding process on the upper spine curve to the middle and top spine joints. After binding, rotating the joints should deform the curves and flex the spline IK skeletons.

3. To make animating the spline IK easier, parent the two-joint skeletons under icons. You should parent the bottom and top skeletons under the hip and head icons. Since there is no icon for the middle skeleton, you should create a new box icon in the upper chest area.

4. Run your box icon code, and transform and shape the icon to fit around the upper chest of the character, naming it **ctSpine**. Then parent the middle skeleton under the spine icon.

Rotating the icons will now flex the lower and upper spine skeletons, but the movement still doesn't look good because the rest of the hierarchy is not yet moving with the controls. Ignore this for now, as you have to complete a few more tasks before parenting all the nodes together.

MAKING THE LOWER SPINE STRETCHY

The curves stretch a little when you rotate the controls. This effect is not very obvious on the neck, but is more noticeable on the lower spine skeleton when the spine icon is moved and rotated. Too much movement causes the joints to become separated from the curve. For this reason, it is advisable to add some stretchy qualities to the skeleton joints. Of course, this is also a very useful technique for creating cartoon-style squash and stretch effects. However, even realistic character rigs look better with a little stretchiness added to their main backbone skeleton.

An easy way to add stretchiness to the lower spine is to write a math expression that uses the length of the curve to drive the scaling in local X axis of the spine joints. If you translate the joints in this direction, it effectively lengthens the skeleton. Translation propagates down the skeleton hierarchy differently than actually scaling the joints, but either technique can produce good stretching controls.

To add stretchiness to the lower spine joints:

1. Create a node on the ctLowSpineCurve curve that contains a channel that registers its length. Select the curve, and run the following MEL command on the command line: `arclen -ch 1;`

2. With the curve still selected, choose Window > Hypergraph: Connections to find a node named curveInfo1, and open it in the Attribute Editor. You will see an arcLength channel that registers the length of the curve (see **FIGURE 4.27**).

FIGURE 4.27 *To add some stretch to the spine, you must first create a curveInfo1 node that has a channel that registers the length of the spline IK curve.*

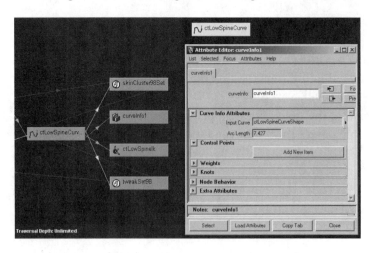

The 7.47 value displayed is the default length of the curve, and will be used in the expression to make the skeleton stretch. Keep in mind that this value will change for different-sized characters.

3. Open the Expression Editor, and write an expression line for each joint in the lower spine skeleton, starting at the second joint. Here is what each line of the expression should look like:

```
ctLowSpine1.tx = 1.36 * ((curveInfo1.arcLength / 7.47) / topNode.sy);
```

The main part of this expression divides the current length channel value by the default value to determine if the curve has been stretched or compressed. This is multiplied by the joint's default translateX value, in this case 1.36, to drive the actual translation. Finally, dividing by the top node scaling in Y will keep the joints sized correctly in relation to the overall rig size. If the top node of the character is scaled to better fit the scene, for instance, the expression will compensate.

4. Copy and paste this expression line for each joint of the lower spine skeleton, only changing the joint name and the default X translation value. When you have finished, name the expression node **stretchySpine**, and click Create and Close.

5. Move and rotate the spine icon to test the stretching on the joints of the skeleton. You should see the Maya skeleton stretch while every two polygon bones move with the joints. When the skin is bound, this movement will produce a smooth stretch.

SETTING THE ADVANCED SPLINE IK TWIST ATTRIBUTES

Currently, if you rotate the icons in Y, the spine skeleton won't rotate in its local X axis to twist the backbone. This is because spline IK twisting is not controlled by the points on the curve, but instead by a special attribute on the IK solver. In the past, it was common to drive the twist-and-roll channels on the handle to control twisting. Now Maya has an even easier option available on the IK handle, called the advanced twist attributes.

To set advanced spline IK twist attributes:

1. In the Hypergraph, right-click the ctLowSpineIk IK handle to open the handle in the Attribute Editor, and click the IK Solver Attributes section to display the disabled Advanced Twist Controls.

2. Turn on the Enable Twist Controls option and set these Advanced Twist controls (see **FIGURE 4.28**):

- Since you are using icons to twist the skeletons, set the World Up Type to Object Rotation Up (Start/End).

- Then set negative Z as the Up Axis and Vector in the next three options. This relates to the X orientation of the skeleton joints.

- Most importantly, type the full name of the hips icon into the first World Up Object field, and type the spine icon name in the second World Up Object field.

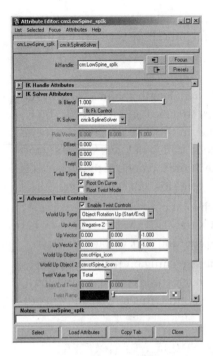

FIGURE 4.28 *Spline IK curves won't twist unless you drive special attributes on the IK handle. You can easily do this by setting the advanced twist attributes in the Attribute Editor.*

3. Click Close to close the Attribute Editor, and repeat steps 1 through 2 on the upper spine IK handle.

This gives you all the nodes required to put together the hierarchy for the advanced backbone and finalize the torso rig.

COMPLETING THE ADVANCED TORSO RIG

To connect all the advanced backbone nodes into the basic hierarchy:

1. All the parts of the rig that used to move with the original backbone skeletons, such as the head and arms, should now move with the spline IK skeletons. The easiest way to do this is to re-parent the ctBackPad0 group node under the end joint of the new lower spine skeleton.

2. To make the original FK backbone joints control the new spline IK, simply parent the spine icon under the ctBack2 joint. Since you are parenting the icon under a joint, insert group node pads between these controls to make sure that the spine icon generates world values when rotating.

3. Rotate the original backbone joints to see if they move the spine icon, which in turn should move the spline IK skeletons. This setup gives you two levels of controls for manipulating the backbone. You should streamline the advanced backbone controls by adding custom channels on the icon; these channels will drive the FK rotation of the backbone joints using SDKs (see **FIGURE 4.29**).

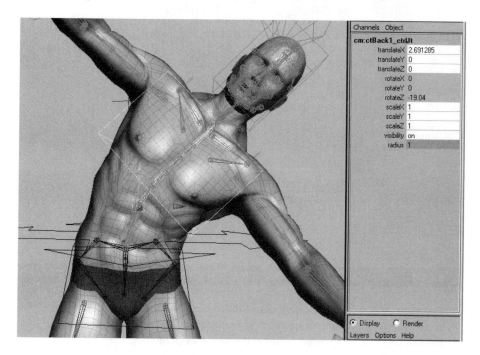

FIGURE 4.29 *Parent the new spine icon under the original FK backbone joints to create two levels of backbone controls.*

4. Parent all other new spline IK nodes under the DoNotMove node at the top of the rig hierarchy. Since you are already controlling the new skeletons through the spline IK curves, it is not necessary to have them also move with parent transformations; that latter could move the nodes twice as far as they should move, called a double transform.

In addition to creating spline IK spine controls, upgrading the torso should also involve adding skeletons to the chest, ribs, and stomach to improve deformations on the skin when the backbone bends (see **FIGURE 4.30**). Draw the skeletons in the same way as done on the advanced face controls, and parent them to the closest spline IK backbone joints.

FIGURE 4.30 *Add and drive skeletons in the chest, ribs, and torso to improve deformations, and to create muscle and skin effects.*

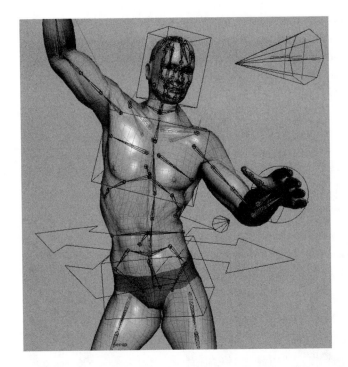

EXERCISE 4.2: SCRIPTING THE ADVANCED HEAD AND TORSO

This exercise examines important details in the head and torso advanced rigging scripts. These two scripts complete the advanced controls, and make the rig ready for binding and adding a character GUI in the next two chapters.

As these scripts follow the same format as previously shown scripts, this exercise examines only the sections that show new techniques. For instance, the code that creates, parents, and drives skeletons in the face and chest will not be shown here. See the actual scripts for more details on this code.

Step 1: Create an Eye Jitter Control

The only new technique used in the CMaraffi_advHead script is a math expression that randomly moves the eye controls to make the eyes shake or jitter. The expression incorporates a rand function, similar to a MEL command, that generates random values between the minimum and maximum limits set in parentheses. For instance, in the following example, the function generates random float values between –10 and 10:

```
rand (-10.0, 10.0);
```

In the advanced head script application, custom channels with a range of –1 to 1 are used in the parentheses instead of static numbers. The random values generated are used to translate the target locators constraining the eyeballs. The code runs three addAttr commands to create three custom channels to use in the expression. The eyeJitter channel is the master channel on the eyes icon for animating the effect, and goes from 0 to 1. This channel drives the jitterMin and jitterMax channels to input values into the random function. Here is the MEL code (starting about line 222 in the cm_advHead procedure):

```
//Eye Jitter: Use expressions to create eye jitter controls:
   addAttr -ln "eyeJitter" -sn "ejt" -at "double" -min 0.0
           -max 1.0 -dv 0.0 -r 1 -w 1 -s 1 -k 1 $eyesIcon;
   addAttr -ln "jitterMin" -sn "jmn" -at "double" -min -1.0
           -max 0.0 -dv 0.0 -r 1 -w 1 -s 1 -k 1 $jitterGp;
   addAttr -ln "jitterMax" -sn "jmx" -at "double" -min 0.0
           -max 1.0 -dv 0.0 -r 1 -w 1 -s 1 -k 1 $jitterGp;
   string $jitExpLn1 = ($jitterGp + ".jitterMin = 0 - " +
           $eyesIcon + ".eyeJitter;\n");
   string $jitExpLn2 = ($jitterGp + ".jitterMax = 0 + " +
           $eyesIcon + ".eyeJitter;\n");
   string $jitExpLn3 = ($jitterGp + ".ty = 0 + rand(" +
           $jitterGp + ".jitterMin," + $jitterGp
           + ".jitterMax);\n");
   string $jitExpLn4 = ($jitterGp + ".tx = 0 + rand(" +
           $jitterGp + ".jitterMin," + $jitterGp
           + ".jitterMax);\n");
   string $jitterExp = ($jitExpLn1 + $jitExpLn2 + $jitExpLn3 +
           $jitExpLn4);
   expression -n "eyeJitter_exp" -s $jitterExp;
```

Running the script creates the following expression in the Expression Editor:

```
ctEyeJitter_group.jitterMin = 0 - ctEyes_icon.eyeJitter;
ctEyeJitter_group.jitterMax = 0 + ctEyes_icon.eyeJitter;
ctEyeJitter_group.ty = 0 +
   rand(ctEyeJitter_group.jitterMin,ctEyeJitter_group.jitterMax);
ctEyeJitter_group.tx = 0 +
   rand(ctEyeJitter_group.jitterMin,ctEyeJitter_group.jitterMax);
```

Once the expression is implemented, you simply increase the eyeJitter channel on the eyes icon to see the eyes move. The reversed signs on the first two lines of the expression cause the minimum and maximum channels to go in different directions when the master eyeJitter channel on the eyes icon is increased, which in turn increases the limits in the random function, producing more jitter. Since the expression requires the interface to update, play the timeline to see the full jitter effect. A large amount of jitter is obviously a very cartoony look, and a common effect used on anime characters. But you can use a little eye jitter on realistic characters to add subtle tension to the eyes.

Step 2: Create the New Backbone Skeletons

The CMaraffi_advTorso script contains a single local procedure that creates all the advanced torso controls, including the spline IK backbone. The first step in creating the advanced torso controls (not shown here) is sourcing scripts, declaring all required names in variables; and renaming joints in the backbone, head, and hips that will become control joints rather than bind joints. This section in the cm_advTorso procedure also creates a new spine icon and fits it around the upper chest area using a circular curve that is part of the FK rig hierarchy.

The next section of code, starting around line 109 in the script, creates the spline IK backbone skeletons. Two loops are used to create the new lower and upper skeletons. The polygon vertebrae intentionally were numbered from 0 to 21 to facilitate running these loops. The code in the loops reference center points on the polygon bones, to position the joints in the center between each vertebra. Lastly, in addition to creating the two main spine skeletons, three new two-joint skeletons also are created in the hips, chest, and head areas. These skeletons will bind the spline IK curves in the next section of the script.

```
//Skels: Create the lower spine skeleton using poly vertebrae 0-12:
   string $targetObj[];
   string $targetPt[];
   int $i;
   for ($i = 0; $i < 13; $i++){//Open loop...
     $targetObj[size($targetObj)] = $vertebrae[$i];
     $targetPt[size($targetPt)] = ".vtx[24]";
     $i = ($i + 1);
   }//Close loop.
   string $lowSpineSkels[] = cm_skelCreate (7,$targetObj,$targetPt,
        $lowSpineName,0,"xdown",0,1);
   string $lowSpineJts[] = sort (`listRelatives -ad -typ "transform"
        $lowSpineSkels[0]`);
 //Create the bottom spine skeleton using the polygon pelvis:
   string $targetObj[] = {$pelvisPoly,$hipsEnd};
   string $targetPt[] = {".vtx[0]","obj"};
   string $botSpineSkel[] = cm_skelCreate (2,$targetObj,$targetPt,
        $botSpineName,0,"xup",0,1);
 //Create the middle spine skeleton using polygon vertebrae 12-15:
   string $targetObj[] = {$vertebrae[12],$vertebrae[15]};
   string $targetPt[] = {".vtx[24]",".vtx[25]"};
```

```
  string $midSpineSkel[] = cm_skelCreate (2,$targetObj,$targetPt,
       $midSpineName,0,"xdown",0,1);
//Create the top spine skeleton using main head skeleton:
  string $targetObj[] = {$headRoot,$headEnd};
  string $targetPt[] = {"obj","obj"};
  string $topSpineSkel[] = cm_skelCreate (2,$targetObj,$targetPt,
       $topSpineName,0,"xdown",0,1);
//Create the upper spine skeleton using polygon vertebrae 15-21:
  clear $targetObj;
  clear $targetPt;
  for ($i = 15; $i < 22; $i++){//Open loop...
    $targetObj[size($targetObj)] = $vertebrae[$i];
    $targetPt[size($targetPt)] = ".vtx[25]";
    $i = ($i + 1);
  }//Close loop.
  string $upSpineSkels[] = cm_skelCreate (4,$targetObj,$targetPt,
       $upSpineName,0,"xdown",0,1);
  string $upSpineJts[] = sort (`listRelatives -ad -typ "transform"
       $upSpineSkels[0]`);
```

Step 3: Add Spline IK to the Spine Skeletons

The next section of the `cm_advTorso` procedure adds spline IK to the two spine skeletons, and smooth-binds the resulting curves. Since the spline IK options are the defaults, it is not necessary to explicitly specify all the flags on the `ikHandle` commands. The `rename` commands are renaming the spline IK curves, since there is no flag on the `ikHandle` command for naming the curves. Finally, the section ends by running `skinCluster` commands to smooth-bind the two curves to the appropriate joints created in the last section of code.

```
//Spline IK: Add spline Ik to the two new spine skeletons:
  string $lowSpineIk[] = `ikHandle -n ($lowSpineName + "_spIk")
        -sol "ikSplineSolver" -pcv false
        -sj $lowSpineSkels[0] -ee $lowSpineSkels[1]`;
  string $upSpineIk[] = `ikHandle -n ($upSpineName + "_spIk")
        -sol "ikSplineSolver" -pcv false
        -sj $upSpineSkels[0] -ee $upSpineSkels[1]`;
//Rename the spline ik curves from default names:
  string $lowSpineCurve = `rename $lowSpineIk[2]
        ($lowSpineName + "_curve")`;
  string $upSpineCurve = `rename $upSpineIk[2]
        ($upSpineName + "_curve")`;
//Bind the curves to the hips, spine, and head root joints:
```

```
    skinCluster -n ($lowSpineName + "_smBind") -dr 4 -mi 5 -omi 1 -rui 1
                $botSpineSkel[0] $midSpineSkel[0] $lowSpineCurve;
    skinCluster -n ($upSpineName + "_smBind") -dr 4 -mi 5 -omi 1 -rui 1
                $midSpineSkel[0] $topSpineSkel[0] $upSpineCurve;
```

Step 4: Create a Stretchy Spine

Once the spline IK skeletons are created, the joints can be made to stretch when the curve is manipulated. Code in the next section of the cm_advTorso procedure does this by first running the arclen command to add a curveInfo node to the lower spine curve, and then using a getAttr command to establish the default length. This length is ultimately used in the math expression to drive the X translation of the lower spine joints. Then the expression lines are created by running several loops. The first loop runs a getAttr command to query each joint's default X translation value; these values are used in each line of the expression. The lines are generated by the second loop and added to the positions in the $spineExpLines string array. Lastly, the array strings are combined in the third loop into a single string, and then run in the expression command.

```
//Spine Stretch: Use expression to drive joint movement:
    string $lengthNode = `arclen -ch 1 $lowSpineCurve`;
    float $lengthVal = `getAttr ($lengthNode + ".arcLength")`;
//Use loop to get tx values on all joints in array:
    float $txValues[];
    string $joint;
    for ($joint in $lowSpineJts){//Open loop...
        $txValues[size($txValues)] = `getAttr ($joint + ".tx")`;
    }//Close loop.
//Use loop to create each line of expression string:
    string $spineExpLines[];
    int $i;
    for ($i = 0; $i < size($lowSpineJts); $i++){//Open for loop...
        $spineExpLines[$i] = ($lowSpineJts[$i] + ".tx = " +
        $txValues[$i] + " * ((" + $lengthNode + ".arcLength / " +
        $lengthVal + ") / " + $topNode + ".sy);\n");
    }//Close loop.
//Use loop to combine expression strings into single string:
    string $expLine;
    string $spineExp;
    for ($expLine in $spineExpLines){//Open loop...
        $spineExp = ($spineExp + $expLine);
    }//Close loop.
    expression -n "spineStretch_exp" -s $spineExp;
```

Step 5: Set the Advanced Twist Attributes

The next section of the cm_advTorso procedure uses a loop to set the advanced twist attributes on both spline IK skeletons. Within the loop, a series of connectAttr commands connect the worldMatrix channels of the icons to the dWorldUpMatrix and dWorldUpMatrixEnd channels of the curves. Channels like these are somewhat obscure, and do not always appear in the History field when you make these connections in the Attribute Editor. Instead, other Maya procedures come up, and you must track down these channels inside those procedures.

```
//Adv Twist: Use loop to set the advanced spline IK controls:
   string $splineIks[] = {$lowSpineIk[0],$upSpineIk[0]};
   string $splineIk;
   for ($splineIk in $splineIks){//Open loop...
     setAttr ($splineIk + ".dTwistControlEnable") 1;
     setAttr ($splineIk + ".dWorldUpType") 4;
     setAttr ($splineIk + ".dWorldUpAxis") 4;
     setAttr ($splineIk + ".dWorldUpVectorY") 0;
     setAttr ($splineIk + ".dWorldUpVectorEndY") 0;
     setAttr ($splineIk + ".dWorldUpVectorZ") -1;
     setAttr ($splineIk + ".dWorldUpVectorEndZ") -1;
   }//Close loop.
//Connect the new spline IK to the hips, spine, and head icons:
   connectAttr -f ($hipsIcon + ".worldMatrix")
             ($lowSpineIk[0] + ".dWorldUpMatrix");
   connectAttr -f ($spineIcon[0] + ".worldMatrix")
             ($lowSpineIk[0] + ".dWorldUpMatrixEnd");
   connectAttr -f ($spineIcon[0] + ".worldMatrix")
             ($upSpineIk[0] + ".dWorldUpMatrix");
   connectAttr -f ($headIcon + ".worldMatrix")
             ($upSpineIk[0] + ".dWorldUpMatrixEnd");
```

Step 6: Parent the Advanced Backbone Nodes

To finalize the advanced spine controls in the cm_advTorso procedure, the main spline IK nodes are first grouped and parented under the DoNotMove node. Then the polygon vertebrae are parented under the appropriate joints, and the new skeletons in the hips, chest, and head are parented under the hips, spine, and head icons. Finally, a parent constraint forces the backPad0 group node to move with the new lower spine skeleton, which in turn makes all the controls in the head and arms follow the new backbone controls. This technique is a variation of the parenting done in the "Building an Advanced Torso Rig" section.

The last two `setAttr` commands in this section keep the curves from inadvertently being animated through any of the parenting connections, by blocking them from inheriting transforms; this prevents a double transform on the spline IK skeletons.

```
//Hierarchy: Create groups for the new icon and skeletons:
   group -p $doNotMove -n "ctSpine_group" $lowSpineSkels[0]
         $upSpineSkels[0] $lowSpineIk[0] $upSpineIk[0]
         $lowSpineCurve $upSpineCurve;
 //Parent the vertebrae under the new skeletons:
   parent $vertebrae[0] $vertebrae[1] $lowSpineSkels[0];
   parent $vertebrae[2] $vertebrae[3] $lowSpineJts[0];
   parent $vertebrae[4] $vertebrae[5] $lowSpineJts[1];
   parent $vertebrae[6] $vertebrae[7] $lowSpineJts[2];
   parent $vertebrae[8] $vertebrae[9] $lowSpineJts[3];
   parent $vertebrae[10] $vertebrae[11] $lowSpineJts[4];
   parent $vertebrae[12] $vertebrae[13] $vertebrae[14]
         $vertebrae[15] $midSpineSkel[0];
   parent $vertebrae[16] $vertebrae[17] $upSpineSkels[0];
   parent $vertebrae[18] $vertebrae[19] $upSpineJts[0];
   parent $vertebrae[20] $vertebrae[21] $upSpineJts[1];
   parent $pelvisPoly $botSpineSkel[0];
   parent $skullPoly $topSpineSkel[0];
   parent $topSpineSkel[0] $headIcon;
 //Parent all other nodes:
   parent $backPad0 $doNotMove;
   parent  $botSpineSkel[0] $hipsIcon;
   parent  $midSpineSkel[0] $spineIcon[0];
 //Parent constrain the back pads to the new lower spine skel:
   parentConstraint -n "ctBackPad0_paCnst" -mo
                    $lowSpineSkels[1] $backPad0;
 //Set transform attributes on curves:
   setAttr ($lowSpineCurve + ".inheritsTransform") 0;
   setAttr ($upSpineCurve + ".inheritsTransform") 0;
```

Step 7: Create Pivot Controls for the Spine Icon

The next section of code in the cm_advTorso procedure uses constraints to create pivot controls for the spine icon. Constraints are useful because they can simulate parenting, but they also have weight channels that let you control the amount of the connection. Constraining a single node to multiple objects, for instance, lets you use a custom channel to drive the weight channels in opposite directions. The result is the connection to one node increases, while the other decreases. You can even make this type of connection to the center pivot of a node, rather than the normal transform channels.

The code first creates and positions three locators at the bottom, middle, and top of the spine icon. The middle locator is then point-constrained to the top and bottom locators, which positions it midway between the two. Then a `connectAttr` command connects the `rotatePivot` channel of the spine icon to the translation of the middle locator. This causes the center pivot of the icon to follow the locator, which in turn follows the other locators through the constraints. The SDK section later in this script creates a custom channel on the spine icon to drive the weight channels on these constraints, which will move the middle locator up and down, and in turn move the pivot of the icon. Because all these channels are keyable, the animator will be able to animate the pivot to rotate the icon in a variety of ways.

```
//Use constraints to control pivot of spine icon:
   string $locNames[] = {$lowSpineName,$midSpineName,$upSpineName};
   string $targets[] = {$lowSpineJts[2],$spineIcon[0],$upSpineSkels[0]};
//Use loop to create locators:
   string $pivotLocs[];
   for ($i = 0; $i < 3; $i++){//Open loop...
     string $locs[] = `spaceLocator -n
         ("ct" + $locNames[$i] + "_loc")`;
     print ("locator created: " + $locs[0] + "\n");
     cm_runLocals ("nodeMover",{$targets[$i],$locs[0],
             "0","0","0"});
     $pivotLocs[size($pivotLocs)] = $locs[0];
   }//Close loop.
//Point constrain the center locator to the other two locators:
   group -p $spineGps[1] -n "ctSpinePivs_group" $pivotLocs[0]
       $pivotLocs[1] $pivotLocs[2];
   string $spineCnst[] = `pointConstraint -n "ctSpinePiv_poCnst"
           $pivotLocs[0] $pivotLocs[2] $pivotLocs[1]`;
//Make the connection to make the locator control the pivot:
   connectAttr -f ($pivotLocs[1] + ".translate")
             ($spineIcon[0] + ".rotatePivot");
```

Step 8: Use Expressions to Create a Spine Stretch Color Warning

Skipping down to about line 500 in the `cm_advTorso` procedure, there is an expression for creating another color warning on the polygon bones. This warning tells the animator when the lower spine has been stretched too far. Similar to the warnings set on the limbs, the expression uses the curve channel to drive the warning, and incorporates an or (||) symbol in the expression to enable triggering the warning whenever the curve is either stretched or compressed beyond set values. Here is what the expression looks like:

```
if (curveInfo1.arcLength > 7.97 || curveInfo1.arcLength < 6.97)
        ctVertabrae_mat.incandescenceR = 1;
else ctVertabrae_mat.incandescenceR = 0;
```

This expression should be read as, "If the arcLength channel of curveInfo1 becomes greater than 7.97 or less than 6.97, then set the vertebrae materials incandescence red channel to 1. Else, set the incandescence red channel to 0."

Reading expressions in plain English like this makes it easy to see what the math expression is actually doing, and is a good starting point for composing your own expressions. Since this is not a cartoon character, the values used for the upper and lower limits in the expression are just slightly beyond the default size of the curve. But the values are really up to you: Feel free to adjust these based on the realism of your character. Here is the code in the script:

```
//Expressions: Spine stretch color warning:
    float $upLimit = ($lengthVal + 0.5);
    float $lowLimit = ($lengthVal - 0.5);
    string $warnColor = "ctVertabrae_mat";
    string $warnExpLine1 = ("if (" + $lengthNode + ".arcLength > "
        + $upLimit + " || " + $lengthNode + ".arcLength < "
        + $lowLimit + ") " + $warnColor + ".ir = 1;\n");
    string $warnExpLine2 = ("else " + $warnColor + ".ir = 0;\n");
    expression -n "stretchWarn_exp" -s ($warnExpLine1 + $warnExpLine2);
```

Step 9: Create an Automatic Breathing Control

The next expression in the cm_advTorso procedure is designed to create breathing controls on several skeletons that were added to the chest area previously in this script. A cosine function is used to create a wave that drives the scaling in X of the joints, making the character appear to breathe in and out. The final expression looks like this:

```
ctChestFront_rootJt.sx = 1 - cos(time * ctTorso_icon.breathSpeed) * .03;
ctStomachFront_rootJt.sx = 1 - cos(time * ctTorso_icon.breathSpeed) * .03;
lfRibSide_rootJt.sx = 1 - cos(time * ctTorso_icon.breathSpeed) * .03;
rtRibSide_rootJt.sx = 1 - cos(time * ctTorso_icon.breathSpeed) * .03;
```

Notice that a time function is being input into the cos or cosine function, and multiplied by a breathSpeed channel on the torso icon. Time references the animation timeline, and makes the character breathe whenever the timeline is played. Multiplying by the breathSpeed channel creates a control for animating the speed of the breathing. Increasing the channel speeds up the breathing, and is only constrained by the limits you set on the driver channel in the initial addAttr command. Here is the code that creates the expression:

```
//Create breathing controls:
   addAttr -ln "breathSpeed" -sn "bsp" -at "double" -min 0.0
          -max 3.0 -dv 0.7 -r 1 -w 1 -s 1 -k 1 $torsoIcon;
   string $breathers[] = {$chestSkel[0],$stomachSkel[0],$ribSkels[0],
          $ribSkels[2]};
   //string $breathSizes[] = {};
   string $breathExpLines[];
   for ($i = 0; $i < 4; $i++){//Open loop...
   $breathExpLines[size($breathExpLines)] = ($breathers[$i] +
      ".sx = 1 - cos(time * " + $torsoIcon + ".breathSpeed) * .03;\n");
   }//Close loop.
   string $breathExpression = stringArrayToString($breathExpLines,"");
   expression -n "breathing_exp" -s $breathExpression;
```

Step 10: Create Optional Auto-Locomotion Torso Controls

The last sections in the cm_advTorso procedure create automatic controls for the torso
to follow the leg icons when they move. These controls force the torso to follow the
legs when they step, dip when the feet move apart, and shift weight to the opposite
leg when a foot is raised. These are optional controls that are turned off by default,
but can be turned on if useful for a specific scene. An autoControls channel is created
on the torso icon to control the effect, and all the connections are multiplied by this
master channel to globally turn the expressions on and off. By default, the channel is
set to 0 or turned off.

The first automatic control in the code is created by direct node connections to keep
the torso positioned between the leg icons in X and Z. This is done by an average
operation using a plusMinusAverage node. In the script a createNode command is
run, and then a setAttr command to the operation channel sets the node to 3, which
indicates averaging. The translate channels of the leg icons are connected through
the average node to the group node parent of the torso icon named torsoAuto0. This
keeps the torso averaged between the two leg icons as the leg icons are moved. The
multiplyDivide node is used to multiply the effect by the autoControls channel so that
it can be turned off.

Here is the code for averaging the torso between the leg icons:

```
//Torso Auto-Connections: Create optional auto controls:
   addAttr -ln "autoControls" -sn "aut" -at "double" -min 0.0
          -max 1.0 -dv 0.0 -r 1 -w 1 -s 1 -k 1 $torsoIcon;
 //Create nodes needed for operation:
   string $average = `createNode plusMinusAverage
          -n "average_util"`;
   string $multiply = `createNode multiplyDivide
```

```
                      -n "average2_util"`;
    //Set operation to average:
      setAttr ($average + ".operation") 3;
    //Connect the output of the left leg to the average node:
      connectAttr -f ($lfLegIcon + ".tx") ($average
                    + ".input3D[0].input3Dx");
      connectAttr -f ($lfLegIcon + ".tz") ($average
                    + ".input3D[0].input3Dz");
    //Connect the output of the right leg to the average node:
      connectAttr -f ($rtLegIcon + ".tx") ($average
                    + ".input3D[1].input3Dx");
      connectAttr -f ($rtLegIcon + ".tz") ($average
                    + ".input3D[1].input3Dz");
    //Set operation to multiply:
      setAttr ($multiply + ".operation") 1;
    //Connect the average node to the multiply node:
      connectAttr -f ($average + ".output3D") ($multiply + ".input1");
    //Connect the auto channel to the multiply node:
      connectAttr -f ($torsoIcon + ".aut") ($multiply + ".input2X");
      connectAttr -f ($torsoIcon + ".aut") ($multiply + ".input2Z");
    //Connect the multiply node to the torsoAuto group node:
      connectAttr -f ($multiply +".outputX") ($torsoAuto0 + ".tx");
      connectAttr -f ($multiply +".outputZ") ($torsoAuto0 + ".tz");
```

The next code in the automatic torso controls section uses math expressions to create a dip and weight-shift effect when the leg icons are moved. These expressions subtract the value of one leg from the other to find out how far the feet are apart from each other to drive the effect. The abs, or absolute value, function removes any negative signs from the distance value.

Here is the final dip expression that controls the Y translation of the group node parented over the torso icon. The expression subtracts the amount that the leg icon moves, dividing the effect by 6 to make the dip more subtle:

```
ctTorsoAuto0_group.ty = (0 - ((abs (lfLeg_icon.tx - rtLeg_icon.tx) + abs
(lfLeg_icon.tz - rtLeg_icon.tz)) / 6)) * ctTorso_icon.aut;
```

And here is the MEL code that creates the expression:

```
//Use expression to create an automatic dip on the torso:
    string $dipExpression = ($torsoAuto0 + ".ty = (0 - ((abs ("
            + $lfLegIcon + ".tx - " + $rtLegIcon + ".tx) + abs ("
            + $lfLegIcon + ".tz - " + $rtLegIcon + ".tz)) / 6)) * "
            + $torsoIcon + ".aut;\n");
    expression -n "dip_exp" -s $dipExpression;
```

The weight-shift conditional expression evaluates how much a leg has been raised in Y, and translates the group node in X. Again, the effect is divided by 4 to make the shift more subtle:

```
if (lfLeg_icon.ty > rtLeg_icon.ty) ctTorsoAuto1_group.tx = (0 -
    (abs (lfLeg_icon.ty - rtLeg_icon.ty) / 4) * ctTorso_icon.aut);
else ctTorsoAuto1_group.tx = (0 + (abs (lfLeg_icon.ty - rtLeg_icon.ty)
    / 4) * ctTorso_icon.aut);
```

And the code that creates the weight-shift expression:

```
//Use expression to create an automatic weight shift on the torso:
    string $wtShiftExp1 = ("if (" + $lfLegIcon + ".ty > "
            + $rtLegIcon + ".ty) " + $torsoAuto1
            + ".tx = (0 - (abs (" + $lfLegIcon + ".ty - "
            + $rtLegIcon + ".ty) / 4) * " + $torsoIcon
            + ".aut);\n");
    string $wtShiftExp2 = ("else " + $torsoAuto1
            + ".tx = (0 + (abs (" + $lfLegIcon + ".ty - "
            + $rtLegIcon + ".ty) / 4) * " + $torsoIcon
            + ".aut);\n");
    expression -n "wtShift_exp" -s ($wtShiftExp1 + $wtShiftExp2);
```

The final code in the `cm_advTorso` procedure creates a control to drive the global scaling of the whole character using a custom channel created on the character icon. This simply scales the top node of the character to better fit the scene, or to export the character to other programs like Motion Builder.

```
//Add global scaling channel on char icon to scale topNode:
    addAttr -ln "globalScale" -sn "sca" -at "double" -min 0.5
            -max 5.0 -dv 1.0 -r 1 -w 1 -s 1 -k 1 $charIcon;
    connectAttr -f ($charIcon + ".sca") ($topNode + ".sx");
    connectAttr -f ($charIcon + ".sca") ($topNode + ".sy");
    connectAttr -f ($charIcon + ".sca") ($topNode + ".sz");
```

The rest of the CMaraffi_advTorso script cleans up the channels on all the remaining icons, lists all the names in the torso hierarchy, and runs the procedure to create the torso rig. This process is similar to that used on all the other advanced scripts, so it will not be reviewed in this chapter. However, take a look at this code to make sure that you are clear on the details.

WRAPPING UP

You should now be familiar with the advanced rigging techniques and scripts. Make sure that you compare the results in the interface with the code that is being run to fully understand the technical process. At this point, you have completed the iconic biped rig, and the character is ready for binding in the next chapter. You will also add other deformers such as blend shapes, geometry-based influence objects, and wrap deformers.

10 IMPORTANT POINTS TO REMEMBER FROM THIS CHAPTER

■ Add skeletons to the basic rig to improve bind deformations and to avoid extensive manual weighting of points.

■ To ensure that channel numbers generate correctly on joints, insert group node parents that are oriented the same as the child joint.

■ Rather than make icons for every control, add custom channels to the main icons, and use them to drive secondary controls.

■ Use SDKs to drive any controls that don't require math computations. SDKs have the advantages of creating animation curves that allow you to edit timing in the connection.

■ Use either math expressions or direct node connections for complex controls, depending on the needs of the production.

■ Lock and hide any channels that animators shouldn't keyframe on the icons, and set some kind of limits on all other icon channels.

■ Use spline IK when you want to combine the flexibility of FK with the ease of IK. In spline IK, you manipulate the points on the curve, not the IK handle.

■ Try to make your advanced scripts modular, so that they create controls for particular body areas.

■ For easy reference, organize global procedures that will be used in all the advanced scripts into one script file.

■ Design your advanced scripts so that they create the center and left-side controls first, and then have arguments to mirror the controls to the right side.

CHAPTER 5

Finishing the IK Biped Rig

THIS CHAPTER TAKES you through the final steps of assigning the rig to the skin with a smooth bind. It shows you details on binding and weighting in both the interface and through MEL scripting. This chapter also introduces you to additional deformation techniques, including indirect binding with a proxy skin, adding geometry-based influences, and using blend shapes to assign morph shapes to the face.

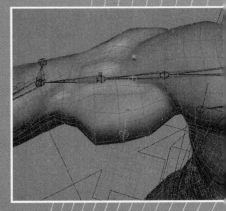

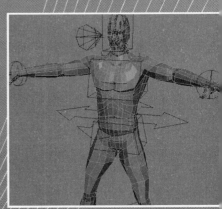

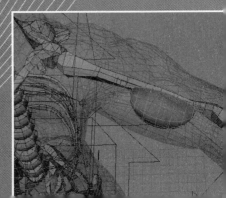

Creating a Final Bind

In Chapter 1, "Starting to Rig a Character," you learned how to do a basic smooth bind and how to test-bind the skin to check deformations. Test-binding after completing the basic IK rig enables you to easily see how the joints influence the skin. Testing continually as you create the advanced IK rig shows how adding joints improves the deformations. At some point in the process of creating the IK rig, you will be ready to perform a final bind and manually edit the weighting. This section details the final bind settings and shows techniques for efficiently setting the final skin weights.

Checking the Skin Model

It can be helpful for the rigging artist to think of rigging as modeling in motion. After binding, the skeletons in the rig deform the skin into different shapes, just as if you had modeled the skin in those poses. The main difference between modeling and rigging, however, is that modeling can add points to the geometry to achieve a desired shape, while rigging cannot. A bound skin must have a set number of points. Thus, all the points required to achieve any shapes or poses must inherently be built into the model. Good character deformations depend as much on the model structure as on the rigging controls. So when preparing to assign the final bind to the character model, you have one last chance to make sure that the skin model is optimized for the intended deformations.

Part of the test binding process is determining whether the rig or the model caused deformation problems. If you determine that the model needs points to be added, removed, or restructured to create the desired deformations, this editing must be done before applying a final bind. For a realistic character, the amount and placement of points and edges on the skin should suffice to bend limbs, flex muscles, and create major wrinkles. On the other hand, to reduce weighting problems, the skin shouldn't have extraneous surface details that could be better done as part of the texture mapping process, such as by using bump or displacement maps for something like a belly button on the stomach or small wrinkles on fingers.

Smooth Binding the Advanced Rig

Although Maya also has an older binding method called rigid binding, smooth binding is the only method you need to understand when assigning your final character bind. Smooth binding is more flexible than rigid binding and produces better deformations on the skin with less editing. It also has the capability to assign the influence of multiple joints to a single point on the bound skin, which smoothly shapes bending limbs. On an arm, for instance, a smooth bind normally assigns points around the elbow to the upper and lower joints, so that their movement averages and doesn't cause intersection problems on the geometry.

When creating your final smooth bind, keep in mind the weighting is always normalized to a value of 1. That is, when Maya assigns percentages of weighting to separate joints, it calculates the total weighting as exactly 1. When you manually edit a skin weight, the software automatically adjusts all the related weight values to continue adding up to 1. For instance, if the weighting to two joints is set to 0.8 and 0.2, and you increase the latter value of 0.2 to 0.6, Maya automatically decreases the value of 0.8 to 0.4. Normalization makes manual weighting of the skin predictable; however, it can be turned off globally, and you can place temporary holds on particular weights when you don't want them to normalize.

To apply a smooth bind to the advanced rig:

1. In the Hypergraph, select the skin of the character, and then hold down the Shift key and click to select all the joints in the advanced rig that are meant to be bound and that are not control joints. This includes all the FK joints in the arms and legs, all the spline IK joints in the torso, and all the FK joints in the head.

If you are binding the skeletons generated from the rigging scripts, an easier way to select all the joints is to run some MEL commands. Since all the joints were given the suffixes _rootJt and _bindJt, you can run a couple MEL select commands specifying the suffixes, and using wildcards (*) for the prefixes and main names. Make sure that you also incorporate the correct namespace name before the colons in these commands:

```
select -cl;
select -r cm_skin;
select -tgl "cm:*_bindJt";
select -tgl "cm:*_rootJt";
```

2. Choose Skin > Bind Skin > Smooth Bind ▢. In the Smooth Bind Options dialog box, set these bind options: Bind To Selected Joints, Closest Distance bind method, Max Influences of 4, and Dropoff Rate of 7.2 (**FIGURE 5.1**). The next section, "Using Smooth Binding Options," details these settings.

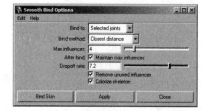

3. Click Bind Skin to smooth bind all selected joints.

4. In Perspective view, display the skin in Smooth Shaded mode, and manipulate the rig controls to check the bind deformations.

Using Smooth Binding Options

You may want to experiment with different bind settings before finalizing your bind. It is important to use the best settings possible for your character rig and model. If your model is a single polygon mesh, like the example model, then you cannot use different bind settings for different parts of the body; only one skinCluster node can be assigned to a model. To use separate settings on the fingers, for instance, you would have to detach the hand's portion of the skin from the rest of the model. It is all right to do this if necessary, but it involves extra work in weighting to prevent the seam from showing when the skin deforms.

Here is an overview of the Smooth Bind options to guide you in creating your final bind.

BIND TO

You can choose from three Bind To options. For simple rigs like the FK rig you created in Chapter 1, it is acceptable to use the default setting of Joint Hierarchy, which binds all the joints in a skeleton regardless of which joint you select. However, for complex rigs like the IK rig you have been building and scripting, you should always use the Selected Joints setting instead, because you want to assign particular joints, while leaving out others. By specifying joints you want to bind, you can keep from binding control joints and end joints. On the advanced rig that has almost 500 nodes, being selective will make your deformer list significantly shorter and easier to deal with when editing weights. The third option, Object Hierarchy, will bind the group nodes and locators in the hierarchy, as well as the joints. Because this binding would cause problems on the advanced rig, do not use this setting.

BIND METHOD

This option has two settings: Closest In Hierarchy and Closest Distance. Both methods assign the amount of skin weighting based on the distance between skeletons and points. Closer joints influence particular points more, while joints farther away influence less. This creates predictable deformations, as well as predictable problems. One frequent problem area is in the fingers, where points on one finger are assigned weighting to joints on a neighboring finger joint. Using Closest In Hierarchy prevents this problem, because it keeps Maya from assigning joints in separate branches of the hierarchy that may also be close in the 3D space.

The Closest Distance method ignores the hierarchy, however. It is being used in the advanced rigging scripts because group nodes inserted throughout the hierarchy causes the Closest In Hierarchy method to not assign joints that should be assigned.

MAX INFLUENCES

Generally for most characters, you should set this option to between 2 to 4 influences. Setting this option to 4 influences, for instance, assigns a maximum of four joints to influence a single point on the model. This is more than enough for most areas of the body to incorporate skeletal joint and muscle deformations on a realistic character. A simpler FK rig can have a lower setting of Max Influences.

AFTER BIND

It's recommended that you select Maintain Max Influences to prevent more joints from being added to points while editing weights. Turning on this option prevents Maya from adding small percentages of weighting to joints that really shouldn't be assigned any weighting. If turned off, the normalizing function may automatically increase the number of joints or influences, and distribute small weight values, especially when using the Paint Weights tool to remove weighting. The result can be a much more complicated weighting scheme, which is difficult to fix.

DROPOFF RATE

A good mid-range setting for most realistic characters is a Dropoff Rate of around 7. Unlike many bind options that won't immediately show different deformation on the skin, changing the Dropoff Rate value can significantly change blending or weighting falloff between joints. A higher setting produces less falloff between joints, which results in a more solid-looking skin when the limbs bend. But setting the rate too high will create intersection problems when limbs bend. Decreasing the rate to around 5 will soften the deformations. At very low settings, such as 3, the limb deformations will begin to have a rubbery look that is more appropriate for cartoon characters.

REMOVE UNUSED INFLUENCES

It's best to leave this default option selected. Turning on the option removes any joints from the bind that are not assigned due to the other settings of Max Influences and Dropoff Rate. So if a joint is out of range and receives no weighting, it is then removed from the list of deformers.

COLORIZE SKELETON

Select this option to display a general overview of the weighting by colorizing the skeletons and points on the skin. The points are colored according to the joint that has the highest percentage of weighting. Using this option is not, however, a substitute for viewing the more detailed weighting in the Paint Weights tool or Component Editor.

Editing the Final Bind

Once you are happy with how the default deformations look on the bound skin, you can start editing the smooth bind by adding influences and manually making edits to the weighting. This section shows how to add a variety of objects as weighted influences, and how to finalize the weighting using the Paint Weights tool and Component Editor.

Adding Joints as Influence Objects

Skeleton joints added after the skin is already bound are called influence objects. You might add joints separately from the initial bind to prevent Maya from calculating their weighting along with the other joints in the rig. If you find during testing that Maya is calculating the weighting badly for some joints, adding them as influence objects gives you more control over their weighting by allowing you to use different bind settings.

To add a joint as an influence object to the right bicep:

1. In Top view, draw a two-joint skeleton for the right bicep that is perpendicular to the bone of the right arm root joint. You should draw the skeleton from the center of the arm out to the middle of the bicep area of the skin, so that scaling the skeleton in X will push the bicep outward when the arm bends. Name the joints in the skeleton **rtBicepRoot** and **rtBicepEnd**.

2. Transform the skeleton so that it fits entirely within the arm (see **FIGURE 5.2**).

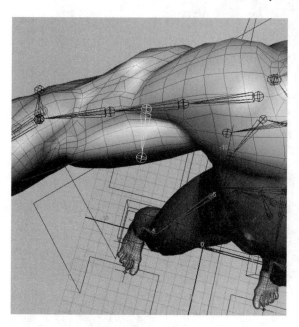

FIGURE 5.2 *Joints can be added as influence objects after the skin is bound, such as this joint placed as a bicep muscle in the arm.*

Freeze the transformations, and parent the root joint of the skeleton under the rtNewUpArm1 joint.

3. Shift-select the root joint and bound skin, and choose Skin > Edit Smooth Skin > Add Influence □.

4. In the Add Influence Options dialog box, deselect the Use Geometry option; always deselect this option when adding a joint as an influence object as it has no points. When using influence objects to create a localized muscle effect, set a very high Dropoff Rate, such as 9.9 (see **FIGURE 5.3**).

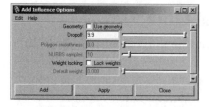

FIGURE 5.3 *Add muscle influence objects with a very high Dropoff Rate, so that the effect applies only to the area of the skin where the muscle should flex.*

5. Click Add to assign the influence object to the skin. Try scaling the bicep root joint in X to see the muscle deformation (see **FIGURE 5.4**).

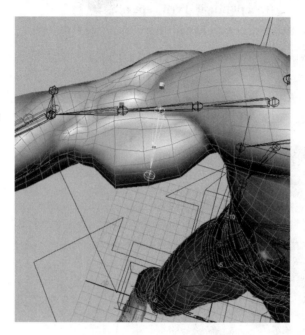

FIGURE 5.4 *Scaling the bicep joint in X creates basic muscle flexing through the default weighting. Some editing may be needed to remove influence in the tricep area of the arm.*

6. Test the influence object to see if the weighting is improved. If not, remove the influence object, and try different settings. First remove any joint (including influence objects) from the bind by Shift-selecting the joint and skin, and choosing Skin > Edit Smooth Skin > Remove Influence. When the influence is removed, Maya automatically recalculates the weighting of the remaining bound joints. To prevent weighting problems, do not delete an influence without first removing it from the bind. With the influence removed from the bind, simply select and delete as you would any object.

7. Use SDKs to drive the bicep influence to scale in X whenever the lower arm joint rotates in Z. Then move the arm icon to see the effect on the skin.

Using Geometry as Influence Objects

Muscles in a real body change shape when they flex. To better simulate such muscle deformations, you can add other types of influence objects, including NURBS and polygon geometry. Actually, you can also add locators and group nodes as influence objects, but this has limited functionality. Geometry-based influences allow you to use the shape of the object, rather than just the transforms, to drive the skin shape. Once added to the bind, such muscle influences will show up in the Paint Skin Weights tool, and can be manually weighted exactly the same as joint influences.

To add a geometry-based influence object as a left bicep muscle:

1. Create a NURBS primitive sphere by choosing Create > NURBS Primitives > Sphere ❒. In the resulting dialog box, set the options to create a half-sphere with the pole facing in X (see **FIGURE 5.5**).

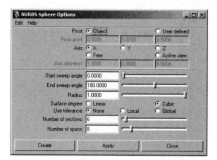

FIGURE 5.5 *Use these sphere settings to create a geometry-based influence object for a bicep muscle.*

2. Transform the half-sphere to fit it inside the bicep area of the left arm, as shown in **FIGURE 5.6**.

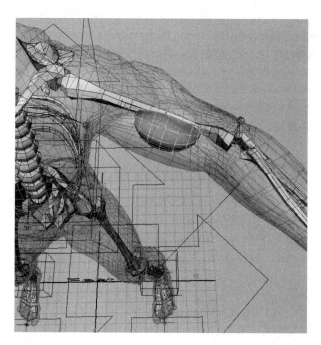

FIGURE 5.6 *Position the sphere entirely within the bicep portion of the left arm.*

3. Freeze the transformations and parent the bicep sphere under the lfNewUpArm1 joint. Name the sphere **lfBicepInf**.

4. With the bicep sphere selected, Shift-select the bound skin, and choose Skin > Edit Smooth Skin > Add Influence ◘.

5. In the Add Influence Options dialog box, select the Use Geometry option, so that Maya will calculate the shape of the sphere. It is not necessary to adjust the Polygon Smoothness or NURBS Samples default settings, which calculate the weighting to match the shape of the object. You would increase these settings only if you were adding an influence object with a very complex shape. Lastly, turn on the Weight Locking check box and set the Default Weight to 0 (see **FIGURE 5.7**). Click Add to assign the bicep sphere as an influence object.

FIGURE 5.7 *Assign the sphere as an influence object using the Geometry setting, and locking the weights to 0.*

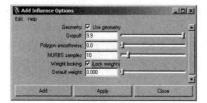

Locking the weights to 0 assigned the bicep sphere as an influence to the skin with no weighting.

6. To manually add the weighting, open the Paint Skin Weights Tool Settings dialog box, and find the bicep in the Influence list. Notice that locking the weight put a hold on the bicep influence object, and selecting the object shows only black, indicating there is no weighting. Unlock the weighting by clicking the Toggle Hold Weights On Selected button located below the list. Then set the Paint Operation to Replace. Using a value of 1, paint the bicep area of the skin so that it is white. To finalize the weighting, change the operation to Smooth, and paint around the edges of the bicep to achieve a soft gray transition (see **FIGURE 5.8**).

7. Scale the bicep sphere in the direction of the front of the arm to see how the influence object is deforming the skin.

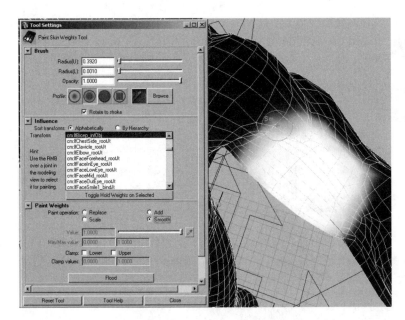

FIGURE 5.8 *Remove the hold on the weights in the Paint Skin Weights Tool options, and manually paint weighting to the bicep skin, smoothing around the edges.*

To drive the shape of the left bicep muscle to flex and deform the skin:

1. To enable the shape of the geometry influence object to deform the points on the skin, turn on the useComponents channel on the skinCluster node. Select the skin, and in the inputs of the Channel Box, click the bind node name to display the channels. Type a value of 1 in the useComponents channel (see **FIGURE 5.9**). Then press the F8 key to switch to Component mode, and translate some points on the bicep influence object to see the skin deform.

To automatically drive the shape of the bicep sphere to flex when the lower arm rotates, and in turn deform the skin, you use SDKs.

2. Select all the points on the bicep influence object, and choose Animate > Set Driven Key > Set to open the Set Driven Key dialog box. If the points are not automatically loaded into the lower driven section, click the Load Driven button. Shift-select all the point names and the XYZ values to drive all the positions of the points. Then load the lower arm joint on the left IK arm as the driver, selecting rotateY as the driver channel.

3. In the Set Driven Key dialog box, click the Key button to set a default position for the driver and driven. Then move the arm icon to bend the arm, and move points on the bicep sphere to create a flexed muscle (see **FIGURE 5.10**).

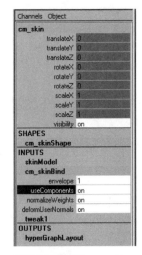

FIGURE 5.9 *Turn on the useComponents channel on the skinCluster node to have the geometry of the influence object drive the deformation on the skin.*

Make sure that you set the skin layer to template mode so you can see both the influence object and the skin deformations while working. Click Key again to set the final SDK.

FIGURE 5.10 *Use set driven keys (SDKs) to drive the points of the bicep influence object to deform when the lower arm rotates.*

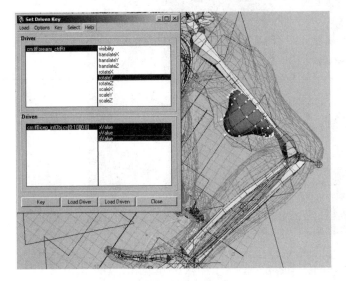

4. Click 0 on the timeline to set the arm icon back to its default position, and move the arm icon to see the muscle effect on the bicep.

This technique is a simple way to create shape animation using SDKs. Later in this chapter in "Creating Blend Shapes," you'll also learn how to create more sophisticated shape animation using blend shapes. To make the muscle effect more realistic, create additional SDKs. For instance, the rotation of the FK forearm joint could also drive the shape of the bicep influence object. You could even have the X rotation of the armTurn joint drive subtle shape changes on the bicep, just as in a real arm when the forearm twists.

Setting Keys to Facilitate Editing Weights

When editing weights with the Paint Skin Weights tool, and later with the Component Editor, it is always helpful to key temporary poses on the timeline. The advanced rigging scripts already set a permanent default key at 0 on all the icon channels. Editing skin weights requires manipulating the icons to see how the editing affects the deformations throughout their range of motion, but manually moving icons forces you to switch out of weight editing mode. You can, however, move the timeline in any mode in Maya. Therefore, setting keys on the icon channels anywhere above 0 on the timeline lets you test the deformations while continuously editing weights. When done, you simply delete the temporary keys.

For instance, if you are editing the weights for the left shoulder, set a key above 0 on the timeline with the arm lowered into a relaxed pose. The following technique uses MEL to streamline this process. The code sets keys on a selected icon at frame 50, even though the timeline remains at frame 0. Then it uses MEL again to remove the temporary key at 50, while leaving the default key at 0. Storing the two sets of code in shelf buttons makes it easy and fast to set the keys while editing weights. Here is how you would set keys on the arm icon when editing shoulder weights:

1. On frame 0, move the arm down to the characters side, and with the icon still selected, run the following MEL commands. The -t, or time, flag on the setKeyframe command ensures that the key is on frame 50, even though you didn't move the timeline:

```
string $sel[] = `ls -sl`;
setKeyframe -t 50 $sel[0];
```

2. Paint weights on the upper chest and shoulder to smooth deformations. When done editing the weights, run the following code to remove the key at 50. The cutkey command with a -cl, or clear, flag deletes any keys in the specified -t, or time range. In this case, any keys from 1 to 100 will be deleted on the selected icon:

```
currentTime 0;
string $sel[] = `ls -sl`;
cutKey -cl -t "1:100" $sel[0];
```

Using the currentTime command to set the timeline back to 0 allows you to easily repeat the keying process on another area of the character.

Using the Paint Skin Weights Tool

The first step in improving weighting on the skin is using the Paint Skin Weights tool, described in "Introduction to Painting Skin Weights" in Chapter 1. Since the example biped character is symmetrical, it is necessary to paint weights only on the left side of the body. A command in the Skin Editing menu lets you mirror the weights to the right side; this is covered later in this chapter in "Editing Weights Using Menu Commands."

The important thing about painting weights is to be precise and methodical. After test-binding you should have a pretty good idea where the problem areas are in the weighting. Fix the major deformation problems first, such as the chest caving in, and address more subtle problems on a second editing pass. Avoid over-painting areas. If the weighting seems to worsen as you paint, undo the brush strokes and start again.

To help you use the Paint Skin Weights tool more effectively, the following sections describe the most useful options (again, see Figure 5.8).

BRUSH

The Brush settings are the same as the standard setting for any artisan tool in Maya, and are mostly meant to be used in relation to a tablet and stylus. You can simply use the default settings: Most rigging artists won't require the same sensitivity in painting weights as a texture artist will require for painting textures. Just set the upper radius (RadiusU) option to scale the brush for the area you want to paint (or hold down the B key in the 3D views to size the brush).

INFLUENCE

The list of influences on a complex character rig can be quite long. The Sort Transforms Alphabetically setting makes it easy to find joints if your rig is well-organized and all the joints are named. Using the prefixes ct, lf, and rt has the added benefit of sorting the names into three groups based on the center, left, and right areas of the body, respectively. You then know that names for the torso and head influences will be found alphabetically under the center names, and the main limb influences will be found alphabetically under the left names. Switching to the Sort By Hierarchy setting attempts to also group influence names according to areas of the body, but may be inconsistent on the advanced biped rig because of the many node connections.

You were introduced to the Toggle Hold Weights On Selected button when removing a hold on a geometry-based influence object (see step 6 of "Using Geometry as Influence Objects," earlier in this chapter). This option can also be useful to place a hold on a joint or influence object when painting weights. A hold can prevent Maya from recalculating a weight that has already been finalized. When you paint an area on the skin, the weights in the neighboring areas automatically normalize. This can be frustrating if you have already set the weighting in those areas. To place a hold on the weights that you don't want to change, select the influence in the list and click the Toggle Hold Weights On

Selected button. The text "(Hold)" will appear next to the joint name. After you finish painting in that area, click the button again to remove the hold.

PAINT WEIGHTS

A good strategy for most weighting problems is to start with the Smooth operation and then move on to the Replace and Add operations. Using the Replace operation to add specific amounts of weighting is more predictable than using the Scale operation. Try to avoid removing weights, as doing so has a greater normalizing effect on neighboring points. If you want to keep the weighting from going beyond specific values, use the Upper and Lower Clamp settings. The Flood button distributes the specified weighting to all the points on the skin, and should be used only if you want to add weighting or remove it from the entire character. This function should not be used on the advanced biped rig.

STROKE, STYLUS PRESSURE, AND DISPLAY

All of these settings can remain at the defaults for painting weights on the advanced biped rig.

Editing Weights in the Component Editor

It's best to use the Component Editor after painting weights to finalize subtle details on the weighting. The editor lets you see the precise numerical weight values influencing each point, and type the exact amount you require to make the skin deform correctly. It is also the best place to view how the weights are normalized.

To view weights in the Component Editor:

1. Switch to Component mode to select some points on the bound skin.

2. Choose Window > General Editors > Component Editor to open the Component Editor.

3. Click the Smooth Skins tab to view a numerical graph of the weighting (see **FIGURE 5.11**).

The left side of the graph lists the points vertically, while across the top the joints are listed horizontally. With a Max Influences setting of 4, each point has no more than four joints with weight values. On the far right of the editor, the values for each point total or normalize to 1.

FIGURE 5.11 *Use the Component Editor to view and edit detailed weight values of selected points.*

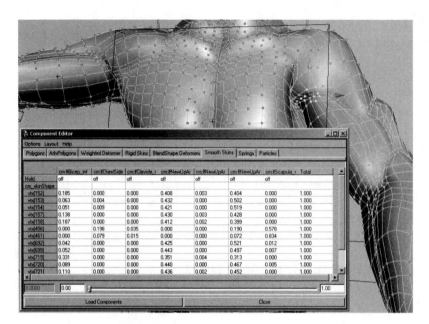

4. To see exactly how the weights continuously normalize, type a decimal value into one of the fields and notice how the other values automatically update to still add up to 1. If you type a 1 into a single field, the other fields update to 0, because there is no longer any weighting to those joints.

In addition to typing in weight values for each point, you can also use the slider at the bottom of the editor to interactively set the weighting for a particular joint.

5. To see the effect on the skin, move the icons to deform the skin, and look at the selected points that are highlighted in Perspective view. Click a joint's name at the top of the editor to select an entire column of weight values, and drag the interactive slider. You should see the highlighted points move as the values change in the column.

As with the Paint Skin Weights tool, you can place a hold on the weights for any joint.

6. To place a hold on the weights of a particular joint or influence object, at the top of the weight column, type **1** in the Hold field. Then type **0** to turn off the hold again.

Editing Weights Using Menu Commands

Several additional commands for editing weights are in the Skin > Edit Smooth Skin menu. These commands should be used in conjunction with editing weights with the Paint Skin Weights tool and Component Editor.

MIRRORING SKIN WEIGHTS

After painting weights on the left side of the characters body, use the Mirror Skin Weights command to weight the right side. Set the Mirror Across option to the YZ plane, the same as when you mirror joints, and mirror positive to negative in the X axis. The remaining Surface Association and Influence Association settings can be left at their default settings of Closest Point On Surface and Closest Joint. These settings will mirror the weights based on the positions of the skin components and influence objects on the other side of the body.

COPYING SKIN WEIGHTS

The Copy Skin Weights command is designed for copying the weights of one skin to another. In the next section, "Using Indirect Deformation Techniques," you'll use this command to copy the weights of a less complex proxy skin to the main skin. This command primarily uses proximity of the body parts in 3D space to calculate where the weight should be assigned. A low-resolution version copied to a high-resolution version of the same skin, using the same rig, has enough similarities to ensure that the weighting interpolates well. For the advanced rig, set the Surface Association to Closest Point and the Influence Associations to One To One, Name, and Closest Joint.

SMOOTHING AND PRUNING SKIN WEIGHTS

Before and after manually editing weights, both the Smooth Skin Weights and Prune Skin Weights commands can be useful. The Smooth Skin Weights command globally averages weights based on a percentage setting between 0 and 1. Weight differences below this value will be smoothed. A setting of 0.5 is the default; lower settings produce more smoothing.

The Prune Small Weights removes weighting to influences that are below a set value. This prevents influences from getting small amounts of weight that really shouldn't be weighted at all. A good setting for this command is a value of 0.1.

Using Indirect Deformation Techniques

Once you understand how to create and edit a basic smooth bind, knowing some additional techniques can make binding and weighting easier. These techniques include using a low-resolution or proxy skin to bind the main skin, and combining other deformation methods, such as blend shapes and a wrap deform. By learning these techniques, you can see how deformers can be connected to enhance the bind, and then come up with your own variations.

Binding with a Proxy Skin

The main difficulty with binding is the time it takes to fix weighting problems on a high-resolution skin. Some professional rigging artists manually weight every single point on the skin using the Component Editor. Depending on the number of points your skin has, this could take a lot of time. Although painting weights speeds up the process somewhat, other techniques can also be used. Binding and weighting a proxy skin with fewer points, and then copying the weights to the main skin, is one way to significantly speed up the weighting process.

Binding through a proxy skin requires first manually creating a low-resolution duplicate of the main skin. Do not try to remove points on the duplicate by using the Maya polygon reduction tools because they tend to remove points randomly. Ideally, you should manually remove points and edges that are not required to bend the main joints, or remodel the skin from scratch. Since this is not a modeling book, a low-resolution proxy skin has been provided in the basikFkRig file on the proxyModel layer (see **FIGURE 5.12**). Use this model to bind and weight the low-resolution skin, and copy the weighting to the main skin.

FIGURE 5.12 *You can simplify the weighting process by binding a low-resolution proxy skin. Maya will automatically interpolate the weighting when copied to the main skin.*

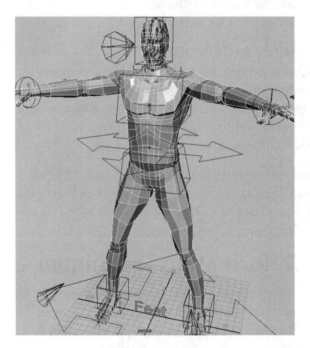

Using this technique, Maya correctly interpolates the copied weighting on the main skin, even though the two skins have different numbers of points.

You have the added advantage of keeping the proxy skin bound to the rig, so you can display it—rather than the main skin—while animating. Using the proxy as reference for the deforming skin uses less system memory, and can ultimately speed up the animation process.

COPYING SKIN WEIGHTS FROM PROXY TO MAIN SKIN

Binding and weighting the proxy skin is the same process as used on the main skin, including painting and mirroring weights. Because the proxy skin has fewer points, however, the process should go faster. Once you have finalized the bind on the proxy skin, you use the Copy Skin Weights command to have Maya interpolate the weighting to the bound main skin:

1. With both the bound proxy and main skins in their default positions, select the proxy skin and Shift-select the main skin. Then choose Skin > Edit Smooth Skin > Copy Skin Weights ☐.

2. In the Copy Skin Weights dialog box, keep the default Surface Association setting of Closest Point On Surface. Set the three Influence Association settings to One To One, Name, and Closest Joint (see **FIGURE 5.13**).

FIGURE 5.13 *Since the rigs for both skins are the same, use the One To One influence as the main copy weights setting.*

Since the rigs are the same for both, the One To One option will find the exact same influences for weighting. If it finds discrepancies, it will then use names, and then joint proximity to copy the weights.

3. Click Copy to copy the weights from the proxy to the main skin. Then move some of the rig controls to see the changes on the main skin.

4. If desired, detach the bind on the proxy skin, and delete it, or keep it to use for animation reference.

SAVING PROXY WEIGHTS TO A FILE

It is easy to copy skin weights in Maya, but it's not so straightforward to save the weights to apply them to the proxy skin of a newly generated rig. It's possible to export and import skin weight maps (the grayscale image you see when you paint skin weights) using the command in the Edit Smooth Skins menu.

But this process is time-consuming for a character with many influences: exporting involves saving an image file for every influence on the smooth bind.

Rather than save images that are only an approximation of the weighting, you can use MEL scripting to write out the exact weight values for each influence to a text file. Later, you can use MEL to open and extract the weight values, and assign them to the proxy skin after it is bound. This process is automated in the CMaraffi_deformSkin script that you will later examine in the chapter exercise "Scripting Skin Deformations."

Morphing Through a Proxy Head

Similar to traditional morphing techniques, using blend shapes is an alternative way to create skin deformations. You model a variety of separate facial expressions, for instance, and then drive the main face skin to morph between those shapes. Using blend shapes is a relatively easy way to achieve complex deformations with a minimal amount of node connections, so it takes very little system resources. Depending on your modeling ability, blend shapes can be a good choice for deforming your character.

Before starting, you must determine whether the skin model presents any issues in creating blend shapes. The main issue with the example model is how best to incorporate blend shapes for just the face, when the entire body is a single piece of geometry. Normally, this would require duplicating the entire mesh to make the target shapes, which would add all the points into the blend shape. This is not a very efficient solution. An alternative is to again create a proxy model that is duplicated from the main skin, and modified to utilize only the head geometry for creating the blend shapes.

To create a proxy head for your blend shapes:

1. Duplicate the skin, naming it proxyHead, and hide the original skin. In Component mode, display polygon faces to select and delete the polygons from the neck down. This becomes the main proxy head that you will later connect to the main model with a wrap deformer.

2. Then duplicate the proxy head to model the blend shape targets. Move each head model to the side so it is easy to see in Perspective view. When modeling different face shapes, focus on particular areas, such as the eyes or mouth, so that you can mix the shapes in the Blend Shape Editor. Also, you can use any modeling tools to shape the heads, as well as deformers such as clusters or skeletons. But do not move the center pivot of the blend shape targets, or change the surface structure by adding or deleting points, as this will create an unpredictable morph.

CREATING BLEND SHAPES ON THE PROXY HEAD

Creating blend shapes involves connecting the shapes of the target models to the shape of the main model through a blend shape node. Since you are using a proxy head, you first will connect the target head shapes to the proxy shape, and then connect the proxy shape to the main skin through the wrap deformer.

To display the proxy heads and prepare for assigning them as blend shapes:

1. Turn on the visibility of the blendHeads layer to see the proxy and target heads (see **FIGURE 5.14**).

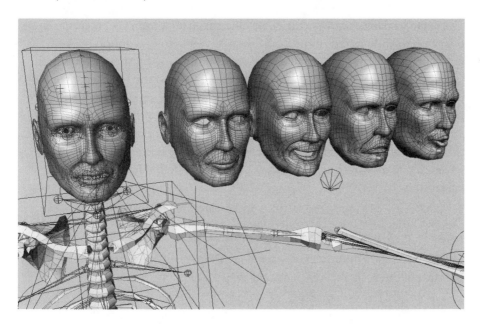

FIGURE 5.14 *Duplicate the main skin and delete polygons to create a proxy head and target heads for blend shapes on the face.*

The proxy head sits on top of the main skin, with the target heads to the right of the proxy head. Notice that the target heads have been modeled to create some basic mouth shapes. This is just a small sampling of the many shapes you can create for the face.

2. If desired, duplicate the main proxy head and create additional shapes for the mouth and the eye areas.

To assign the target heads as blend shapes on the proxy head:

1. Shift-select all the target heads from left to right, and then Shift-select the proxy head last. Choose Create Deformers > Blend Shape ❐.

2. In the Create Blend Shape dialog box, first type **mouthShapes** to name the blend shape node. Leave the rest of the options at their default settings (see **FIGURE 5.15**).

FIGURE 5.15 *For the face of the character, use the default Blend Shape options.*

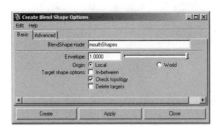

The default Local Origin setting copies the shape data from the targets to the proxy head while ignoring the transforms. If you turn this option on, the heads will move on top of the target head as it is changing shape. Leaving the In Between option deselected creates parallel sliders on the blend shape node that can be additively mixed. This is useful for mixing shapes on different areas of the face, such as mixing mouth with eye shapes. Since the target heads are exact duplicates of the main head, leaving Check Topology selected ensures that the numbered points are connected one to one. Leave Delete Targets deselected; you may need to adjust the target shapes before finalizing the face controls.

3. Click Create to apply the settings and create the blend shape node.

USING THE BLEND SHAPE EDITOR
The Blend Shape Editor is a convenient GUI for viewing, editing, and animating the channels created on the blend shape node.

To use the Blend Shape Editor:

1. Choose Window > Animation Editors > Blend Shape to open the editor.

A vertical slider, named according to the target head, appears for each head shape. Maya arranges the sliders parallel to each other from left to right, in the same order as you selected the targets. By default, the blend shape channels go from 0 to 1, with 0 being no shape and 1 being the full shape. A field below each slider lets you type values beyond the default limits, to achieve more extreme shapes than were actually modeled.

2. To view the blend shape node and channels in the Channel Box, click Select (see **FIGURE 5.16**).

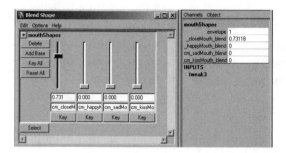

FIGURE 5.16 *In the Blend Shape Editor you can use sliders to animate the channels on the blend shape node.*

3. To animate blend shapes, move the sliders and either click individual Key buttons, or click Key All to set a key on all the shape channels. To set all the sliders back to 0, click Reset All.

4. To edit blend shapes in the editor, click Add Base to create a new blend shape and target head from mixing existing sliders. Or to delete the blend shape node, click Delete.

Other commands for editing blend shapes are found in the Edit Deformers menu, including adding, removing, and swapping target shapes.

To edit blend shapes in the Edit Deformers menu:

1. Select any blend shape target head, Shift-select the proxy head, and choose Edit Deformers > Blend Shape > Remove ⬛.
The options let you specify the blend shape node if the scene has multiple nodes. In this case where there is only one blend shape node, leave the options off and click Apply and Close. Notice that the slider and channel have been removed.

2. To add the same shape back again (or to add a new shape that you modeled), select the target, Shift-select the proxy head, and choose Edit Deformers > Blend Shape > Add. Set the options only if you have more than one blend shape node in the scene. Notice the blend shape has been added last in the sliders and channels.

3. To move the last target shape forward in the slider order, with the target shape selected, Shift-select the target head next to it in Perspective view, and choose Edit Deformers > Blend Shape > Swap. It should move forward one in the ordering.

ADDING IN-BETWEEN SHAPES

When moving the blend shape sliders, you may have noticed an inherent issue with using blend shapes on a face. The morph may not move naturally because the points move in a straight line from shape to shape. Rarely does skin move this way on a face: the muscles in a face stretch over bones, which cause the muscles to flex on an arc. To make the face movement more natural, you must create and insert in-between shapes that help to simulate such arcs.

To create and add an in-between shape to an existing blend shape channel:

1. Move a slider, such as the happyMouth slider, to a 0.5 value; manipulating an existing slider to create an in-between shape is easier than modeling one from scratch. Then duplicate the main proxy head, which will create a new target head with the half-smile shape. Move the in-between target to the side where you can work on it, and manipulate the points around the mouth to make it go less upward and more outward.

2. To add the in-between target to the smile blend shape, Shift-select the target and then the main proxy head, and choose Edit Deformers > Blend Shape > Add ☐. In the dialog box, turn on Add In-Between Target. To add the in-between shape to the second blend shape on the node, which is the smile, type a Target Index of **2**. Set the In-Between weight to 0.5, turn on Check Topology, and click Apply and then Close.

3. Move the smile slider to test the blend. It should cause the mouth on the proxy head to first deform outward before arcing upward into a smile.

Since the connection between the target shapes and main head remains, you can continue to adjust points on the in-between shape until it looks natural.

CONNECTING THE PROXY HEAD TO THE SKIN

Once the blend shapes are working on the proxy head, you need to have them drive the face shapes on the bound skin. You cannot effectively use a blend shape between the proxy head and bound skin because of the difference in point structure and numbering. But a wrap deformer can make such a connection. A wrap deformer allows one piece of geometry to drive the points of another piece of geometry based on point proximity. The deformer will enable the proxy head to drive only the corresponding head points on the bound skin.

To use a wrap deformer to connect the blend shapes to the bound skin:

1. Select the bound skin and then Shift-select the proxy head. Choose Create Deformers > Wrap ❐. Set the options as shown in **FIGURE 5.17**.

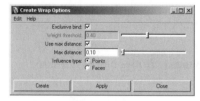

FIGURE 5.17 *Use the Exclusive Bind setting when creating a wrap deformer to connect the points of the proxy head to the head points on the bound skin.*

Since the point structure of the proxy head perfectly matches the head points of the skin, select Exclusive Bind to drive the points one to one. If the points on the surfaces differ, you would instead deselect this option and set a Weight Threshold. Setting a very low Max Distance setting of 0.1 or so will calculate faster. Use Points as the Influence Type to calculate.

2. Click Create to make the wrap deformer connection. Don't worry if you see the head part of the main skin stretch when you first apply the deformer.

3. Once the connection is made, select the proxy head and notice in the Channel Box that the transform node has several new deformers.

4. In the Channel Box, change the inflTyp channel to 2 (see **FIGURE 5.18**); on changing this value, in Perspective view you should see the head part of the skin go back to normal. Keep the Dropoff and Smoothness values at the defaults of 4 and 0.

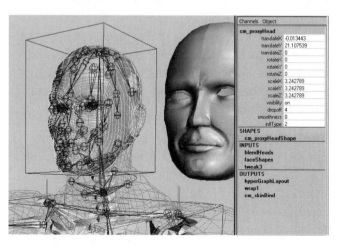

FIGURE 5.18
When adding a wrap deformer, be sure to set the infType channel for the proxy head to 2 so that Maya evaluates the skin correctly.

Since multiple deformers are now connected to the skin, it is important to ensure that they are evaluated in the correct order. When adding other deformers to a bound skin, make sure that Maya evaluates the bind after the other deformers.

5. To check how the deformers are ordered, right-click the skin, and choose Inputs > All Input. The resulting input list is a stack, which means that the order goes from bottom to top. Because you did the wrap deformer after the bind, the wrap will be at the top.

6. Use the middle mouse button to drag the wrap deformer below the skin-Cluster node in the list (see **FIGURE 5.19**).

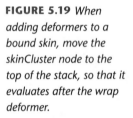

FIGURE 5.19 *When adding deformers to a bound skin, move the skinCluster node to the top of the stack, so that it evaluates after the wrap deformer.*

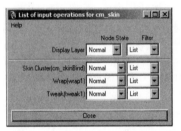

7. Test the new connections by moving some of the rig controls like the torso icon, and then moving the blend shape sliders to see the face shapes deform the bound skin.

COMBINING BLEND SHAPES WITH JOINT DEFORMATIONS

It is not very good interface design to force the animator to switch to a separate GUI like the Blend Shape Editor to animate the face shapes. It is much easier to provide custom face channels on the head icon that drive the blend shape channels, so that all the face controls are available in one place. You can even make the custom face channels drive the blend shapes to go slightly beyond their 0 and 1 default limits to create some useful extreme shapes. Do this in the same way you created all the other SDKs in the advanced rig controls in Chapter 4, "Adding Advanced Rig Controls."

In addition, you can experiment with combining the skeleton face controls with the blend shape controls, to leverage both their strengths. Skeletons can move the face points on an arc while the blend shape deforms them, creating some interesting combinations. This can be done simply, by manually keying the separate channels together (see **FIGURE 5.20**), or by the more sophisticated process of having the skeleton channels drive the blend shape channels using SDKs. Experiment with both to see how they work.

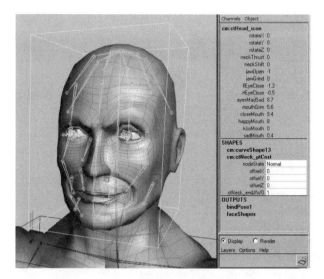

FIGURE 5.20 *Add face channels to the head icon to drive the blend shape channels using SDKs.*

EXERCISE 5.1: SCRIPTING SKIN DEFORMATIONS

There is a limit to how much you can script the deformation process, because some aspects of weighting and blend shapes need to be done manually. If your rigging scripts are going to work with a variety of biped skin models where the point numbering and structure will differ on each skin, then you cannot incorporate exact weight values ahead of time in the code. However, the indirect binding method using a proxy skin does let you script some of the weighting process, because the proxy point structure will remain accurate for many biped characters. You just have to adjust the points on the proxy to fit as closely as possible to the general shape of the main character skin before binding.

In this exercise you will examine the CMaraffi_deformSkin script, which automates some of the binding process through the setup GUI controls (see **FIGURE 5.21**).

The script has several global procedures that bind both the main skin and proxy skin, assign stored weights from a file to the proxy, copy the weights from proxy to the main skin, and assign facial blend shapes on a proxy head to the main skin through a wrap deform. Two procedures for writing proxy skin weights to a file and smoothing weights will not be reviewed here. Make sure that you run all the procedures in the setup GUI before examining the actual script.

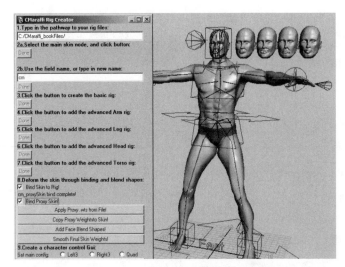

FIGURE 5.21 *Run the bind script through the setup GUI to bind both the proxy and main skin, to copy weights after editing and to add blend shapes.*

Step 1: Smooth Bind the Skin

The cm_bindSkin procedure is run to smooth bind both the main skin and proxy skin when you click the appropriate check boxes in the setup GUI. A conditional statement at the beginning of the procedure uses an integer argument of 1 or 0 to set the name of the skin to bind. If the argument is set to 1, then the low-resolution proxy skin name is set into the $skinName variable. If the argument is set to 0, then the main high-resolution skin is retrieved from the environment, and set into the $skinName variable.

```
//Global proc used for binding the skin to the rig:
global proc cm_bindSkin (int $proxy){//Open procedure...
 //Enable proxy GUI check box after binding skin:
   checkBox -e -en 1 "cm_proxyCheckBox";
 //Set global names for binding:
   string $rigName = `getenv "cm_rigName"`;
   string $nSpace = ($rigName + ":");
   string $skinName;
   string $bindName;
 //Use conditional to choose skin or proxy for binding:
   if ($proxy == 1){//Open conditional:
   //Set proxy to bind:
     $skinName = ($rigName + "_proxySkin");
     $bindName = ($rigName + "_proxyBind");
```

```
//Enable other binding GUI buttons:
   button -e -vis 0 "cm_applyWeightsButton";
   button -e -en 1 -vis 1 -bgc 0.0 1.0 0.0
         "cm_applyWeightsButton";
   button -e -vis 0 "cm_proxyWeightsButton";
   button -e -en 1 -vis 1 -bgc 0.0 1.0 0.0
         "cm_proxyWeightsButton";
   button -e -vis 0 "cm_smoothWeightsButton";
   button -e -en 1 -vis 1 -bgc 0.0 1.0 0.0
         "cm_smoothWeightsButton";
}//Close conditional.
else {//Open conditional:
//Set main skin to bind:
   $skinName = `getenv "cm_skinName"`;
   $bindName = ($rigName + "_skinBind");
}//Close conditional.
```

The next section of code in the cm_bindSkin procedure uses a conditional to verify
that the skin has not already been bound, which could cause errors. It first runs a
findRelatedSkinCluster command on the skin name, which returns any skinCluster
nodes, and catches the name in a $bindTest variable. The conditional statement
checks whether the $bindTest variable is empty, and runs the binding code if the
condition is true. The actual code for binding is done the same way as shown in the
interface, by selecting all the root and bind joints with wildcards (*), and running a
skinCluster command with the flags set to the same values as the interface options.

```
//Check to see if skin is already bound:
   string $bindTest = `findRelatedSkinCluster($skinName)`;
   if (size($bindTest) == 0) {//Open conditional:
     select -r $skinName;
     select -tgl ($nSpace + "*_rootJt");
     select -tgl ($nSpace + "*_bindJt");
     string $skinCluster[] = `skinCluster -n $bindName -dr 7.2
         -mi 4 -omi 1 -tsb -ih -rui 1`;
     select -cl;
     putenv "cm_bindName" $skinCluster[0];
     text -e -l ($skinName + " bind complete!") "cm_bindFeedback";
     print ($skinName + " is smooth bound to "
         + $rigName + " rig!\n");
```

The rest of the cm_bindSkin procedure runs a nested conditional to see if any objects
contain the _infObj suffix, and if so, runs a skinCluster command in edit mode to
add influence objects using the -ai, or add influence, flag, as well as other flags to
lock the weights to 0. Then the procedure runs a skinPercent command with a -prw,

or prune weights, flag to remove weights below 0.1 percent. Lastly, the second part of the initial conditional used to check if the skin is bound prints warnings if a skinCluster node was found.

```
    //Add influences that are locked to 0 weighting:
    string $infObjs[] = `ls ($nSpace + "*_infObj")`;
    if (size ($infObjs) > 0){//Open conditional:
        string $inf;
        for ($inf in $infObjs){//Open loop...
            skinCluster -e -ai $inf -lw 1 -wt 0.0 -dr 9.9
                        $skinCluster[0];
            print ("Influence object " + $inf +
                " added with 0 weighting.\n");
        }//Close loop.
        select -cl;
    }//Close conditional.
    else print "No influence objects to add.\n";
    //Edit the bind by globally pruning weights below .1:
    skinPercent -prw 0.1 $skinCluster[0] $skinName;
    }//Close conditional.
    else {//Open conditional:
        text -e -l ("Bind already exists on " + $skinName + "!")
            "cm_bindFeedback";
        warning ("Bind already exists on " + $skinName + "!");
    }//Close conditional.
 //Edit next buttons in the setup GUI:
    button -e -vis 0 "cm_blendWrapButton";
    button -e -en 1 -vis 1 -bgc 0.0 1.0 0.0
            "cm_blendWrapButton";
}//Close procedure.
```

Step 2: Detach the Bind

To facilitate test-binding, the cm_bindDetach procedure is run when the check boxes in the setup GUI are deselected. This procedure follows the same structure as the bind procedure, in that it has an integer argument that is run through a conditional statement to detach either the proxy or main skin. The skinCluster command is run in edit mode with a –ub, or unbind, flag to detach the skin. Notice, however, that it is being run inside a catch command that is nested inside a conditional. The catch command is useful for catching and preventing errors from stopping the script. In this case, if you try to detach a bind that doesn't exist on a skin, the command will produce an error. By running it inside the catch command, the error will be ignored. Running the whole thing inside the conditional statement, you can print a warning if the catch runs. Otherwise, the procedure detaches the skin.

```
//Global proc for detaching the bind:
global proc cm_bindDetach (int $proxy){//Open procedure...
 //Set global names for detaching:
   string $rigName = `getenv "cm_rigName"`;
   string $skinName;
 //Use conditional choose skin or proxy for binding:
   if ($proxy == 1){//Open conditional:
     $skinName = ($rigName + "_proxySkin");
     button -e -vis 0 "cm_applyWeightsButton";
     button -e -en 0 -vis 1 -bgc 1.0 0.0 0.0
           "cm_applyWeightsButton";
     button -e -vis 0 "cm_proxyWeightsButton";
     button -e -en 0 -vis 1 -bgc 1.0 0.0 0.0
           "cm_proxyWeightsButton";
   }//Close conditional.
   else {//Open conditional:
     $skinName = `getenv "cm_skinName"`;
     button -e -vis 0 "cm_proxyWeightsButton";
     button -e -en 0 -vis 1 -bgc 1.0 0.0 0.0
           "cm_proxyWeightsButton";
     button -e -vis 0 "cm_smoothWeightsButton";
     button -e -en 0 -vis 1 -bgc 1.0 0.0 0.0
           "cm_smoothWeightsButton";
   }//Close conditional.
   if ( catch( `skinCluster -e -ub $skinName` ) ) {
      text -e -l ("Bind does not exist on " + $skinName + "!")
           "cm_bindFeedback";
      warning ("Bind does not exist on " + $skinName + "!");
   }//Close if.
   else {//Open else...
      text -e -l ("Bind has been removed from " + $skinName + ".")
           "cm_bindFeedback";
      print ("Bind has been removed from " + $skinName + "\n");
   }//Close else.
   select -cl;
}//Close procedure.
```

Step 3: Assign Proxy Weights from File

The cm_getProxyWts procedure retrieves weights printed to a .wts file and assigns
the weights to the proxy skin. The procedure opens the file for reading, and retrieves
the first line, storing it in a $weightData string variable. The string is tokenized into
three parts, which converts the pieces into $vertex, $joint, and $weight variables.

The variables are then assigned to the proxy skin using a skinPercent command with a -tv, or transform value, flag. The rest of the lines are retrieved from the file using a while loop. The conditional statement in the loop checks for empty weight data, to prevent spaces at the end of the file from causing an error.

```
global proc cm_getProxyWts(){//Open procedure...
 //Get the name of the rig and file path from the environment:
   string $rigName = `getenv "cm_rigName"`;
   string $filePath = `getenv "cm_filePath"`;
   string $proxyName = ($rigName + "_proxySkin");
   string $proxyBind = `findRelatedSkinCluster($proxyName)`;
   string $fileName = "proxyWeights";
   string $readFile = ($filePath + $rigName + "_" + $fileName + ".wts");
 //Read names from .rig file:
   int $fileId = `fopen $readFile "r"`;
   string $weightData = `fgetline $fileId`;
 //Use tokenize to remove new line character:
   string $buffer[];
   tokenize ($weightData,"\n",$buffer);
   $weightData = $buffer[0];
 //Use tokenize to break up data into three variables:
   string $data[];
   tokenize ($weightData,",",$data);
   int $vertex = $data[0];
   string $joint = $data[1];
   float $weight = $data[2];
 //Assign weighting to each point and print result:
   skinPercent -tv $joint $weight $proxyBind
       ($proxyName + ".vtx[" + $vertex + "]");
   print ($proxyName + ".vtx[" + $vertex + "] weighted to " + $joint
       + " with weight " + $weight + " on " + $proxyBind + "\n");
   int $i = 0;
   while ( size($weightData) > 0 ) {//Open loop...
       $i++;
       $weightData = `fgetline $fileId`;
     //Use tokenize to remove new line character:
       tokenize ($weightData,"\n",$buffer);
       $weightData = $buffer[0];
       if ($weightData == ""){//Open conditional...
           print "No more weights in file.\n";
       }//Close conditional.
       else {//Open conditional...
         //Use tokenize to break up data into three variables:
           tokenize ($weightData,",",$data);
```

```
            $vertex = $data[0];
            $joint = $data[1];
            $weight = $data[2];
        //Assign weighting to each point and print result:
            skinPercent -tv $joint $weight $proxyBind
                    ($proxyName + ".vtx[" + $vertex + "]");
            print ($proxyName + ".vtx[" + $vertex + "] weighted to "
                    + $joint + " with weight " + $weight + " on "
                    + $proxyBind + "\n");
        }//Close conditional.
    }//Close loop.
    fclose $fileId;
    print "All points weighted on proxy from file!\n";
}//Close procedure.
```

Step 4: Copy Proxy Weights to Skin

The cm_copyWeights procedure uses the findRelatedSkinCluster command to get the
names of the proxy and skin binds, and runs them in a copySkinWeights command.
The procedure uses the same settings for –sa (surface association) and –ia (influence
association), as detailed in "Copying Skin Weights" earlier in this chapter.

```
//Global proc for copying weights from proxy to main skin:
global proc cm_copyWeights (){//Open procedure...
    string $rigName = `getenv "cm_rigName"`;
    string $skinName = `getenv "cm_skinName"`;
    string $proxyName = ($rigName + "_proxySkin");
 //Check to see if both skin are bound:
    string $skinBind = `findRelatedSkinCluster($skinName)`;
    string $proxyBind = `findRelatedSkinCluster($proxyName)`;
    if ((size($skinBind) == 0) || (size($proxyBind) == 0))
    {//Open conditional:
      text -e -l "Cannot copy weights!" "cm_bindFeedback";
      warning ("Cannot copy weights, skin not bound!");
    }//Close conditional.
    else {//Open conditional:
    //Run command to copy weights:
      copySkinWeights -ss $proxyBind -ds $skinBind -nm -sm
          -sa "closestPoint" -ia "oneToOne" -ia "name" -ia "closestJoint";
      text -e -l "Weights copied from proxy!" "cm_bindFeedback";
      print "Weights copied from proxy to main skin!";
    }//Close conditional.
}//Close procedure.
```

Step 5: Add Blend Shapes Through a Wrap Deformer

The cm_blendWrap procedure starts by setting names and listing all the blend shape targets using the _blend suffix. It runs the blendShape command to create the face-Shapes blend shape node with the first target and the proxy head. The other target heads are then added in a loop by editing the node.

```
//Global proc used for adding blend shapes through a wrap deform:
global proc cm_blendWrap (){//Open procedure...
 //Set names for creating blend shapes:
   string $skinName = `getenv "cm_skinName"`;
   string $skinCluster = `findRelatedSkinCluster($skinName)`;
   string $defaultHead = "cm_proxyHead";
 //List all target shapes and create blend shape node:
   string $mouthTargets[] = `ls "cm_*_blend"`;
   string $faceBlend[] = `blendShape -n "faceShapes"
        $mouthTargets[0] $defaultHead`;
   print ("Blend shape node " + $faceBlend[0] + " created containing "
            + $mouthTargets[0] + "\n");
 //Add all other shapes to blend shape node using loop:
     int $i;
     for ($i = 1; $i < size ($mouthTargets); $i++){//Open loop...
        blendShape -e -t $defaultHead $i
            $mouthTargets[$i] 1.0 $faceBlend[0];
        print ($mouthTargets[$i] + " added as a blend shape to "
            + $faceBlend[0] + "\n");
     }//Close loop.
```

The next section of code in the cm_blendWrap procedure creates the wrap deformer to connect the proxy head to the bound skin. The source line is being used because the wrap deformer command is a procedure named performCreateWrap, and must be put into memory when run in a script. Running the command with an integer argument of 0 tells Maya to create the deformer between the selected objects with the default settings. The listConnections command retrieves the name of the wrap deformer node so that it can be used in the series of setAttr commands to set the deformer options. As performCreateWrap is a procedure, you won't find any documentation on it in the MEL Command Reference. But you can run a whatIs command on the name, and open the procedure to examine what it is doing in more detail.

```
//Connect blend shape head to main skin with a wrap deformer:
   select -r $skinName;
   select -tgl $defaultHead;
 //Source and run wrap deformer MEL procedure:
   source "performCreateWrap.mel";
   performCreateWrap 0;
```

```
//Find wrap node and set attributes:
   string $wrap[] = `listConnections -t "wrap" $defaultHead`;
   string $blendWrap = $wrap[0];
   setAttr ($blendWrap + ".envelope") 1;
   setAttr ($blendWrap + ".weightThreshold") 0.7;
   setAttr ($blendWrap + ".maxDistance") 0.1;
   setAttr ($blendWrap + ".exclusiveBind") 1;
   setAttr ($defaultHead + ".dropoff") 4;
   setAttr ($defaultHead + ".smoothness") 0;
   setAttr ($defaultHead + ".inflType") 2;
```

The last section of code in the cm_blendWrap procedure runs a reorderDeformers command to place the skinCluster node last in the inputs stack, and then creates channels on the head icon to drive the blend shape channels using the SDKs.

```
//Make sure wrap is evaluated before the bind:
   reorderDeformers $skinCluster $blendWrap $skinName;
   select -cl;
   print ("Blend shapes connected to " + $skinName +
         " using wrap deform " + $wrap[0] + "\n");
 //Create and connect face channels on the head icon:
   eval ("source CMaraffi_processNames");
   eval ("source CMaraffi_advGlobals");
   string $basicRigNames[] = cm_getNames("basicRig");
   string $headIcon = cm_returnName ($basicRigNames,"Head","icon");
   for ($i = 0; $i < size ($mouthTargets); $i++){//Open loop...
       string $mainName[];
       tokenize $mouthTargets[$i] "_" $mainName;
       string $shortName = startString($mainName[1], 3);
       float $driverVals[] = {-5.0,0.0,10.0};
       float $drivenVals[] = {-0.5,0.0,1.5};
       cm_setDrivens ($headIcon,$mainName[1],$faceBlend[0],
             $mouthTargets[$i],$driverVals,$drivenVals,1,
             $shortName,-5,10,0,0);
       setKeyframe -t 0 ($headIcon + "." + $mainName[1]);
   }//Close loop.
 //Disable setup GUI button:
   button -e -l "Done" -en 0 "cm_blendWrapButton";
}//Close procedure.
```

WRAPPING UP

At this stage you should understand how to rig and bind a biped character in the Maya interface and through MEL scripting. In the final chapter, you will learn additional scripting commands for laying out graphic controls into an advanced character animation GUI.

10 IMPORTANT POINTS TO REMEMBER FROM THIS CHAPTER

- Smooth binding assigns percentages of weighting to multiple joints, and normalizes the weight values to add up to 1.

- A skin model can be connected to only one bind or skinCluster node.

- Joints are added as influence objects to the bind by editing the skinCluster node.

- You can add other types of nodes as influence objects, including NURBS and polygons.

- Lock the weighting of influence objects at 0 to keep Maya from assigning any weight to the influences, and then weight them manually.

- Paint skin weights first to rough out and smooth weighting, and then use the Component Editor to finalize the weight values.

- To simplify weighting, you can bind and weight a low-resolution proxy skin, and then copy the weights to the main skin.

- Creating separate mouth and eye blend shapes allows you to mix complex shapes on the face.

- A wrap deformer drives points on one object with the points on another object based on proximity.

- When adding multiple deformers to a bound skin, always make sure that the skinCluster node is evaluated last in the inputs stack.

6

Scripting an Advanced Character GUI

YOU HAVE BEEN using a basic setup GUI since your introduction to GUI commands in Chapter 2, "Learning to Script in MEL." This last chapter gets you started designing a custom animation GUI for your character rig by scripting more advanced controls and layouts. You will learn how to add custom images to basic controls like check boxes and buttons, and how to connect MEL sliders to attributes on the rig icons. You will also learn more complex layout commands, and how to combine layouts to design a sophisticated multipanel window to contain your GUI controls.

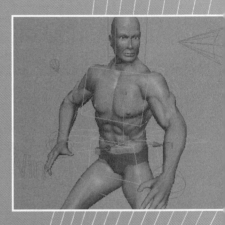

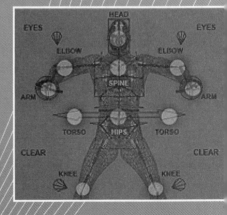

Creating More GUI Controls

This section first reviews some important points about the basic controls used in the setup GUI, and then discusses alignment flags that help to efficiently display the parts of a control group, such as found in a radio button group. You will also learn new commands for adding menus and custom images to the GUI. In addition, you will see how to create a variety of sliders that will allow you to control and animate all the attributes on the rig icons.

Briefly look at the section on creating a basic GUI in Chapter 2, "MEL Scripting a Basic GUI," and open the CMaraffi_setupRigGui script introduced in that chapter. Make sure that you understand the main commands and flags being used before learning the new GUI commands.

Reviewing Basic Controls in the Setup GUI

Beyond the window and showWindow commands that create and display a GUI window, the commands used in the CMaraffi_setupRigGui script are for organizing and creating controls that run your scripts. The controls are stacked vertically flush left in the window using a columnLayout command, which is the most basic layout command in Maya. It is so basic that it doesn't even require any flags to work as intended. By far the most frequently used control in the setup GUI are buttons that run script and procedures in their -c, or command, flags when clicked. Similar flags are used on the check boxes and radio button groups. The check boxes employ -onc and -ofc, or on-off command, flags to run procedures when checked; the radio button group has -on1, -on2, and -on3 flags that run commands when the first, second, or third buttons are turned on.

In addition to buttons and check boxes, the setup GUI script uses textField commands to input a rig name and file path to your scripts by querying the -tx, or text, flag. Querying also is done on the -v, or value, flag of check boxes to determine if they are turned on or off, and the -sl, or select, flag of radio buttons to find out which button the user chose. Both querying and editing controls require adding a string at the end of the GUI commands to name them. By far the most common flag used on all the GUI controls is the label flag, -l. The label flag is used by the text command to add instructions to the setup GUI, as well as to add descriptive labels and instructions on all the other controls.

Using Alignment Flags on a Control Group

In the CMaraffi_setupRigGui script, the radioButtonGrp command contains flags not used on the other commands. Here is the code again:

```
radioButtonGrp -p $layout -sl 0 -nrb 3 -cal 1 "left" -cw4 100 70 70 70
-en 0 -l "Set main config:" -la3 "Left3" "Right3" "Quad"
-on1 "button -e -en 1 cm_charGuiButton"
-on2 "button -e -en 1 cm_charGuiButton"
-on3 "button -e -en 1 cm_charGuiButton" $configRadios;
```

Notice the -cal and -cw4, or column alignment and width, flags in the command. These flags are used to adjust the individual GUI elements within the group of controls that make up the radio buttons. Any command that has Grp in the name, and even some that do not, are created by assembling multiple graphic elements in a hidden column layout. Adding column alignment and width flags lets you adjust the pieces horizontally within the hidden columns to reduce empty spaces, or to make more room for larger labels. In this case, the column alignment flag sets the first column containing the main label flush left, and the column width flag sets the necessary space to contain the individual labels and buttons.

Adding a Window Menu

A new method for running commands in your GUI is to create a menu of choices that run MEL commands or procedures. A common place to add such a menu is on the title bar of a window.

Adding a menu to the title bar of a window involves adding a -mb, or menu bar, flag to create an empty menu, and then running a menu command followed by a series of menuItem commands to incorporate menu choices. It is not necessary to precede the menu command with a layout command, because the menu attaches automatically to the window.

```
//GUI example showing a window menu bar:
 window -t "Menu Bar Example" -mb 1;
  menu -l "Create Primitive:" -to 1;
   menuItem -l "Create sphere..." -c "sphere";
   menuItem -l "Create cube..." -c "polyCube";
   menuItem -l "Create cone" -c "polyCone";
 showWindow;
```

FIGURE 6.1 *It is easy to add menu controls to the title bar of a window.*

In this simple example, an empty window has a menu for creating three types of primitives (see **FIGURE 6.1**).

Both new commands have familiar flags for labels and running commands, while the menu command has a new -to, or tear, off flag that makes the menu detachable.

Incorporating Custom Images

In Chapter 2, you learned how to customize the look of buttons by changing their -bgc, or background color, flags. You can give your GUI an even more unique design by incorporating images you create, rather than using Maya's default graphic icons for everything. You can attach your own graphics to some controls, like buttons and check boxes, as well as implement static images as headers instead of using text commands.

Special button and check box commands, called symbol controls, have flags that let you specify a pathway to a custom image file. You can create your images in any image program, such as Adobe® Photoshop®, and save them in Windows bitmap (.bmp) file format. You can also use Maya's fcheck program to convert the images to other types, such as the Maya native icon (.xpm) file format; however, converting to this format will reduce image quality because it does not support as many colors as the bitmap format. (Note: Macintosh versions of the scripts use the XPM format.)

Here is an example of using images for a static window header, a check box that controls the visibility of curves in Perspective view, and a button that opens a Graph Editor (see **FIGURE 6.2**):

FIGURE 6.2 *Image and symbol commands have image flags to specify a custom graphic for your controls.*

```
//GUI examples of using custom image files:
string $filePath = "C:/CMaraffi_bookFiles/";
window -t "Image GUI Examples";
columnLayout;
image -w 450 -h 70 -i ($filePath + "winImage.BMP");
symbolCheckBox -v 0 -w 165 -h 35 -ofi ($filePath + "hideRig.BMP")
```

```
    -oni ($filePath + "showRig.BMP")
    -onc "modelEditor -e -nurbsCurves 0 modelPanel4"
    -ofc "modelEditor -e -nurbsCurves 1 modelPanel4";
              symbolButton -i ($filePath + "graphEd.BMP") -w 165
                 -h 30 -c "GraphEditor";
showWindow;
```

To create a static image header, simply use the command image with a –i, or image, flag to reference the location of the custom bitmap file. It is important when using commands that reference image files that you always include width and height flags that specify the exact image size. Otherwise, Maya tends to crop parts of the image when displaying the window. The symbolCheckBox command references different images using the –ofi and –oni, or off-on image, flags. These flags let you automatically swap out the images when the check box is clicked. The symbolButton command works just like a regular button command, except it has an image flag to reference a bitmap file. Maya automatically creates a graphic button edge around your custom image.

Creating Slider Controls

Sliders are the most common controls in a character-animation GUI because they enable generating a range of float values. This quality makes them ideal for connecting to most rig controls, including transform and custom channels on icons. To take advantage of these capabilities, you can choose from several types of MEL slider commands in Maya. This section shows three sliders of increasing complexity. All the sliders controls presented in these sections, and later used in the character GUI scripts, will be sliders grouped with fields. Although there are sliders that are not grouped with fields in Maya, such sliders have limited uses because they cannot display values as you move the slider handle.

GENERATING DECIMAL VALUES WITH FLOAT SLIDERS

The simplest slider command to learn is a floatSliderGrp, which creates a control consisting of a label, field, and slider. Here is an example that runs the command with different values in the arguments to create three stacked sliders containing a variety of limits and decimal step values (see **FIGURE 6.3**):

FIGURE 6.3

The floatSliderGrp *command creates a slider and field that generate decimal numbers.*

```
//Create sliders and fields with different limits and steps:
window -t "Basic Slider GUI Example";
 columnLayout;
  floatSliderGrp -l "Float Slider from -10 to 10:" -cal 1 "left" -f 1
    -min -10.0 -max 10.0 -v 0 -s .1;
  floatSliderGrp -l "Float Slider from 0 to 1:" -cal 1 "left" -f 1
    -min 0.0 -max 1.0 -v 0 -s .01;
  floatSliderGrp -l "Float Slider from -1 to 0:" -cal 1 "left" -f 1
    -min -1.0 -max 0.0 -v 0 -s .001;
showWindow;
```

The -f, or field, flag creates a field to display and input values. The -min and -max flags set the minimum and maximum limits on the slider, which are required to display a slider bar, while the -v flag sets the default value. Notice that the -s, or step, flag sets the amount of decimal values displayed in the field. Moving the slider handle generates the appropriate decimal values, but they are not connected to anything else in Maya. This kind of slider is good for inputting values into script procedures or commands. After the slider is set, you query the -v, or value, flags to store the result in a float variable or argument for further processing in the script.

CONNECTING SLIDERS TO ATTRIBUTES

The second slider command, attrFieldSliderGrp, has many of the same flags as the floatSliderGrp command. However, this command has an additional -at, or attribute, flag, which can be used to easily connect the slider to an attribute or channel in Maya.

Here is an example of using this slider command to control the three translation values of a sphere (see **FIGURE 6.4**):

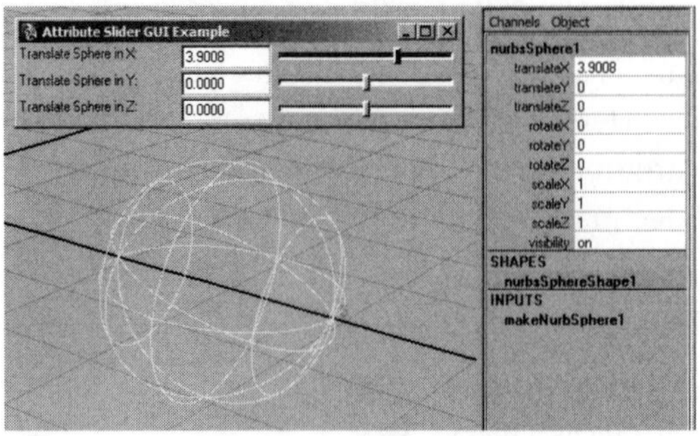

FIGURE 6.4

The attrFieldSliderGrp *command has an attribute flag that makes it easy to control the transform attributes of an object.*

```
//Connect sliders to translation attributes:
string $sphere[] = `sphere`;
window -t "Attribute Slider GUI Example";
 columnLayout;
  attrFieldSliderGrp -l "Translate Sphere in X:" -cal 1 "left"
    -min -10.0 -max 10.0 -s .1 -at ($sphere[0] + ".tx");
  attrFieldSliderGrp -l "Translate Sphere in Y:" -cal 1 "left"
    -min -10.0 -max 10.0 -s .1 -at ($sphere[0] + ".ty");
  attrFieldSliderGrp -l "Translate Sphere in Z:" -cal 1 "left"
    -min -10.0 -max 10.0 -s .1 -at ($sphere[0] + ".tz");
showWindow;
```

Keep in mind that connecting a slider to an attribute is not like connecting attributes with the Connection Editor or SDKs, which constrains or keys the driven channel. Instead, MEL sliders are an alternative interface for moving the attribute directly, just like scrubbing a channel in the Channel Box. In fact, changing the connected attribute in the Channel Box updates the slider. Because the connection goes both ways, this slider command does require a value flag.

USING SLIDER-BUTTON GROUPS

The previous slider command may be easy to connect to attributes, but it lacks some functionality for character controls. The third slider command, floatSliderButtonGrp, is the command used in the advanced character GUI scripts. This command adds two buttons to the end of the field and slider controls. These buttons are useful for incorporating reset and key capabilities for animating the rig controls. Although you could add this functionality as separate buttons to any of the previous sliders, it would involve a more complicated layout to make the buttons always display beside each slider.

Here is an example that places the slider command inside a procedure, with arguments for all the main slider options. A second command is also incorporated into the procedure to connect the slider to an attribute, as this slider command has no attribute flag. Then the procedure is run to create the actual sliders (see **FIGURE 6.5**):

FIGURE 6.5 *Use the* floatSliderButtonGrp *command to create character-animation sliders that have a key and reset button as part of the slider group.*

```
//Slider-button Group GUI Example:
global proc cm_mySlider (string $label, int $min, int $max,
      string $objAttr, int $reset, string $name)
{//Open procedure...
 //Create slider using arguments:
  floatSliderButtonGrp  -l $label -f 1 -s .01 -min $min -max $max
   -cal 1 left -cw5 65 40 160 50 35 -bl "Reset"
   -bc ("setAttr " + $objAttr + " " + $reset)
   -sbc ("setKeyframe " + $objAttr) -sbd 1
   -i "SETKEYSMALL.xpm" $name;
 //Connect slider to the node attribute:
  connectControl $name $objAttr;
}//Close procedure.
//Run procedures in window to animate sphere:
string $sphere[] = `sphere`;
window -t "Slider-button Group GUI Example";
 columnLayout;
 //Run slider procedure to create and connect sliders:
  cm_mySlider ("Translate Y",-10,10,($sphere[0] + ".tx"),0,"mySliderX");
  cm_mySlider ("Translate X",-10,10,($sphere[0] + ".ty"),0,"mySliderY");
  cm_mySlider ("Translate Z",-10,10,($sphere[0] + ".tz"),0,"mySliderZ");
showWindow;
```

The floatSliderButtonGrp command has additional flags to create and display the buttons. The first is a regular button with a -bl, or button label, flag being set to "Reset", and a -bc, or button command, employing a setAttr command that sets the attribute back to its default value. The second button is a symbol button with an image flag specifying one of Maya's built-in graphic icons: "SETKEYSMALL.xpm". When you reference one of Maya's icons, it is not necessary to include the entire file path before the name. The -sbc, or symbol button, command runs a setKeyframe command to set a key at the current timeline frame on the attribute that the slider controls.

The second command in the procedure is a connectControl command, which is designed to connect the new slider to the attribute by specifying the slider name followed by the object-attribute string. After this command is run, all the controls on the slider function. A similar procedure will be used in the advanced GUI scripts to create and connect all the character sliders to the icon channels.

Designing a Character GUI

The setup GUI uses column layout to create a linear series of basic controls that takes the user through several predesigned rig creation steps. A character-animation GUI, however, must contain a wide variety of nonlinear controls that are accessible within one or two mouse clicks. To design such a GUI, you need to understand how to implement many different types of layouts within a single window. You must be able to position controls within those layouts horizontally as well as vertically, and provide scroll bars when some controls inevitably go off screen.

Designing a character GUI requires that you organize primary controls such as sliders into groups within frames, tabs, or panels. You should allow secondary controls to be hidden from view until needed using collapsible frames. You also need to supply at least one panel containing a 3D view in which to pose the character, as well as a panel containing a timeline to facilitate setting keys (see **FIGURE 6.6**).

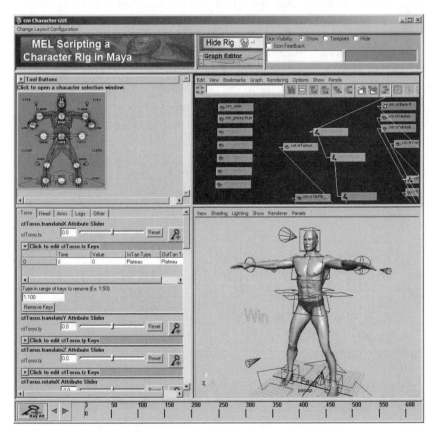

FIGURE 6.6 *Designing an advanced character GUI requires nesting a variety of layouts and controls within a single window.*

Working with Layouts

In this section, you will start implementing the character GUI requirements by learning how to position controls in a variety of basic layouts, and learn how to combine layouts through parenting. Then you will insert, or nest, basic layouts inside frames, panels, and tabs.

Parenting Basic Layouts

Parenting GUI elements is similar to parenting nodes in the Hypergraph. The window is always at the top of the hierarchy, followed by at least one child layout, and then either more layouts or controls. Layouts can be child to other layouts, and controls are always child to a layout. This hierarchy structure is pretty straightforward when you are only using a single column layout for all the controls, such as in the setup GUI. In this case, Maya can deduce the parenting structure without the need for you to add any clarification. It is when multiple layouts are nested within a single layout that you must specify the exact parenting, or you may get an error message that keeps your window from opening.

FIGURE 6.7 *In this window, row layout places the top buttons in a single row from left to right, while column layout puts the bottom buttons is a single column flush left. The* scrollLayout *command creates scroll bars around all the controls.*

Multiple nested layouts are like branches in a hierarchy coming off of a single parent layout. In this case, you must add a -p, or parent, flag to each GUI command to specify the direct parent, or run a setParent command to assign multiple children to a single parent. The following example shows three types of basic layouts used to arrange some empty buttons into rows and columns, with scroll bars around all the controls (see **FIGURE 6.7**).

```
//GUI example showing parenting of basic layouts to a window:
string $win = "MyWindow";
string $scroll = "myScrollL";
string $col = "myMainColumnL";
string $row = "myRowL";
string $col2 = "myColumnL2";
//Parenting - |$win|$scroll|$col| (then two branches) |$row and |$col2:
if (`window -ex $win`) deleteUI $win;
window -t "Basic Layout Example" -wh 300 200 $win;
 scrollLayout -p $win $scroll;
  columnLayout -p $scroll $col;
    rowLayout -p $col -nc 6 -cw6 55 55 55 55 55 55 $row;
      button -w 50; button -w 50; button -w 50; button -w 50;
      button -w 50; button -w 50;
```

```
        setParent..;
    columnLayout -p $col $col2;
        text -l ""; button -w 50; button -w 50; button -w 50;
        button -w 50; button -w 50;
        setParent $col2;
showWindow $win;
```

The direct child of the window command is a scrollLayout command, which creates scroll bars that are enabled if any controls go beyond the edge of the window. Child to the scroll layout is a columnLayout command, which is the main parent layout of the two layouts containing all the buttons. This is where the hierarchy splits into two branches. Although parent flags have been used on the scroll and column layouts, they weren't really required to prevent an error message. However, the rowLayout command and second columnLayout command must have the parenting specified to the first column layout.

The buttons in this example are parented to the appropriate layouts using a setParent command instead of inserting individual parent flags. This command is useful for parenting multiple controls under one parent layout. Simply run the command after the last control to be parented by either specifying the named layout, or by using setParent.. to specify parenting to the layout that is up one level in the hierarchy. The row layout arranges the first set of buttons in a single horizontal row using the -nc, or number of columns, flag to place each button in a hidden column. You must use this flag to create a row, and it must be set to the exact number of controls to be placed in the row. The -cw6 flag sets the width in pixels of each of the hidden columns, so that they fit the width of the buttons.

The other set of buttons are stacked vertically with a column layout. Notice that an empty text command has been inserted into the layout to create the space at the top of the column. This is a simple technique for adding spaces into a layout, since Maya automatically fills in the places of the layout with the next control in the script.

At times, you will want to create multiple wrapped columns or multiple wrapped rows. The rowColumnLayout command can do either based on the flags specified. Here is an example that shows how this command can wrap the controls (look at the numbering on the buttons in **FIGURE 6.8**):

FIGURE 6.8 *Look at the numbering on the buttons to see how* rowColumnLayout *wraps controls based on whether you use column or row flags.*

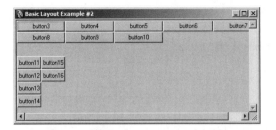

```
//GUI example showing basic wrapping of rows and columns:
string $win = "MyWindow";
string $scroll = "myScrollL";
string $col = "myMainColumnL";
string $rowCol1 = "wrapRows";
string $rowCol2 = "wrapCols";
if (`window -ex $win`) deleteUI $win;
window -t "Basic Layout Example #2" -wh 500 250 $win;
 scrollLayout -p $win $scroll;
  columnLayout -p $scroll $col;
    rowColumnLayout -p $col -nc 5 $rowCol1;
      button -w 50; button -w 50; button -w 50; button -w 50;
    button -w 50; button -w 50; button -w 50; button -w 50;
      setParent $rowCol1;
    rowColumnLayout -p $col -nr 5 $rowCol2;
      text -l ""; button -w 50; button -w 50; button -w 50;
    button -w 50; text -l ""; button -w 50; button -w 50;
      setParent $rowCol2;
showWindow $win;
```

One thing to remember when using this command is that you cannot use both row and column flags on the same rowColumnLayout command, or you will get an error. You must choose whether to use a -nc flag to place the controls in columns that wrap to the next row, or use a -nr, or number of rows, flag to place the controls in rows that wrap to the next column. Use whichever flag will most easily produce the arrangement you want for your GUI design. The rowColumnLayout command will be used with a -nc flag in the advanced character GUI script to arrange symbol buttons into a picture of the character that can be clicked to select the rig icons.

Using Intermediate Layouts

Intermediate layouts separate basic layouts and controls into frames, panels, and tabs. This function makes it easier to fit many different types of controls into a limited amount of window space, and lets you include other important GUI features like 3D views. Frames have the capability of being collapsed, so that you can hide secondary controls. Panels are useful for separating the main parts of your window into sections that contain groups of different type controls. Tabs allow you to put many instances of the same type controls in an overlapping space.

NESTING CONTROLS IN COLLAPSING FRAMES

A frame is a labeled box that appears around a set of controls in a window. You create a frame by running a frameLayout command, and specify it as the parent of a basic layout that contains controls. Here is an example of a frame around buttons in rowColumnLayout (see **FIGURE 6.9**):

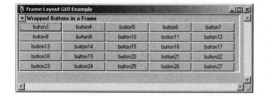

FIGURE 6.9 *Frame layout creates a box around the controls that can be collapsed by clicking the arrow button.*

```
//GUI example showing how to nest controls within a frame:
string $win = "MyWindow";
string $scroll = "myScrollL";
string $frame = "myFrameL";
string $rowCol = "myRowColL";
if (`window -ex $win`) deleteUI $win;
window -t "Frame Layout GUI Example" -wh 550 200 $win;
 scrollLayout -p $win $scroll;
   //Create a collapsible frame containing wrapped buttons:
    frameLayout -p $scroll -w 515 -l "My Frame"
        -cll 1 -cl 0 -bs "in" $frame;
     rowColumnLayout -p $frame -nc 5 $rowCol;
     //Use loop to create 25 buttons:
       int $i;
       for ($i = 0; $i < 25; $i++){//Open loop...
           button -w 50;
       }//Close loop.
     setParent $rowCol;
showWindow $win;
```

The buttons in this example use a loop to wrap 25 buttons in 5 columns. The entire set of buttons sits within a frame labeled "My Frame," which appears receded in the window as a result of the -bs, or border style, flag being set to "in". Also notice the drop-down arrow beside the label that indicates the frame can be collapsed, which is a result of turning on the -cll, or collapsible, flag in the code. Another flag, -cl, or collapsed, makes the frame open when the window is displayed, rather than closed. Turn on this flag to set the default state of the frame to collapsed, and thus hide secondary controls until they are needed.

ORGANIZING A WINDOW WITH PANELS

The paneLayout command lets you organize groups of controls into distinct panels in the window. This command enables you to easily create a multipanel window simply by specifying a -cn, or configuration, flag setting. The flag expects a predefined string argument, such as "single", "left3", "top4", or "quad". Be sure to look up the command in the MEL Command Reference to see all the available configurations. Once you set a configuration, you can populate the panels with layouts and controls, or commands that create views such as the perspective or Hypergraph views.

The most important thing to understand when using the paneLayout command is that Maya places the controls within the panels as they are ordered in the script, starting in the upper left panel going either left to right, top to bottom, or clockwise (depending on the configuration). To set the panel contents into place, you should use a setParent command specifying the named pane layout. Here is a simple example using a left3 configuration (see **FIGURE 6.10**):

FIGURE 6.10 *A pane layout command lets you create a variety of multipanel views based on the configuration flag argument, as this example of a* left3 *configuration shows.*

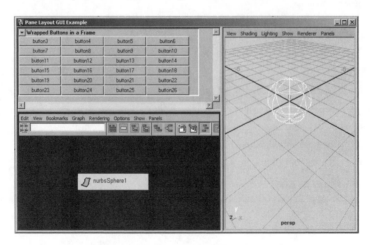

```
//Procedure to run in multi-panel window example:
proc cm_myPanelContents (){//Open procedure...
string $frame = "myFrameL";
string $rowCol = "wrapRows";
 scrollLayout;
   //Create a collapsible frame containing wrapped buttons:
    frameLayout -w 425 -l "Wrapped Buttons in a Frame"
        -cll 1 -cl 0 -bs "in" $frame;
     rowColumnLayout -p $frame -nc 4 $rowCol;
      //Use loop to create 24 buttons:
       int $i;
       for ($i = 0; $i < 24; $i++){//Open loop...
           button -w 50;
       }//Close loop.
     setParent $rowCol;
}//End procedure.
//----------------------------------------
//Multi-panel GUI window using pane layout:
string $win = "myWindow";
string $pane = "myPaneL";
if (`window -ex $win`) deleteUI $win;
window -t "Pane Layout GUI Example" -wh 800 600 $win;
 paneLayout -cn "left3" -ps 1 60 40 $pane;
  //1st controls panel upper left:
    cm_myPanelContents;
  setParent $pane;
  //2nd perspective view panel right:
    modelPanel;
  setParent $pane;
  //3rd Hypergraph panel lower left:
    scriptedPanel -typ "hyperGraphPanel";
  setParent $pane;
showWindow $win;
```

In addition to the configuration flag, this example has a -ps, or pane size, flag to set the width and height of the first panel. You do not have to set this flag for every panel because the values specified are percentages of the window. So if you set the first panel to be 60% width and 40% height, then the other panels automatically adjust to total 100% in both directions. The contents of the three panels in this example are buttons within a frame in the top-left panel, a perspective view in the large right panel, and a Hypergraph view in the bottom-left panel. You can navigate within the custom views in the same manner as in the standard Maya views.

OVERLAPPING CONTROLS IN TABS

Incorporating overlapping tabs into your GUI is useful for placing large groups of controls in a single panel, such as sliders connected to the many icon channels in the rig. Placing controls in tabs is more complicated than creating the other layouts, because it requires running and editing several layout commands, including `tabLayout` and `formLayout`.

Here is an example that uses a procedure to create 10 vertically stacked sliders inside 2 tabs (see **FIGURE 6.11**):

FIGURE 6.11 *This example of sliders being created in a tab layout shows how using tabs allows adding many sliders to a small space like a panel in a window.*

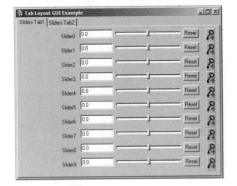

```
//Procedure to create sliders in tabs GUI example:
proc cm_mySliderContents (){//Open procedure...
    string $col = "myColumnL";
  //Create a collapsible frame containing wrapped buttons:
    columnLayout $col;
    //Use loop to create 10 sliders:
     int $i;
     for ($i = 0; $i < 10; $i++){//Open loop...
        floatSliderButtonGrp -l ("Slider" + $i) -min -10 -max 10
           -f 1 -bl "Reset" -sbd 1 -i "SETKEYSMALL.xpm";
     }//Close loop.
    setParent $col;
    setParent..;
```

```
}//End procedure.
//----------------------------------------
//Create a window with two tabs:
string $win = "myWindow";
if (`window -ex $win`) deleteUI $win;
window -t "Tab Layout GUI Example" -wh 500 400 $win;
 string $form = `formLayout`;
 string $tabs = `tabLayout -imw 5 -imh 5`;
 formLayout -e -af $tabs "top" 0 -af $tabs "left" 0
     -af $tabs "bottom" 0 -af $tabs "right" 0 $form;
//Create 1st tab contents using slider procedure:
     string $tab1 = `columnLayout`;
         cm_mySliderContents;
     setParent $tabs;
//Create 2nd tab contents using slider procedure:
     string $tab2 = `columnLayout`;
         cm_mySliderContents;
     setParent $tabs;
 //Add labels for the tabs:
     tabLayout -e -tl $tab1 "Sliders Tab1" -tl
     $tab2 "Sliders Tab2" $tabs;
showWindow $win;
```

In the window code after the slider procedure, the formLayout and tabLayout commands are initially run with minimal flags. Then the formLayout command is run again in edit mode to attach the tabs. Form layout is a fundamental command that is used to create very precise layouts. It is more complicated than the other layout commands because you have to specify how to attach every piece of the layout using the -af, or attach form, flag. Using form layout, however, lets you create custom layouts that other commands cannot achieve.

Once the tabs are attached, the contents of each tab must be specified, and the tab labels must be set. Each tab contains sliders in column layout by running the cm_mySliderContents procedure, followed by a setParent command specifying the tab layout name. The labels for each tab are specified at the end of the window code with a tabLayout command in edit mode using -tl, or tab label, flags.

Designing an Advanced GUI

Designing an advanced character GUI involves nesting layouts to organize the necessary controls in the window as efficiently as possible. It also involves adding functionality to some controls that require constant feedback from the software, which in MEL is done by running a `scriptJob` command.

Nesting Intermediate Layouts

The advanced character GUI scripts show controls stacked within collapsible frames, which in turn are placed in a tab within a panel, which is within another panel. This nesting of layouts within other layouts often is necessary to achieve the desired GUI functionality. Even though Maya provides several configurations for arranging multiple panels in a window, you may decide to venture outside those limits for your GUI design.

For instance, the advanced character GUI has a large panel across the top containing a header graphic, followed by some global controls positioned in columns and rows. The GUI also has three panels in the middle that contain slider controls, a selection graphic, and a perspective view. Lastly, there is a large panel across the bottom that contains animation controls and a timeline. To achieve this type of design requires you nest pane layout commands. Here is a simplified version of the same GUI layout with only a scaled button for contents of each panel (see **FIGURE 6.12**):

FIGURE 6.12 *Nesting pane layouts let you insert a* left3 *configuration into the middle panel of a* horizontal3 *configuration.*

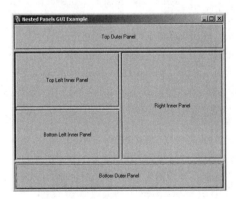

```
//Nest a left3 pane layout inside of a horizontal3:
string $pane1 = "myOuterPaneL";
string $pane2 = "myInnerPaneL";
```

```
string $win = "myWindow";
if (`window -ex $win`) deleteUI $win;
window -t "Nested Panels GUI Example" -wh 500 400 $win;
 //Run pane layout to create three stacked panels:
  paneLayout -configuration "horizontal3"
   -paneSize 1 100 15 -paneSize 2 100 65 $pane1;
 //Create and parent the small top outer panel:
    button -l "Top Outer Panel";
  setParent $pane1;
  //Run pane layout to create three middle panels:
    paneLayout -configuration "left3" $pane2;
     //Create and parent the first inner panel:
       button -l "Top Left Inner Panel";
    setParent $pane2;
     //Create and parent the second inner panel:
       button -l "Right Inner Panel";
    setParent $pane2;
     //Create and parent the third inner panel:
       button -l "Bottom Left Inner Panel";
    setParent $pane2;
 //Set the large center panel containing inner panels:
  setParent $pane1;
 //Create and parent the small bottom panel:
    button -l "Bottom Outer Panel";
  setParent $pane1;
showWindow $win;
```

Remember that it is the order of the commands in the script that determines what goes in the panels. In this case, the first configuration (horizontal3) creates three stacked panels that are ordered from top to bottom. If you want to place another pane layout configuration within the middle or second panel, you must run the command right after the first setParent $pane1 command. The remaining setParent commands are used to assign the contents of each panel to the correct pane layout. Of course, once your panel design is working, the next step would be to replace the button commands with procedures that contain all the layouts and controls you want to place inside the panels.

Running Script Jobs

A script job stays continuously in memory to run MEL commands or procedures when a specified type of event occurs in Maya. For instance, the script job may be set to run whenever the timeline is played, or when you select something in the 3D views. In the advanced GUI scripts, events like these trigger procedures that open a GUI window, and print help feedback to the command line when rig icons are selected. Incorporating such script jobs into your rigging controls can add real-time functionality that cannot be achieved in any other way through MEL. When using script jobs, however, you must manage how the jobs affect Maya's performance. Too many jobs in memory, or jobs left in memory that are no longer needed, can cause system problems.

CREATING SCRIPT JOBS

You place a script job in memory by running the scriptJob command specifying a -e, or event, flag and argument, followed by the command or procedure the event should trigger. Looking up the command in the documentation will show you a long list of possible events to choose from in Maya. In the advanced character GUI scripts, however, only the "Selection Changed" event is used. This type of event is useful for running a conditional statement that checks whether a target object was selected, and then runs additional code if the condition evaluates as true.

Here is a simple example of such a script job:

```
//Create sphere for script job example:
 string $obj[] = `sphere`;
 select -cl;
//Put name into environment to use in procedure:
 putenv "cm_myObj" $obj[0];
//Procedure to list and check selected, and print if sphere:
 global proc cm_findSelected (){//Open procedure...
     string $sel[] = `ls -sl`;
     string $myObj = `getenv "cm_myObj"`;
     if ($sel[0] == $myObj) {//Open conditional...
         print "My script job is working!\n";
     }//Close conditional.
   }//Close procedure.
//Script job to run procedure for event:
```

```
  int $myJob = `scriptJob -kws -e "SelectionChanged" cm_findSelected`;
  print ("My job number is: " + $myJob);
//Result: My job number is: 34 //
```

In this example, a sphere is created, and the name is put into memory using a putenv command. Then a cm_findSelected global procedure is created that lists whatever is selected, gets the sphere name from the environment, and runs a conditional statement to check if the sphere was selected. If the conditional evaluates as true, then the procedure prints that your script job is working. Once the procedure is in memory, the actual script job itself is put into memory to run the procedure whenever the user selects anything in Maya. Notice that the return statement for the script job is being caught in a $myJob integer variable for printing, rather than a string variable. The reason is that there are no naming flags on the scriptJob command, and the return statement is a randomly assigned job number (in this case, 34).

MANAGING JOBS IN MEMORY

The most important thing to consider when using script jobs is how to remove the jobs from memory when you have finished using them. Since you cannot name a script job, you must catch the job number in an integer variable when it is created, and store it somewhere so you can remove it later from memory, known as killing it. To manually kill your script job, run the command again with a -k, or kill, flag specifying the job number:

```
scriptJob -k 34;
```

If a job is to be used only while your GUI window is open, you can parent the job to your window using the -p, or parent, flag at creation. The parented job will automatically get killed when the window is closed or deleted. If you cannot kill the job manually or attach it to a GUI window, then be sure to add a -kws, or kill-with-scene, flag at creation to have the job removed from memory when the scene is changed. To check whether your script job is still in memory, run the scriptJob command with a -lj, or list-all-jobs, flag:

```
scriptJob -lj;
```

Running this flag displays a list of about 30 to 40 protected jobs that are always running in the software, with any user-created jobs at the end of the list. You can also remove all custom jobs by running a -ka, or kill-all, flag.

EXERCISE 6.1: SCRIPTING THE ADVANCED CHARACTER GUI

In this exercise you will examine the two advanced character GUI scripts: CMaraffi_characterGui and CMaraffi_mainGuiPanels. The two scripts create the nested multipanel layout with all the controls for animating the character (see **FIGURE 6.13**).

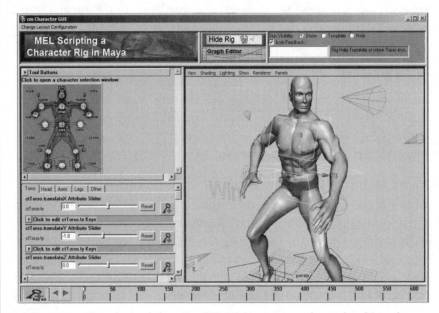

FIGURE 6.13 *The advanced character GUI scripts create an advanced multipanel window that lets you animate with both icon and MEL controls.*

The first script contains all the procedures for creating the window and outer panel configuration, including the graphic header and visibility controls in the top panel, and the timeline controls in the bottom panel. The second script contains all the procedures to create the nested panel configuration and contents, including selection controls, sliders for all the icon attributes, and a perspective view for posing the character. Make sure that you run the scripts and try out all the controls in the advanced character GUI before examining the code that creates them.

Step 1: Create the Top Panel Controls

The first five procedures in the CMaraffi_characterGui script create the controls in the top outer panel of the GUI. The first is a global procedure that contains the code to run in a script job for printing icon help feedback to the command line. It lists whatever is selected and runs a match command on the result to find the main name of the icon. Then it runs that name through a `switch` statement to print the appropriate help feedback.

```
//1.Global procedure for icon help feedback in top panel:
global proc cm_iconFeedBack (){//Open procedure...
  //Get the name of the rig from the environment:
    string $rigName = `getenv "cm_rigName"`;
  //List selected to run through switch statement:
    string $sel[] = `ls -sl`;
  //Create array of icon main names to match:
    string $matchNames[] = {"Char","Eyes","Feet","Head","Hips",
        "Torso","Arm","Elbow","Knee","Leg"};
  //Use loop and switch to print feedback for selected object:
      int $i;
      for ($i = 0; $i < size($matchNames); $i++){//Open loop...
      //Match selected name with part of name in array:
       string $match = `match $matchNames[$i] $sel[0]`;
      //Run match in switch cases to print feedback:
       switch ($match) {//Open switch...
         case "Char":
           print "Rig Help:Translate or rotate Character icon.\n";
         break;
         case "Eyes":
           print "Rig Help:Translate or scale-X Eyes icon.\n";
         break;
         case "Feet":
           print "Rig Help:Translate Feet icon.\n";
         break;
         case "Head":
           print "Rig Help:Rotate Head icon.\n";
         break;
         case "Hips":
           print "Rig Help:Translate or rotate Hips icon.\n";
         break;
         case "Torso":
           print "Rig Help:Translate or rotate Torso icon.\n";
         break;
         case "Arm":
           print "Rig Help:Translate Arm icon.\n";
         break;
         case "Elbow":
           print "Rig Help:Translate Elbow icon.\n";
         break;
         case "Knee":
           print "Rig Help:Translate Knee icon.\n";
         break;
         case "Leg":
```

```
            print "Rig Help:Translate or rotate Leg icon.\n";
          break;
        }//Close switch.
      }//Close loop.
}//Close procedure.
```

The next two global procedures start and stop the icon feedback by running and killing a script job. These procedures are run through a check box in the top panel of the GUI. Turning on the check box runs the cm_runFeedBack procedure, which creates a script job that specifies a "SelectionChanged" event. The job number is caught in a $feedJob integer variable, but then converted to a $job string variable to store the job in memory using a putenv command. Turning off the GUI check box runs the cm_stopFeedBack procedure, which gets the job number out of memory and kills the job. Notice that the job number is again converted from a string to an integer when retrieved from memory.

```
//2.Global procedure for starting icon feedback script job:
global proc cm_runFeedBack (){//Open procedure...
  string $winName = "cm_characterWindow";
 //Run script job whenever selection changed, and parent job to window:
  int $feedJob = `scriptJob -p $winName -event "SelectionChanged"
      cm_iconFeedBack`;
 //Convert integer job number to string, and put in memory:
  string $job = $feedJob;
  putenv "cm_iconFeedJob" $job;
}//Close procedure.
  print "cm_runFeedBack global proc is now in Maya's memory.\n";
 //************************************************************************
//3.Global procedure for stopping icon feedback script job:
global proc cm_stopFeedBack (){//Open procedure...
 //Get script job number out of memory:
  string $job = `getenv "cm_iconFeedJob"`;
 //Convert string to integer, and kill job:
  int $feedJob = $job;
  scriptJob -kill $feedJob;
}//Close procedure.
```

The cm_topPanel local procedure creates a graphic header and other controls within three horizontal panels using a vertical3 configuration on another paneLayout command. The beginning of the procedure shows names and background color values being retrieved from memory. Since this panel uses many custom images, the names are also declared at the beginning of the procedure. All the layouts and controls have background color flags so they will accept any color chosen with the Choose GUI Color button in the setup GUI. If no color is chosen, the layouts and controls are assigned a default Maya gray color.

Then the contents of the three panels are specified (each ending with setParent commands to $mainLayout): the first runs an image command to bring up the custom header graphic; the second runs symbol commands to create a check box for controlling the rig visibility in the custom Perspective view and a button that opens a graph editor; the third creates a radio button group to control skin visibility, a check box to run the icon feedback, and a command line to see the feedback.

```
//4.Local procedure for creating contents of top outer panel:
proc cm_topPanel (){//Open procedure...
  //Get strings from the environment:
    string $skinName = `getenv "cm_skinName"`;
    string $filePath = `getenv "cm_filePath"`;
    float $r = `getenv "cm_r"`;
    float $g = `getenv "cm_g"`;
    float $b = `getenv "cm_b"`;
  //Set layout and image names into variables:
    string $mainLayout = "cm_topPaneL";
    string $nestLayout = "cm_topRowL";
    string $winImg = ($filePath + "winImage.BMP");
    string $hideImg = ($filePath + "hideRig.BMP");
    string $showImg = ($filePath + "showRig.BMP");
    string $graphImg = ($filePath + "graphEd.BMP");
  //Create three panels for images, and selection-visibility controls:
    paneLayout -cn "vertical3" -w 700 -ps 1 44 100
                -ps 3 40 100 $mainLayout;
      columnLayout -bgc $r $g $b;
        image -w 450 -h 70 -i $winImg;
    setParent $mainLayout;
      columnLayout -cw 165 -bgc $r $g $b;
        symbolCheckBox -v 0 -w 165 -h 35 -ofi $hideImg -oni $showImg
          -onc "modelEditor -e -nurbsCurves 0 -polymeshes 1 cm_perspView"
          -ofc "modelEditor -e -nurbsCurves 1 -polymeshes 1 cm_perspView";
        symbolButton -i $graphImg -w 165 -h 35 -c "GraphEditor";
    setParent $mainLayout;
      columnLayout -bgc $r $g $b;
        radioButtonGrp -l "Skin Visibility:" -w 300
              -cal 1 "left" -cw4 75 55 70 55 -nrb 3 -sl 1
              -la3 "Show" "Template" "Hide" -bgc $r $g $b
              -on1 {("setAttr " + $skinName
                  + ".v 1; toggle -state off -template " + $skinName)}
              -on2 {("setAttr " + $skinName
                  + ".v 1; toggle -state on -template " + $skinName)}
              -on3 {("setAttr " + $skinName
                  + ".v 0; toggle -state off -template " + $skinName)};
```

```
        checkBox -v 0 -w 125 -bgc $r $g $b -l "Icon Feedback:"
                -al "left" -onc "cm_runFeedBack"
                -ofc "cm_stopFeedBack" "cm_checkJob";
        commandLine -w 350 -h 30 -bgc $r $g $b;
    setParent $mainLayout;
}//Close procedure.
```

Step 2: Create the Bottom Panel Controls

The cm_bottomPanel local procedure creates the animation controls and timeline on a single horizontal row from left to right. Notice that the first symbol button is designed to set a key on all the icon channels, and that the commands run in the -c flag of the button are first declared in string variables. This technique of separating commands into shorter strings can be used whenever you want to run multiple commands in a single flag argument, which makes the argument easier to manage. Also, notice that the internal quotation marks on some of the commands have a backslash in front of them. This prevents Maya from recognizing them until the string is processed as an argument. Without the backslash, the internal quotation marks would confuse Maya, causing an unterminated string error.

The timeline controls are also symbol buttons using Maya's standard icons, while the timeline itself is an instance of the main timeline created by a timePort command. When turned on, the -gt, or global time, flag and the -sn, or snap, flag cause the time port to update the main timeline and to snap to integer values on the frames.

```
//5.Local procedure for creating contents of bottom outer panel:
proc cm_bottomPanel (){//Open procedure...
 //Get the names from the environment:
   string $rigName = `getenv "cm_rigName"`;
   string $filePath = `getenv "cm_filePath"`;
 //Set layout and image names:
   string $layout = "cm_BotRowL";
   string $keyAllImg = ($filePath + "KeyAll.BMP");
   string $timeBackImg = "TIMEREV.xpm";
   string $timeForwImg = "TIMEPLAY.xpm";
   string $timeStopImg = "TIMESTOP.xpm";
 //Set commands into string for running Key-all procedure:
   string $getRig = "string $rigName = `getenv \"cm_rigName\"`;";
   string $listIcons =
          "string $iconNames[] = `ls ($rigName + \":*_icon\")`;";
   string $curTime = "int $time = `currentTime -q`;";
   string $keyAll = "cm_keyArray ($iconNames,$time);";
 //Create timeline controls across the button horizontally:
   rowLayout -nc 4 -ad4 4 -cw4 75 25 25 600 -cat 4 "left" 30 $layout;
```

```
        symbolButton -p $layout -i $keyAllImg
            -c {($getRig + $listIcons + $curTime + $keyAll)};
        symbolCheckBox -p $layout -ofi $timeBackImg -oni $timeStopImg
            -onc "play -f 0" -ofc "play -st 0";
        symbolCheckBox -p $layout -ofi $timeForwImg -oni $timeStopImg
            -onc "play -f 1" -ofc "play -st 0";
        timePort -p $layout -sn 1 -gt 1 "cm_timePort";
}//Close procedure.
```

Step 3: Create the Outer Panel Layout

The cm_characterWin local procedure runs the main window code to create the advanced character GUI. A paneLayout command with a horizontal3 configuration argument is used to create the top, middle, and bottom panels. The top and bottom panels run the procedures from Steps 1 and 2 of this exercise, while the middle panel requires sourcing the second GUI script to run the cm_mainGuiPanels global procedure. The nested panels are created according to the $config argument coming from the setup rig GUI. Also notice that a menu is created on the window title bar that allows the user to change the nested configuration by running this same procedure again with a different argument.

```
//6. Local procedure for character GUI window with a nested panels:
proc cm_characterWin (string $config){//Open procedure...
  //Source file containing nested panels global procedures:
    eval ("source CMaraffi_mainGuiPanels");
  //Get names from the environment:
    string $rigName = `getenv "cm_rigName"`;
    float $r = `getenv "cm_r"`;
    float $g = `getenv "cm_g"`;
    float $b = `getenv "cm_b"`;
  //Set names of window and layout:
    string $winName = "cm_characterWindow";
    string $layout = "cm_nestPaneL";
  //Create main character GUI window:
        if (`window -ex $winName`) deleteUI -wnd $winName;
        window -t ($rigName + " Character GUI") -mb 1 $winName;
        menu -l "Change Layout Configuration" -to 1;
    menuItem -l "Left 3 Layout" -c "cm_characterWin(\"left3\")";
    menuItem -l "Right 3 Layout" -c "cm_characterWin(\"right3\")";
    menuItem -l "Quad Layout" -c "cm_characterWin(\"quad\")";
        //Put character controls in three stacked panels:
            paneLayout -p $winName -cn "horizontal3" -bgc $r $g $b
                    -ps 1 100 12 -ps 2 100 80 $layout;
                //Run global proc:
```

```
              cm_topPanel;
        setParent $layout;
          //Run global proc:
            cm_mainGuiPanels($config);
        setParent $layout;
          //Run global proc:
            cm_bottomPanel;
        setParent $layout;
     //Edit size and placement of window:
      window -e -wh 1024 700 -tlc 50 50 $winName;
     showWindow $winName;
}//Close procedure.
```

Step 4: Use a Window Icon to Open the GUI

The next several procedures in the CMaraffi_characterGui script create a new text icon that the user can select to open the character-animation GUI. The cm_windowIcon local procedure creates a window icon using the text "Win", moves it to the side of the character, and parents it to the DoNotMove node in the rig hierarchy. Since the code creating the window icon is the same as used for other icons, this procedure will not be shown in this exercise.

The next three global procedures use a script job to automatically open the GUI when the new window icon is selected. Run by the script job, the cm_autoOpenWin procedure contains code that lists whatever is selected, and runs a conditional to see if the selected object is the window icon. If true, the character GUI global procedure is run. Notice that a clear selection command has been added after the GUI is opened to prevent the procedure from running multiple times, which could occur if the icon remained selected.

The cm_runAutoWin and cm_stopAutoWin procedures create and kill the script job that runs the previous procedure. The procedure that runs the scriptJob command, cm_runAutoWin, uses a -kws, or kill-with-scene, flag because the job must run when the GUI window is closed. The cm_stopAutoWin procedure is run before the cm_runAutoWin procedure to delete any old script jobs before running a new one, so they don't build up in memory every time you use the window icon to open the GUI.

```
//8.Global procedure for opening GUI by selecting the window icon:
global proc cm_autoOpenWin (){//Open procedure...
  string $winIcon = `getenv "cm_winIconName"`;
  string $sel[] = `ls -sl`;
  if ($sel[0] == $winIcon) {//Open conditional...
    cm_characterGui;
    select -cl;
```

```
    }//Close conditional.
}//Close procedure.
    print "cm_autoOpenWin global proc is now in Maya's memory.\n";
//************************************************************************
//9.Global procedure for starting automatic window script job:
global proc cm_runAutoWin (){//Open procedure...
    int $winJob = `scriptJob -kws -event "SelectionChanged" cm_autoOpenWin`;
    string $job = $winJob;
    putenv "cm_autoWinJob" $job;
}//Close procedure.
    print "cm_runAutoWin global proc is now in Maya's memory.\n";
//************************************************************************
//10.Global procedure for stopping automatic window script job:
global proc cm_stopAutoWin (){//Open procedure...
    string $job = `getenv "cm_autoWinJob"`;
    int $winJob = $job;
    if ($winJob == 0) print "No script job exists!\n";
    else if (`scriptJob -ex $winJob`) scriptJob -kill $winJob;
}//Close procedure.
```

The next procedure is run the first time the GUI window is opened, and after the window icon is created. The cm_runGuiNode procedure creates a script node in the Expression Editor that will be saved with the scene. The scriptNode command includes an –st, or state, flag set to 2; this is the same as choosing in the Expression Editor to Execute On: GUI/Open-Close, which automatically runs the node when the scene is opened. This command ensures that the window icon will still work if the scene is saved and opened again.

The code saved in the script node is entered as a string argument in the –bs, or before script, flag. At the beginning of the procedure, a series of strings are declared that are assembled into a single string argument for this flag. The strings put all the necessary data into memory that are required to open the GUI, and also run the cm_runAutoWin procedure to start the script node that checks for selection of the window icon.

```
//11.Local procedure for creating a script node in scene:
proc cm_runGuiNode (){//Open procedure...
  //Get the names from the environment:
    string $rigName = `getenv "cm_rigName"`;
    string $filePath = `getenv "cm_filePath"`;
    string $skinName = `getenv "cm_skinName"`;
    string $winIcon = `getenv "cm_winIconName"`;
    string $newMayaPath = `getenv "MAYA_SCRIPT_PATH"`;
    string $r = `getenv "cm_r"`;
    string $g = `getenv "cm_g"`;
    string $b = `getenv "cm_b"`;
```

```
//Create strings to use in script node:
  string $string1 = ("putenv cm_rigName "
         + $rigName + ";\n");
  string $string2 = ("putenv cm_filePath "
         + "\"" + $filePath  + "\"" + ";\n");
  string $string3 = ("putenv cm_skinName "
         + $skinName + ";\n");
  string $string4 = ("putenv cm_winIconName "
         + $winIcon + ";\n");
  string $string5 = ("putenv MAYA_SCRIPT_PATH "
         + "\"" + $newMayaPath + "\"" + ";\n");
  string $string6 = ("putenv cm_r " + "\"" + $r + "\""
         + "; putenv cm_g " + "\"" + $g + "\"" + "; putenv cm_b "
         + "\"" + $b + "\"" + ";\n");
  string $string7 = "eval (\"source CMaraffi_characterGui\");\n";
  string $string8 = "cm_runAutoWin;\n";
//Create script node containing string of commands for GUI:
  string $scriptNode = ($string1 + $string2 + $string3
     + $string4 + $string5 + $string6 + $string7 + $string8);
  scriptNode -n ($rigName + "_runGuiIcon") -st 2
     -bs $scriptNode;
//Change setup GUI script node to be on demand:
  setAttr runSetupGui.scriptType 0;
}//Close procedure.
```

Step 5: Run All GUI Procedures to Create the Multipanel Window

The last procedure in the CMaraffi_characterGui script is the main global procedure that runs all the GUI code and opens the advanced character window. The procedure consists of some conditional statements that first check whether the window icon exists. If it does, this means that the GUI has been created previously, so the procedure just opens the GUI with the default left3 configuration. Otherwise, the GUI is being created for the first time, so the procedure queries the radio buttons in the setup GUI to use as the configuration for the middle nested panels. Also, the window icon and script node is created, and the setup GUI is deleted.

Notice toward the end of this procedure that a toggle command with a –te, or template, flag is run to template the window icon, which is designed to prevent the user from accidentally selecting the window icon again. The icon stays in the template state until the GUI window is closed. This functionality is created by the scriptJob command at the end of this procedure that uses the –uid, or UI-delete, flag to determine when the window is closed and then start the script jobs associated with the window icon.

```
//12.Main global procedure for creating the character GUI:
global proc cm_characterGui (){//Open procedure...
  //Get names from environment:
    string $rigName = `getenv "cm_rigName"`;
  //Run global procedure to create window icon for opening GUI:
    string $winIcon;
    if(`objExists ($rigName + ":ctOpenWin_icon")`){//Open conditional...
      print "Window icon already exists.\n";
      $winIcon = `getenv "cm_winIconName"`;
      cm_characterWin ("left3");
    }//Close conditional.
    else {//Open conditional...
      $winIcon = cm_windowIcon();
     //Query radio buttons to get nested layout configuration:
        string $getRadios = `radioButtonGrp -q -sl "cm_configRadios"`;
     //Process setup GUI data with conditionals:
        if ($getRadios == 3) {cm_characterWin ("quad");}
        else if ($getRadios == 2) {cm_characterWin ("right3");}
          else {cm_characterWin ("left3");}
     //Delete setup GUI:
        deleteUI "cm_setupGuiWin";
     //Create script node for window icon to save with scene:
        cm_runGuiNode;
    }//Close conditional.
 //Toggle visibility to template window icon while window open:
   toggle -st 1 -te $winIcon;
 //Run script job to show window icon when window closed:
   scriptJob -kws -uid "cm_characterWindow"
            {("toggle -st 0 -te " + $winIcon +
            "; cm_stopAutoWin; cm_runAutoWin")};
}//Close procedure.
```

Step 6: Create the Nested Selection Panel

The second advanced character GUI script, CMaraffi_mainGuiPanels, creates all the contents of the nested middle panels.

The `cm_selectGrid` global procedure creates a separate popup window named `cm_selectWindow` that contains selection controls made from symbol buttons. The images on the buttons were created in Adobe Photoshop by slicing a labeled character image into 5 columns and 7 rows, for a total of 35 images. The bitmap images were saved and numbered starting in the upper-left corner, from left to right, and wrapping down to the next row. To reassemble the images, a `rowColumnLayout` command with a number-of-columns flag set to 5 is run in a loop with a string array that specifies the selection commands associated with each image. The conditional statement within the loop sorts which symbol buttons should clear selection, and which should select an icon. The cm_returnName procedure pulls out the full icon name from a listed array of icon names.

```
//1.Global procedure for bottom outer panel contents:
global proc cm_selectGrid (){//Open procedure...
 //Get the names from the environment:
   string $rigName = `getenv "cm_rigName"`;
   string $filePath = `getenv "cm_filePath"`;
 //Set window, layout, and image names:
   string $winName = "cm_selectWindow";
   string $mainLayout = "cm_gridColumn";
   string $rowColLayout = "cm_gridRowCol";
 //Create image selection grid GUI window:
   if (`window -ex $winName`) deleteUI -wnd $winName;
   window -t ($rigName + " Selection GUI") $winName;
     columnLayout $mainLayout;
   //List to create an array of all the icons:
     string $iconNames[] = `ls ($rigName + ":*_icon")`;
   //Use a loop to create a selection grid using symbol buttons:
     string $selectGrid[] = {"Eyes","rtElbow","Head","lfElbow","Eyes",
         "clear","rtElbow","Spine","lfElbow","clear",
         "rtArm","rtArm","Spine","lfArm","lfArm",
         "clear","Torso","Hips","Torso","clear",
         "clear","clear","Hips","clear","clear",
         "clear","rtKnee","Feet","lfKnee","clear",
         "Char","rtLeg","Feet","lfLeg","Char"};
     text -l "Click the parts of the character you want to select:"
         -fn "smallBoldLabelFont" -w 400 -al "left";
     rowColumnLayout -nc 5 -cw 1 69  -cw 2 65 -cw 3 86
                   -cw 4 66 -cw 5 68 $rowColLayout;
     int $i;
     for ($i = 0; $i < size($selectGrid); $i++){//Open loop...
       //Run conditional to clear selection or select icon:
         if ($selectGrid[$i] == "clear") symbolButton -c "select -cl"
               -i ($filePath + "selGrid" + $i + ".bmp");
         else {//Open conditional...
           //Run procedure in processNames script to match icon name:
             string $select = cm_returnName
                   ($iconNames,$selectGrid[$i],"icon");
           //Create button with image for selecting icon:
             symbolButton -i ($filePath + "selGrid" + $i + ".bmp")
```

```
                -c ("select -r " + $select);
            }//Close conditional.
        }//Close loop.
        setParent $rowColLayout;
    setParent $mainLayout;
    //Edit size and placement of window:
        window -e -wh 360 450 -tlc 200 200 $winName;
    showWindow $winName;
}//Close procedure.
```

The next procedure, `cm_selectPanel`, creates the selection panel that contains tool buttons in a collapsed frame, and a symbol button that opens the `cm_selectWindow` window. Creating standard tool buttons involves running a `toolCollection` command followed by the `toolButton` command specifying the Maya tool name and graphic icon. The tool buttons created in this particular frame are placed in a row using row column layout. Running several `setParent` commands is necessary to keep the symbol button outside the tool button frame.

```
//2.local proc containing selection and tool buttons grid for main panel:
proc cm_selectPanel (){//Open procedure...
 //Source any scripts needed to create GUI:
    eval ("source CMaraffi_processNames");
 //Get the name of the rig from the environment:
    string $rigName = `getenv "cm_rigName"`;
    string $filePath = `getenv "cm_filePath"`;
 //Layout strings:
    string $mainLayout = "cm_selectColumn";
    string $frameLayout = "cm_toolFrame";
    string $frameColumn = "cm_toolColumn";
    string $manipToolImg = "SHOWMANIP.xpm";
    string $selectToolImg = "aselect.xpm";
    string $moveToolImg = "move_M.xpm";
    string $rotateToolImg = "rotate_M.xpm";
 //Set parent layouts:
    scrollLayout;
    columnLayout $mainLayout;
 //Create collapsible frame containing tool buttons:
    frameLayout -w 375 -l "Tool Buttons" -cll true -cl true
            -bs "out" $frameLayout;
      columnLayout $frameColumn;
        rowColumnLayout -nc 4;
          text -l "Move Tools:" -fn "smallBoldLabelFont" -w 50 -al "left";
          text -l " "; text -l " "; text -l " ";
        //Create standard Maya tool buttons within frame:
```

```
          toolCollection;
          toolButton -t "ShowManips" -iol "Transform"
        -ti1 "ShowManips" $manipToolImg;
          toolButton -t "selectSuperContext" -iol "Select"
        -ti1 "selectSuperContext" $selectToolImg;
          toolButton -t "moveSuperContext" -iol "Translate"
        -ti1 "moveSuperContext" $moveToolImg;
          toolButton -t "RotateSuperContext" -iol "Rotate"
        -ti1 "RotateSuperContext" $rotateToolImg;
      //Specify parenting for the nested layouts:
        setParent $frameColumn;
      setParent $frameLayout;
    setParent $mainLayout;//End collapsible frame.
      text -l "Click to open a character selection window:"
          -fn "smallBoldLabelFont" -w 400 -al "left";
    //Use symbol button to open floating selection window:
      symbolButton -i ($filePath + "selectGrid.bmp") -c "cm_selectGrid";
}//Close procedure.
```

Step 7: Create the Nested Sliders Panel

The next four procedures in the CMaraffi_mainGuiPanels script create a slider and key editing controls for every attribute on the rig icons, and organize groups of sliders into particular tabs in tab layout.

The first two procedures create the individual slider, and then use the slider return statements to create some key editing controls in a collapsed frame. The cm_slider procedure runs a floatSliderButtonGrp command followed by a connectControl command to create and connect the slider to an icon channel. Notice that the string array being returned is fed directly into the arguments of the next cm_keyOutliner procedure, which then lists any keys set on the channel controlled by the slider.

The keyframeOutliner command creates the key list, while a field and button are also provided to specify a range of keys to remove by running a cutKey command. Be aware that if you cut off all the keys, the key outliner control will cease to update correctly, because it requires at least one key on the animation curve it is listing. So always leave the default key on frame 0 when editing keys.

```
//3.Local proc for creating slider to control icon attributes:
proc string[] cm_slider (string $label, float $min, float $max,
      string $object,string $attr, string $name, float $reset)
{//Open procedure...
  //Create slider with arguments:
  floatSliderButtonGrp  -l $label -f true -s .1 -min $min
```

```
      -max $max -v $reset -cal 1 left -cw5 90 40 160 50 35
   -bl "Reset" -cc ("select " + $object)
         -bc ("setAttr " + $object + "." + $attr + " " + $reset)
         -sbc ("setKeyframe " + $object + "." + $attr) -sbd true
         -i "SETKEYSMALL.xpm" $name;
    //Connect slider to icon attribute:
     connectControl $name ($object + "." + $attr);
    //Return arguments to use in key editing procedure:
     string $return[] = {$label,$object,$attr,$name,$reset};
     return $return;
}//Close procedure.
   print "cm_slider local proc is now in Maya's memory.\n";
   //*************************************************************************
   //4.Local proc for creating a frame containing key editing controls:
   proc cm_keyOutliner (string $label,string $object, string $attr,
                  string $slider, float $reset){//Open procedure...
    //Set some names and command strings into variables:
     string $animCurve = ($object + "." + $attr);
     string $queryField = ("string $range = `textField -q -tx "
          + $slider + "_keyField`;");
     string $cutKey = ("cutKey -cl -t $range -at " + $attr + " " + $object);
    //Create collapsible frame with list of keys, and editing controls:
         frameLayout -w 375 -l ("Click to edit " +
                $label + " Keys")
                -cll true -cl true -bs "in" -bgc .73 .71 .7;
            columnLayout;
         //List keys with the key outliner:
            keyframeOutliner -w 375 -h 75 -display "narrow"
                    -animCurve $animCurve;
            separator -w 350;
         //Create field to cut range of keys:
            text -l "Type in range of keys to remove (Ex: 1:50):";
            textField -w 100 -tx "1:100" ($slider + "_keyField");
            button -l "Remove Keys" -c {($queryField + $cutKey)};
         setParent..;
         setParent..;
}//Close procedure.
```

The cm_createSliders procedure lists all the transform and custom attributes on the icons, and runs the names through the previous two procedures to create all the sliders and key outliner controls. All the procedure requires is the main part of an icon name as an argument, which it matches with a list of icons. Then it runs a series of listAttr commands on the icon using both transform flags, and –ud, or user-defined, flags, to get all the appropriate attributes. The procedure ignores any attributes that have been hidden and locked in the advanced scripts. Next, two commands, transformLimits and attributeQuery, run in separate loops to find all the limits set on the transform and custom channels, for use as minimum and maximum arguments in the slider procedure.

```
//5.Local proc for creating all sliders for each rig icon:
proc cm_createSliders (string $iconName){//Open procedure...
  //Get the name of the rig and path from the environment:
    string $rigName = `getenv "cm_rigName"`;
  //List to create an array of all the icons:
    string $iconNames[] = `ls ($rigName + ":*_icon")`;
      //Use loop to create and print to .attr files for each icon:
        int $i;
        for ($i = 0; $i < size($iconNames); $i++){//Open for loop...
          //Tokenize to remove namespace on icon names:
            string $buffer[];
            int $numTokens = `tokenize $iconNames[$i] ":" $buffer`;
                string $mainName = $buffer[1];
          //Tokenize to remove suffix on icon names:
            string $buffer2[];
            int $numTokens = `tokenize $buffer[1] "_" $buffer2`;
                string $shortName = $buffer2[0];
          //Check if match with procedure argument:
            if ($shortName == $iconName){//Start nested conditional...
            //List all transform and custom attributes for each icon:
              string $transformAttrs[] = `listAttr -v -k -sn
-st "tx" -st "ty" -st "tz"
-st "rx" -st "ry" -st "rz"
-st "sx" -st "sy" -st "sz" $iconNames[$i]`;
                string $longTrAttrs[] = `listAttr -v -k
-st "translateX" -st "translateY" -st "translateZ"
-st "rotateX" -st "rotateY" -st "rotateZ"
-st "scaleX" -st "scaleY" -st "scaleZ" $iconNames[$i]`;
                string $customAttrs[] = `listAttr -ud -v -k
                  -sn $iconNames[$i]`;
                string $longCuAttrs[] = `listAttr -ud -v -k
                  $iconNames[$i]`;
              //Query transform attr limits and default value:
                int $i2;
                for ($i2 = 0; $i2 < size($transformAttrs); $i2++)
                {//Open nested loop...
          float $trLimits[] = `transformLimits -q ("-" +
                $transformAttrs[$i2]) $iconNames[$i]`;
                float $trCurrent = `getAttr ($iconNames[$i] +
```

```
                            "." + $transformAttrs[$i2])`;
            //Create slider(label,min,max,object,attr,sliderName,reset):
              text -l ($shortName + "." + $longTrAttrs[$i2] +
                " Attribute Slider") -w 300 -al "left"
                -fn "boldLabelFont";
              string $sliderReturn[] = cm_slider
                    (($shortName + "." + $transformAttrs[$i2]),
                    $trLimits[0],$trLimits[1],$iconNames[$i],
                    $transformAttrs[$i2],($shortName + "_" +
                    $transformAttrs[$i2] + "_slider"),$trCurrent);
              cm_keyOutliner
                ($sliderReturn[0],$sliderReturn[1],$sliderReturn[2],
                $sliderReturn[3],$sliderReturn[4]);
              separator -w 400 -st "double";
            }//Close loop.
          //Query custom attr limits and default values:
          int $i2;
          for ($i2 = 0; $i2 < size($customAttrs); $i2++)
          {//Open nested loop...
      float $cuLimits[] = `attributeQuery
                -n $iconNames[$i] -r $customAttrs[$i2]`;
      float $cuCurrent[] = `attributeQuery
                -n $iconNames[$i] -ld $customAttrs[$i2]`;
          //Create slider(label,min,max,object,attr,sliderName,reset):
            text -l ($shortName + "." + $longCuAttrs[$i2] +
              " Attribute Slider") -w 300 -al "left"
              -fn "boldLabelFont";
            string $sliderReturn[] = cm_slider
                  (($shortName + "." + $customAttrs[$i2]),
                  $cuLimits[0],$cuLimits[1],$iconNames[$i],
                  $customAttrs[$i2],($shortName + "_" +
                  $customAttrs[$i2] + "_slider"),$cuCurrent[0]);
            cm_keyOutliner
              ($sliderReturn[0],$sliderReturn[1],$sliderReturn[2],
              $sliderReturn[3],$sliderReturn[4]);
            separator -w 400 -st "double";
          }//close nested loop.
        }//Close conditional.
      }//Close loop.
}//Close procedure.
```

The cm_slidersPanel procedure organizes the sliders into tabs by grouping the icons according to the torso, head, arms, legs, and others. The procedure places the main icon names in arrays, and then runs them through the cm_createSliders procedure as arguments, which lists all their attributes and creates the slider and key editing controls. The cm_slidersPanel procedure processes the slider procedure using loops nested inside column and tab layouts, to create and stack the slider controls in the appropriate tabs.

```
//6.Local proc that places sliders in tab layout for slider panel:
proc cm_slidersPanel (){//Open procedure...
 //Specify which icons will be grouped into a tab:
    string $torsoIcons[] = {"ctTorso","ctHips","ctSpine"};
    string $headIcons[] = {"ctHead","ctEyes"};
    string $armIcons[] = {"lfArm","lfElbow","rtArm","rtElbow"};
    string $legIcons[] = {"lfLeg","lfKnee","rtLeg","rtKnee"};
    string $otherIcons[] = {"ctChar","ctFeet"};
 //Create tab layout with sliders in tabs:
   scrollLayout;
   string $form = `formLayout`;
   string $tabs = `tabLayout -imw 5 -imh 5`;
   formLayout -e -w 375 -af $tabs "top" 0 -af $tabs "left" 0
       -af $tabs "bottom" 0 -af $tabs "right" 0 $form;
   //Create the torso tab containing sliders:
    string $createTab1 = `columnLayout`;
      string $iconName1;
      for ($iconName1 in $torsoIcons){//Open loop...
          cm_createSliders($iconName1);
      }//Close loop.
    setParent..;
   //Create the head tab containing sliders:
    string $createTab2 = `columnLayout`;
      string $iconName2;
      for ($iconName2 in $headIcons){//Open loop...
          cm_createSliders($iconName2);
      }//Close loop.
    setParent..;
   //Create the arm tab containing sliders:
    string $createTab3 = `columnLayout`;
      string $iconName3;
      for ($iconName3 in $armIcons){//Open loop...
          cm_createSliders($iconName3);
      }//Close loop.
    setParent..;
   //Create the leg tab containing sliders:
    string $createTab4 = `columnLayout`;
      string $iconName4;
      for ($iconName4 in $legIcons){//Open loop...
```

```
                cm_createSliders($iconName4);
        }//Close loop.
      setParent..;
    //Create the other tab containing sliders:
    string $createTab5 = `columnLayout`;
        string $iconName5;
        for ($iconName5 in $otherIcons){//Open loop...
            cm_createSliders($iconName5);
        }//Close loop.
      setParent..;
  //Edit tab labels:
    tabLayout -e -tl $createTab1 "Torso" -tl $createTab2 "Head"
              -tl $createTab3 "Arms" -tl $createTab4 "Legs"
              -tl $createTab5 "Other" $tabs;
}//close procedure.
```

Step 8: Configure the Main Nested Layout

The final two procedures create the nested panel configuration containing all the controls from the selection and slider procedures. The cm_setCommands procedure places commands for creating the perspective and Hypergraph views into run-time commands to use in the final global procedure. Run-time commands let you custom-name frequently used commands and save them in a file in your Maya preferences folder, so they are available whenever Maya launches. This procedure is just a simple example of how to create and use two run-time commands.

The last cm_mainGuiPanels procedure is the main global procedure in the CMaraffi_mainGuiPanels script. The procedure takes a $config argument from the other script, and runs it through a series of conditional statements to arrange the panels in the best way possible for each configuration. For instance, the run-time command that creates a custom perspective view, "cm_view", is run in the large panel for the left3 and right3 pane layouts. This placement provides more room to pose the character. Also notice that to process correctly, run-time commands must be run inside an eval command. The final modelEditor commands in this procedure optimizes the GUI perspective view by making it display a smooth-shaded model, and by hiding all the joints and locators so that only NURBS curves, polygons, and NURBS surfaces show in the view.

```
//7.Local proc to create run-time commands for panel views:
proc cm_setCommands (){//Open procedure...
  //Creates a perspective view used in main window:
    if (!`runTimeCommand -ex "cm_view"`){//Open conditional...
        runTimeCommand -d 0 -cat "User" -ann "Custom perspective view"
          -c ("modelPanel \"cm_perspView\"") "cm_view";
```

```
        }//Close conditional.
    //Creates a hypergraph view used in main window:
      if (!`runTimeCommand -ex "cm_hyperG"`){//Open conditional...
          runTimeCommand -d 0 -cat "User" -ann "Custom hypergraph view"
              -c ("scriptedPanel -typ \"hyperGraphPanel\"") "cm_hyperG";
      }//Close conditional.
}//Close procedure.
    print "cm_setCommands local proc is now in Maya's memory.\n";
    //*************************************************************************
//8.Main global procedure creating configuration of inner panels:
global proc cm_mainGuiPanels (string $config){//Open procedure...
    //Run proc to put run-time commands in memory:
      cm_setCommands;
    //Use conditionals to set panel configuration of main section of GUI:
      if ($config == "right3"){//Open conditional...
        if (`panel -exists "cm_perspView"`) deleteUI -pnl "cm_perspView";
      //Create the right3 configuration, and order the contents:
        paneLayout -p "cm_nestPaneL" -cn $config -ps 2 40 60 "cm_mainPaneL";
          //Evaluate run-time command:
            eval ("cm_view");
        setParent "cm_mainPaneL";
          //Run slider proc:
            cm_slidersPanel;
        setParent "cm_mainPaneL";
          //Run select proc:
            cm_selectPanel;
        setParent "cm_mainPaneL";
      }//Close conditional.
      else if ($config == "left3"){//Open conditional...
        if (`panel -exists "cm_perspView"`) deleteUI -pnl "cm_perspView";
      //Create the left3 configuration, and order the contents:
        paneLayout -p "cm_nestPaneL" -cn $config -ps 1 40 40 "cm_mainPaneL";
          //Run select proc:
            cm_selectPanel;
        setParent "cm_mainPaneL";
          //Evaluate run-time command:
            eval ("cm_view");
        setParent "cm_mainPaneL";
          //Run slider proc:
            cm_slidersPanel;
        setParent "cm_mainPaneL";
      }//Close conditional.
      else {//Open conditional...
        if (`panel -exists "cm_perspView"`) deleteUI -pnl "cm_perspView";
```

```
    //Create the quad configuration, and order the contents:
    paneLayout -p "cm_nestPaneL" -cn $config -ps 1 40 40 "cm_mainPaneL";
        //Run select proc:
            cm_selectPanel;
    setParent "cm_mainPaneL";
        //Evaluate run-time command:
            eval ("cm_hyperG");
    setParent "cm_mainPaneL";
        //Evaluate run-time command:
            eval ("cm_view");
    setParent "cm_mainPaneL";
        //Run slider proc:
            cm_slidersPanel;
    setParent "cm_mainPaneL";
  }//Close conditional.
//Set up the custom perspective view by shading skin and hiding joints:
  modelEditor -e -da "smoothShaded" -ao false "cm_perspView";
  modelEditor -e -alo 0 "cm_perspView";
  modelEditor -e -nc 1 -pm 1 -ns 1 "cm_perspView";
}//Close procedure.
```

WRAPPING UP

If you made it this far in the book… congratulations! You are well on the road to becoming a MEL-savvy character-rigging artist. Once you have this skill in your toolbox, you can use the same coding techniques to script almost any technical job in Maya. Like any language, however, if you don't use it often and regularly, you will get rusty and eventually forget it. Also, if you find that you really enjoy MEL scripting, then you may want to investigate other coding languages, like Python. This will expand your programming knowledge, and give you access to scripting in other 3D applications, such as in Motion Builder to facilitate integrating motion capture data with a rig in Maya. Good luck and happy coding!

10 IMPORTANT POINTS TO REMEMBER FROM THIS CHAPTER

- Add column alignment and column width flags on groups of GUI controls to adjust the pieces to fit better in a layout.

- Images, symbol buttons, and symbol check boxes are good for adding custom design elements to your advanced character GUI.

- Sliders are the best control for icon channels, because they generate the same type of float values.

- Add parent flags or `setParent` commands whenever nesting layouts, to prevent Maya from giving you an error message.

- Row column layout creates multiple rows or columns by wrapping the controls. Both row and column flags cannot be used on the same command.

- Collapsible frame layout is great for hiding secondary controls that don't need to be used often.

- Tab and scroll layouts let you fit many sliders in a single panel.

- The configuration flag is most important on the `paneLayout` command.

- Nesting pane layouts lets you design almost any configuration.

- Script jobs let you run MEL commands and procedures triggered by Maya events, but you must properly manage the jobs in memory.

Index